Papers in metaph

This is part of a three-volume collection of most of David Lewis's papers in philosophy, except for those which previously appeared in his *Philosophical Papers* (Oxford University Press, 1983 and 1986). They are now offered in a readily accessible form.

This second volume is devoted to Lewis's work in metaphysics and epistemology. Topics covered include properties, ontology, possibility, truthmaking, probability, the mind–body problem, vision, belief, and knowledge.

The purpose of this collection, and the volumes that precede and follow it, is to disseminate more widely the work of an eminent and influential contemporary philosopher. The volume will serve as a useful work of reference for teachers and students of philosophy.

David Lewis is Professor of Philosophy at Princeton University.

CAMBRIDGE STUDIES IN PHILOSOPHY

General editor ERNEST SOSA (Brown University)

Advisory editors:

JONATHAN DANCY (University of Keele)
JOHN HALDANE (University of St. Andrews)
GILBERT HARMAN (Princeton University)
FRANK JACKSON (Australian National University)
WILLIAM G. LYCAN (University of North Carolina at Chapel Hill)
SYDNEY SHOEMAKER (Cornell University)
JUDITH J. THOMSON (Massachusetts Institute of Technology)

RECENT TITLES:

Papers in metaphysics and epistemology

DAVID LEWIS

CAMBRIDGE
UNIVERSITY PRESS

PUBLISHED BY THE PRESS SYNDICATE OF THE UNIVERSITY OF CAMBRIDGE
The Pitt Building, Trumpington Street, Cambridge CB2 1RP, United Kingdom

CAMBRIDGE UNIVERSITY PRESS
The Edinburgh Building, Cambridge CB2 2RU, UK   http://www.cup.cam.ac.uk
40 West 20th Street, New York, NY 10011–4211, USA   http://www.cup.org
10 Stamford Road, Oakleigh, Melbourne 3166, Australia

© David Lewis 1999

First published 1999

Printed in the United States of America

Typeset in Bembo 10.5/13 pt., in Penta [RF]

*A catalog record for this book is available from
the British Library.*

Library of Congress Cataloging-in-Publication Data
Lewis, David K., 1941–
Papers in metaphysics and epistemology / David Lewis.
p.   cm. – (Cambridge studies in philosophy)
A collection of the author's papers, most of which were previously published.
Includes bibliographical references and index.
ISBN 0-521-58248-2 (hardbound). – ISBN 0-521-58787-5 (pbk.)
1. Metaphysics.   2. Knowledge, theory of.   I. Title.   II. Series.
BD111.L45   1999   98-25689
110 – dc21   CIP

ISBN 0 521 58248 2 hardback
ISBN 0 521 58787 5 paperback

For the philosophers, past and present,
of Sydney and Canberra

Contents

Introduction

This collection reprints almost all my previously published papers in metaphysics and epistemology, except for those that were previously reprinted in another collection.[1] There is also one previously unpublished paper. Still omitted are three book reviews and four rejoinders.[2] I have taken the opportunity to correct typographical errors and editorial alterations. But I have left the philosophical content as it originally was, rather than trying to rewrite the papers as I would write them today.

The first six papers have to do with properties. 'New Work for a Theory of Universals' marked a big turning point in my philosophical position. Formerly I had been persuaded by Goodman and others that all properties were equal: it was hopeless to try to distinguish 'natural' properties from gruesomely gerrymandered, disjunctive

---

1 David Lewis, *Philosophical Papers*, volumes I and II (Oxford University Press, 1983 and 1986).

2 Review of W. H. Capitan and D. D. Merrill, eds., *Art, Mind, and Religion, Journal of Philosophy* 66 (1969), pp. 22–27; review of R. E. Olson and A. M. Paul, eds., *Contemporary Philosophy in Scandinavia, Theoria* 41 (1975), pp. 39–60 (with Stephanie Lewis); review of John Bigelow, *The Reality of Numbers, Australasian Journal of Philosophy* 67 (1989), pp. 487–489; 'Possible-World Semantics for Counterfactual Logics: A Rejoinder', *Journal of Philosophical Logic* 6 (1977), pp. 359–363; 'Levi Against U-Maximization', *Journal of Philosophy* 80 (1983), pp. 531–534; 'Vague Identity: Evans Misunderstood', *Analysis* 48 (1988), pp. 128–130; and 'Counterpart Theory, Quantified Modal Logic, and Extra Argument Places', *Analysis* 53 (1993), pp. 69–71.

properties.[3] Eventually I was persuaded, largely by D. M. Armstrong, that the distinction I had rejected was so commonsensical and so serviceable – indeed, was so often indispensable – that it was foolish to try to get on without it. We should accept it as primitive if need be; or we should admit that we understand whatever else it may take to explain it. What else? – Here we have several choices: among them, a suitable version of a primitive similarity relation; or perhaps a sparse theory of universals, as advocated by Armstrong.[4]

'Putnam's Paradox' expands the part of 'New Work' devoted to arguing that the distinction between natural and gerrymandered properties – if indeed we're prepared to grant that we can understand such a distinction – serves to answer Putnam's famous 'model-theoretic argument' for extreme semantic indeterminacy, and thence for the automatic truth of ideal theories.

I noted that one way to characterize natural properties was to help ourselves to Armstrong's theory of universals. But in 'Against Structural Universals' I note that one part of that theory gives trouble: the part about structural universals. Those are universals built up somehow – the problem is *how*? – out of simpler universals. I note that a similar theory of structural *tropes* – particular property-instances – has no parallel problem; and, further, that accepting a sparse theory of tropes would be another good way to give ourselves the distinction between natural and gerrymandered properties. In my brief 'Comment on Armstrong and Forrest' I suggest that my worries about structural universals can be paralleled by worries about states of affairs.

Another distinction among properties is the distinction between intrinsic and extrinsic (also called 'relational') properties. 'Extrinsic Properties' argues that a definition offered by Jaegwon Kim doesn't work. My first response, in 'New Work for a Theory of Universals', was that we should deem perfectly natural properties to be *ipso facto* intrinsic, and proceed from there. But recently Langton and I have come to think that, although Kim's idea won't work as it stands, a

---

3 Nelson Goodman, *Fact, Fiction, and Forecast* (Harvard University Press, 1955), Chapter 3.

4 D. M. Armstrong, *Universals and Scientific Realism* (Cambridge University Press, 1978).

modified version of it will capture the intrinsic–extrinsic distinction at least among non-disjunctive properties. Then we can go on to say that intrinsic properties generally are those that supervene upon the non-disjunctive intrinsic properties of a thing.

The next four papers address the question of ontological commitment: what entities we're committed to the existence of when we decide to use languages or accept theories that appear to talk about controversial entities. 'Noneism or Allism?' attacks those who claim in general to be entitled to talk about nonexistent objects without compromising their denials of existence. There's a problem about how to translate their language into ours, and the best translation is one that reinterprets away their apparent denials of existence.

Peter Unger and Peter Geach have posed the 'problem of the many'. A cat is on the mat; the cat is shedding, so some hairs are on the way to falling off and hence are questionably parts of the cat; the cat taken as including any one of these questionable hairs and the cat taken as excluding it have equal claim to be called cats, and they are not identical; so instead of one cat on the mat we have many! I say: yes, but these cats overlap so extensively that they are *almost* identical to one another; so it is *almost* true that there is just one cat on the mat; the many are almost one; what we commonsensically want to say is near enough to right.

My review, with Stephanie Lewis, of Casati and Varzi, *Holes and other Superficialities*, is a sequel to our paper 'Holes'.[5] The main point made is that, no matter what we say about the ontological status of holes themselves, it will at any rate be true that the truth of hole-statements supervenes upon the arrangement of matter.

'Rearrangement of Particles' criticizes E. J. Lowe's solution to the problem of intrinsic change. If something endures identically through time while gaining or losing an intrinsic property, we have a *prima facie* contradiction: the very same thing both has and lacks an intrinsic property. Lowe said we could dodge the problem by confining our attention to identically enduring particles. They may undergo rearrangement over time, but they never change their intrinsic properties.

5 David and Stephanie Lewis, 'Holes', *Australasian Journal of Philosophy* 48 (1970), pp. 206–212.

3

I say this move fails. Lowe rejects temporal parts, and since the particles that compose a persisting thing exist before and after the thing does, Lowe is in no position to identify the thing with its particles. So his solution for the unchanging particles leaves him still without a solution for the changing thing.

The next two papers discuss D. M. Armstrong's views about possibility, states of affairs, and truthmaking. Armstrong treats alternative possible worlds as fictitious recombinations of the universals that are the building blocks of the actual world. In my critical notice of his book on possibility, I explore a number of questions, among them these. What is the fiction – one big fiction of many worlds, many little fictions of one world each, or something more complicated? To what extent does his treatment of alternative possibilities as recombinations of actual ingredients leave room for the seeming possibility that there might have been universals other than those there actually are? To what extent is Armstrong's combinatorial theory of possibility compromised by his theory of 'strong' laws of nature?

I suggest, further, that Armstrong's combinatorialism is compromised by his requirement that every contingent truth should have a 'truthmaker': that is to say, there should be something whose existence entails that truth. In 'A World of Truthmakers?', my review of his book on states of affairs, I expand this objection. I say that the demand for truthmakers just *is* a demand for necessary connections that violate the principles of combinatorialism. We have to compromise one or the other, and my (reluctant) preference is to compromise the demand for truthmakers.

The next paper, 'Humean Supervenience Debugged', partially resolves a conflict between my commitment to objective single-case probabilities (chances) and my commitment to Humean Supervenience.[6] It would be nice to think that, in a world like ours, all else supervenes upon the spatiotemporal arrangement of local qualities instantiated by point-sized things. But what about chances and the laws governing them? Do these supervene, somehow, upon the frequencies and symmetries in the arrangement of local qualities? Then we have a

---

6 This conflict is the 'big bad bug' described in my *Philosophical Papers*, Vol. II (Oxford University Press, 1986), pp. *xiv* – *xvii*.

dilemma. We have present chances of various different future histories; and upon the different total past-present-and-future histories, different present chance distributions would supervene. Do we then have some present chance of the present chances being other than they actually are? – That seems peculiar, and indeed it turns out to conflict with a principle about chance that I take to be fundamental. So that principle has to be compromised. But how much? I argue here that, in realistic cases, the correction required may be so very slight as to be tolerable.

The next four papers deal with the mind–body problem. I am an 'Australian materialist': I have long held that mental states are states, presumably physical states of the brain, definable as occupants of certain folk-psychological causal roles. 'Psychophysical and Theoretical Identifications' presents this as a special case of a general method for defining theoretical terms. 'Reduction of Mind' discusses my long-standing position in the light of various contemporary discussions.

The most formidable opposition to any form of mind–body identity comes from the friends of qualia. It would be incredible to say that they are entirely wrong. In 'What Experience Teaches' and in 'Should a Materialist Believe in Qualia?' I argue that I can concede quite a lot to the friends of qualia – though not, of course, all that they ask! – without compromising materialism.

In the next paper, 'Naming the Colours', I analyse the colours and colour-experiences likewise as occupants of folk-theoretical causal roles. If an anti-materialist theory of qualia were true, and in particular if colour-experience revealed the essences of the qualia (or of the colours themselves), a satisfying account of the meanings of colour-names would be close at hand. Since this account is unavailable to a materialist like me, I must provide a substitute. I argue that the key to an adequate materialistic account of the meanings of colour-names lies in philosophy of language: we must avoid a certain sort of over-ambition about the semantic common knowledge that permits linguistic coordination.

The next two papers deal with the ontology of visual experience. There are two rival conceptions of what is given in vision. One is that the content of visual experience consists of an arrangement of colours. The other is that it consists of a percept: a proposition about the arrangement of things in the world before the eyes. Although I favour the second conception, in 'Percepts and Colour Mosaics in Visual

5

Experience' I find a place within the percept theory for the first sort of content as well, and for the idea that every percept is somehow equivalent to a definite colour-mosaic-percept. Within the percept theory, we can distinguish between seeing that a thing of so-and-so sort is present, and seeing a certain particular thing. In part, this is a matter of the veridicality of the perception; but a distinction remains even within unveridical perceptions. Hintikka has explained this in terms of cross-identification between alternative possibilities compatible with the content of the experience. In 'Individuation by Acquaintance and by Stipulation' I argue that the requisite cross-identification depends on prior cross-identification of the subject; and that this is best handled by taking the alternative possibilities to be *de se*, egocentric, possibilities. They are not possible ways for the world to be, rather they are possible ways for the subject to be vis-à-vis his surroundings.

The next two papers deal with questions about rational belief. The well-known model of belief as subjective probability is justified in part by 'Dutch book' theorems. These say that if someone is guided in betting by his degrees of belief, but his degrees of belief do not obey the usual axioms of probability, then he can be exploited by offers of bets which he will find acceptable but which result in a certain loss. Often it's said that this justification applies also to the policy of revising degrees of belief by conditionalizing on one's total evidence; but the sources cited, if any, seem not to be saying exactly that. In 'Why Conditionalize?' I provide the missing argument.

Saul Kripke's Pierre puzzle seems to show that we can fall blamelessly into contradictory belief, not because of irrationality but because of mere linguistic ignorance. Those who hear of the puzzle usually want to say that even if there is some sense in which the victim's state is one of contradictory belief, surely there is some other good sense in which it is not. In 'What Puzzling Pierre Does Not Believe' I propose a way to make good on this inclination.

The final paper, 'Elusive Knowledge', proposes an analysis of knowledge. *Pace* the many complicated analyses now on offer, it seems as if the concept of knowledge is simple enough for small children to master. I suggest that the complicated phenomena we have observed arise from the interaction between a very simple analysis and the complex pragmatics of context-dependent ignoring. '*S* knows that *P*' means simply that there is no possibility that *S* is wrong that *P* – Psst! except for those possibilities that we are now (properly) ignoring.

David Lewis
Princeton, November 1997

1

New work for a theory of universals

INTRODUCTION

D. M. Armstrong offers a theory of universals as the only adequate answer to a 'compulsory question' for systematic philosophy: the problem of One over Many.[1] I find this line of argument unpersuasive. But I think there is more to be said for Armstrong's theory than he himself has said. For as I bear it in mind considering various topics in philosophy, I notice time and again that it offers solutions to my problems. Whatever we may think of the problem of One over Many, universals can earn their living doing other much-needed work.

I do not say that they are indispensable. The services they render could be matched using resources that are Nominalistic in letter, if perhaps not in spirit.[2] But neither do I hold any presumption

First published in *The Australasian Journal of Philosophy* 61 (1983), pp. 343–377. Reprinted with kind permission from *The Australasian Journal of Philosophy*.

I am indebted to comments by Gilbert Harman, Lloyd Humberstone, Frank Jackson, Mark Johnston, Donald Morrison, Kim Sterelny, and others; and especially to discussion and correspondence with D. M. Armstrong over several years, without which I might well have believed to this day that set theory applied to *possibilia* is all the theory of properties that anyone could ever need.

1 D. M. Armstrong, *Universals and Scientific Realism* (Cambridge University Press, 1978), henceforth cited as '*Universals*'; see also his "Against 'Ostrich' Nominalism: A Reply to Michael Devitt", *Pacific Philosophical Quarterly* 61 (1980) pp. 440–449.

2 In this paper, I follow Armstrong's traditional terminology: 'universals' are repeatable entities, wholly present wherever a particular instantiates them; 'Nominalism' is the

against universals, to the effect that they are to be accepted only if we have no alternative. I therefore suspend judgement about universals themselves. I only insist that, one way or another, their work must be done.

I shall investigate the benefits of adding universals to my own usual ontology. That ontology, though Nominalistic, is in other respects generous. It consists of *possibilia* – particular, individual things, some of which comprise our actual world and others of which are unactualised[3] – together with the iterative hierarchy of classes built up from them. Thus I already have at my disposal a theory of properties as classes of *possibilia*. Properties, so understood, are not much like universals. Nor can they, unaided, take over the work of universals. Nevertheless they will figure importantly in what follows, since for me they are part of the environment in which universals might operate.

The friend of universals may wonder whether they would be better employed not as an addition to my ontology of *possibilia* and classes, but rather as a replacement for parts of it. A fair question, and an urgent one; nevertheless, not a question considered in this paper.

In the next section, I shall sketch Armstrong's theory of universals, contrasting universals with properties understood as classes of *possibilia*. Then I shall say why I am unconvinced by the One over Many argument. Then I shall turn to my principal topic: how universals could help me in connection with such topics as duplication, supervenience, and divergent worlds; a minimal form of materialism; laws and causation; and the content of language and thought. Perhaps the list could be extended.

rejection of such entities. In the conflicting modern terminology of Harvard, classes count as 'universals' and 'Nominalism' is predominantly the rejection of classes. Confusion of the terminologies can result in grave misunderstanding; see W. V. Quine, 'Soft Impeachment Disowned', *Pacific Philosophical Quarterly* 61 (1980) pp. 450–451.

3 Among 'things' I mean to include all the gerrymandered wholes and undemarcated parts admitted by the most permissive sort of mereology. Further, I include such physical objects as spatiotemporal regions and force fields, unless an eliminative reduction of them should prove desirable. Further, I include such nonphysical objects as gods and spooks, though not – I hope – as parts of the same world as us. Worlds themselves need no special treatment. They are things – big ones, for the most part.

Language offers us several more or less interchangeable words: 'universal'; 'property', 'quality', 'attribute', 'feature', and 'characteristic'; 'type', 'kind', and 'sort'; and perhaps others. And philosophy offers us several conceptions of the entities that such words refer to. My purpose is not to fix on one of these conceptions; but rather to distinguish two (at opposite extremes) and contemplate helping myself to both. Therefore some regimentation of language is called for; I apologise for any inconvenience caused. Let me reserve the word 'universal' for those entities, if such there be, that mostly conform to Armstrong's account. And let me reserve the word 'property' for classes – any classes, but I have foremost in mind classes of things. To have a property is to be a member of the class.[4]

Why call them 'properties' as well as 'classes'? – Just to underline the fact that they need not be classes of *actual* things. The property of being a donkey, for instance, is the class of *all* the donkeys. This property belongs to – this class contains – not only the actual donkeys of this world we live in, but also all the unactualised, otherworldly donkeys.

Likewise I reserve the word 'relation' for arbitrary classes of ordered pairs, triples, . . . Thus a relation among things is a property of 'tuples of things. Again, there is no restriction to actual things. Corresponding roughly to the division between properties and relations of things, we have the division between 'monadic' and 'polyadic' universals.

Universals and properties differ in two principal ways. The first difference concerns their instantiation. A universal is supposed to be wholly present wherever it is instantiated. It is a constituent part (though not a spatiotemporal part) of each particular that has it. A property, by contrast, is spread around. The property of being a donkey is partly present wherever there is a donkey, in this or any other world. Far from the property being part of the donkey, it is closer to

---

4 My conception of properties resembles the doctrine of Class Nominalism considered in *Universals*, I, pp. 28–43. But, strictly speaking, a Class Nominalist would be someone who claims to solve the One over Many problem simply by means of properties taken as classes, and that is far from my intention.

the truth to say that the donkey is part of the property. But the precise truth, rather, is that the donkey is a member of the property.

Thus universals would unify reality (*cf. Universals*, I, p. 109) in a way that properties do not. Things that share a universal have not just joined a single class. They literally have something in common. They are not entirely distinct. They overlap.

By occurring repeatedly, universals defy intuitive principles. But that is no damaging objection, since plainly the intuitions were made for particulars. For instance, call two entities *copresent* if both are wholly present at one position in space and time. We might intuit offhand that copresence is transitive. But it is not so, obviously, for universals. Suppose for the sake of argument that there are universals: round, silver, golden. Silver and round are copresent, for here is a silver coin; golden and round are copresent, for there is a gold coin; but silver and golden are not copresent. Likewise, if we add universals to an ontology of *possibilia*, for the relation of being part of the same possible world.[5] I and some otherworldly dragon are not worldmates; but I am a worldmate of the universal golden, and so is the dragon. Presumably I needed a mixed case involving both universals and particulars. For why should any two universals ever fail to be worldmates? Lacking such failures, the worldmate relation among universals alone is trivially transitive.

The second difference between universals and properties concerns their abundance. This is the difference that qualifies them for different work, and thereby gives rise to my interest in having universals and properties both.

---

5 If universals are to do the new work I have in store for them, they must be capable of repeated occurrence not only within a world but also across worlds. They would then be an exception to my usual principle – meant for particulars, of course – that nothing is wholly present as part of two different worlds. But I see no harm in that. If two worlds are said to overlap by having a coin in common, and if this coin is supposed to be wholly round in one world and wholly octagonal in the other, I stubbornly ask what shape it is, and insist that shape is not a relation to worlds. (See my 'Individuation by Acquaintance and by Stipulation', *Philosophical Review* 92 (1983), pp. 3–32 (reprinted in this volume as Chapter 22).) I do not see any parallel objection if worlds are said to overlap by sharing a universal. What contingent, nonrelational property of the universal could we put in place of shape of the coin in raising the problem? I cannot think of any.

A distinctive feature of Armstrong's theory is that universals are sparse. There are the universals that there must be to ground the objective resemblances and the causal powers of things, and there is no reason to believe in any more. All of the following alleged universals would be rejected:

not golden,	first examined before 2000 A.D.;
golden or wooden,	being identical,
metallic,	being alike in some respect,
self-identical,	being exactly alike,
owned by Fred,	being part of,
belonging to class C,	owning,
grue,	being paired with by some pair in R

(where C and R are utterly miscellaneous classes). The guiding idea, roughly, is that the world's universals should comprise a minimal basis for characterising the world completely. Universals that do not contribute at all to this end are unwelcome, and so are universals that contribute only redundantly. A satisfactory inventory of universals is a non-linguistic counterpart of a primitive vocabulary for a language capable of describing the world exhaustively.

(That is rough: Armstrong does not dismiss redundant universals out of hand, as the spirit of his theory might seem to demand. Conjunctive universals – as it might be, golden-and-round – are accepted, though redundant; so are analysable structural universals. The reason is that if the world were infinitely complex, there might be no way to cut down to a minimal basis. The only alternative to redundancy might be inadequacy, and if so we had better tolerate redundancy. But the redundancy is mitigated by the fact that complex universals consist of their simpler – if perhaps not absolutely simple – constituents. They are not distinct entities. See *Universals*, II, pp. 30–42 and 67–71.)

It is quite otherwise with properties. Any class of things, be it ever so gerrymandered and miscellaneous and indescribable in thought and language, and be it ever so superfluous in characterising the world, is nevertheless a property. So there are properties in immense abundance. (If the number of things, actual and otherwise, is beth-2, an estimate I regard as more likely low than high, then the number of properties of things is beth-3. And that is a big infinity indeed, except to students

12

of the outer reaches of set theory.) There are so many properties that those specifiable in English, or in the brain's language of synaptic interconnections and neural spikes, could be only an infinitesimal minority.

Because properties are so abundant, they are undiscriminating. Any two things share infinitely many properties, and fail to share infinitely many others. That is so whether the two things are perfect duplicates or utterly dissimilar. Thus properties do nothing to capture facts of resemblance. That is work more suited to the sparse universals. Likewise, properties do nothing to capture the causal powers of things. Almost all properties are causally irrelevant, and there is nothing to make the relevant ones stand out from the crowd. Properties carve reality at the joints – and everywhere else as well. If it's distinctions we want, too much structure is no better than none.

It would be otherwise if we had not only the countless throng of all properties, but also an élite minority of special properties. Call these the *natural* properties.[6] If we had properties and universals both, the universals could serve to pick out the natural properties. Afterwards the universals could retire if they liked, and leave their jobs to the natural properties. Natural properties would be the ones whose sharing makes for resemblance, and the ones relevant to causal powers. Most simply, we could call a property *perfectly* natural if its members are all and only those things that share some one universal. But also we would have other less-than-perfectly natural properties, made so by families of suitable related universals.[7] Thus we might have an imperfectly

---

6 See *Universals*, I, pp. 38–41; Anthony Quinton, 'Properties and Classes', *Proceedings of the Aristotelian Society* 48 (1957) pp. 33–58; and W. V. Quine, 'Natural Kinds', in his *Ontological Relativity* (Columbia University Press, 1969). See also George Bealer, *Quality and Concept* (Oxford University Press, 1982), especially pp. 9–10 and 177–187. Like me, Bealer favours an inegalitarian twofold conception of properties: there are abundant 'concepts' and sparse 'qualities', and the latter are the ones that 'determine the logical, causal, and phenomenal order of reality' (p. 10). Despite this point of agreement, however, Bealer's views and mine differ in many ways.

7 Here I assume that some solution to the problem of resemblance of universals is possible, perhaps along the lines suggested by Armstrong in *Universals*, II, pp. 48–52 and 101–131; and that such a solution could be carried over into a theory of

natural property of being metallic, even if we had no such single universal as metallic, in virtue of a close-knit family of genuine universals one or another of which is instantiated by any metallic thing. These imperfectly natural properties would be natural to varying degrees.

Let us say that an *adequate* theory of properties is one that recognises an objective difference between natural and unnatural properties; preferably, a difference that admits of degree. A combined theory of properties and universals is one sort of adequate theory of properties.

But not the only sort. A Nominalistic theory of properties could achieve adequacy by other means. Instead of employing universals it could draw primitive distinctions among particulars. Most simply, a Nominalist could take it as a primitive fact that some classes of things are perfectly natural properties; others are less-than-perfectly natural to various degrees; and most are not at all natural. Such a Nominalist takes 'natural' as a primitive predicate, and offers no analysis of what he means in predicating it of classes. His intention is to select the very same classes as natural properties that the user of universals would select. But he regards the universals as idle machinery, fictitiously superimposed on the primitive objective difference between the natural properties and the others.[8]

Alternatively, a Nominalist in pursuit of adequacy might prefer to rest with primitive objective resemblance among things. (He might not think that 'natural' was a very natural primitive, perhaps because it is to be predicated of classes.) Then he could undertake to define natural properties in terms of the mutual resemblance of their members and the failure of resemblance between their members and their nonmembers. Unfortunately, the project meets with well-known technical difficulties. These can be solved, but at a daunting price in complexity and artificiality of our primitive. We cannot get by with the familiar dyadic 'resembles'. Instead we need a predicate of resemblance that is both contrastive and variably polyadic. Something like

resemblance of perfectly natural properties, even if we take naturalness of properties as primitive.

8 This is the Moderate Class Nominalism considered in *Universals*, I, pp. 38–41. It is akin to the view of Quinton, *op. cit.*; but plus the unactualised members of the natural classes, and minus any hint that 'natural' could receive a psychologistic analysis.

x_1, x_2, . . . resemble one another and do not likewise resemble any of y_1, y_2, . . .

(where the strings of variables may be infinite, even uncountable) must be taken as understood without further analysis.[9] If adequate Nominalism requires us to choose between this and a primitive predicate of classes, we might well wonder whether the game is worth the candle. I only say we might wonder; I know of no consideration that seems to me decisive.

---

9 Such a theory is a form of Resemblance Nominalism, in Armstrong's classification, but it is unlike the form that he principally considers. See *Universals*, I, pp. 44–63. For discussions of the problem of defining natural classes in terms of resemblance, and of the trickery that proves useful in solving this problem, see Nelson Goodman, *The Structure of Appearance* (Harvard University Press, 1951), Chapters IV–VI; W. V. Quine, 'Natural Kinds'; and Adam Morton, 'Complex Individuals and Multigrade Relations', *Noûs* 9 (1975) pp. 309–318.

To get from primitive resemblance to perfectly natural properties, I have in mind a definition as follows. We begin with R as our contrastive and variably polyadic primitive. We want it to turn out that $x_1, x_2, . . . Ry_1, y_2, . . .$ iff some perfectly natural property is shared by all of x_1, x_2, . . . but by none of $y_1, y_2, ...$ We want to define N, another variably polyadic predicate, so that it will turn out that $Nx_1, x_2, . . .$ iff x_1, x_2, . . . are all and only the members of some perfectly natural property. Again we must allow for, and expect, the case where there are infinitely many x's. We define $Nx_1, x_2, . . .$ as:

$$\exists y_1, y_2, . . . \forall z \, (z, x_1, x_2, . . . Ry_1, y_2, . . . \equiv z = x_1 \vee z = x_2 \vee . . .).$$

Then we finish the job by defining a perfectly natural property as a class such that, if x_1, x_2, . . . are all and only its members, then Nx_1, $x_2, ...$

We might have taken N as primitive instead of R. But would that have been significantly different, given the interdefinability of the two? On the other hand, taking N as primitive also seems not significantly different from taking perfect naturalness of classes as primitive. It is only a difference between speaking in the plural of individuals and speaking in the singular of their classes, and that seems no real difference. Is plural talk a disguised form of class talk? Or *vice versa*? (See the discussion in *Universals*, I, pp. 32–34; also Max Black, 'The Elusiveness of Sets', *Review of Metaphysics* 24 (1971) pp. 614–636; Eric Stenius, 'Sets', *Synthese* 27 (1974), pp. 161–188; and Kurt Gödel, 'Russell's Mathematical Logic', in P. A. Schilpp, ed., *The Philosophy of Bertrand Russell* (Cambridge University Press, 1944).) At any rate, it is not at all clear to me that Moderate Class Nominalism and Resemblance Nominalism in its present form are two different theories, as opposed to a single theory presented in different styles.

At this point, you may see very well why it could be a good idea to believe in universals as well as properties; but you may see no point in having properties as well as universals. But properties have work of their own, and universals are ill-suited to do the work of properties.

It is properties that we need, sometimes natural and sometimes not, to provide an adequate supply of semantic values for linguistic expressions. Consider such sentences as these:

(1) Red resembles orange more than it resembles blue.
(2) Red is a colour.
(3) Humility is a virtue.
(4) Redness is a sign of ripeness.

Prima facie, these sentences contain names that cannot be taken to denote particular, individual things. What is the semantic role of these words? If we are to do compositional semantics in the way that is best developed, we need entities to assign as semantic values to these words, entities that will encode their semantic roles. Perhaps sometimes we might find paraphrases that will absolve us from the need to subject the original sentence to semantic analysis. That is the case with (1), for instance.[10] But even if such paraphrases sometimes exist – even if they

10 In virtue of the close resemblance of red and orange, it is possible for a red thing to resemble an orange one very closely; it is not possible for a red thing to resemble a blue one quite so closely. Given our ontology of *possibilia*, all possibilities are realised. So we could paraphase (1) by

(1') Some red thing resembles some orange thing more than any red thing resembles any blue thing.

so long as it is understood that the things in question needn't be part of our world, or of any one world. Or if we did not wish to speak of unactualised things, but we were willing to take ordinary-language modal idioms as primitive, we could instead give the paraphrase:

(1") A red thing can resemble an orange thing more closely than a red thing can resemble a blue thing.

It is necessary to use the ordinary-language idioms, or some adequate formalization of them, rather than standard modal logic. You cannot express (1") in modal logic (excluding an enriched modal logic that would defeat the point of the para-

always exist, which seems unlikely – they work piecemeal and frustrate any systematic approach to semantics.

Armstrong takes it that such sentences provide a subsidiary argument for universals, independent of his main argument from the One over Many problem (*Universals*, I, pp. 58–63; also "Against 'Ostrich' Nominalism"[11]). I quite agree that we have here an argument for something. But not for universals as opposed to properties. Properties can serve as the requisite semantic values. Indeed, properties are much better suited to the job than universals are. That is plain even from the examples considered. It is unlikely that there are any such genuine universals as the colours (especially determinable colours, like red, rather than determinate shades), or ripeness, or humility. Armstrong agrees (*Universals*, I, p. 61) that he cannot take (1)–(4) as straightforwardly making reference to universals. He must first subject them to paraphrase. Even if there always is a paraphrase that does refer to, or quantify over, genuine universals, still the need for paraphrase is a threat to systematic semantics. The problem arises exactly because universals are sparse. There is no corresponding objection if we take the requisite semantic values as properties.

Other sentences make my point more dramatically.

(5) Grueness does not make for resemblance among all its instances.
(6) What is common to all who suffer pain is being in some or another state that occupies the pain role, presumably not the same state in all cases.

The point is not that these sentences are true – though they are – but that they require semantic analysis. (It is irrelevant that they are not ordinary language.) A universal of grueness would be anathema; as

phrase by quantifying over degrees of resemblance or whatnot) because you cannot express cross-world relations, and in particular cannot express the needed cross-world comparison of similarity.

11 He derives the argument, and a second semantic argument to be considered shortly, from Arthur Pap, 'Nominalism, Empiricism, and Universals: I', *Philosophical Quarterly* 9 (1959) pp. 330–340, and F. C. Jackson, 'Statements about Universals', *Mind* 86 (1977) pp. 427–429.

would a universal such that, necessarily, one has it if he is in some state or other that occupies the pain role in his case.[12] But the corresponding properties are no problem.

Indeed, we have a comprehension schema applying to any predicate phrase whatever, however complicated. (Let it even be infinitely long; let it even include imaginary names for entities we haven't really named.) Let x range over things, P over properties (classes) of things. Then:

$$\exists_1 P\square\ \forall x\ (x\ \text{has}\ P \equiv \emptyset x).$$

We could appropriately call this 'the property of $\emptyset$-ing' in those cases where the predicate phrase is short enough to form a gerund, and take this property to be the semantic value of the gerund. Contrast this with the very different relationship of universals and predicates set forth in *Universals*, II, pp. 7–59.

Consider also those sentences which *prima facie* involve second-order quantification. From *Universals*, I, p. 62, and "Against 'Ostrich' Nominalism" we have these.

(7) He has the same virtues as his father.
(8) The dresses were of the same colour.
(9) There are undiscovered fundamental physical properties.
(10) Acquired characteristics are never inherited.
(11) Some zoological species are cross-fertile.

Prima facie, we are quantifying either over properties or over universals. Again, paraphrases might defeat that presumption, but in a piecemeal way that threatens systematic semantics. In each case, properties could serve as the values of the variables of quantification. Only in case (9) could universals serve equally well. To treat the other cases, not to mention

(12) Some characteristics, such as the colours, are more disjunctive than they seem.

---

12 Or better, in the case of creatures of his kind. See my 'Mad Pain and Martian Pain', in Ned Block, ed., *Readings in Philosophy of Psychology*, I (Harvard University Press, 1980).

as quantifications over universals, we would again have to resort to some preliminary paraphrase. (Armstrong again agrees: *Universals*, I, p. 63.) This second semantic argument, like the first, adduces work for which properties are better qualified than universals.

Which is not to deny that a partnership might do better still. Let it be granted that we are dealing with quantifications over properties. Still, these quantifications – like most of our quantifications – may be tacitly or explicitly restricted. In particular, they usually are restricted to natural properties. Not to perfectly natural properties that correspond to single universals, except in special cases like (9), but to properties that are at least somewhat more natural than the great majority of the utterly miscellaneous. That is so for all our examples, even (12). Then even though we quantify over properties, we still need either universals or the resources of an adequate Nominalism in order to say which of the properties we mostly quantify over.

I also think that it is properties that we need in characterising the content of our intentional attitudes. I believe, or I desire, that I live in one of the worlds in a certain class, rather than any world outside that class. This class of worlds is a property had by worlds. I believe, or I desire, that my world has that property. (The class of worlds also may be called a *proposition*, in one of the legitimate senses of that word, and my 'propositional attitude' of belief or desire has this proposition as its 'object'.) More generally, subsuming the previous case, I believe or I desire that I myself belong to a certain class of *possibilia*. I ascribe a certain property to myself, or I want to have it. Or I might ascribe a property to something else, or even to myself, under a relation of acquaintance I bear to that thing.[13] Surely the properties that give the content of attitudes in these ways cannot be relied on to be perfectly natural, hence cannot be replaced by universals. It is interesting to ask whether there is any lower limit to their naturalness (see the final section of this paper), but surely no very exacting standard is possible. Here again properties are right for the job, universals are not.

13 See my 'Attitudes *De Dicto* and *De Se*', *Philosophical Review* 88 (1979) pp. 513–543; and 'Individuation by Acquaintance and by Stipulation'.

Armstrong's main argument for universals is the 'One over Many'. It is because I find this argument unconvincing that I am investigating alternative reasons to accept a theory of universals.

Here is a concise statement of the argument, taken by condensation from "Against 'Ostrich' Nominalism", pp. 440–441. A very similar statement could have been drawn from the opening pages of *Universals*.

I would wish to start by saying that many different particulars can all have what appears to be the same nature and draw the conclusion that, as a result, there is a *prima facie* case for postulating universals. We are continually talking about different things having the same property or quality, being of the same sort or kind, having the same nature, and so on. Philosophers draw the distinction between sameness of token and sameness of type. But they are only making explicit a distinction which ordinary language (and so, ordinary thought) perfectly recognises. I suggest that the fact of sameness of type is a Moorean fact: one of the many facts which even philosophers should not deny, whatever philosophical account or analysis they give of such facts. Any comprehensive philosophy must try to give some account of Moorean facts. They constitute the compulsory questions in the philosophical examination paper.

From this point of departure, Armstrong makes his case by criticising rival attempts to answer the compulsory question, and by rejecting views that decline to answer it at all.

Still more concisely, the One over Many problem is presented as the problem of giving some account of Moorean facts of apparent sameness of type. Thus understood, I agree that the question is compulsory; I agree that Armstrong's postulation of shared universals answers it; but I think that an adequate Nominalism also answers it.

An effort at systematic philosophy must indeed give an account of any purported fact. There are three ways to give an account. (1) 'I deny it' – this earns a failing mark if the fact is really Moorean. (2) 'I analyse it thus' – this is Armstrong's response to the facts of apparent sameness of type. Or (3) 'I accept it as primitive'. Not every *account* is an *analysis*! A system that takes certain Moorean facts as primitive, as unanalysed, cannot be accused of failing to make a place for them. It neither shirks the compulsory question nor answers it by denial. It does give an account.

An adequate Nominalism, of course, is a theory that takes Moorean facts of apparent sameness of type as primitive. It predicates mutual resemblance of the things which are apparently of the same type; or it predicates naturalness of some property that they all share, *i.e.* that has them all as members; and it declines to analyse these predications any further. That is why the problem of One over Many, rightly understood, does not provide more than a *prima facie* reason to postulate universals. Universals afford one solution, but there are others.

I fear that the problem does not remain rightly understood. Early in *Universals* it undergoes an unfortunate double transformation. In the course of a few pages (*Universals*, I, pp. 11–16) the legitimate demand for an account of Moorean facts of apparent sameness of type turns into a demand for an analysis of predication in general. The analysandum becomes the schema '*a* has the property *F*'. The turning point takes only two sentences (p. 12):

How is [the Nominalist] to account for the apparent (if usually partial) identity of numerically different particulars? How can two different things both be white or both be on a table?

And very soon (pp. 16–17) those who 'refuse to countenance universals but who at the same time see no need for any reductive analyses [of the schema of predication]', those according to whom 'there are no universals but the proposition that *a* is *F* is perfectly all right as it is' stand accused of dodging the compulsory question.

When the demand for an account – for a place in one's system – turned into a demand for an analysis, then I say that the question ceased to be compulsory. And when the analysandum switched, from Moorean facts of apparent sameness of type to predication generally, then I say that the question ceased to be answerable at all. The transformed problem of One over Many deserves our neglect. The ostrich that will not look at it is a wise bird indeed.

Despite his words, I do not think that Armstrong really means to demand, either from Nominalists or from himself, a *fully* general analysis of predication. For none is so ready as he to insist that not just any

21

shared predicate makes for even apparent sameness of type. (That is what gives his theory its distinctive interest and merit.) It would be better to put the transformed problem thus: one way or another, all predication is to be analysed. Some predications are to be analysed away in terms of others. Here we have one-off analyses for specific predicates – as it might be, for 'grue'. But all those predications that remain, after the one-off analyses are finished, are to be analysed wholesale by means of a general analysis of the schema 'a has property F'.

There is to be no unanalysed predication. Time and again, Armstrong wields this requirement against rival theories. One theory after another falls victim to the 'relation regress': in the course of analysing other predications, the theory has resort to a new predicate that cannot, on pain of circularity, be analysed along with the rest. So falls Class Nominalism (including the version with primitive naturalness that I deem adequate): it employs predications of class membership, which predications it cannot without circularity analyse in terms of class membership. So falls Resemblance Nominalism: it fails to analyse predications of resemblance. So fall various other, less deserving Nominalisms. And so fall rival forms of Realism, for instance Transcendent, Platonic Realism: this time, predications of participation evade analysis. Specific theories meet other, specific objections; suffice it to say that I think these inconclusive against the two Nominalisms that I called adequate. But the clincher, the one argument that recurs throughout the many refutations, is the relation regress. And this amounts to the objection that the theory under attack does not achieve its presumed aim of doing away with all unanalysed predication and therefore fails to solve the transformed problem of One over Many.

Doing away with all unanalysed predication is an unattainable aim, and so an unreasonable aim. No theory is to be faulted for failing to achieve it. For how could there be a theory that names entities, or quantifies over them, in the course of its sentences, and yet altogether avoids primitive predication? Artificial tricks aside,[14] the thing cannot be done.

14 Let S be the syntactic category of sentences, let N be the category of names, and for any categories x and y, let x/y be the category of expressions that attach to

What's true is that a theory may be faulted for its overabundant primitive predications, or for unduly mysterious ones, or for unduly complicated ones. These are not fatal faults, however. They are to be counted against a theory, along with its faults of overly generous ontology or of disagreement with less-than-Moorean commonsensical opinions. Rival philosophical theories have their prices, which we seek to measure. But it's all too clear that for philosophers, at least, there ain't no such thing as a free lunch.

How does Armstrong himself do without primitive predication? – He doesn't. Consider the predicate 'instantiates' (or 'has'), as in 'particular *a* instantiates universal *F*' or 'this electron has unit charge'. No one-off analysis applies to this specific predicate. 'Such identity in nature [as results from the having of one universal in many particulars] is literally inexplicable, in the sense that it cannot be further explained.' (*Universals*, I, p. 109.) Neither do predications of 'instantiates' fall under Armstrong's general analysis of (otherwise unanalysed) predication. His is a *non-relational* Realism: he declines, with good reason, to postulate a dyadic universal of instantiation to bind particulars to their universals. (And if he did, it would only postpone the need for primitive predication.) So let all who have felt the bite of Armstrong's relation regress rise up and cry *'Tu quoque!'* And let us mark well that Armstrong is prepared to give *one* predicate 'what has been said to be the privilege of the harlot: power without responsibility. The predicate is informative, it makes a vital contribution to telling us what is the case, the world is different if it is different, yet ontologically it is supposed not to commit us. Nice work: if you can get it.' (Compare Armstrong on Quine's treatment of predication, "Against 'Ostrich' Nominalism", p. 443.)

Let us dump the project of getting rid of primitive predication, and

y-expressions to make *x*-expressions. Predicates, then, are category *S/N*. (Or (*S/N*)/*N* for two-place predicates, and so on.) To embed names (or variables in the category of names) into sentences without primitive predication, take any category *Q* which is neither *S* nor *N*, nor *S/N*, and let there be primitives of categories *Q/N* and *S/Q*. Or take Q_1 and Q_2, different from *S* and *N* and *S/N* and each other, and let the primitives be of categories Q_1/N, Q_2/Q_1, and S/Q_1. Or. . . . I cannot see how this trickery could be a genuine alternative to, rather than a disguise for, primitive predication.

return to the sensible – though not compulsory – project of analysing Moorean facts of apparent sameness of type. Now does the relation regress serve Armstrong better? I think not. It does make better sense within the more sensible project, but it still bites Armstrong and his rivals with equal force. Let the Nominalist say 'These donkeys resemble each other, so likewise do those stars, and there analysis ends.' Let the Platonist say 'This statue participates in the Form of beauty, likewise that lecture participates in the Form of truth, and there analysis ends.' Let Armstrong say 'This electron instantiates unit charge, likewise that proton instantiates tripartiteness, and there analysis ends.' It is possible to complain in each case that a fact of sameness of type has gone unanalysed, the types being respectively resemblance, participation, and instantiation. But it is far from evident that the alleged facts are Moorean, and still less evident that the first two are more Moorean than the third. None of them are remotely the equals of the genuine Moorean fact that, in some sense, different lumps of gold are the same in kind.

Michael Devitt has denounced the One over Many problem as a mirage better left unseen.[15] I have found Devitt's discussion instructive and I agree with much of what he says. But Devitt has joined Armstrong in transforming the One over Many problem. He takes it to be the problem of analysing the schema

a and b have the same property (are of the same type), F-ness

otherwise than by means of a one-off analysis for some specific F. To that problem it is fair to answer as he does that

a is F; b is F

is analysis enough, once we give over the aim of doing without primitive predication. But Devitt has set himself too easy a problem. If we attend to the modest, untransformed One over Many problem, which is no mirage, we will ask about a different analysandum:

15 " 'Ostrich Nominalism' or 'Mirage Realism'?", *Pacific Philosophical Quarterly* 61 (1980) pp. 433–439. Devitt speaks on behalf of Quine as well as himself; Quine indicates agreement with Devitt in 'Soft Impeachment Disowned'.

a and *b* have some common property (are somehow of the same type)

in which it is not said what *a* and *b* have in common. This less definite analysandum is not covered by what Devitt has said. If we take a clearly Moorean case, he owes us an account: either an analysis or an overt resort to primitive predication of resemblance.

DUPLICATION, SUPERVENIENCE, AND DIVERGENT WORLDS

Henceforth I shall speak only of my need for the distinction between natural and unnatural, or more and less natural, properties. It is to be understood that the work I have in store for an adequately discriminatory theory of properties might be new work for a theory of universals, or it might instead be work for the resources of an adequate Nominalism.

I begin with the problem of analysing duplication. We are familiar with cases of approximate duplication, *e.g.* when we use copying machines. And we understand that if these machines were more perfect than they are, the copies they made would be perfect duplicates of the original. Copy and original would be alike in size and shape and chemical composition of the ink marks and the paper, alike in temperature and magnetic alignment and electrostatic charge, alike even in the exact arrangement of their electrons and quarks. Such duplicates would be exactly alike, we say. They would match perfectly, they would be qualitatively identical, they would be indiscernible.

But they would not have exactly the same properties, in my sense of the word. As in the case of any two things, countless class boundaries would divide them. Intrinsically, leaving out their relations to the rest of the world, they would be just alike. But they would occupy different spatio-temporal positions; and they might have different owners, be first examined in different centuries, and so on.

So if we wish to analyse duplication in terms of shared properties, it seems that we must first distinguish the *intrinsic* (or 'internal') properties from the *extrinsic* (or 'external' or 'relational') properties. Then we may say that two things are duplicates iff they have precisely the same intrinsic properties, however much their extrinsic properties might differ. But our new problem of dividing the properties into intrinsic and extrinsic is no easier than our original problem of analysing duplication. In fact, the two problems are joined in a tight little circle of interdefinability. Duplication is a matter of sharing intrinsic properties; intrinsic properties are just those properties that never differ between duplicates. Property P is intrinsic iff, for any two duplicate things, not necessarily from the same world, either both have P or neither does. P is extrinsic iff there is some such pair of duplicates of which one has P and the other lacks P.[16]

16 Given duplication, we can also subdivide the extrinsic properties, distinguishing pure cases from various mixtures of extrinsic and intrinsic. Partition the things, of this and other worlds, into equivalence classes under the relation of duplication. A property may divide an equivalence class, may include it, or may exclude it. A property P is extrinsic, as we said, if it divides at least some of the classes. We have four subcases. (1) P divides every class; then we may call P *purely extrinsic.* (2) P divides some classes, includes some, and excludes none; then P is the disjunction of an intrinsic property and a purely extrinsic property. (3) P divides some, excludes some, and includes none; then P is the conjunction of an intrinsic property and a purely extrinsic property. (4) P divides some, includes some, and excludes some; then P is the conjunction of an intrinsic property and an impurely extrinsic property of the sort considered in the second case, or equivalently is the disjunction of an intrinsic property and an impurely extrinsic property of the sort considered in the third case.

We can also classify relations as intrinsic or extrinsic, but in two different ways. Take a dyadic relation, *i.e.* a class or ordered pairs. Call the relation *intrinsic to its relata* iff, whenever a and a' are duplicates (or identical) and b and b' are duplicates (or identical), then both or neither of the pairs $<a,b>$ and $<a',b'>$ stand in the relation. Call the relation *intrinsic to its pairs* iff, whenever the pairs $<a,b>$ and $<a', b'>$ themselves are duplicates, then both or neither of them stand in the relation. In the second case, a stronger requirement is imposed on the pairs. For instance they might fail to be duplicate pairs because the distance between a and b differs from the distance between a' and b', even though a and a' are duplicates and b and b' are duplicates. In traditional terminology, 'internal relations' are intrinsic to their *relata*; 'external relations' are intrinsic to their pairs but not to their *relata*; and relations extrinsic even to their pairs, such as the relation of belonging to the same owner, get left out of the classification altogether.

Our definition of intrinsic properties in terms of duplication closely resembles the definition of 'differential properties' given by Michael Slote in 'Some Thoughts on Goodman's Riddle', *Analysis* 27 (1967) pp. 128–132, and in *Reason and Scepti-*

If we relied on our physical theory to be accurate and exhaustive, we might think to define duplication in physical terms. We believe that duplicates must be alike in the arrangement of their electrons and quarks – why not put this forward as a definition? But such a 'definition' is no analysis. It presupposes the physics of our actual world; however physics is contingent and known a *posteriori*. The definition does not apply to duplication at possible worlds where physics is different, or to duplication between worlds that differ in their physics. Nor does it capture what those ignorant of physics mean when they speak – as they do – of duplication.

The proper course, I suggest, is to analyse duplication in terms of shared properties; but to begin not with the intrinsic properties but rather with natural properties. Two things are qualitative duplicates if they have exactly the same perfectly natural properties.[17]

Physics is relevant because it aspires to give an inventory of natural properties – not a complete inventory, perhaps, but a complete enough inventory to account for duplication among actual things. If physics succeeds in this, then duplication within our world amounts to sameness of physical description. But the natural properties themselves are what matter, not the theory that tells us what they are. If Materialism were false and physics an utter failure, as is the case at some deplorable worlds, there would still be duplication in virtue of shared natural properties.

On my analysis, all perfectly natural properties come out intrinsic. That seems right. The converse is not true. Intrinsic properties may

---

cism (George Allen & Unwin, 1970). But where I quantify over *possibilia*, Slote applies modality to ordinary, presumably actualist, quantifiers. That makes a difference. An extrinsic property might differ between duplicates, but only when the duplicates inhabit different worlds; then Slote would count the property as differential. An example is the property of being a sphere that inhabits a world where there are pigs or a cube that inhabits a world without pigs.

See my 'Extrinsic Properties', *Philosophical Studies* 44 (1983) pp. 197–200 (reprinted in this volume as Chapter 5), for further discussion of the circle from duplication to intrinsicness and back.

17 Likewise $<a,b>$ and $<a', b'>$ are duplicate pairs iff a and a' have exactly the same perfectly natural properties, and so do b and b', and also the perfectly natural relations between a and b are exactly the same as those between a' and b'.

be disjunctive and miscellaneous and unnatural, so long as they never differ between duplicates. The perfectly natural properties comprise a basis for the intrinsic properties; but arbitrary Boolean compounds of them, however unnatural, are still intrinsic. Hence if we adopt the sort of adequate Nominalism that draws a primitive distinction between natural and unnatural properties, that is not the same thing as drawing a primitive distinction between intrinsic and extrinsic properties. The former distinction yields the latter, but not *vice versa*.

Likewise if we adopt the sort of adequate Nominalism that begins with a suitable relation of partial resemblance, that is not the same thing as taking duplication itself as primitive. Again, the former yields the latter, but not *vice versa*.

If instead we reject Nominalism, and we take the perfectly natural properties to be those that correspond to universals (in the sense that the members of the property are exactly those things that instantiate the universal), then all the properties that correspond to universals are intrinsic. So are all the Boolean compounds – disjunctions, negations, etc. – of properties that correspond to universals. The universals themselves are intrinsic *ex officio*, so to speak.

But here I must confess that the theory of universals for which I offer new work cannot be exactly Armstrong's theory. For it must reject extrinsic universals; whereas Armstrong admits them, although not as irreducible. (See *Universals*, II, pp. 78–79.) I think he would be better off without them, given his own aims. (1) They subvert the desired connection between sharing of universals and Moorean facts of partial or total sameness of nature. Admittedly, there is such a thing as resemblance in extrinsic respects: things can be alike in the roles they play *vis-à-vis* other things, or in the origins they spring from. But such resemblances are not what we mean when we say of two things that they are of the same kind, or have the same nature. (2) They subvert the desired immanence of universals: if something instantiates an extrinsic universal, that is not a fact just about that thing. (3) They are not needed for Armstrong's theory of laws of nature; any supposed law connecting extrinsic universals of things can be equivalently re-placed by a law connecting intrinsic structures of larger systems that have those things as parts.

Thus I am content to say that if there are universals, intrinsic duplicates are things having exactly the same universals. We need not say '. . . exactly the same *intrinsic* universals' because we should not believe in any other kind.

Not only is duplication of interest in its own right; it also is needed in dealing with other topics in metaphysics. Hence such topics create a derived need for natural properties. I shall consider two topics where I find need to speak of duplication: supervenience and divergent worlds.

First, supervenience. A supervenience thesis is a denial of independent variation. Given an ontology of *possibilia*, we can formulate such theses in terms of differences between possible individuals or worlds. To say that so-and-so supervenes on such-and-such is to say that there can be no difference in respect of so-and-so without difference in respect of such-and-such. Beauty of statues supervenes on their shape, size, and colour, for instance, if no two statues, in the same or different worlds, ever differ in beauty without also differing in shape or size or colour.[18]

A supervenience thesis is, in a broad sense, reductionist. But it is a stripped-down form of reductionism, unencumbered by dubious denials of existence, claims of ontological priority, or claims of translatability. One might wish to say that in some sense the beauty of statues is nothing over and above the shape and size and colour that beholders appreciate, but without denying that there is such a thing as beauty, without claiming that beauty exists only in some less-than-fundamental way, and without undertaking to paraphrase ascriptions of beauty in terms of shape etc. A supervenience thesis seems to capture what the cautious reductionist wishes to say.

Even if reductionists ought to be less cautious and aim for translation, still it is a good idea to attend to the question of supervenience. For if supervenience fails, then no scheme of translation can be correct and we needn't go on Chisholming away in search of one. If supervenience succeeds, on the other hand, then some correct scheme must

18 For a general discussion of supervenience, see Jaegwon Kim, 'Supervenience and Nomological Incommensurables', *American Philosophical Quarterly* 15 (1978) pp. 149–156.

exist; the remaining question is whether there exists a correct scheme that is less than infinitely complex. If beauty is supervenient on shape etc., the worst that can happen is that an ascription of beauty is equivalent to an uncountably infinite disjunction of maximally specific descriptions of shape etc., which descriptions might themselves involve infinite conjunctions.

Interesting supervenience theses usually involve the notion of qualitative duplication that we have just considered. Thus we may ask what does or doesn't supervene on the qualitative character of the entire world, throughout all of history. Suppose that two possible worlds are perfect qualitative duplicates – must they then also have exactly the same distributions of objective probability, the same laws of nature, the same counterfactuals and causal relations? Must their inhabitants have the same *de re* modal properties? If so, it makes sense to pursue such projects as a frequency analysis of probability, a regularity analysis of laws of nature, or a comparative similarity analysis of causal counterfactuals and *de re* modality. If not, such projects are doomed from the start, and we needn't look at the details of the attempts. But we cannot even raise these questions of supervenience unless we can speak of duplicate worlds. And to do that, I have suggested, we need natural properties.

(Note that if possible worlds obey a principle of identity of qualitative indiscernibles, then all these supervenience theses hold automatically. If no two worlds are duplicates, then *a fortiori* no two are duplicates that differ in their probabilities, laws, . . . , or anything else.)

We might also ask whether qualitative character supervenes on anything less. For instance, we might ask whether global qualitative character supervenes on local qualitative character. Say that two worlds are *local duplicates* iff they are divisible into corresponding small parts in such a way that (1) corresponding parts of the two worlds are duplicates, and (2) the correspondence preserves spatiotemporal relations. (The exact meaning depends, of course, on what we mean by 'small'.) If two worlds are local duplicates, then must they be duplicates *simpliciter*? Or could they differ in ways that do not prevent local duplication – e.g. in external relations, other than the spatiotemporal relations themselves, between separated things? Again, we must make sense of duplication – this time, both in the large and in the small – even to ask the question.[19]

Next, divergent worlds. I shall say that two possible worlds *diverge* iff they are not duplicates but they do have duplicate initial temporal segments. Thus our world and another might match perfectly up through the year 1945, and go their separate ways thereafter.

Note that we need no identity of times across worlds. Our world through our 1945 duplicates an initial segment of the other world; that otherworldly segment ends with a year that indeed resembles our 1945, but it is part of otherworldly time, not part of our time. Also, we need no separation of time and space that contravenes Relativity – we have initial temporal segments, of this or another world, if we have spatiotemporal regions bounded by spacelike surfaces that cut the world in two.

I distinguish *divergence* of worlds from *branching* of worlds. In branching, instead of duplicate segments, one and the same initial segment is allegedly shared as a common part by two overlapping worlds. Branching is problematic in ways that divergence is not. First, because an inhabitant of the shared segment cannot speak unequivocally of *the* world he lives in. What if he says there will be a sea fight tomorrow, meaning of course to speak of the future of his own world, and one of the two worlds he lives in has a sea fight the next day and the other doesn't? Second, because overlap of worlds interferes with the most salient principle of demarcation for worlds, *viz.* that two possible individuals are part of the same world iff they are linked by some chain of external relations, *e.g.* of spatiotemporal relations. (I know of no other example.) Neither of these difficulties seems insuperable, but both are better avoided. That makes it reasonable to prefer a theory of nonoverlapping divergent worlds to a theory of branching worlds. Then we need to be able to speak of qualitative duplication of world-segments, which we can do in terms of shared natural properties.

19 Such a thesis of supervenience of the global on the local resembles the 'holographic hypothesis' considered and rejected by Saul Kripke in 'Identity Through Time', presented at the 1979 conference of the American Philosophical Association, Eastern Division, and elsewhere.

Divergent (or branching) worlds are of use in defining Determinism. The usual definitions are not very satisfactory. If we say that every event has a cause, we overlook probabilistic causation under Indeterminism. If we speak of what could be predicted by a superhuman calculator with unlimited knowledge of history and the laws of nature, we overlook obstacles that might prevent prediction even under Determinism, or else we try to make nonvacuous sense of counterfactuals about what our predictor could do if he had some quite impossible combination of powers and limitations.

A better approach is as follows. First, a system of laws of nature is Deterministic iff no two divergent worlds both conform perfectly to the laws of that system. Second, a world is Deterministic iff its laws comprise a Deterministic system. Third, Determinism is the thesis that our world is Deterministic.[20]

(Alternative versions of Determinism can be defined in similar fashion. For instance, we could strengthen the first step by prohibiting convergence as well as divergence of law-abiding worlds. Or we could even require that no two law-abiding worlds have duplicate momentary slices without being duplicates throughout their histories. Or we could define a weaker sort of Determinism: we could call a world *fortuitously* Deterministic, even if its laws do not comprise a Deterministic system, iff no world both diverges from it and conforms to its laws. The laws and early history of such a world suffice to determine later history, but only because the situations in which the laws fall short of Determinism never arise. We might equivalently define fortuitous Determinism as follows: for any historical fact F and any initial segment S of the world, there are a true proposition H about the history of S and a true proposition L about the laws of nature, such that H and L together

---

20 This approach is due, in essence, to Richard Montague, 'Deterministic Theories', in *Decisions, Values and Groups*, II (Pergamon Press, 1962), and in his *Formal Philosophy* (Yale University Press, 1974). But Montague did not speak as I have done of duplication of initial segments of worlds in virtue of the sharing of certain élite properties. Instead, he used sameness of description in a certain vocabulary, which vocabulary was left as an unspecified parameter of his analysis. For he wrote as a logician obliged to remain neutral on questions of metaphysics.

strictly imply F.[21] Does this definition bypass our need to speak of duplication of initial segments? Not so, for we must ask what it means to say that H is about the history of S. I take that to mean that H holds at both or neither of any two worlds that both begin with segments that are duplicates of S.)

Divergent worlds are important also in connection with the sort of counterfactual conditional that figures in patterns of causal dependence. Such counterfactuals tend to be temporally asymmetric, and this is what gives rise to the asymmetry of causation itself. Counterfactuals of this sort do not 'backtrack': it is not to be said that if the present were different a different past would have led up to it, but rather that if the present were different, the same past would have had a different outcome. Given a hypothesised difference at a certain time, the events of future times normally would be very different indeed, but the events of past times (except perhaps for the very near past) would be no different. Thus actuality and its counterfactual alternatives are divergent worlds, with duplicate initial segments.[22]

MINIMAL MATERIALISM

There is a difficulty that arises if we attempt to formulate certain reductionist views, for instance Materialism, as supervenience theses. A solution to this difficulty employs natural properties not only by way of duplication but in a more direct way also.

Roughly speaking, Materialism is the thesis that physics – something not too different from present-day physics, though presumably

---

21 A closely related definition appears in Peter van Inwagen, 'The Incompatibility of Free Will and Determinism', *Philosophical Studies* 27 (1975) pp. 185–199.

22 See my 'Counterfactual Dependence and Time's Arrow', *Noûs* 13 (1979) pp. 455–476; Jonathan Bennett's review of my *Counterfactuals, Canadian Journal of Philosophy* 4 (1974) pp. 381–402; P. B. Downing, 'Subjunctive Conditionals, Time Order, and Causation', *Proceedings of the Aristotelian Society* 59 (1959) pp. 125–140; Allan Gibbard and William Harper, 'Counterfactuals and Two Kinds of Expected Utility', in C. A. Hooker, J. T. Leach, and E. F. McClennen, eds., *Foundations and Applications of Decision Theory* (Reidel, 1978), and in W. L. Harper, R. Stalnaker, and G. Pearce, eds., *Ifs* (Reidel, 1981); and Frank Jackson, 'A Causal Theory of Counterfactuals', *Australasian Journal of Philosophy* 55 (1977) pp. 3–21.

somewhat improved – is a comprehensive theory of the world, complete as well as correct. The world is as physics says it is, and there's no more to say. World history written in physical language is all of world history. That is rough speaking indeed; our goal will be to give a better formulation. But before I try to say more precisely what Materialism is, let me say what it is not. (1) Materialism is not a thesis of finite translatability of all our language into the language of physics. (2) Materialism is not to be identified with any one Materialist theory of mind. It is a thesis that motivates a variety of theories of mind: versions of Behaviourism, Functionalism, the mind–body identity theory, even the theory that mind is all a mistake. (3) Materialism is not just the theory that there are no things except those recognised by physics. To be sure, Materialists don't believe in spirits, or other such nonphysical things. But antimaterialists may not believe in spirits either – their complaint needn't be that physics omits some of the things that there are. They may complain instead that physics overlooks some of the ways there are for physical things to differ; for instance, they may think that physical people could differ in what their experience is like. (4) That suggests that Materialism is, at least in part, the thesis that there are no natural properties instantiated at our world except those recognised by physics. That is better, but I think still not right. Couldn't there be a natural property X (in the nature of the case, it is hard to name an example!) which is shared by the physical brains in worlds like ours and the immaterial spirits that inhabit other worlds? Or by thisworldly quarks and certain otherworldly particles that cannot exist under our physics? Physics could quite properly make no mention of a natural property of this sort. It is enough to recognise the special case applicable to our world, X-*cum*-physicality, brainhood or quarkhood as it might be. Then if by physical properties we mean those properties that are mentioned in the language of physics, a Materialist ought not to hold that all natural properties instantiated in our world are physical properties.

At this point, it ought to seem advisable to formulate Materialism as a supervenience thesis: no difference without physical difference. Or, contraposing: physical duplicates are duplicates *simpliciter*. *A fortiori*, no mental difference without physical difference; physical duplicates are mental duplicates. The thesis might best be taken as applying to whole possible worlds, in order to bypass such questions as whether mental life is to some extent extrinsic to the subject. So we have this first of several attempted formulations of Materialism:

M1. Any two possible worlds that are exactly alike in all respects recognised by physics are qualitative duplicates.

But this will not do. In making Materialism into a thesis about how just any two worlds can and cannot differ, *M1* puts Materialism forward as a necessary truth. That is not what Materialists intend. Materialism is meant to be a contingent thesis, a merit of our world that not all other worlds share. Two worlds could indeed differ without differing physically, if at least one of them is a world where Materialism is false. For instance, our Materialistic world differs from a nonmaterialistic world that is physically just like ours but that also contains physically epiphenomenal spirits.

There is a noncontingent supervenience thesis nearby that might appeal to Materialists:

M2. There is no difference, *a fortiori* no mental difference, without some nonmental difference. Any two worlds alike in all nonmental respects are duplicates, and in particular do not differ in respect of the mental lives of their inhabitants.

This seems to capture our thought that the mental is a pattern in a medium, obtaining in virtue of local features of the medium (neuron firings) and perhaps also very global features (laws of nature) that are too small or too big to be mental themselves. But *M2* is not Materialism. It is both less and more. Less, obviously, because it never says that the medium is physical. More, because it denies the very possibility of what I shall call *Panpsychistic* Materialism.

It is often noted that psychophysical identity is a two-way street: if all mental properties are physical, then some physical properties are mental. But perhaps not just some but *all* physical properties might be mental as well; and indeed every property of anything might be at once physical and mental. Suppose there are indeed worlds where this is so. If so, presumably there are many such worlds, not all duplicates, differing *inter alia* in the mental lives of their inhabitants. But all differences between such worlds are mental (as well as physical), so none

35

are nonmental. These worlds will be vacuously alike in all nonmental respects, for lack of any nonmental respects to differ in. Then *M2* fails. And not just at the troublemaking worlds; *M2* is noncontingent, so if it fails at any worlds, it fails at all – even decent Materialistic worlds like ours. Maybe Panpsychistic Materialism is indeed impossible – how do you square it with a broadly functional analysis of mind? – but a thesis that says so is more than just Materialism.

A third try. This much is at least true:

> *M3.* No two Materialistic worlds differ without differing phys-
> ically; any two Materialistic worlds that are exactly alike
> physically are duplicates.

But *M3* is not a formulation of Materialism, for the distinction between Materialistic and other worlds appears within *M3*. All we learn is that the Materialistic worlds comprise a class within which there is no difference without physical difference. But there are many such classes. In fact any world, however spirit-ridden, belongs to such a class.

A fourth try. Perhaps we should confine our attention to nomologically possible worlds, thus:

> *M4.* Among worlds that conform to the actual laws of nature,
> no two differ without differing physically; any two such
> worlds that are exactly alike physically are duplicates.

But again we have something that is both less and more than Materialism. Less, because *M4* could hold at a world where Materialism is false but where spiritual phenomena are correlated with physical phenomena according to strict laws. More, because *M4* fails to hold at a Materialistic, spirit-free world if the laws of that world do not preclude the existence of epiphenomenal spirits. Our world might be such a world, a world where spirits are absent but not outlawed.[23]

So far, a supervenience formulation of Materialism seems elusive. But I think we can succeed if we join the idea of supervenience with the idea that a nonmaterialistic world would have something extra,

---

23 This objection against *M4* as a formulation of 'the ontological primacy of the microphysical' appears in Terence Horgan, 'Supervenience and Microphysics', *Pacific Philosophical Quarterly* 63 (1982) pp. 29–43.

something that a Materialistic world lacks. It might have spirits; or it might have physical things that differ in nonphysical ways, for instance in what their experience is like. In either case there are extra natural properties, properties instantiated in the nonmaterialistic world but nowhere to be found in the Materialistic world. Let us say that a property is *alien* to a world iff (1) it is not instantiated by any inhabitant of that world, and (2) it is not analysable as a conjunction of, or as a structural property constructed out of, natural properties all of which are instantiated by inhabitants of that world. (I need the second clause because I am following Armstrong, *mutatis mutandis*, in declining to rule out perfectly natural properties that are conjunctive or structurally complex. See *Universals*, II, pp. 30–42 and 67–71. It would be wrong to count as alien a complex property analysable in terms of nonalien constituents.) If our world is Materialistic, then it is safe to say that some of the natural properties instantiated in any nonmaterialistic world are properties alien to our world. Now we can proceed at last to formulate Materialism as a restricted and contingent supervenience thesis:

> M5. Among worlds where no natural properties alien to our world are instantiated, no two differ without differing physically; any two such worlds that are exactly alike physically are duplicates.[24]

We took Materialism to uphold the comprehensiveness of 'something not too different from present-day physics, though presumably somewhat improved'. That was deliberately vague. Materialist metaphysicians want to side with physics, but not to take sides within

24 This formulation resembles one proposed by Horgan, *op. cit.* The principal difference is as follows. Horgan would count as alien (my term, not his) any property cited in the fundamental laws of otherworldly microphysics that is not also explicitly cited in the fundamental laws of this worldly microphysics. Whether the property is instantiated in either world doesn't enter into it. But must an alien property figure in laws of otherworldly *physics*? Must it figure in any otherworldly laws at all? It seems that a Materialistic world might differ without differing physically from a world where there are properties alien in my sense but not in Horgan's – perhaps a world where laws are in short supply.

physics. Within physics, more precise claims of completeness and correctness may be at issue. Physics (ignoring latter-day failures of nerve) is the science that aspires to comprehensiveness, and particular physical theories may be put forward as fulfilling that aspiration. If so, we must again ask what it means to claim comprehensiveness. And again, the answer may be given by a supervenience formulation: no difference without physical difference as conceived by such-and-such grand theory. But again it must be understood as a restricted and contingent supervenience thesis, applying only among worlds devoid of alien natural properties.

Thus the business of physics is not just to discover laws and causal explanations. In putting forward as comprehensive theories that recognise only a limited range of natural properties, physics proposes inventories of the natural properties instantiated in our world. Not complete inventories, perhaps. But complete enough to account for all the duplications and differences that could arise in the absence of alien natural properties. Of course, the discovery of natural properties is inseparable from the discovery of laws. For an excellent reason to think that some hitherto unsuspected natural properties are instantiated – properties deserving of recognition by physics, the quark colours as they might be – is that without them, no satisfactory system of laws can be found.

This is reminiscent of the distinctive a *posteriori*, scientific character of Armstrong's Realism (*Universals*, I, pp. 8–9, and *passim*). But in the setting of an ontology of *possibilia*, the distinction between discovering what universals or natural properties there actually are and discovering which ones are actually instantiated fades away. And the latter question is a *posteriori* on any theory. What remains, and remains important, is that physics discovers properties. And not just any properties – natural properties. The discovery is, for instance, that neutrinos are not all alike. That is not the discovery that different ones have different properties in my sense, belong to different classes. We knew that much a *priori*. Rather, it is the surprising discovery that some *natural* property differentiates some neutrinos from others. That discovery has in fact been made; I should like to read an account of it by some philosopher who is not prepared to adopt a discriminatory attitude toward properties and who thinks that all things are equally similar and dissimilar to one another.

LAWS AND CAUSATION

The observation that physics discovers natural properties in the course of discovering laws may serve to introduce our next topic: the analysis of what it is to be a law of nature. I agree with Armstrong that we need universals, or at least natural properties, in explaining what lawhood is, though I disagree with his account of how this is so.

Armstrong's theory, in its simplest form,[25] holds that what makes certain regularities lawful are second-order states of affairs $N(F,G)$ in which the two ordinary, first-order universals F and G are related by a certain dyadic second-order universal N. It is a contingent matter which universals are thus related by the lawmaker N. But it is necessary – and necessary *simpliciter*, not just nomologically necessary – that if $N(F,G)$ obtains, then F and G are constantly conjoined. There is a necessary connection between the second-order state of affairs $N(F,G)$ and the first-order lawful regularity $\forall x(Fx \supset Gx)$; and likewise between the conjunctive state of affairs $N(F,G)$ & Fa and its necessary consequence Ga.

A parallel theory could be set up with natural properties in place of Armstrong's first- and second-order universals. It would have many of the attractive features that Armstrong claims on behalf of his theory, but at least one merit would be lost. For Armstrong, the lawful necessitation of Ga by Fa is a purely local matter: it involves only a, the universals F and G that are present in a, and the second-order lawmaking universal that is present in turn in (or between) these two universals. If we replace the universals by properties, however natural, that locality is lost. For properties are classes with their membership

---

25 *Universals*, II, pp. 148–157. A more developed form of the theory appears in D. M. Armstrong, *What Is a Law of Nature?* (Cambridge University Press, 1983). Similar theories have been proposed in Fred I. Dretske, 'Laws of Nature', *Philosophy of Science* 44 (1977) pp. 248–268, and in Michael Tooley, 'The Nature of Laws', *Canadian Journal of Philosophy* 4 (1977) pp. 667–698.

spread around the worlds, and are not wholly present in *a*. But I do not think this a conclusive objection, for our intuitions of locality often seem to lead us astray. The selective regularity theory I shall shortly advocate also sacrifices locality, as does any regularity theory of law.

What leads me (with some regret) to reject Armstrong's theory, whether with universals or with natural properties, is that I find its necessary connections unintelligible. Whatever N may be, I cannot see how it could be absolutely impossible to have $N(F,G)$ and Fa without Ga. (Unless N just *is* constant conjunction, or constant conjunction plus something else, in which case Armstrong's theory turns into a form of the regularity theory he rejects.) The mystery is somewhat hidden by Armstrong's terminology. He uses 'necessitates' as a name for the lawmaking universal N; and who would be surprised to hear that if F 'necessitates' G and a has F, then a must have G? But I say that N deserves the name of 'necessitation' only if, somehow, it really can enter into the requisite necessary connections. It can't enter into them just by bearing a name, any more than one can have mighty biceps just by being called 'Armstrong'.

I am tempted to complain in Humean fashion of alleged necessary connections between distinct existences, especially when first-order states of affairs in the past supposedly join with second-order states of affairs to necessitate first-order states of affairs in the future. That complaint is not clearly right: the sharing of universals detracts from the distinctness of the necessitating and the necessitated states of affairs. But I am not appeased. I conclude that necessary connections can be unintelligible even when they are supposed to obtain between existences that are not clearly and wholly distinct.[26]

26 Armstrong's more developed theory in *What Is a Law of Nature?* complicates the picture in two ways. First, the second-order state of affairs $N(F,G)$ is itself taken to be a universal, and its presence in its instances detracts yet further from the distinctness of the necessitating and the necessitated states of affairs. Second, all laws are defeasible. It is possible after all to have $N(F,G)$ and Fa without Ga, namely if we also have $N(E\&F,H)$ and Ea, where H and G are incompatible. (The law that F's are G's might be *contingently* indeafeasible, if no such defeating state of affairs $N(E\&F,H)$ obtains; but no law has its indefeasibility built in essentially.) It remains true that there are alleged necessary connections that I find unintelligible, but they are more complicated than before. To necessitate a state of affairs, we need not

40

Thus I do not endorse Armstrong's way of building universals, or alternatively natural properties, into the analysis of lawhood. Instead I favour a regularity analysis. But I need natural properties even so.

Certainly not just any regularity is a law of nature. Some are accidental. So an adequate regularity analysis must be selective. Also, an adequate analysis must be collective. It must treat regularities not one at a time, but rather as candidates to enter into integrated systems. For a given regularity might hold either as a law or accidentally, depending on whether other regularities obtain that can fit together with it in a suitable system. (Thus I reject the idea that lawhood consists of 'law-likeness' plus truth.) Following Mill and Ramsey,[27] I take a suitable system to be one that has the virtues we aspire to in our own theory-building, and that has them to the greatest extent possible given the way the world is. It must be entirely true; it must be closed under strict implication; it must be as simple in axiomatisation as it can be without sacrificing too much information content; and it must have as much information content as it can have without sacrificing too much simplicity. A law is any regularity that earns inclusion in the ideal system. (Or, in case of ties, in every ideal system.) The ideal system need not consist entirely of regularities; particular facts may gain entry if they contribute enough to collective simplicity and strength. (For instance, certain particular facts about the Big Bang might be strong candidates.) But only the regularities of the system are to count as laws.

We face an obvious problem. Different ways to express the same content, using different vocabulary, will differ in simplicity. The problem can be put in two ways, depending on whether we take our

only the first- and second-order states of affairs originally considered, but also a negative existential to the effect that there are no further states of affairs of the sort that could act as defeaters.

27 John Stuart Mill, *A System of Logic* (Parker, 1843) Book III, Chapter IV, Section 1; F. P. Ramsey, 'Universals of Law and of Fact', in his *Foundations* (Routledge & Kegan Paul, 1978). Ramsey regarded this theory of law as superseded by the different theory in his 'General Propositions and Causality', also in *Foundations*, but I prefer his first thoughts to his second. I present a theory of lawhood along the lines of Ramsey's earlier theory in my *Counterfactuals* (Blackwell, 1973) pp. 73–75. A revision to that discussion is needed in the probabilistic case, which I here ignore.

systems as consisting of propositions (classes of worlds) or as consisting of interpreted sentences. In the first case, the problem is that a single system has different degrees of simplicity relative to different linguistic formulations. In the second case, the problem is that equivalent systems, strictly implying the very same regularities, may differ in their simplicity. In fact, the content of any system whatever may be formulated very simply indeed. Given system S, let F be a predicate that applies to all and only things at worlds where S holds. Take F as primitive, and axiomatise S (or an equivalent thereof) by the single axiom $\forall x F x$. If utter simplicity is so easily attained, the ideal theory may as well be as strong as possible. Simplicity and strength needn't be traded off. Then the ideal theory will include (its simple axiom will strictly imply) all truths, and a *fortiori* all regularities. Then, after all, every regularity will be a law. That must be wrong.

The remedy, of course, is not to tolerate such a perverse choice of primitive vocabulary. We should ask how candidate systems compare in simplicity when each is formulated in the simplest eligible way; or, if we count different formulations as different systems, we should dismiss the ineligible ones from candidacy. An appropriate standard of eligibility is not far to seek: let the primitive vocabulary that appears in the axioms refer only to perfectly natural properties.

Of course, it remains an unsolved and difficult problem to say what simplicity of a formulation is. But it is no longer the downright insoluble problem that it would be if there were nothing to choose between alternative primitive vocabularies.

(One might think also to replace strict implication by deducibility in some specified calculus. But this second remedy seems unnecessary given the first, and seems incapable of solving our problem by itself.)

If we adopt the remedy proposed, it will have the consequence that laws will tend to be regularities involving natural properties. Fundamental laws, those that the ideal system takes as axiomatic, must concern perfectly natural properties. Derived laws that follow fairly straightforwardly also will tend to concern fairly natural properties. Regularities concerning unnatural properties may indeed be strictly implied, and should count as derived laws if so. But they are apt to escape notice even if we someday possess a good approximation to the ideal system. For they will be hard to express in a language that has words mostly for not-too-unnatural properties, as any language must. (See the next section.) And they will be hard to derive, indeed they may not be finitely derivable at all, in our deductive calculi. Thus my account explains, as Armstrong's does in its very different way, why the scientific investigation of laws and of natural properties is a package deal; why physicists posit natural properties such as the quark colours in order to posit the laws in which those properties figure, so that laws and natural properties get discovered together.

If the analysis of lawhood requires natural properties, then so does the analysis of causation. It is fairly uncontroversial that causation involves laws. That is so according to both of the leading theories of causation: the deductive-nomological analysis, on which the laws are applied to the actual course of events with the cause and effect present; and the counterfactual analysis that I favour, on which the laws are applied to counterfactual situations with the cause hypothesised away. These counterfactual alternatives may need to break actual laws at the point where they diverge from actuality, but the analysis requires that they evolve thereafter in accordance with the actual laws.[28]

According to my counterfactual analysis, causation involves natural properties in a second way too. We need the kind of counterfactuals that avoid backtracking; else the analysis faces fatal counterexamples involving epiphenomenal side-effects or cases of causal preemption. As I have already noted, these counterfactuals are to be characterised in terms of divergent worlds, hence in terms of duplicate initial world-segments, hence in terms of shared natural properties.

Causation involves natural properties in yet another way. (Small wonder that I came to appreciate natural properties after working on the analysis of causation!) Causation holds between events. Unless we distinguish genuine from spurious events, we will be left with too many putative causes. You put a lump of butter on a skillet, and the butter melts. What event causes this? There is one event that we can call a moving of molecules. It occurs in the region where the skillet is, just before the butter melts. This is an event such that, necessarily,

---

28 See my 'Causation', *Journal of Philosophy* 70 (1973) pp. 556–567; reprinted in Ernest Sosa, ed., *Causation and Conditionals* (Oxford University Press, 1975).

it occurs in a spatiotemporal region only if that region contains rapidly moving molecules. Surely this event is a cause of the melting of the butter.

Heat is that phenomenon, whatever it may be, that manifests itself in certain familiar characteristic ways. Let us say: heat is that which occupies the heat-role. (It won't matter whether we take the definite description plain, as I prefer, or rigidified.) In fact, but contingently, it is molecular motion that occupies the heat-role. It might have been molecular nonmotion, or caloric fluid, or what you will. Now consider an alleged second event, one that we may call a having-the-occupant-of-the-heat-role. This second event occurs just when and where the first does, in the region where the hot skillet is. It occurs there in virtue of the two facts (1) that the skillet's molecules are moving rapidly, and (2) that the region in question is part of a world where molecular motion is what occupies the heat-role. But this second event differs from the first. The necessary conditions for its occurrence are different. Necessarily, it occurs in a region only if that region contains whatever phenomenon occupies the heat-role in the world of which that region is part. So in those worlds where caloric fluid occupies the heat-role and molecular motion does not, the first event occurs only in regions with molecular motion whereas the second occurs only in regions with caloric fluid.

Certainly the first event causes the melting of the butter, but shall we say that the second event does so as well? No; that seems to multiply causes beyond belief by playing a verbal trick. But if there really are two events here, I cannot see why the second has less of a claim than the first to be a cause of the melting of the butter. It is out of the question to say that the first and the second events are one and the same – then this one event would have different conditions of occurrence from itself. The best solution is to deny that the alleged second event is a genuine event at all. If it isn't, of course it can't do any causing.

Why is the first event genuine and the second spurious? Compare the properties involved: containing rapidly moving molecules versus containing whatever phenomenon occupies the heat-role. (I mean these as properties of the spatiotemporal region; other treatments of events would take instead the corresponding properties of the skillet, but my point would still apply.) The first is a fairly natural, intrinsic property. The second is highly disjunctive and extrinsic. For all sorts of different phenomena could occupy the heat-role; and whether the phenomenon going on in a region occupies the role depends not only on what goes on in the region but also on what goes on elsewhere in the same world. Thus the distinction between more and less natural properties gives me the distinction between genuine and spurious events that I need in order to disown an overabundance of causes. If a property is too unnatural, it is inefficacious in the sense that it cannot figure in the conditions of occurrence of the events that cause things.[29]

THE CONTENT OF LANGUAGE AND THOUGHT

Hilary Putnam has given an argument which he regards as a refutation of a 'radically non-epistemic' view of truth, but which I regard rather as a *reductio* against Putnam's premises.[30] In particular, it refutes his assumption that '*we* interpret our languages or nothing does' ('Models and Reality', p. 482) so that any constraint on reference must be established by our own stipulation in language or thought. Gary Merrill has suggested that Putnam may be answered by appeal to a constraint that depends on an objective structure of properties and relations in

29 See the discussion of impotence of dispositions in Elizabeth W. Prior, Robert Pargetter, and Frank Jackson, 'Three Theses About Dispositions', *American Philosophical Quarterly* 19 (1982) pp. 251–257. If a disposition is not identified with its actual basis, there is a threat of multiplication of putative causes similar to that in my example. We would not wish to say that the breaking of a struck glass is caused both by its fragility and by the frozen-in stresses that are the basis thereof; and if forced to choose, we should choose the latter. I suggest that the fragility is inefficacious because it is too unnatural a property, too disjunctive and extrinsic, to figure in the conditions of occurrence of any event.

30 Hilary Putnam, 'Realism and Reason', in his *Meaning and the Moral Sciences* (Routledge & Kegan Paul, 1978), and 'Models and Reality', *Journal of Symbolic Logic* 45 (1980) pp. 464–482. The reader is warned that the argument as I present it may not be quite as Putnam intended it to be. For I have made free in reading between the lines and in restating the argument in my own way.

the world.[31] I agree, and find here another point at which we need natural properties.

Putnam's argument, as I understand it, is as follows. First, suppose that the only constraint on interpretation of our language (or perhaps our language of thought) is given by a description theory of reference of a global and futuristic sort. An 'intended interpretation' is any interpretation that satisfies a certain body of theory: *viz.* the idealised descendant of our current total theory that would emerge at the end of inquiry, an ideal theory refined to perfection under the guidance of all needed observation and our best theoretical reasoning. If so, intended interpretations are surprisingly abundant. For *any* world can satisfy *any* theory (ideal or not), and can do so in countless very different ways, provided only that the world is not too small and the theory is consistent. Beyond that, it doesn't matter what the world is like or what the theory says. Hence we have radical indeterminacy of reference. And we have the coincidence that Putnam welcomes between satisfaction under all intended interpretations and 'epistemic truth'. For the ideal theory is the whole of 'epistemic truth', the intended interpretations are just those interpretations of our language that satisfy the ideal theory, and (unless the world is too small or ideal theory is inconsistent) there are some such interpretations.

I take this to refute the supposition that there are no further constraints on reference. But Putnam asks: how *could* there be a further constraint? How could we ever establish it? By stipulation, by saying or thinking something. But whatever we say or think will be in language (or language of thought) that suffers from radical indeterminacy of interpretation. For the saving constraint will not be there until we succeed in establishing it. So the attempted stipulation must fail. The most we can do is to contribute a new chapter to current and ideal theory, a chapter consisting of whatever we said or thought in our stipulation. And this new theory goes the way of all theory. So we cannot establish a further constraint; and '*we* interpret our language or nothing does'; so there cannot be any further constraint. We cannot lift ourselves by our bootstraps, so we must still be on the ground.

31 G. H. Merrill, 'The Model-Theoretic Argument Against Realism', *Philosophy of Science* 47 (1980) pp. 69–81.

Indeed we cannot lift ourselves by our bootstraps, but we are off the ground, so there must be another way to fly. Our language does have a fairly determinate interpretation (a Moorean fact!) so there must be some constraint not created *ex nihilo* by our stipulation.

What can it be? Many philosophers would suggest that it is some sort of causal constraint. If so my case is made, given my arguments in the previous section: we need natural properties to explain determinacy of interpretation. But I doubt that it really is a causal constraint, for I am inclined to think that the causal aspect of reference *is* established by what we say and think. Thus: I think of a thing as that which I am causally acquainted with in such-and-such way, perhaps perceptually or perhaps through a channel of acquaintance that involves the naming of the thing and my picking up of the name. I refer to that thing in my thought, and derivatively in language, because it is the thing that fits this causal and egocentric description extracted from my theory of the world and of my place in the world.[32]

I would instead propose that the saving constraint concerns the referent – not the referrer, and not the causal channels between the two. It takes two to make a reference, and we will not find the constraint if we look for it always on the wrong side of the relationship. Reference consists in part of what we do in language or thought when we refer, but in part it consists in eligibility of the referent. And this eligibility to be referred to is a matter of natural properties.

That is the suggestion Merrill offers. (He offers it not as his own view, but as what opponents of Putnam ought to say; and I gratefully accept the offer.) In the simplest case, suppose that the interpretation of the logical vocabulary somehow takes care of itself, to reveal a standard first-order language whose nonlogical vocabulary consists entirely of predicates. The parts of the world comprise a domain; and sets, sets of pairs, . . . , from this domain are potential extensions for the predicates. Now suppose we have an all-or-nothing division of properties into natural and unnatural. Say that a set from the domain is *eligible* to be the extension of a one-place predicate iff its members are just those things in the domain that share some natural property; and likewise for many-place predicates and natural relations. An *eligible interpretation*

---

32 See Stephen Schiffer, 'The Basis of Reference', *Erkenntnis* 13 (1978) pp. 171–206.

is one that assigns none but eligible extensions to the predicates. A so-called 'intended' interpretation is an eligible interpretation that satisfies the ideal theory. (But the name is misleading: it is not to be said that our intentions establish the constraint requiring eligibility. That way lies the futile bootstrap-tugging that we must avoid.) Then if the natural properties are sparse, there is no reason to expect any over-abundance of intended interpretations. There may even be none. Even ideal theory runs the risk of being unsatisfiable, save in 'unintended' ways. Because satisfaction is not guaranteed, we accomplish something if we manage to achieve it by making a good fit between theory and the world. All this is as it should be.

The proposal calls for refinement. First, we need to provide for richer forms of language. In this we can be guided by familiar trans-lations, for instance between modal language with higher-order quan-tification and first-order language that explicitly mentions *possibilia* and classes built up from them. Second, it will not do to take naturalness of properties as all-or-nothing. Here, above all, we need to make nat-uralness – and hence eligibility – a comparative matter, or a matter of degree. There are salient sharp lines, but not in the right places. There is the line between the perfectly natural properties and all the rest, but surely we have predicates for much-less-than-perfectly natural prop-erties. There is the line between properties that are and that are not finitely analysable in terms of perfectly natural properties, but that lets in enough highly unnatural properties that it threatens not to solve our problem. We need gradations; and we need some give and take be-tween the eligibility of referents and the other factors that make for 'intendedness', notably satisfaction of appropriate bits of theory. (Ideal theory, if we keep as much of Putnam's story as we can.) Grueness is not an absolutely ineligible referent (as witness my reference to it just now) but an interpretation that assigns it is to that extent inferior to one that assigns blueness instead. *Ceteris paribus*, the latter is the 'in-tended' one, just because it does better on eligibility.

Naturalness of properties makes for differences of eligibility not only among the properties themselves, but also among things. Com-pare Bruce with the cat-shaped chunk of miscellaneous and ever-changing matter that follows him around, always a few steps behind. The former is a highly eligible referent, the latter is not. (I haven't succeeded in referring to it, for I didn't say just which such chunk 'it' was to be.) That is because Bruce, unlike the cat-shaped chunk, has a boundary well demarcated by differences in highly natural properties. Where Bruce ends, there the density of matter, the relative abundance of the chemical elements, . . . abruptly change. Not so for the chunk. Bruce is also much more of a locus of causal chains than is the chunk; this too traces back to natural properties, by the considerations of the previous section. Thus naturalness of properties sets up distinctions among things. The reverse happens also. Once we are away from the perfectly natural properties, one thing that makes for naturalness of a property is that it is a property belonging exclusively to well-demarcated things.

You might well protest that Putnam's problem is misconceived, wherefore no need has been demonstrated for resources to solve it. Putnam seems to conceive of language entirely as a repository of theory, and not at all as a practice of social interaction. We have the language of the encyclopedia, but where is the language of the pub? Where are the communicative intentions and the mutual expectations that seem to have so much to do with what we mean? In fact, where is thought? It seems to enter the picture, if at all, only as the special case where the language to be interpreted is hard-wired, unspoken, hidden, and all too conjectural.

I think the point is well taken, but I think it doesn't matter. If the problem of intentionality is rightly posed there will still be a threat of radical indeterminacy, there will still be a need for saving constraints, there will still be a remedy analogous to Merrill's suggested answer to Putnam, and there will still be a need for natural properties.

Set language aside and consider instead the interpretation of thought. (Afterward we can hope to interpret the subject's language in terms of his beliefs and desires regarding verbal communication with others.) The subject is in various states, and could be in various others, that are causally related to each other, to the subject's behaviour, and to the nearby environment that stimulates his senses. These states fit into a functional organisation, they occupy certain causal roles. (Most likely they are states of the brain. Maybe they involve something that is language-like but hard-wired, maybe not. But the nature of the states is beside the point.) The states have their functional roles in the subject as he now is, and in the subject as he is at other times and as he might have been under other circumstances, and even in other creatures of the same kind as the subject. Given the functional roles of the states, the problem is to assign them content. Propositional content, some would say; but I would agree only if the propositions can be taken as egocentric ones, and I think an 'egocentric proposition' is simply a property. States indexed by content can be identified as a belief that this, a desire for that, a perceptual experience of seeming to confront so-and-so, an intention to do such-and-such. (But not all ordinary ascriptions of attitudes merely specify the content of the subject's states. Fred and Ted might be alike in the functional roles of their states, and hence have states with the same content in the narrowly psychological sense that is my present concern, and hence believe alike *e.g.* by each believing himself to have heard of a pretty town named 'Castlemaine'. Yet they might be acquainted via that name with different towns, at opposite ends of the earth, so that Fred and not Ted believes that Castlemaine, Victoria, is pretty.) The problem of assigning content to functionally characterised states is to be solved by means of constraining principles. Foremost among these are principles of fit. If a state is to be interpreted as an intention to raise one's hand, it had better typically cause the hand to go up. If a state (or complex of states) is to be interpreted as a system of beliefs and desires – or better, degrees of belief and desire – according to which raising one's hand would be a good means to one's ends, and if another state is to be interpreted as an intention to raise one's hand, then the former had better typically cause the latter. Likewise on the input side. A state typically caused by round things before the eyes is a good candidate for interpretation as the visual experience of confronting something round; and its typical impact on the states interpreted as systems of belief ought to be interpreted as the exogenous addition of a belief that one is confronting something round, with whatever adjustment that addition calls for.

So far, so good. But it seems clear that preposterous and perverse misinterpretations could nevertheless cohere, could manage to fit the functional roles of the states because misassignment of content at one point compensates for misassignment at another. Let us see just how this could happen, at least under an oversimplified picture of interpretation as follows. An interpretation is given by a pair of functions C and V. C is a probability distribution over the worlds, regarded as encapsulating the subject's dispositions to form beliefs under the impact of sensory evidence: if a stream of evidence specified by proposition E would put the subject into a total state S – for short, if E *yields* S – we interpret S to consist in part of the belief system given by the probability distribution $C(-/E)$ that comes from C by conditionalising on E. V is a function from worlds to numerical desirability scores, regarded as encapsulating the subject's basic values: if E yields S, we interpret S to consist in part of the system of desires given by the $C(-/E)$-expectations of V. Say that C and V *rationalise* behaviour B after evidence E iff the system of desires given by the $C(-/E)$-expectations of V ranks B at least as high as any alternative behaviour. Say that C and V *fit* iff, for any evidence-specifying E, E yields a state that would cause behaviour rationalised by C and V after E. That is our only constraining principle of fit. (Where did the others go? – We built them into the definitions whereby C and V encapsulate an assignment of content to various states.) Then any two interpretations that always rationalise the same behaviour after the same evidence must fit equally well. Call two worlds *equivalent* iff they are alike in respect of the subject's evidence and behaviour, and note that any decent world is equivalent *inter alia* to horrendously counterinductive worlds and to worlds where everything unobserved by the subject is horrendously nasty. Fit depends on the total of C for each equivalence class, and on the C-expectation of V within each class, but that is all. Within a class, it makes no difference which world gets which pair of values of C and V. We can interchange equivalent worlds *ad lib* and preserve fit. So, given any fitting and reasonable interpretation, we can transform it into an equally fitting perverse interpretation by swapping equivalent worlds around so as to enhance the probabilities of counterinductive worlds, or the desirabilities of nasty worlds, or both. *Quod erat demonstrandum.*

(My simplifications were dire: I left out the egocentricity of belief and desire and evidence, the causal aspect of rationalised behaviour, the role of intentions, change of basic values, limitations of logical competence,. . . . But I doubt that these omissions matter to my conclusion. I conjecture that if they were remedied, we could still transform reasonable interpretations into perverse ones in a way that preserves fit.)

If we rely on principles of fit to do the whole job, we can expect radical indeterminacy of interpretation. We need further constraints, of the sort called principles of (sophisticated) charity, or of 'humanity'.[33] Such principles call for interpretations according to which the subject has attitudes that we would deem reasonable for one who has lived the life that he has lived. (Unlike principles of crude charity, they call for imputations of error if he has lived under deceptive conditions.) These principles select among conflicting interpretations that equally well conform to the principles of fit. They impose *a priori* – albeit defeasible – presumptions about what sorts of things are apt to be believed and desired; or rather, about what dispositions to develop beliefs and desires, what inductive biases and basic values, someone may rightly be interpreted to have.

It is here that we need natural properties. The principles of charity will impute a bias toward believing that things are green rather than grue, toward having a basic desire for long life rather than for long-life-unless-one-was-born-on-Monday-and-in-that-case-life-for-an-even-number-of-weeks. In short, they will impute eligible content, where ineligibility consists in severe unnaturalness of the properties the subject supposedly believes or desires or intends himself to have. They will impute other things as well, but it is the imputed eligibility that matters to us at present.

Thus the threat of radical indeterminacy in the assignment of content to thought is fended off. The saving constraint concerns the content – not the thinker, and not any channels between the two. It takes two to index states with content, and we will not find the constraint if we look for it always on the wrong side of the relationship. Believing this or desiring that consists in part in the functional roles of the states whereby we believe or desire, but in part it consists in the eligibility

33 See my 'Radical Interpretation', *Synthese* 23 (1974) pp. 331–344; and Richard E. Grandy, 'Reference, Meaning and Belief', *Journal of Philosophy* 70 (1973) pp. 439–452.

of the content. And this eligibility to be thought is a matter, in part, of natural properties.

Consider the puzzle whereby Kripke illustrates Wittgenstein's paradox that 'no course of action could be determined by a rule, because every course of action can be made out to accord with the rule'.[34] A well-educated person working arithmetic problems intends to perform addition when he sees the '+' sign. He does not intend to perform quaddition, which is just like addition for small numbers but which yields the answer 5 if any of the numbers to be quadded exceeds a certain bound. Wherefore does he intend to add and not to quadd? Whatever he says and whatever is written in his brain can be perversely (mis)interpreted as instructing him to quadd. And it is not enough to say that his brain state is the causal basis of a disposition to add. Perhaps it isn't. Perhaps if a test case arose he would abandon his intention, he would neither add nor quadd but instead would put his homework aside and complain that the problems are too hard.

The naive solution is that adding means going on in the same way as before when the numbers get big, whereas quadding means doing something different; there is nothing present in the subject that constitutes an intention to do different things in different cases; therefore he intends addition, not quaddition. We should not scoff at this naive response. It is the correct solution to the puzzle. But we must pay to regain our naiveté. Our theory of properties must have adequate resources to somehow ratify the judgement that instances of adding are all alike in a way that instances of quadding are not. The property of adding is not perfectly natural, of course, not on a par with unit charge or sphericality. And the property of quadding is not perfectly unnatural. But quadding is worse by a disjunction. So quaddition is to that extent less of a way to go on doing the same, and therefore it is to that extent less of an eligible thing to intend to do.

It's not that you couldn't possibly intend to quadd. You could. Suppose that today there is as much basis as there ever is to interpret you as intending to add and as meaning addition by your word 'addition' and quaddition by 'quaddition'; and tomorrow you say to your-

---

34 See Saul A. Kripke, 'Wittgenstein on Rules and Private Language: An Elementary Exposition', in Irving Block, ed., *Perspectives on Wittgenstein* (Blackwell, 1981).

self in so many words that it would be fun to tease the philosophers by taking up quadditon henceforth, and you make up your mind to do it. But you have to go out of your way. Adding and quadding aren't on a par. To intend to add, you need only have states that would fit either interpretation and leave it to charity to decree that you have the more eligible intention. To intend to quadd, you must say or think something that creates difficulties of fit for the more eligible intention and thereby defeats the presumption in its favour. You must do something that, taking principles of fit and presumptions of eligibility and other principles of charity together, tilts the balance in favour of an interpretation on which you intend to quadd. How ironic that we were worried to find nothing positive to settle the matter in favour of addition! For the lack of anything positive that points either way just *is* what it takes to favour addition. Quaddition, being less natural and eligible, needs something positive in its favour. Addition can win by default.

What is the status of the principles that constrain interpretation, in particular the charitable presumption in favour of eligible content? We must shun several misunderstandings. It is not to be said (1) that as a contingent psychological fact, the contents of our states turn out to be fairly eligible, we mostly believe and desire ourselves to have not-too-unnatural properties. Still less should it be said (2) that we should daringly presuppose this in our interpreting of one another, even if we haven't a shred of evidence for it. Nor should it be said (3) that as a contingent psychological fact we turn out to have states whose content involves some properties rather than others, and that is what makes it so that the former properties are more natural. (This would be a psychologistic theory of naturalness.) The error is the same in all three cases. It is supposed, wrongly as I think, that the problem of interpretation can be solved without bringing to it the distinction between natural and unnatural properties; so that the natural properties might or might not turn out to be the ones featured in the content of thought according to the correct solution, or so that they can afterward be defined as the ones that are so featured. I think this is overoptimistic. We have no notion how to solve the problem of interpretation while regarding all properties as equally eligible to feature in content. For that would be to solve it without enough constraints. Only if we have an independent, objective distinction among properties, and we impose the presumption in favour of eligible content *a priori* as a constitutive constraint, does the problem of interpretation have any solution at all. If so, then any correct solution must automatically respect the presumption. There's no contingent fact of psychology here to be believed, either on evidence or daringly.

Compare our selective and collective theory of lawhood: lawhood of a regularity just consists in its fitting into an ideally high-scoring system, so it's inevitable that laws turn out to have what it takes to make for high scores. Likewise, I have suggested, contenthood just consists in getting assigned by a high-scoring interpretation, so it's inevitable that contents tend to have what it takes to make for high scores. And in both cases, I've suggested that part of what it takes is naturalness of the properties involved. The reason natural properties feature in the contents of our attitudes is that naturalness is part of what it is to feature therein. It's not that we're built to take a special interest in natural properties, or that we confer naturalness on properties when we happen to take an interest in them.

2

Putnam's paradox

INTRODUCTION

Hilary Putnam has devised a bomb that threatens to devastate the realist philosophy we know and love.[1] He explains how he has learned to stop worrying and love the bomb. He welcomes the new order that it would bring (RT&H, Preface). But we who still live in the target area do not agree. The bomb must be banned.

Putnam's thesis (the bomb) is that, in virtue of considerations from the theory of reference, it makes no sense to suppose that an empirically ideal theory, as verified as can be, might nevertheless be false because the world is not the way the theory says it is. The reason given is, roughly, that there is no semantic glue to stick our words onto their referents, and so reference is very much up for grabs; but there is one force constraining reference, and that is our intention to refer in such a way that we come out right; and there is no countervailing force; and the world, no matter what it is like (almost), will afford *some*

First published in *The Australasian Journal of Philosophy* 62 (1984), pp. 221–236. Reprinted with kind permission from *The Australasian Journal of Philosophy*.

1 Hilary Putnam, 'Realism and Reason', *Proceedings of the American Philosophical Association* 50 (1977) pp. 483–498, reprinted in Putnam, *Meaning and the Moral Sciences* (Routledge & Kegan Paul, 1978), henceforth 'R&R', cited with page numbers from *Meaning and the Moral Sciences*; 'Models and Reality', *Journal of Symbolic Logic* 45 (1980) pp. 464–482, henceforth 'M&R'; and *Reason, Truth and History* (Cambridge University Press, 1981), henceforth 'RT&H'.

scheme of reference that makes us come out right; so how can we fail to come out right?[2]

Putnam's thesis is incredible. We are in the presence of paradox, as surely as when we meet the man who offers us a proof that there are no people, and in particular that he himself does not exist.[3] It is out of the question to follow the argument where it leads. We know in advance that there is something wrong, and the challenge is to find out where. If the paradox-monger is good at his work, we stand to learn something; and indeed, I think that Putnam's paradox affords an important lesson.

In the first half of the paper I shall give my account of what I take to be the core of Putnam's argument, and I shall say how I think it fails. In the second half of the paper, I shall raise some questions about aspects of Putnam's presentation that puzzle me.

Three caveats. (1) I warn the reader that I am not sure how well I understand Putnam.[4] Sometimes, different things he says seem to point in different directions. What is more, I shall state what I take to be his argument in my own way. I hope the line of argument I discuss is Putnam's, even if rather freely paraphrased. But whether it is his or not, I think it worthy of attention. (2) I shall acquiesce in Putnam's linguistic turn: I shall discuss the semantic interpretation of language rather than the assignment of content to attitudes, thus ignoring the possibility that the latter settles the former. It would be better, I think,

---

2 Compare the malicious joke: 'Mr. Z claims to have found a counterexample to my theory. But he has misunderstood me, he has not interpreted my words as I intended. For I intended that there be no counterexamples.'

3 Peter Unger, 'Why There Are No People', *Midwest Studies in Philosophy* 4 (1979), pp. 177–222; and 'I Do Not Exist', in G. F. Macdonald, ed., *Perception and Identity* (Macmillan, 1979).

4 I find it especially hard to make RT&H mesh with R&R and M&R, but I do think they are supposed to mesh. The third full paragraph of RT&H, p. 7, indicates a connection. Also, RT&H was in draft before Putnam read Goodman's *Ways of Worldmaking* (see RT&H, p. xii); the latter was published in 1978, and might have been available in manuscript to a sympathetic colleague earlier than that; so RT&H is more nearly simultaneous with R&R and M&R than their publication dates would suggest.

to start with the attitudes and go on to language. But I think that would relocate, rather than avoid, the problem; wherefore I may as well discuss it on Putnam's own terms.[5] (3) I shall ignore the complex details of model-theoretic semantics for natural language. I suppose that a proper treatment would require interpretations in which the semantic values are elaborate set-theoretic constructions.[6] But I shall acquiesce in Putnam's supposition that we can get by with model theory in its 'basic form' (R&R, p. 124): we have a domain of 'parts of the world', things which may serve as referents for singular terms, and classes of which may serve as referents for general terms. Such a supposition might matter, if model-theoretic results were as important to Putnam's argument as he suggests. But I load the dice in Putnam's favour, if at all; so I play fair.

GLOBAL DESCRIPTIVISM REFUTED

We are familiar with the idea of a description theory of reference – for short, *descriptivism* – and, especially, with a local form thereof. Suppose, *pace* Putnam, that somehow we already have an extensive language with fairly determinate reference. Then we may add new language to the old, a little at a time, by introducing undefined terms in our theorising. Thereby we associate clusters of old-language descriptions with our new terms; and thereby, if the world cooperates, we bestow reference on the new terms. 'Jack the Ripper did this, that, and the other' says the detective; his point is in part to hypothesise that there is someone who did this, that, and the other, and in part to stipulate that the one who did, if such there be, is to become the referent of 'Jack the Ripper'. The new term 'Jack the Ripper' is to acquire the referent, if any, of the old-language description 'the one who did this, that, and the other'. The intended interpretation of the augmented language is to be an extension of the old interpretation of the old language, if such there be, that makes the new Jack-the-Ripper theory come true.

---

5 For a discussion of the 'relocated' problem and its solution, see the final section of my 'New Work for a Theory of Universals', *Australasian Journal of Philosophy* 61 (1983), pp. 343–377 (reprinted in this volume as Chapter 1).

6 More or less as in my 'General Semantics', *Synthese* 22 (1970), pp. 18–67.

Seven points should be noted. (1) There may or may not be rigidification. If there is, that will avoid confusion between people who have attached the same term to the same referent by means of different descriptions. For nothing will be true as one person means it but false as the other means it, not even when the term appears in modal contexts.[7] (2) The term-introducing descriptive theory may be egocentric (for instance, it might include 'Water is abundant on this planet'); (3) it may make reference (in old language) to word tokens or thought tokens; and (4) it may involve relations of causal acquaintance. Taking points (2) – (4) together, we note for instance that 'Beech trees are the causal source in such-and-such way of tokens in my speech and thought of "beech tree" ' might be part of the bit of descriptive theory that, for me, attaches a referent to 'beech tree'; and so, *mutatis mutandis*, with 'elm tree'. (5) The description needn't fit perfectly. 'Jack the Ripper' might take as referent the one who comes closest to doing this, that, and the other, if no better candidate is available. The intended interpretation of the augmented language, then, is to be that extension of the old interpretation that comes as close as can be to making the new Jack-the-Ripper theory come true. (6) There might be two candidates that both fit perfectly; more likely, there might be two imperfect candidates with little to choose between them and no stronger candidate to beat them both. If so, we end up with indeterminate reference (in addition to whatever results from indeterminacy of the old interpretation of the old language): the new term refers equally to both candidates. Hartry Field's example of Newtonian 'mass' illustrates this possibility.[8] Note well that this is moderate indeterminacy, in which the rival interpretations have much in common; it is not the radical indeterminacy that leads to Putnam's paradox. I take it that the existence of moderate indeterminacy is not to be denied. Finally, and most important for what follows, (7) it may happen that new terms acquire their referents by description not singly but in families. Suppose that our detective hypothesised that the murders

---

7 I owe the point to H. W. Noonan, 'Rigid Designation', *Analysis* 39 (1979), pp. 174–182.

8 Hartry Field, 'Theory Change and the Indeterminacy of Reference', *Journal of Philosophy* 70 (1973), pp. 462–481.

were the joint work of a couple: Jack the Ripper and Jill the Slasher, as he chose to call them. 'Jack did this,' he says, 'Jill did that and the other, and Jack and Jill are related thus'. Then, if the world provides suitable candidates, 'Jack' and 'Jill' gain referents together. The intended interpretation of the doubly augmented language is to be an extension of the old interpretation of the old language, if such there be, that makes the new Jack-and-Jill theory come true.

Description theories of reference are supposed to have been well and truly refuted. I think not: we have learnt enough from our attackers to withstand their attacks. I think that a descriptivism that takes to heart the seven points just listed is still tenable, and is indeed a substantial part of the truth about reference.

Be that as it may, a local descriptivism is disappointingly modest. It tells us how to get more reference if we have some already. But where did the old language get *its* reference?

It is therefore tempting to try the same method on a grander scale. We can introduce terms in little families. How about bigger families? How about the biggest family of all – the entire vocabulary of the language? Then we needn't worry how the old vocabulary got its reference. Because there isn't any old vocabulary. (Or perhaps the old vocabulary is just the first-order logical vocabulary. Putnam seems to assume this, but without telling us why that vocabulary is special, or how it got its reference.) We go on just as before. The intended interpretation will be the one, if such there be, that makes the term-introducing theory come true. (Or: . . . come near enough to true. Or: the intended interpretation*s* will be the one*s*, if such there be, . . . with indeterminacy if there are more than one.) But this time, the term-introducing theory is total theory! Call this account of reference: *global* descriptivism.

And it leads straight to Putnam's incredible thesis. For *any* world (almost), whatever it is like, can satisfy *any* theory (almost), whatever it says. We said: 'the intended interpretation will be the one, *if such there be,* . . .' Never mind the proviso – there *will* be. It is (almost) certain that the world will afford the makings of an interpretation that will make the theory come true. In fact, it will afford countless such interpretations. *Ex hypothesi* these interpretations are intended. So there is (almost) no way that the theory can fail to come true on its intended interpretations. Which is to say: (almost) no way that the theory can fail to come true *simpliciter*. This is Putnam's so-called 'model-theoretic argument'.[9]

So global descriptivism is false; or Putnam's incredible thesis is true; or there is something wrong with the presuppositions of our whole line of thought. Unlike Putnam, I resolutely eliminate the second and third alternatives. The one that remains must therefore be the truth. Global descriptivism stands refuted. It may be part of the truth about reference, but it cannot be the whole story. There must be some additional constraint on reference: some constraint that might, if we are unlucky in our theorising, eliminate *all* the allegedly intended interpretations that make the theory come true.

FURTHER CONSTRAINTS – JUST MORE THEORY?

Putnam has constraints to offer: he speaks often of 'operational and theoretical constraints' (for instance, see R&R, p. 126; M&R, pp. 466, 469, 471, and 473). It is hard to tell from his words whether these are supposed to constrain reference or theory. Probably he thinks they do both: they constrain ideal theory, ideal theory is the term-introducing descriptive theory to which global descriptivism applies, so in this indirect way they constrain reference also. So these constraints work within global descriptivism. They are not an addition or alternative to it. We must seek elsewhere for salvation from indeterminacy and over-easy truth. We need further constraints.

Putnam thinks there can be no such further constraints. Global descriptivism is the only possible account of reference (apart from accounts that rely on supernatural aid). Constraints that work within it are the only possible constraints on reference. His reason is that global descriptivism is imperialistic: it will annex any satisfactory alternative account of constraints on reference.

9 The argument was anticipated (apart from mathematical detail having to do with the qualification '*almost* any world') in M. H. A. Newman, "Mr. Russell's 'Causal Theory of Perception' ", *Mind* 37 (1928), pp. 137–148. Newman's argument is discussed in William Demopoulos and Michael Friedman, 'The Concept of Structure in *The Analysis of Matter*', *Philosophy of Science* 52 (1985), pp. 621–639.

Suppose that we say it is constraint C that saves the day – a causal constraint, perhaps, or what have you. We offer an account of how constraint C works, a bit of theory in fact. If this bit of theory looks good, it will deserve to be incorporated into total theory. Suppose it is. Then an intended interpretation must make C-theory come true, along with the rest of total theory. But it will still be true, as much as ever, that (almost) any world can satisfy (almost) any theory. Adding C-theory to the rest of total theory doesn't help. It is still trivially easy for a world to make total theory come true, and in fact to do so in countless ways. And the point is general: it applies to any constraint (or, at least, to any otherwise satisfactory constraint) that might be proposed. Constraint C is to be imposed by accepting C-theory, according to Putnam. But C-theory is just more theory, more grist for the mill; and more theory will go the way of all theory.

To which I reply: C is *not* to be imposed just by accepting C-theory. That is a misunderstanding of what C is. The constraint is *not* that an intended interpretation must somehow make our account of C come true. The constraint is that an intended interpretation must conform to C itself.

That is why global descriptivism does not automatically annex its successful rivals. That is why global descriptivism, unaided by further constraints, is not the only possible theory of reference. That is why some further constraint on reference might save the day. Since Putnam's paradoxical thesis is patently false, we can be confident that there is indeed some further constraint, whether or not we can find out what it is.

Is that all? What I have just said (and others before me, *e.g.* Devitt,[10] in the course of advocating particular constraints) may not carry conviction. It may seem that Putnam is onto something deep and right. He is not just missing an easy distinction: satisfying C-theory versus conforming to C. Is there really a distinction here?

I think there is. But there are two reasons for doubting the distinction. One is simply misguided; the other is instructively wrong.

The misguided reason comes from the dialectic of philosophy.

10 Michael Devitt, 'Realism and the Renegade Putnam: A Critical Study of *Meaning and the Moral Sciences*', *Noûs* 17 (1983), pp. 291–301.

The rules of disputation sometimes give the wrong side a winning strategy. In particular, they favour the sceptic. They favour the ordinary sceptic about empirical knowledge; they favour the logical sceptic, Carroll's tortoise or a present-day doubter of non-contradiction; and they favour the sceptic about determinate reference. It goes as follows. The Challenger asks how determinate reference is possible. The Respondent answers by giving an account of his favourite constraint. The Challenger says: 'Unless the words of your answer had determinate reference, you have not answered me unequivocally. So I challenge you now to show how the words of your answer had determinate reference. If you cannot, I can only take you to have proposed an addition to total theory – *that* I can understand, but that is futile.' If the Respondent answers just as before, he begs the question and loses. If he answers differently, he does not win, for he gets another challenge just like the one before. And so it goes. The Challenger is playing by the rules, and the Respondent cannot win. And yet the Respondent may indeed have given a correct account of the constraint that makes determinate reference possible, couched in language that does indeed have determinate reference in virtue of the very constraint that it describes! (Here I follow Devitt (*op. cit.*), generalising his account of the dialectical deadlock in case a causal constraint is proposed.) Moral: truth is one thing, winning disputations is another.

But there is a deeper and better reason to say that any proposed constraint is just more theory. Take your favourite theory of reference. Let us grant that it is true. But let us ask: what makes it true? And the tempting answer is: *we* make it true, by our referential intentions. We can refer however we like – language is a creature of human convention – and we have seen fit to establish a language in which reference works *thus*. Somehow, implicitly or explicitly, individually or collectively, we have made this theory of reference true by stipulation. '*We* interpret our languages or nothing does' (M&R, p. 482).

The main lesson of Putnam's Paradox, I take it, is that this purely voluntaristic view of reference leads to disaster. If it were right, any proposed constraint *would* be just more theory. Because the stipulation that establishes the constraint would be something we say or think, something we thereby add to total theory.

Referring isn't just something we do. What we say and think not only doesn't settle what we refer to; it doesn't even settle the prior question of *how* it is to be settled what we refer to. Meanings – as the saying goes – just ain't in the head.

WHAT MIGHT THE SAVING CONSTRAINT BE?

Many philosophers would suggest at once that the saving constraint has to do with the causal chains that lead into the referrer's head from the external things that he refers to. At a minimum, some interpretations would be disqualified on causal grounds, and global descriptivism would select from those remaining. Or perhaps a causal account of reference ought to overthrow global descriptivism altogether.

If we subject a causal theory of reference (or a more modest causal constraint) to the 'just more theory' treatment, we get what I call causal descriptivism. That is: descriptivism, global or local, in which the descriptions are largely couched in causal terms. The lesson of Putnam's Paradox for causal theorists of reference is: don't trade in your genuine causal theory for causal descriptivism. But I myself would prefer causal descriptivism over a genuine causal theory. The causal theory often works, but not as invariably as philosophers nowadays tend to think. Sometimes an old-fashioned descriptivism works better; sometimes there are puzzling intermediate cases in which causal and descriptive considerations seem to tug in opposite directions.[11] When causal theories work, causal descriptivism works too.[12] When not, we need mixed theories, halfway houses between the 'new theory of reference' and the old. Causal descriptions seem ideally suited to mix into clusters with noncausal descriptions.

Given my preference for causal descriptivism – which indeed is just more description, just more theory – I must seek elsewhere for my saving constraint. I am inclined to favour a different kind of constraint

11 Such cases are presented in Peter Unger, 'The Causal Theory of Reference', *Philosophical Studies* 43 (1983), pp. 1–45.

12 Even Saul Kripke grudgingly admits this: see footnote 38 to 'Naming and Necessity' in D. Davidson and G. Harman, eds., *Semantics of Natural Language* (Reidel, 1972). However, he doubts that a non-circular theory of *either* sort exists.

proposed by G. H. Merrill.[13] (More precisely, he advises realists to propose it, but notes that he himself is no realist.) This constraint looks not to the speech and thought of those who refer, and not to their causal connections to the world, but rather to the referents themselves. Among all the countless things and classes that there are, most are miscellaneous, gerrymandered, ill-demarcated. Only an elite minority are carved at the joints, so that their boundaries are established by objective sameness and difference in nature. Only these elite things and classes are eligible to serve as referents. The world – any world – has the makings of many interpretations that satisfy many theories; but most of these interpretations are disqualified because they employ in-eligible referents. When we limit ourselves to the eligible interpreta-tions, the ones that respect the objective joints in nature, there is no longer any guarantee that (almost) any world can satisfy (almost) any theory. It becomes once again a worthy goal to discover a theory that will come true on an eligible interpretation, and it becomes a daring and risky hope that we are well on the way toward accomplishing this.

Merrill makes eligibility an all-or-nothing matter; I would prefer to make it a matter of degree. The mereological sum of the coffee in my cup, the ink in this sentence, a nearby sparrow, and my left shoe is a miscellaneous mess of an object, yet its boundaries are by no means unrelated to the joints in nature. It is an eligible referent, but less eligible than some others. (I have just referred to it.) Likewise the metal things are less of an elite, eligible class than the silver things, and the green things are worse, and the grue things are worse still – but all these classes belong to the elite compared to the countless utterly mis-cellaneous classes of thing that there are. *Ceteris paribus*, an eligible interpretation is one that maximises the eligibility of referents overall. Yet it may assign some fairly poor referents if there is good reason to. After all, 'grue' is a word of our language! *Ceteris* aren't *paribus*, of course; overall eligibility of referents is a matter of degree, making total theory come true is a matter of degree, the two desiderata trade off. The correct, 'intended' interpretations are the ones that strike the best

13 G. H. Merrill, 'The Model-Theoretic Argument Against Realism', *Philosophy of Science* 47 (1980), pp. 69–81. For further discussion of Merrill's solution, see the final section of my 'New Work for a Theory of Universals'.

balance. The terms of trade are vague; that will make for moderate indeterminacy of reference; but the sensible realist won't demand perfect determinacy.[14]

There seems to be a problem. To a physicalist like myself, the most plausible inegalitarianism seems to be one that give a special elite status to the 'fundamental physical properties': mass, charge, quark colour and flavour, . . . (It is up to physics to discover these properties, and name them; physicalists will think that present-day physics at least comes close to providing a correct and complete list.) But these elite properties don't seem to be the ones we want. Only in recent times have we had words for quark colour and flavour, but we have long had words for sticks and stones, cats, books, stars, . . . The solution, I suggest, is that we used to lack words for some very eligible referents because the correct interpretations of our language were the ones that did best on balance, not the ones that did best at best. Indeed, physics discovers which things and classes are the most elite of all; but others are elite also, though to a lesser degree. The less elite are so because they are connected to the most elite by chains of definability. Long chains, by the time we reach the moderately elite classes of cats and pencils and puddles; but the chains required to reach the utterly in-eligible would be far longer still.

It is not to be said that our theorising makes the joints at which the world is to be carved. That way lies the 'just more theory' trap. Putnam would say: "very well, formulate your theory of 'objective joints in nature', what they are and where they are; and stipulate if you will that your referents are to be 'eligible'. But total theory with this addition goes the way of all theory: it is satisfiable with the greatest of ease in countless ways. And these countless ways, of course, assign countless different extensions to 'joint in nature', 'eligible', and the rest." No: the proposed constraint is that referents are to be eligible, not just that eligibility-theory is to be satisfied somehow, not just that the referents of 'cat' etc. are to be included among the referents of 'eligible'.

---

14 It is not clear how much indeterminacy might be expected to remain. For instance, what of Quine's famous example? His rabbit-stages, undetached rabbit-parts, and rabbit-fusion seem only a little, if any, less eligible than rabbits themselves.

If I am looking in the right place for a saving constraint, then realism needs realism. That is: the realism that recognises a nontrivial enterprise of discovering the truth about the world needs the traditional realism that recognises objective sameness and difference, joints in the world, discriminatory classifications not of our own making. I do not quite say that we need traditional realism about universals.[15] For perhaps a nominalism that takes objective resemblance as primitive could do the job instead. But we need something of that sort. What it takes to solve Putnam's paradox is an objective inegalitarianism of classifications, in which grue things (or worse) are not all of a kind in the same way that bosons, or spheres, or bits of gold, or books are all of a kind.

I take it that Putnam classes the solution I advocate with solutions that rely on supernatural graspings or intuitings. He assimilates the view that 'the world . . . sorts things into kinds' to the preposterous view that the world gives things their names (RT&H, p. 53)! Recently, he has called my talk of elite classes 'spooky' and 'medieval-sounding'.[16] Well, sticks and stones may break my bones. . . . Anyway, what's wrong with sounding medieval? If the medievals recognised objective joints in the world − as I take it they did, realists and nominalists alike − more power to them. But I don't suppose that inegalitarianism of classifications is an especially medieval notion − rather, egalitarianism is a peculiarity of our own century.

Putnam has also said that inegalitarianism of classifications is contrary to physicalism. That would bother me, if true. But what's true is the opposite: *egalitarianism* is contrary to physicalism. For physicalists take physics − as it now is, or as it will be − at face value. And physics professes to discover the elite properties. What is the content of this part of physical science, according to an egalitarian?[17]

---

15 As it might be, the theory of D. M. Armstrong, *Universals and Scientific Realism* (Cambridge University Press, 1978), discussed in my 'New Work for a Theory of Universals'.

16 In remarks presented at the annual conference of the American Philosophical Association, Eastern Division, Baltimore, 1982.

17 See the discussion of formulations of materialism in my 'New Work for a Theory of Univerals', in which I argue that inegalitarianism of classifications must be presupposed in stating materialism.

That completes the first part of the paper. Now I shall take up five questions about why Putnam proceeds as he does – questions that leave me uncertain how well I have understood what he is up to.

WHY 'MODEL-THEORETIC'?

The premise that joins with global descriptivism to yield disaster is *not* any big theorem of model theory. In particular, it is not the theorem that gets star billing in M&R, the Skolem-Löwenheim Theorem. In fact, what's needed is pretty trivial. As I put it before: (almost) any world can satisfy (almost) any theory. The first 'almost' means 'unless the world has too few things'; the second means 'unless the theory is inconsistent'. This premise is obtained as follows. A consistent theory is, by definition, one satisfied by some model; an isomorphic image of a model satisfies the same theories as the original model; to provide the makings for an isomorphic image of any given model, a domain need only be large enough.

The real model theory adds only a couple of footnotes that are not really crucial to the argument. First, by the Completeness Theorem, we could if we wished redefine 'consistent' in syntactic terms. Second, by the Skolem-Löwenheim Theorem, our 'unless the world has too few things' is less of a qualification than might have been supposed: any infinite size is big enough. But the qualification wasn't very important in the first place. If Putnam's thesis had been that an ideal theory can misdescribe the world only by getting its size wrong, that would have been incredible enough. And in fact that *is* Putnam's thesis: for all he has said, it is still possible for ideal theory to misdescribe a finite world as infinite. Who cares whether the possibility of similar mistakes among the infinite sizes also is granted? We thought it was possible to misdescribe the world in ways having nothing to do with its size.

Anyway, the applicability of the model theory depends on treating exactly the first-order logical vocabulary as 'old' language, with antecedently determinate reference. As Robert Farrell[18] has emphasised,

---

18 Robert Farrell, 'Blanket Skolemism', presented at the annual conference of the Australasian Association of Philosophy, Sydney, 1980.

Putnam has no right to give this vocabulary special treatment. Perhaps he only did it for the sake of the argument, giving away points just because he would not need them.

WHY JUST IDEAL THEORIES?

You should have spotted a shift in my formulations of Putnam's incredible thesis. The official formulation was this: it makes no sense to suppose that an *empirically ideal* theory might nevertheless be false. But the conclusion of the model-theoretic argument applies to *any* consistent term-introducing total theory to which global descriptivism applies. It makes no sense (small worlds aside) to suppose that *any* such theory might be false, whether or not it is ideal. Idealness of the theory doesn't figure in the proof.

Perhaps Putnam has chosen to underplay his hand. Perhaps he does think of the model-theoretic argument as showing that our total accepted theory cannot be false, whether or not it is ideal (unless it is inconsistent, or the world is too small). But the special case of an ideal theory is the case that distinguishes realists from Peirceans, so that is the case he chooses to discuss. This hypothesis nicely fits the text of R&R, pp. 125–126. Even so, I think it is most likely a misunderstanding.

For one thing, why does he pass up the opportunity to say that the 'incoherent picture' held by his realist opponents commits them to the absurdity that even non-ideal theories are true on their intended interpretations, if that is what he thinks?

More likely, the model-theoretic argument is supposed to work only for ideal theories. But how could that be? A theory does *not* need to be ideal, merely consistent, in order to be satisfiable in any (big enough) world. So maybe the first premise of the argument, global descriptivism, is only supposed to work for ideal theories. But then how could it say anything about the vocabulary of our actual, present total theory, which doubtless isn't quite ideal? Perhaps as follows.

Descriptivism, local or global, might be *futuristic*. That is, the term-introducing theory which is supposed to come true on intended interpretations, if such there be, might be not the theory by which the terms actually were introduced, but rather some improved descendant that is expected to exist in the future. It might even be some ideally improved descendant that is never expected to actually exist, but that would result if the process of improvement went on forever. Imagine that our detective says: "My present hypothesis is that Jack the Ripper – as I propose to call him – did this, that, and the other. Of course, I realise that most likely that's not quite right. But if we start with this hypothesis, and improve it bit by bit in accordance with the evidence and the canons of scientific detection, eventually we may have a Jack-the-Ripper theory that can be improved no further. Maybe we will have it; maybe we never will, but I can speak of it even so. By 'Jack the Ripper' I intend to refer to the one described by that ultimate Jack-the-Ripper theory that we may never see." Likewise there could be a futuristic global descriptivism. Perhaps that is what Putnam has in mind. (I don't see any explicit futurism in R&R; I do in RT&H, pp. 30–32, but not in the context of the model-theoretic argument; in M&R, p. 475, there is explicit consideration of futuristic and non-futuristic alternatives.) I think it is what he should have in mind, for a reason to be stated shortly.

WHY ANTI-REALIST?

Why does the model-theoretic argument attack realism? By definition, of course: 'It is this feature [that an ideal theory might be false] that distinguishes metaphysical realism, as I am using the term, from the mere belief that there *is* an ideal theory . . . ' (R&R, p. 125). But what makes *that* a definition of any form of *realism*?

My point is emphatically not that 'Internal realism is all the realism we want or need' (R&R, p. 130). Internal realism, I take it, is realism feigned. The plan is to speak exactly as the realists do (except in the philosophy room – I have no idea how that lapse can be justified); and to do so in good conscience, in the hope that one's words are destined to join the ideal theory, and so are 'epistemically true'; but to do so without any intention of describing the world by saying something that will be true only if the world is one way rather than the other. (But of course the Internalist will *say* that he intends to be 'describing the world . . .'. His plan is to speak *exactly* as the realists do!)

My point is rather that even if the model-theoretic argument worked, it would not blow away the whole of the realist's picture of the world and its relation to theory. Something vital would be destroyed, but a lot would be left standing. There would still be a world, and it would not be a figment of our imagination. It would still have many parts, and these parts would fall into classes and relations – too many for comfort, perhaps, but too many is scarcely the same as none. There would still be interpretations, assignments of reference, intended and otherwise. Truth of a theory on a given interpretation would still make sense, and in a non-epistemic way. Truth on all intended interpretations would still make sense. Despite Putnam's talk of the 'collapse' of an 'incoherent picture', he has given us no reason to reject any of these parts of the picture. The only trouble he offers is that there are too many intended interpretations, so that truth on the intended interpretations is too easily achieved. That is trouble, sure enough. But is it *anti-realist* trouble, except by tendentious definition? It seems to me exactly opposite to traditional anti-realism.

The traditional anti-realist doubts or denies that there is any world save a figment of our imagination. Or he doubts or denies that the world divides into parts except insofar as we divide it, or that those parts fall into any classes or relations except such as are somehow of our own making. Or he doubts or denies that we can achieve reference to parts of the world, he questions that there can be even one intended referential interpretation. Or he doubts or denies that we can ever achieve truth on intended interpretations, or that we can ever have reason to believe that we have done so.

Across the board, wherever traditional anti-realism sees privation, Putnam argues instead from overabundance. It is only at the end that the opposites meet. They agree that it is unreasonable for science to aim at accurate description of reality, as opposed to the 'epistemic truth' of ideal theory. But why is that? Is it because accurate description is so difficult that we could not attain it, or could not reasonably expect to, even if we attain 'epistemic truth'? Or is it rather because accurate description is easy, automatically attained along with 'epistemic truth' and adding nothing extra?

Putnam should say the latter. He gives us no argument that discredits the realist's conception of truth of a theory on an interpretation which assigns referents in the world. His strategy should be to co-opt that conception, not to oppose it. He ought to say: '*Contra* realist orthodoxy, truth *simpliciter* is equivalent to, or simply is, epistemic truth. That is not because there is anything epistemic about truth-on-an-interpretation. Nor is it because truth *simpliciter* is anything else than truth on all intended interpretations. Rather it is because intendedness of interpretations is an epistemic matter.'

Maybe this *is* Putnam's strategy. His presentations of the model-theoretic argument in R&R and M&R can very well be read accordingly. If so, then global descriptivism needs to be futuristic, else truth on all intended interpretations will coincide with 'epistemic truth' only in the sweet by and by when we have ideal theory. This is my postponed reason why I think Putnam should have the futuristic version of global descriptivism in mind.

But if Putnam's strategy really is as I have just imagined, then there is a lot of poetic licence in some of what he says. It is an exaggeration to say that the realist picture 'collapses' (R&R, pp. 126 and 130). That suggests destruction more total than has actually been accomplished. And it is quite uncalled for to say, however metaphorically, that 'the mind and the world jointly make up the mind and the world' (RT&H, p. xi). No; we make theories, not worlds. The *metaphysics* of realism survives unscathed. What does suffer, if Putnam has his way, is realist semantics and epistemology.[19]

WHY ARE SUPERNATURAL CONSTRAINTS EXEMPT?

Putnam presents the model-theoretic argument as bad news for moderate, naturalistic realists: 'it is, unfortunately, the *moderate* realist position which is put into deep trouble . . .' (M&R, p. 464). Verificationists who aspire only to 'epistemic truth' have nothing to fear. But neither, he says, do those immoderate realists who claim to achieve determinate reference by supernatural means – by grasping, by intuiting, by direct contact, by magic, by noetic rays, by sixth sense, call it what you will. *Their* only problem is that their views are scientifically disreputable.

---

19 In this section I am indebted to Devitt's insistence that it is really very peculiar to take realism as an issue about semantic theory.

Why is that? Is it just that Putnam magnanimously declines to fight the weak? Or would supernatural intercourse between thinker and referent actually afford some way around Putnam's argument? I do not see how supernatural acquaintance with referents could do any better than the natural sort. Why is it a better way to achieve determinate reference if we get cat Nana into the grasp of our noetic rays than if we hold her in our hands? Why is it better if we intuit her with our sixth sense than if we see her with our eyes and hear her with our ears?

We know what Putnam says if we try to base determinate reference on natural causal connection: the theory of the causal constraint on reference is just more theory, as subject as any theory to overabundant, conflicting intended interpretations. But why are supernatural constraints exempt from parellel treatment? What's the good of holding up yet another sign, thus

$$\boxed{\text{DIRECTLY GRASPS}}$$

or perhaps

$$\boxed{\text{INTUITS}}$$

if it is still open to Putnam to challenge the determinate reference of the words written on the sign? (*Cf.* R&R, p. 127.) What can the proposed supernatural constraint be, if not the useless requirement that grasping-theory, or whatever, shall be made to come true along with the rest of (futuristic?) total theory?

I have argued, of course, that it is fair to reject the 'just more theory' treatment, whatever constraint it may be applied to. Presumably Putnam disagrees. But he has said nothing to show why the treatment applies only to natural constraints.

Perhaps Putnam thinks that supernaturalists are immune from the 'just more theory' treatment because they deny the premise that 'we interpret our languages or nothing does', or in other words that constraints on reference obtain only because we stipulate that they do. That would be a good reason to grant them exemption. I reply that a naturalist also can deny it on behalf of natural constraints, as I have done.

WHAT IS THE VAT ARGUMENT?

In R&R, setting forth the picture to be refuted by the model-theoretic argument, Putnam mentions brains in a vat:

> . . . indeed, it is held [by the metaphysical realist] that we might be *unable* to represent THE WORLD correctly at all (*e.g.* we might all be 'brains in a vat', the metaphysical realist tells us). (p. 125)

And a little later, still in connection with the model-theoretic argument,

> Suppose we . . . are and always were 'brains in a vat'. Then how does it come about that *our* word 'vat' refers to *noumenal* vats and not to vats in the image? (p. 127)

So when RT&H opens with a discussion of brains in a vat, we know what to expect. Brains in a vat are a stock example of radical deception. The model-theoretic argument is meant to show that radical deception is impossible. (More precisely: that radical deception is possible only when the deceived fall radically short of 'epistemic truth', which *ex hypothesi* the brains do not.) We expect Putnam to introduce the model-theoretic argument in dramatic fashion by using it to argue that even a brain in a vat is not radically deceived; and hence that it is nonsense to fear that we are radically deceived brains in a vat.

We might also expect that Putnam would anticipate the objection that the model-theoretic argument ignores causal constraints on reference; and that he might wish to postpone his 'just more theory' rejoinder, since it is tricky and he is obviously writing in part for nonspecialists; and that he might therefore offer an interim reply to the advocate of causal constraints, a reply that works only in this special case. And he does have such a reply. Even if a causal theory is correct and relevant – *contra* the 'just more theory' rejoinder – it doesn't help in this case. For it tends to show that we and the brains do not refer to the same things when we use the same words, since they are causally isolated from our referents. (Here I imagine Putnam to concede temporarily that our own reference is governed at least partly by causal constraints.) So at least some apparent examples of deception are mitigated, rather than worsened, by applying causal constraints on reference. If the brain says (in his inner speech) 'I am in Vienna', we might carelessly suppose that he means what we do and is therefore mistaken. (The brain and his vat are not in Vienna.) For he cannot think of Vienna, for he cannot refer to it, for *ex hypothesi* he is causally isolated from it.

All this, I repeat, is what we might reasonably expect. It is not what Putnam gives us. The argument in Chapter 1 of RT&H is not the model-theoretic argument.[20] The causal theory of reference is not used *ad hominem* against a hypothetical objector who hopes to use it to defend determinate reference. It is defended vigorously, then it carries the whole weight of the argument that the brains in the vat are not deceived.

Putnam's defence of the causal theory of reference is fair. Even if he really thinks it is just more theory, and couched in language with radically indeterminate reference, he may still think it is good theory, in all probability 'epistemically true'. Surely he does think so.

But how can the causal theory of reference, unaided, carry the whole weight of the argument? I see how it can be used to exonerate the brains from various specific accusations of error. "The brain says that by 'Vienna' he refers to Vienna and he doesn't." – "No, he *does* refer to what *he* calls 'Vienna', and so he speaks the truth. For what he calls 'Vienna' isn't the city that he is isolated from, but rather is part of the computer program that is the source of his 'Vienna'-tokens and his mental 'Vienna'-dossier."

Or even, perhaps, "He says that he isn't a brain in a vat, but he is." – "No, he's right; for by 'vat' he means not the sort of thing he is in, but rather the sort of thing that is the source of his 'vat'-tokens and his 'vat'-dossier. That sort of thing is, again, a sort of part of the computer program, and he isn't in one of those."

So far, so good. But it's not good enough just to show that the

---

20 For a genuine model-theoretic argument that brains in a vat are not deceived, see Paul Horwich, 'How to Choose Between Empirically Equivalent Theories', *Journal of Philosophy* 74 (1982), pp. 61–77.

brain doesn't make certain specific errors – he might make ever so many other errors, and be very radically deceived indeed.

In fact, showing that the brain avoids certain specific errors *is* enough to meet Putnam's stated goals in Chapter 1 of RT&H. He doesn't promise more than he delivers. But it isn't enough to contribute to Putnam's overall strategy. So what if we have to be a bit careful in saying just what mistakes a radically deceived brain in a vat does and doesn't make? No worries for realism there! Anybody can grant the point. I willingly do.

I suspect that Putnam thinks that the causal theory of reference can be used over and over, in similar fashion to the examples just considered, to exonerate the brain from all accusations of error whatsoever. (Except when the brain falls short of 'epistemic truth'.) If that is what Putnam means us to think, then Chapter 1 of RT&H fits nicely into his plan of battle. The causal-theoretic argument against massive error takes its place as partner to the model-theoretic argument, at least for a certain class of cases.

But I think we have been given no reason whatever to suppose that causal-theoretic exonerations can be produced *en masse*. The requisite causal theory of reference does not exist. We have a fairly well developed causal theory of reference for ordinary proper names, *e.g.* of people and places;[21] and we have a sketchy causal theory of reference for names of chemical substances and plant and animal species. The causal theory of reference for the whole of language is *not* just over the next hill. We don't know whether there is any such theory to be had, still less how credible it would seem or what it would say.

Suppose I accuse the brain of error when he says 'I am in Vienna', not because he isn't in the city that *we* call 'Vienna' but because he isn't *in* that part of a computer program that *he* calls 'Vienna'. You appeal to the causal theory of reference for the word 'in', saying that he *is* in the relation that *he* calls 'in' to the appropriate piece of program. I say it's a fraud. You may hope someday to possess a credible causal

---

21 I have in mind the theory of Michael Devitt, *Designation* (Columbia University Press, 1981). But I don't endorse even Devitt's theory; recall that I'm inclined to prefer causal descriptivism.

theory of reference that yields that result, but I do not believe you now possess even a glimmering of how this theory will go.

(One reason to doubt that you will ever have it: whatever happens in special cases, causal theories usually make it easy to be wrong about the things we refer to.)

And so it will go, I think, time and again. The exonerations of error to be had from extant causal theories of reference will be few and far between. The model-theoretic argument against massive error is fatally flawed, I think; but the causal-theoretic argument is barely a starter.

3

Against structural universals

INTRODUCTION

At the 1983 conference of the Auseralasian Association of Philosophy, there were two papers about the project of using abstract entities as ersatz possible worlds. One was mine, which distinguished three versions of ersatzism and raised different objections against different ones.[1] The other was Peter Forrest's, which proposed that structural universals should serve as ersatz worlds; the actualised one is instantiated by the concrete world, the rest are uninstantiated (or instantiated only by proper parts of the concrete world – I omit this complication henceforth).[2]

Forrest and I both wondered where his proposal would fall in my classification, and which of my objections I might raise against it. I found it unexpectedly difficult to give a straight answer. I ended up posing trilemmas, and needing to know more about the doctrine of structural universals on which Forrest's proposal was to be based.

First published in *The Australasian Journal of Philosophy* 64 (1986), pp. 25–46. Reprinted with kind permission from *The Australasian Journal of Philosophy*.

In writing this paper, I have been much helped by discussion with D. M. Armstrong, John Bigelow, Peter Forrest, and Mark Johnston.

1 David Lewis, 'Ersatz Modal Realism: Paradise on the Cheap?' given at the 1983 A.A.P. Conference, Adelaide; a much revised version appears as Chapter III of Lewis, *On the Plurality of Worlds* (Blackwell, 1986).

2 Peter Forrest, 'Ways Worlds Could Be', *Australasian Journal of Philosophy* 64 (1986), pp. 15–24.

I concluded that, after all, I had little objection to Forrest's use of structural universals, for the most part uninstantiated, as abstract ersatz worlds. Instead, I objected to the structural universals themselves. But I needed to distinguish different versions of the doctrine of structural universals and raise different objections against different ones. And I found that, for the most part, what I had to say would parallel what I had to say against different versions of ersatzism.

Not long before, in 'New Work for a Theory of Universals',[3] I had taken a favourable but noncommittal view of D. M. Armstrong's theory of universals – a theory which accepts structural universals, though not uninstantiated ones.[4] I said that it gave us one tenable way to draw an indispensable distinction between natural and unnatural classes. But I said that this distinction also could be had within a class nominalist theory, if we helped ourselves to a disagreeably complicated primitive notion of similarity. (The best way to do this might be to take naturalness of classes itself as primitive.) Armstrong's theory burdened us with more ontology; whereas an adequate form of class nominalism burdened us with a rather artificial-seeming primitive distinction. I took seriously the merits and drawbacks of both alternatives, and reckoned that between them the honours were about even. That judgement is now up for reconsideration.

I should have commended a sparse theory of tropes as a third alternative, no less meritorious than the two I considered. *Tropes* are supposed to be particularised properties: nonspatiotemporal parts of their instances which cannot occur repeatedly, but can be exact duplicates. I have in mind more or less the trope theory taught by D. C. Williams,[5] except for one thing: if natural classes of things are to be

---

3 *Australasian Journal of Philosophy* 61 (1983) pp. 343–377 (reprinted in this volume as Chapter 1).

4 D. M. Armstrong, *Universals and Scientific Realism*, two volumes (Cambridge University Press, 1978). Armstrong's principal discussion of structural universals is Volume II, pp. 69–71; see also Volume I, p. 117; Volume II, p. 39; and Volume II, pp. 120–127.

5 See D. C. Williams, 'On the Elements of Being', *Review of Metaphysics* 7 (1953) pp. 3–18 and 171–192, reprinted in Williams, *Principles of Empirical Realism* (Charles Thomas, 1966). Other versions of trope theory have recently been put forward in Keith Campbell, 'The Metaphysic of Abstract Particulars', *Midwest Studies in*

defined in terms of classes of duplicate tropes, then trope theory needs to be made sparse and selective in just the way that Armstrong's theory of universals is sparse and selective. Else there might be classes of duplicate disjunctive tropes, or of duplicate negative tropes, that would mark out unduly miscellaneous classes of things. Like a theory of universals, a theory of tropes burdens us with ontology that plain nominalism avoids; like class nominalism, it requires a primitive of similarity. However, its primitive of similarity – exact duplication of tropes – looks far less artificial, hence more acceptable, than primitive naturalness of classes.

If Armstrong is right in his arguments that a theory of universals ought to include structural universals, and if I am also right that structural universals are trouble, then together we bring bad news for universals. Trouble over structural universals would tend to show that the honours are not even after all, so that in my pursuit of natural classes, I ought to employ either primitive naturalness or tropes, and leave the universals out of it.

The discussion to follow is motivated by an interest in both projects: Forrest's pursuit of ersatz worlds, and my pursuit of natural classes. The projects differ. Forrest's project requires many structural universals to be uninstantiated, mine does not. Armstrong, of course, does not accept uninstantiated universals of any sort. So, although I must of course heed Armstrong's views on structural universals, my aim will not be just to discuss his theory.

WHAT ARE STRUCTURAL UNIVERSALS?

What is a structural universal supposed to be? In the first place, it is a universal: something that does, or at least can, occur repeatedly. It is instantiated by different particulars, at different spatiotemporal positions; and wherever it is instantiated, there the whole of it is present. When it is instantiated, it is a nonspatiotemporal part of the particular that instantiates it.[6]

Philosophy 6 (1981) pp. 477–488; and in Mark Johnston, *Particulars and Persistence*, Princeton dissertation, 1983.
6 I mean what Armstrong calls the 'thick' particular, not the 'thin' particular which

In the second place, it is a distinctive kind of universal. Anything that instantiates it must have proper parts; and there is a necessary connection between the instantiating of the structural universal by the whole and the instantiating of other universals by the parts. Let us say that the structural universal *involves* these other universals – a suitably nondescript word, leaving us free to ask later what 'involvement' may be. It is not required, or not at this stage, that the involved universals should themselves be simple. It is also not required that the involved universals should all be monadic. That is one special case; but often, a structural universal will involve dyadic (or, more generally, *n*-adic) universals as well. If it does, then for something to instantiate the structural universal is partly a matter of the properties of the parts of that thing, and partly a matter of how those parts are externally – say, spatiotemporally – related.

(Distinguish two senses in which a universal might be called 'simple'. It might be one that does not involve any others; that is, not a structural universal. This is what I have meant, and will mean henceforth. Or it might be mereologically *atomic*: it might have no proper parts, no parts other than itself. I would suppose that on any theory, simple universals come out atomic; but we shall later consider one theory according to which structural universals also are atomic.)

Example: suppose we have monadic universals *carbon* and *hydrogen*, instantiated by atoms of those elements; and a dyadic universal *bonded*, instantiated by pairs of atoms between which there is a covalent bond. (I should really be talking about momentary stages, but let's leave time out of it for simplicity.) Then we have, for instance, a structural universal *methane*, which is instantiated by methane molecules. It involves the three previously mentioned universals as follows: necessarily, something instantiates *methane* if and only if it is divisible into five spatial parts c, h_1, h_2, h_3, h_4 such that c instantiates *carbon*, each of the *h*'s instantiates *hydrogen*, and each of the c-h pairs instantiates *bonded*.

results from the mereological subtraction of the universals. See *Universals and Scientific Realism*, Volume I, pp. 114–115.

81

Why should anybody believe in structural universals? Why not prefer a theory of universals even sparser than Armstrong's, which admits only simple universals?[7] Such a theory is simple and elegant. Why not be content with it?

One reason which might be given need not detain us long:

(1) There is a universal for every predicate we can formulate, including complex predicate phrases; or for every class that things belong to. There are such predicates as 'is a methane molecule'; there are such classes as the class of all methane molecules. So there are the corresponding universals, and these must be structural.

But to hold a sparse theory of universals is, among other things, to reject the premise that there is a universal to correspond to just any predicate or class. And any theorist of universals as *immanent* had better hold a sparse theory; it is preposterous on its face that a thing has as many nonspatiotemporal parts as there are different predicates that it falls under, or different classes that it belongs to.

A second reason is better:

(2) The main job of a theory of universals is to give an account of resemblance; and things may resemble one another by being alike in their structure, by being composed of like parts arranged in a like way. We need structural universals so that we can give an account of this sort of structural resemblance as the sharing of universals.

But it is one thing to say that resemblance is to be explained in terms of shared universals; it is another thing to say that whenever two particulars are alike, those particulars *themselves* share a universal. Why not say that structural resemblance of A and B is to be explained not as sharing of universals between the whole of A and the whole of B, but

---

7 As in the principal system of Nelson Goodman, *The Structure of Appearance* (Harvard University Press, 1951), except that I am considering a structure not of appearance but of reality generally.

rather as sharing of universals between corresponding parts of A and of B? (Or more generally, as sharing of n-adic universals between corresponding n-tuples of parts.) Only the simplest way of explaining resemblance in terms of shared universals requires there to be shared structural universals.

Another reason is Forrest's:

(3) Structural universals can serve as ersatz possible worlds and individuals, affording an objectual treatment of modality without requiring us to believe in an implausible abundance of otherworldly concrete particulars.

I do not dispute this – provided, of course, that an appropriate conception of structural universals could be had. I only warn that such ersatz worlds will not give us all the benefits of the real thing. In particular, I do not think Forrest's plan can afford an eliminative analysis of modality. For one thing, we may find appeals to modality within some conceptions of structural universals themselves – see below. But also, a theory of ersatz worlds needs to be able to explain what it means to say that so-and-so is the case *according to* (for short: *at*) an ersatz world. I can see how we might say, without modality, what it is to be an ersatz world at which such-and-such a pattern of instantiation of simple universals – such-and-such a spatiotemporal arrangement of masses, charges, and so forth – obtains. But what is it to be an ersatz world according to which there is a talking donkey? Or one according to which a turtle supports the Earth? I doubt that Forrest would countenance *being a talking donkey*, or *being a turtle*, as genuine universals; certainly Armstrong would not. So I do not see what alternative Forrest has to the modal answer:

Such an ersatz world is a structural universal such that, necessarily, any particular that instantiates it has a talking donkey as a part, or has a turtle supporting (a counterpart of) the Earth as a part.

But if we waive this objection and grant that structural universals could do all that we should ask of ersatz worlds, still that is an odd reason to believe in them. Ersatz worlds are meant to serve the cause of actualism; and we would expect an actualist first to settle the ontology of this world, and afterward to cut his treatment of modality to fit. If the demands of a treatment of modality control an actualist's theory of what universals there are for this worldly things to instantiate, he seems to put his modal cart before his actual horse. Further, even if structural universals could do for ersatz worlds, other alternatives might do as well. For one thing, a theory of simple universals ought to provide an ideal setting for 'combinatorial' ersatzism; and, while that has problems of its own, I think it is as at least as well off as any version of Forrest's ersatzism of structural universals. Indeed, on one version – the 'linguistic conception' discussed below – structural universals and combinatorial ersatz worlds come out very much alike.

Armstrong, of course, would never suggest that we need a universal for every predicate. And it is only after he has already accepted structural universals that he commits himself to explaining structural resemblance in the simple way.[8] Nor could he endorse Forrest's program, since it takes unactualised ersatz worlds to be uninstantiated universals. His reasons for accepting structural universals are different. He has three, of which I take some to be more persuasive than others. In order of increasing weight:

(4) Another job for a theory of universals is to provide resources for the anti-Humean theory of laws of nature which Dretske, Tooley, and Armstrong have advanced. This theory says that we have a (fundamental) law that F's are G's when a certain second-order lawmaking relation N holds between two first-order universals F and G. But if we confined ourselves to the case where F and G are simples, surely we could only get the simplest of laws, and it's unreasonable to think that we could cover all the laws of nature there are, still less all there might be, in such a simple way.[9]

---

8 *Universals and Scientific Realism*, Volume II, p. 96.

9 See *Universals and Scientific Realism*, Volume II, pp. 149–153; Fred I. Dretske, 'Laws of Nature', *Philosophy of Science* 44 (1977) pp. 248–268; Michael Tooley, 'The Nature of Laws', *Canadian Journal of Philosophy* 4 (1977) pp. 667–698; and D. M. Armstrong, *What is a Law of Nature?* (Cambridge University Press, 1983).

I think this is a good reason, within the DTA theory of lawhood; my reasons for finding it unconvincing are just my reasons for preferring a fancy regularity theory to the DTA theory.[10] Even within the DTA theory, however, I think it is less than decisive. Another option is to have not just the one lawmaker relation, but a family of them, and put the complexity that is missing from the simple F's and G's into the N's that apply to them. I take it that it would be possible to develop the DTA theory in such a way, but that the requisite family of fancy N's would be a most unwelcome complication.

(5) For structural universals, if not for universals in general, it is possible to say something about what makes one universal similar to, or incompatible with, another. Armstrong uses the example of structural universals of length. If one stick is 9 meters long and another is 8 meters long, then, necessarily, a large part of the first stick is 8 meters long; and, necessarily, no stick is 8 meters long and also is 9 meters long. These necessities both follow from the necessary connections between the universals of length and other universals they involve: a stick 9 meters long must have two distinct proper parts, one of them 8 meters long and one of them 1 meter long. That is what makes the universals 9 *meters long* and 8 *meters long* be both similar and incompatible. A parallel account could be given for resemblance and incompatibility of shapes, and perhaps also colours.[11]

But don't we really need to understand how universals in general, whether structural or simple, can be similar or incompatible? For instance, positive and negative charge might be incompatible simple universals. If we need a general account, then the value of an account that works only for a special case is limited.

(6) Can we be sure that there *are* any simples? If not, then we cannot dispense with structural universals in favour of the simples they involve; because they don't involve simples, just

10 See my 'New Work for a Theory of Universals', p. 366.
11 *Universals and Scientific Realism*, Volume II, pp. 120–127.

other structural universals. Take our previous example. We certainly didn't get down to simples: a carbon atom consists of electrons, protons, and neutrons in a certain structure of bonding; protons and neutrons consist in turn of quarks; it is speculated that quarks in turn are composite. . . . Maybe there is no end to this complexity. Maybe there are no simples, just structures of structures *ad infinitum*. (Or maybe there are simples but not enough of them – if *electronhood* were simple but *protonhood* were a matter of structures *ad infinitum*, that would be enough to defeat the plan of dispensing with *hydrogen* in favour of the simples it involves.) Even if we believe in (enough) simples, should we adopt a doctrine of universals that presupposes this, and leaves no room for even the possibility of infinite complexity?[12]

I take this last reason to be weightiest by far. Infinite complexity does seem, offhand, to be a genuine possibility. I might contemplate treating it as negotiable: if structural universals are trouble, and simple universals retain their charm, so much the worse for the alleged possibility that there are no simples! But that seems objectionably high-handed, if not downright intolerable.

Suppose we do acknowledge the possibility. That imposes a demand on a theory of universals – a severe demand, if I am right that structural universals are trouble. (It is unseemly that so far-fetched a possibility, as I take it to be, should do so much to constrain our theory of the constitution of this world.) If, like Armstrong, you think that universals afford the only tenable answer to the compulsory question about what it is for things to be alike, then you will have to meet the demand as best you can. If, like me, you think that universals afford one of three *prima facie* tenable answers, you will want to take a closer look at the other alternatives.

I note that class nominalism, with a primitive distinction between natural and unnatural classes, has no problem with infinite complexity. It might happen that whenever we have a natural class, its members

12 *Universals and Scientific Realism*, Volume II, pp. 67–68.

are composite individuals, and their parts (and pairs, triples, . . . of their parts) fall in turn into natural classes.

Likewise a trope theory has no problem with infinite complexity. It might happen that every trope is divisible into interrelated spatio-temporal parts, and that any two duplicate tropes are divisible in such a way that their corresponding parts are duplicates in turn.

THE LINGUISTIC CONCEPTION

Now I shall present three different conceptions of what a structural universal is, against which I shall raise different objections. I cannot prove these conceptions are the only ones available; it's just that I can't think of another. So one way to answer me would be to produce a fourth. I call these three conceptions (echoing my earlier classification of versions of ersatzism) *linguistic, pictorial,* and *magical.*

On the linguistic conception, a structural universal is a set-theoretic construction out of simple universals, in just the way that a (parsed) linguistic expression can be taken as a set-theoretic construction out of its words.[13] In fact, we think of the structural universal as being a complex predicate, in a language in which the words are the simple universals. Or rather, the simple universals are *some* of the words; they comprise the nonlogical vocabulary. We also need logical words – the usual connectives, quantifiers, and variables – and we need mereological predicates of identity, inclusion, and overlap. These words can be anything the resources of set-theoretic construction have to offer, it doesn't matter what. A language, in this generalised sense, needn't be something we can speak or write! What matters is that we have parsing and interpretation. The words of the language are interpreted by stipulation, and part of our stipulation is that each simple universal is to be a predicate which is satisfied by just the particulars that instantiate it. (Simple dyadic universals are two-place predicates, satisfied by pairs of particulars; and so on.) Complex expressions, including those that

13 As in my 'General Semantics', *Synthese* 22 (1970) pp. 18–67, reprinted in my *Philosophical Papers*, Volume I (Oxford University Press, 1983); or as in M. J. Cresswell, *Languages and Logics* (Methuen, 1973).

we take as the structural universals, are interpreted in a derivative way. Recursive rules are stipulated whereby the interpretation of a parsed expression depends on the interpretations of its immediate constituents under the parsing, and in one step or several we get down to the stipulated interpretations of the words from which that expression is built up. Thus we specify, in particular, what it is for something to satisfy a complex predicate in the language.

It is these predicates (or certain favoured ones of them, say the ones that are suitably nondisjunctive) that we take to be the structural universals; and to satisfy the predicate is to instantiate the universal. We have the required necessary connections between the instantiating of a structural universal by the whole and the instantiating of simpler universals by its parts. And there is no mystery about how these connections can be necessary: they hold by definition. They are just consequences of a semantic recursion which defines satisfaction of complex predicates in terms of satisfaction of the simple ones that are the vocabulary from which the complex predicate is built up; in other words, which defines the instantiation of structural universals in terms of the instantiation of simple universals they involve.

It is an easy matter to believe in structural universals, so understood. The hard thing would be not to believe in them. Once we have the simples, we need only believe in set-theoretic constructions out of things we believe in. There is no extra ontic commitment, apart from the commitment to sets that most of us accept as unavoidable.

Is it fair to call these constructions *universals*? I think so. It may stretch a point, given that they are sets whereas simple universals are individuals; but if so, that is a point we stretch routinely. A set of located individuals is itself located, in the plural way appropriate to a set: the set *is* where its members *are*. (It might be better to flout grammar and say that the set *are* where its members are.) Likewise for the higher ranks: a set of sets is where its members of members are, and in general a set-theoretic construction is where the individuals are whence it is constructed. In the case of one of our putative structural universals, those individuals are its simples; and as universals, they are wholly present in each of their instances; and among their instances are the appropriate parts of any instance of the structural universal; and that is how the structural universal itself is wholly present in each of its instances. The structural universal occurs repeatedly, as a universal should. Therefore it deserves the name.[14]

So far, so good; but the trouble with the linguistic conception should now be plain to see. Its structural universals are constructed out of simples. Armstrong's principal need for structural universals is exactly to cover the possibility that there are no simples, or not enough simples; and constructions out of simples are worthless to meet that need. Just when the need for structural universals is greatest, the wherewithal to make them is lacking.

If we put aside worries about infinite complexity, the structural universals of the linguistic conception might be some use. They could do for ersatz worlds, provided we are content to limit ourselves to possibilities which are fully given by arrangements of some stock of actually existing simples (and provided we do not aspire to an eliminative analysis of modality); this amounts to a version of 'combinatorial' ersatzism. They are shared between things that are similar in the way that methane molecules, for instance, are, by being isomorphic in a pattern of instantiation of simples. Their sharing of substructures (constituent linguistic expressions) can provide a theory of similarity and incompatibility of lengths, shapes, or perhaps colours. They could be made the *relata* of a lawmaking universal, provided that a DTA theorist were prepared to allow such dubious entities as sets to instantiate genuine universals. But none of these manoeuvres really seems to depart from a very sparse theory of universals that confines itself to simples. Formulations are simplified, but we gain no additional strength. What we have are make-believe structural universals for those who do not accept the real thing.

14 John Bigelow has noted a peculiarity: on the linguistic conception, a structural universal is apt to be present not only in its instances but elsewhere as well. Our universal *methane* will be wholly present, because its simples are, not only where there is a methane molecule but also wherever there is any sort of molecule that is made of carbon and hydrogen bonded together. So far as I can see, this is no real problem; we just have to take care to distinguish instantiation from mere presence.

On the pictorial conception, a structural universal is isomorphic to its instances. The methane atom consists of one carbon atom and four hydrogen atoms, with the carbon bonded to each of the four hydrogens; the structural universal *methane* likewise consists of several parts, one for each of the five atoms, and one for each of the four bonds. Compare a ball-and-spring model: one large central ball, and four smaller balls attached to it by springs. This model is a three-dimensional picture. It represents a methane molecule – any methane molecule, not any one in particular – by isomorphism.

The ball-and-spring model is a particular, and is wholly distinct from any of the methane molecules to which it is isomorphic. (Only in a much colder climate could we make it out of frozen methane.) The structural universal *methane*, on the other hand, is an immanent universal as well as an isomorph. It is wholly present as a nonspatio-temporal part of each methane molecule that instantiates it.

Since it is a universal, capable of repeated occurrence, its parts must be universals too. For wherever the whole is present, there the parts are present; so the parts must occur just as repeatedly as the whole; which they could not do if they were particulars. Then what can the parts be? An answer is immediate: they are the universals that are instantiated by the parts of the methane molecule. When the whole of the molecule instantiates the whole of the universal, the parts of the molecule instantiate the appropriate parts of the universal. The structural universal *methane*, we have supposed, involves three simpler universals: the monadic universals *carbon* and *hydrogen*, and the dyadic universal *bonded*. These are its parts. The central atom of any methane molecule instantiates *carbon*, the other four atoms instantiate *hydrogen*, and the four carbon–hydrogen pairs instantiate *bonded*. In this way, part by part under the isomorphic correspondence, the whole molecule instantiates the whole universal *methane*.

On this conception a structural universal is an individual, not a set. It is mereologically composite. The simpler universals it involves are present in it as proper parts. It is nothing over and above them, in the straightforward sense that it is nothing but their mereological sum.

These simpler universals may not yet be simples. In fact there may be no simples at all; this time, we have a conception that would permit infinite complexity. A universal is simple iff it is mereologically atomic; on this conception, we have no need to distinguish the two notions.

So far, so good. We have our structural universals, and we do not require them to be reducible to simples. But if there are simples, the structural universals are nothing over above their simple parts, just as a molecule is nothing over and above its atoms. A whole is an extra item in our ontology only in the minimal sense that it is not identical to any of its proper parts; but it is not distinct from them either, so when we believe in the parts it is no extra burden to believe in the whole. Likewise in general a structural universal is nothing over and above its simpl*er* parts, whether or not any of its parts are simple *simpliciter*. Further, we avoid the resources of set theory, with its queer way of spinning vast riches out of little or nothing; and we avoid the modal magic that I shall denounce later.

In the days when I was unworried about structural universals, I think I held the pictorial conception of them, though not in a perfectly explicit way. Does Armstrong hold the pictorial conception? Certainly his writing very often suggests it; certainly he affirms parts of it; and I cannot see how to extract an alternative conception from what he says. But also he sees what is wrong with it, and in that connection rejects one part of it. So we mustn't say outright that he holds it; what is unclear to me is how much of it he repudiates.

What *is* wrong? I hope I have been explicit enough to make the trouble stand out like a sore thumb. It is as follows. Each methane molecule has not one hydrogen atom but four. So if the structural universal *methane* is to be an isomorph of the molecules that are its instances, it must have the universal *hydrogen* as a part not just once, but four times over. Likewise for *bonded*, since each molecule has four bonded pairs of atoms. But what can it mean for something to have a part four times over? What are there four of? There are not four of the universal *hydrogen*, or of the universal *bonded*; there is only one. The pictorial conception as I have presented it has many virtues, but consistency is not among them.

Armstrong's discussion of the trouble is brief. He takes a simple example, one where the structure involves only a single monadic universal. (He rejects a dyadic universal of nonidentity.) He writes:

> Consider the structural property of *being (just) two electrons*, a property possessed by all two-member collections of electrons. We cannot say that this property involves the same universal, *being an electron*, taken twice over, because a universal is one, not many. We can only say that the more complex universal involves the notion of two particulars of a certain sort, two instances of the same universal state of affairs.[15]

What 'we can only say' is all very well; but it does not take the place of what 'we cannot say'. I should like to know what he thinks we *can* say, not about notions and not about instances, but about the universals themselves. Is it so or is it not that *being an electron* (taken only once) is part of *being two electrons*? If it is not, does that mean that the two universals (as opposed to their instances, or our concepts of them) are wholly distinct? If it is part, is it a proper part? Or is it the whole? If it is a proper part, what other part is there? If it is the whole, how do the two universals nevertheless differ?

It is part of Armstrong's theory that universals generally, and structural universals along with the rest, are abstractions from their particular instances.[16] Does this doctrine of abstraction somehow give us licence to set aside questions about the mereology of the abstracted universals themselves, and to speak only about the unproblematic mereology of the instances? Might it dissolve our difficulty? That depends what is meant when Armstrong says that a universal is an 'abstraction from' its instances. I know three things that could be meant, and three only. But two of them cannot be what Armstrong means, and the third cannot help us.[17]

(1) When one thing is said to be abstracted from others, the abstraction could be a mere verbal fiction. We could speak as if of some

15 *Universals and Scientific Realism*, Volume II, pp. 69–70.

16 I find this stated most explicitly not in *Universals and Scientific Realism*, but in *What is a Law of Nature?*, pp. 83–84.

17 Note well that my question concerns the relational phrase 'abstraction from'. On this occasion, I shall not even enter that quagmire of senses in which things are said to be 'abstract entities' although not abstracted *from* anything in particular.

one 'surman' named Geach, when really the only entities we refer to are the many Geaches.[18] We could refer to them in an indeterminate and partial way, no more to one Geach than to another, and keep out of trouble by only saying things to which the differences between Geaches make no difference. We could even say there is only one, that being among the things that comes out true on every resolution of the indeterminancy of our reference. (Alternatively, we could say it by counting not by identity but by the namesake relation.) Then the surman Geach is nothing at all; or else he is some one of the many Geaches but we needn't ever settle which one. If this were meant when Armstrong tells us that a universal is an abstraction from its instances, then indeed our trouble over the mereology of structural universals would dissolve. For they and their parts alike would be dismissed as fictions and we would be left with the unproblematic mereology of the instances. But if this were meant, then also Armstrong would be a false friend of universals, and a most disingenuous nominalist; which assuredly he is not.

(2) When mathematicians abstract one thing from others, they take an equivalence class. The one direction common to many lines in the Euclidean plane is the equivalence class of those lines under the relation of being parallel. This way, our one abstracted from the many is at least not a fictitious entity (unless classes themselves are fictions). But it is only superficially a one; underneath, a class are still many. Otherwise my comment is as before. If Armstrong were a disingenuous class nominalist, that would indeed dissolve questions about the mereology of structural universals. But he isn't.

(3) What Armstrong *can* mean, without betraying his principles, is that the one universal is abstracted from its many instances in a mereological sense: all of them share it as a common part. That *is* Armstrong's view: he often speaks of immanent universals wholly present in their instances, and of the partial identity between different instances of the same universal. If he sometimes hesitates to say outright that a universal is part of its instances, I suppose that is just to placate those

18 See P. T. Geach, *Logic Matters* (Blackwell, 1972), pp. 222–223 and 245–246. Of course it is not required that we join Geach in his rejection of absolute identity in order to regard surmen as mere verbal fictions.

who insist on limiting the word 'part' to spatiotemporal parts, or to spatial parts, or even to well-demarcated spatial parts; and who go all bewildered when they hear the word used in its fully general sense. But to say that a universal such as *being an electron* or *being two electrons* is an abstraction from its instances, and to mean thereby that each universal is part of its instances, does nothing at all to answer or to dissolve our question whether the one universal is part of the other.

VARIANTS OF THE PICTORIAL CONCEPTION

Perhaps there is some hope of a repair. How would it be if we dropped the isomorphism of the universal to its instances, but continued to hold that a structural universal is a mereological composite, having as parts the simpler universals that it involves? There are the three universals *carbon, hydrogen,* and *bonded*; the universal *methane* is composed of exactly these three parts, each entering into it only once; and it remains that whenever the universal is present in its instance its parts also are present, being instantiated by the appropriate parts of the instance, or pairs of parts.

But now consider butane. Its molecules consist of four carbon atoms in a straight chain, with adjacent atoms bonded; the end carbon atoms are bonded also to three hydrogen atoms each, and the middle ones to two. So we might have wanted to say that the structural universal *butane* consists of the universal *carbon* four times over, the universal *hydrogen* ten times over, and the dyadic universal *bonded* thirteen times over. But if we dump this strange talk of parts many times over, we'll just say that it consists of the three universals *carbon, hydrogen,* and *bonded* – just like the universal *methane*. So here we have two different universals, as witness the fact that some molecules instantiate the one and some the other; and both of them are composed of exactly the same three parts!

But how can two different things be composed of exactly the same parts? I know how two things can be made of parts that are qualitatively just the same – that is no problem – but this time, the two things are supposed to be made not of duplicate parts, but of numerically identical parts. That, I submit, is unintelligible.

Two bad rejoinders. (1) Sets do it. – I do not agree. It is a mistake to say that sets afford a precedent wherein many things are composed, presumably in some special unmereological sense, out of the very same parts. What's true is that two sets – indeed, countless different sets – can be generated out of the very same individuals. We see this already with unit sets. Take Bruce, one individual: then we have his unit set, the unit set of his unit set, and so *ad infinitum*. But is this a case in which different things are composed of the same parts? No – it's not composition at all! When a unit set is made out of its sole member, one thing is made out of *one* thing; whereas composition is the combining of many things into one. If we want to find composition among sets, we must look elsewhere. The parts of a set are its (nonempty) subsets, and thus every many-membered set is composed, ultimately, of its unit subsets. This is genuine composition: many combined into one. It obeys all the canons of mereology. In particular, no two sets are ever composed of the very same subsets. The generation of sets out of their elements, as opposed to their subsets, is not some unmereological form of composition. Rather it is a mixture of the two things we have distinguished: the generation of unit sets from their members, which is not composition at all (God knows what it is); and the genuine, mereological composition of many-membered sets out of their unit subsets. Both of these together, applied in alternation, yield the entire hierarchy of (nonempty) sets. The set of Bruce and myself is the mereological sum of our unit sets; the set of Armstrong and Forrest and the aforementioned set is likewise a sum of three unit sets, one of which is the unit set of a sum of unit sets; and so on up the ranks.

(2) Different things can be made of the same parts at different times, as when the tinkertoy house is taken apart and put back together as a tinkertoy car. – I say that what's true is not that two things are made out of the very same parts, but rather that two things are made out of different parts, different temporal segments of the same persisting bits of tinkertoy. Admittedly, that answer is premised on a controversial view about how things persist through time. But if you reject that view, and think instead that the bits of tinkertoy endure identically through time, you still oughtn't to say that two things are made of the very same parts. Rather, *one* thing is made of those parts. This thing is not a house or a car *simpliciter*. Rather, it bears the house-at relation to some times and the car-at relation to other times. If you think that

95

persistence is identical endurance, you keep having to transform plain classifications of things into fancy external relations of things to times, and so it is here.

Here is a second attempt at repair. We might restore the talk of parts many times over; agree that two different things cannot be made of the very same parts taken once each, but insist that two things can be made of the same parts if there is a difference in how many times over some part is taken. Such is the difference between the structural universals *methane* and *butane*. Further, we might take the 'many times over' adverbially: if *A* has *B* as part four times over that doesn't mean we have four of anything; the relevant entities are *A* and *B*, there is only one of *B*, but 'four times over' is the *way* that *A* has *B* as a part.

I think such talk of having parts in one or another way is empty; and I should like to know what it can have to do with the fact that in the instances, we do have four of something. (I would suspect modal magic, of the sort to be discussed later.) But let that pass; there is a simpler objection. Consider isobutane. Where butane has a straight chain, isobutane branches. Its molecules consist of a central carbon atom bonded to three outlying carbon atoms; the central carbon atom is bonded also to one hydrogen atom, and each outlying carbon atom is bonded to three hydrogen atoms. So the structural universal *isobutane* consists of the universal *carbon* four times over, the universal *hydrogen* ten times over, and the dyadic universal *bonded* thirteen times over – just like the universal *butane*. But these two structural universals are different, as witness the different molecules that instantiate them. Even if our adverbial differences made sense, they would not solve our problem.

Here is a third attempt at repair. Again, we talk of having parts in one or another way, rather than composition *simpliciter*. And again we posit a *sui generis*, unmereological form of composition, whereby many things can be made out of the very same parts. Suppose that we have several different combining operations, each of which applies to several universals to yield a new universal. Each operation singly obeys a principle of uniqueness: for any given arguments, in a given order, it yields at most one value. But if we apply the operations repeatedly, starting with the same initial stock of universals, we can produce many different structural universals depending on the order in which the operations are applied.[19] Whenever we apply the operations, we get a structural universal which involves the universals to which the operation was applied; the latter are in that sense simpler. But there is no need to assume that we start with simples, or that there are any.

My objection to this is that I do not see by what right the operations are called *combining* operations. An operation applies to several universals; it yields a new universal. But if what goes on is unmereological, in what sense is the new one *composed* of the old ones? In what unmereological sense are they present in it? After all, not just any operation that makes new things from old is a form of composition! There is no sense in which my parents are parts of me, and no sense in which two numbers are parts of their greatest common factor; and I doubt that there is any sense in which Bruce is part of his unit set.

If the friend of '*sui generis* composition' does not mean it seriously when he says that the new universal is composed of the old ones, if he takes this to be a dispensable metaphor, if he does not insist that the old universals are still present in the new one, well and good. Then he is no longer any sort of pictorialist; rather, he favours the magical conception of structural universals, and I shall address his view later.

But if he does insist that his unmereological composition is nevertheless composition, in a perfectly literal sense, then I need to be told why. Saying so doesn't make it so. What is the *general* notion of composition, of which the mereological form is supposed to be only a special case? I would have thought that mereology already describes composition in full generality. If sets were composed in some unmereological way out of their members, that would do as a precedent to show that there can be unmereological forms of composition; but I have challenged that precedent already.

19 The operations that build structural universals out of the simpler universals they involve might be formally parallel to some of the operations that are used to build compound predicates in variable-free formulations of predicate logic; for instance, in the system of W. V. Quine, 'Variables Explained Away', in Quine, *Selected Logic Papers* (Random House, 1966). (Here I am indebted to Peter Forrest.)

Here is a final attempt. I do not see that it faces any decisive refutation; but it strays a long way from any ordinary theory of universals, and eventually it becomes so bizarre that I cannot take it seriously. We might restore genuine isomorphism between the structural universal and its instances, and face the consequences. Let us concede that when the universal *methane* involves the universal *hydrogen*, we don't just have the one universal *hydrogen* after all. We *do* have four of something, and all four are parts of the universal *methane*. (And there are ten that are parts of the universal *butane*, not to mention the universal *dodecane*, or various high polymers!) Our new problem of one over many within the structural universal itself is to be solved by accepting the many.

Before, I argued that the parts of a universal had to be as capable of repeated occurrence as the universal itself; and that conclusion stands. So when we have many of something, instead of the one universal *hydrogen*, the many are still universals. Or at any rate they're not particulars. But it's not clear that they're universals either, because they're all alike. Universals were meant to explain similarity and duplication, and in such a way that two particulars are duplicates if and only if they share the very same universals. But then we'd better not have duplicate universals; else things could be duplicates without sharing the very same universals, if instead they had duplicate universals. It's hard to know what to call things that make like universals in the way they occur repeatedly, yet make like particulars in the way they duplicate one another. Let me call them *amphibians*.

We need four hydrogen amphibians as parts of the universal *methane*, one for each of the four hydrogen atoms in the molecules that instantiate it. In the special case of *methane* we might still get by with the one universal *carbon;* but for the case of *butane* we need carbon amphibians, and presumably it would be best to treat all cases alike.

How about *bonded*? Do we also need some dyadic amphibians? I think not – not if we are prepared to let the one universal *bonded* relate amphibians in the same way that it relates particulars. In that case, the fourfold occurrence of *bonded* in the universal *methane* can be understood on a par with its fourfold occurrence in a particular molecule of methane: the one universal is instantiated by four different pairs. And we'd better let *bonded* relate amphibians, else we're still in trouble over the universals *butane* and *isobutane*. It would be no good just saying that each of them consists of four carbon amphibians, ten hydrogen amphibians, and thirteen dyadic amphibians of bonding. That does at least give us the required numerical difference between the two, if they were made of numerically different amphibians; but it leaves us with a mystery about why one universal is instantiated by the straight-chain butane molecules and the other by branched-chain isobutane molecules. We'd better have straight and branched chains of amphibians within the universals – as taking isomorphism seriously would require – and for that we need bonded amphibians, and if we have bonded amphibians we don't also need amphibians of bonding.

So we come to this: a structural universal is composed of parts; some of these parts are the amphibians which replace our original monadic universals; amphibians may be related by n-adic universals, in which case those n-adic universals also are parts of the structural universal. When the structural universal is instantiated by a particular, the particular consists of parts that correspond one–one to the amphibians that are parts of the universal. Each amphibian is wholly present, as a nonspatiotemporal part, in the corresponding part of the particular – perhaps we may still call this 'instantiation'. And the parts of the particular are related by the same n-adic universals that relate the corresponding parts of the universal.[20]

We face some fascinating questions. (1) What becomes of our original monadic universals, such as the one universal *hydrogen*? Do we have them as well as their amphibians, perhaps instantiated by their amphibians? (2) Does the same amphibian ever occur as part of two different structural universals? (3) If we have two hydrogen atoms in two different methane molecules, is there indeed a distinction between the case in which they instantiate the same amphibian of the structural

20 Are amphibians tropes? No, though there are some points in common. Like tropes and particulars, amphibians may be duplicated; like tropes and ordinary universals, amphibians may be nonspatiotemporal parts of things; like ordinary universals but *unlike* tropes, amphibians may occur repeatedly. Even if, like Campbell and Johnston, we say that tropelike things may persist by enduring identically, and to that extent may be wholly present at different times, we don't quite get amphibians; for amphibians can be repeated where there is no question of one thing persisting, as when one and the same hydrogen amphibian is present wherever there is a methane molecule.

universal *methane* and the case in which they instantiate different ones? I do not mean to put these questions forward as unanswerable. I might even suggest answers. But I shall not. I shall suggest indeed that the questions are too bizarre to take seriously. The theory that asks them just has to be barking up the wrong tree. There comes a time not to go on following where the argument leads!

I conclude that no version of the pictorial conception is satisfactory; it's no good thinking that a structural universal is composed of simpler universals which are literally parts of it.[21]

THE MAGICAL CONCEPTION

On the magical conception, a structural universal has no proper parts. It is this conception on which 'simple' must be distinguished from 'atomic'. A structural universal is never simple; it involves other, simpler, universals. (Simpler, perhaps not *simple*.) But it is mereologically atomic. The other universals it involves are not present in it as parts. Nor are the other universals set-theoretic constituents of it; it is not a set but an individual. There is no way in which it is composed of them.

Or rather, no way that is at all literal. We can speak of 'composition' to the extent, and only to the extent, that it is metaphorical; and what

---

21 There is a different place for mereology in a theory of universals. Suppose we have two monadic universals F and G; and we want a conjunctive universal $F \& G$ that is instantiated by just those things that instantiate both F and G. Then it would be quite natural to take $F \& G$ as the mereological sum of F and G. (More generally, we could conjoin n-adic universals by summation, so long as n is the same for all conjuncts.) Thus we insure that the conjuncts must be present wherever the conjunction is, and also that the conjunction is nothing over and above its conjuncts; both of which conclusions are desirable. Universals are mereologically atomic only if they are nonconjunctive; there may or may not be any such, for here too we may allow a possibility of infinite complexity.

I have no quarrel with any of this. We have no need for conjuncts taken many times over, or for isomeric conjunctive universals that differ because they have the very same conjuncts differently arranged, so we avoid the troubles that threaten composition of structural universals. For simplicity, however, I shall ignore conjunctive universals in what follows.

it is metaphorical for is the involving of one universal by another. If we say that the universal *methane* consists of the universals *carbon, hydrogen*, and *bonded*, the most that we may mean is that an *instance* of *methane* must consist, in a certain way, of *instances* of the others. Involving, in turn, is a matter of necessary connection between the instantiating of one universal and the instantiating of another; and on the magical conception, the universals so connected are wholly distinct atomic individuals.

Therein lies the magic. Why *must* it be that if something instantiates *methane*, then part of it must instantiate *carbon*? According to the linguistic conception, that is built into a recursive specification of what it means to instantiate *methane*. Fair enough. According to the pictorial conception, that is because *carbon* is part of *methane*, and the whole cannot be wholly present without its part. Fair enough. But on the present conception, this necessary connection is just a brute modal fact.

If you said that wherever *carbon* is instantiated, *bromine* must necessarily be instantiated next to it, that would make good enough sense as a matter of nomological necessity. There is no such law of nature, but there could have been. But suppose you said that it was a matter of necessity *simpliciter* – absolute 'logical' or 'metaphysical' necessity. Then what you say is not only false; it is entirely unintelligible how it could be true. Why couldn't anything over here coexist with anything else over there, and in particular why couldn't the presence of an instance of *carbon* over here coexist with the absence of any instance of *bromine* over there?

To be sure, the case of a structural universal and the simpler universals it involves is not quite that bad. The particulars in question are not distinct: the instance of *carbon* is supposed to be a proper part of the instance of *methane*. But how does that help, when the universals in question *are* wholly distinct? What is it about the universal *carbon* that gets it involved in necessary connections with *methane*? Why *carbon*? Why not some other universal, say *rubidium*? After all, the universal *carbon* has nothing more in common with the universal *methane* than the universal *rubidium* has! They are three distinct atomic individuals, and that is that. There is no conceivable reason why the universal *methane* should, by the strictest necessity, drag the universal *rubidium* around with it wherever it goes. How does it manage, then to drag around *carbon*?

It may seem that I am making a great fuss over something very easy. By definition, methane consists of carbon and hydrogen bonded together in a certain arrangement, so of course we must have an atom of carbon as part of every molecule of methane. Carbon atoms instantiate the universal *carbon*, methane molecules instantiate the universal *methane*, so of course there must be an instance of the one universal as part of every instance of the other. What could be easier than that?

But you can make any problem look easy if you state it so as to presuppose that it is already solved. To name one universal *'methane'* and the other *'carbon'* (or, more longwindedly, *'being a methane molecule'* and *'being a carbon atom'*) is to name them descriptively, in other words tendentiously. To be sure, no two universals deserve those two names unless the first drags the second around with it; unless it is somehow necessary, *inter alia*, that every instance of the first contains an instance of the second as its central part. Of course. But our question is: how can two universals – universals understood as atomic – possibly deserve those two names? How can two universals, which we might at first call by the neutral names 'Matthew' and 'Carl', possibly enter into the necessary connection which would entitle us to call them *'methane'* and *'carbon'* instead? It only conceals our problem if we call them that from the start. The magician makes our problem vanish by verbal sleight of hand.

Structural universals, conceived magically, make a striking test case in philosophical method. It is really very clear what sort of necessary connections are required, and how these connections are to be used in explaining how a structural universal involves simpler universals. It ought to be child's play to formalise this conception systematically in a suitable modal language. And that is all that many philosophers would ask. But that just goes to show that their standards of intelligibility are incomplete. Although we understand just what necessary connections are supposed to obtain, we are given no notion how they possibly could. I might say that the magical conception carries an unacceptable price in mystery; or perhaps I would do better to deny that there is any *conception* here at all, as opposed to mere words.

Forrest's plan to use structural universals as ersatz possible worlds requires us to accept uninstantiated structural universals. These are the unactualised ersatz worlds, and they are in the overwhelming majority. Armstrong, on the other hand, has a general objection to uninstantiated universals, structural or simple. In this final section, let us consider whether uninstantiated structural universals are any more problematic than instantiated ones.

(I hasten to say that my question concerns universals that are uninstantiated *simpliciter*. There is surely no special problem about universals that are instantiated in foreign countries but uninstantiated here. Likewise, if I am right that ours is but one of many possible worlds, there is no special problem about universals that are instantiated in other worlds but uninstantiated in actuality. Forrest and Armstrong, disbelieving as they do in the other worlds, face the question whether they ought to believe in universals that might have been instantiated but happen not to be. For me there is no such question: whatever might have been, *is*.)

We might hope to extract an argument against uninstantiated universals from Armstrong's doctrine that universals are abstractions from their instances. Perhaps we might argue that an abstraction cannot exist if there is nothing whence it is abstracted: this instance or that may be dispensable, since the universal is wholly present in each one, but it is nonsense to say that it is an abstraction from its instances if it has no instances. But again I do not know what we can mean by 'abstraction' that would meet the needs of the argument. If abstracted universals were equivalence classes or verbal fictions, then indeed they could not exist without particulars to be abstracted from; but if so, we have no genuine universals at all. We would do better to mean that universals are nonspatiotemporal parts of their particular instances, and the abstraction of them is just mereological subtraction. But if 'abstraction' means that, it supports no argument against uninstantiated universals. Every hand is part of a human body, suitably integrated with the rest of it. It can be 'abstracted' from the body, so to speak, by mereological subtraction of the rest of the body. But a hand that is in fact part of a body might have existed on its own, or at any rate a duplicate or counterpart of it might have existed on its own; and something that is intrinsically just like the hands that are parts of bodies might exist without being part of a body. And why couldn't the same be true of nonspatiotemporal parts? The argument against uninstantiated universals requires that if something is an abstraction, then it is so *essentially* and couldn't exist without being so. But if abstractions are just parts of things (or, nonspatiotemporal parts of things) then it seems that if something is an abstraction, it is so contingently. We would need some independent argument against uninstantiated universals to establish that they were abstractions essentially.

A universal is wholly present wherever it is instantiated, and present nowhere else. Therefore an uninstantiated universal is present nowhere. But that is not a strong reason to deny its existence. It is an open question whether everything that exists has some sort of spatiotemporal location. The empty set, and the pure sets generally, are supposed to be unlocated; if so, maybe that is bad news for the pure sets, or maybe it is bad news instead for the thesis that everything is located.

(I myself would deny that unlocated things are part of this possible world, or any other; but that is irrelevant, since I do not claim that everything there is must be part of some or another world. The pure sets might perhaps be a counterexample.)

I would raise a different objection against uninstantiated universals.[22] Wherefore are they *universals* at all? When we are told what it means to be a universal, we are told, mainly, that universals are wholly present repeatedly, as nonspatiotemporal parts of things at different times and places; and also we are told that this repetition of universals makes for similarity. But uninstantiated universals satisfy no part of this description. Far from being wholly present repeatedly, and thereby making similarities, they are not present anywhere.

(To a lesser extent, my complaint applies also against universals with only one instance. There is no repetition, and no similarity or duplication made by such repetition. But the one-instanced universal is at least wholly present as a nonspatiotemporal part of something.)

---

22 The argument that follows is due in large part to Mark Johnston.

I thought I knew what universals were – but if there are some of them that go against all I have been told about their distinctive behaviour, we'd better begin again!

I know the answer, of course. An uninstantiated (or one-instanced) universal is supposed to deserve the name because it *might* be instantiated many times over. It *might* be wholly present repeatedly, and thereby make similarities. It *might* do what universals distinctively do, even if in fact it happens not to.

This means that the definition of a universal is modal. A universal is something that satisfies a certain *de re* modal condition; it has a certain potentiality, whether or not this is realised. So far, so good. But what makes it so that one thing has the potentiality for repeated presence and another thing lacks it, when in fact neither thing is repeatedly present? Is that just a brute modal fact? I would hope not. For the most part, things have their potentialities in virtue of their nonmodal characteristics.

(I would explain that as follows: something might satisfy a condition iff it has a counterpart that does; it is resemblance that makes counterparts; and it is the intrinsic and extrinsic characteristics of two things that make resemblance between them. But I suppose that many who would not care to explain *de re* modality in that way would nevertheless agree that things have their potentialities in virtue of the nonmodal characteristics they actually have.)

If brute potentialities are to be rejected, then the modal answer is a halfway house. It rests on some better answer, in terms of the nonmodal characteristics that universals actually have. Then we might as well give the better answer directly. It should be as follows. There are the universals that are repeatedly present; and there are the uninstantiated universals that are not repeatedly present, indeed are present nowhere. But these are all things of one and the same kind. The universals that exhibit the distinctive behaviour of their kind, and those that don't but might have done, are united by a common nature. That is the reason why the latter deserve the name of universals; and it is also the nonmodal fact in virtue of which the latter might have behaved as the former do.

But what does 'of a kind' mean here? Usually, in a theory of universals, things of a kind are supposed to share a universal. So is it that the uninstantiated universals share a second-order universal of *universalhood* with the instantiated ones? That would be an unwelcome complication at best, and leads straightway to a Third Man regress. Or must we have recourse to some primitive notion of sameness of kinds – a sort of similarity – which is not to be explained in terms of shared universals? I myself have no great objection to primitive similarity, if it is offered as an *alternative* to a theory of universals. But what are universals for, if not to afford an account of similarity? To buy into universals, and yet appeal to a primitive similarity between the uninstantiated and the instantiated ones, is to buy a dog and do the barking yourself.

If we are dealing with simples, I see no other way to explain how the instantiated and the uninstantiated ones are of a kind. Therefore I think it is quite unsatisfactory to believe in uninstantiated simple universals. There is no good way to say what makes them be universals at all.

But if we are dealing with structural universals, we may be better off. We may have new ways to say how the uninstantiated and the instantiated ones are of a kind. Certainly that is so on the linguistic conception: we can say that they are constructed alike, in accordance with the same syntactic rules, out of the same vocabulary of simples. The linguistic conception is thus entitled to uninstantiated structural universals if, but only if, they are built out of instantiated simples.

Likewise for the pictorial conception. It is unintelligible how structural universals could be composed mereologically out of simpler universals; but try to imagine, nevertheless, that somehow they are. Then why not say that uninstantiated and instantiated structural universals are of a kind, because they are composed in the same (mysterious) way out of simpler universals? Eventually we must descend to instantiated universals, perhaps simples or perhaps just simpler structural universals. (The latter alternative covers the case of infinite complexity, which the linguistic conception can't handle.) Provided we reach instantiated universals sooner or later, it seems that we do not get any extra problem when our more complex structural universals are uninstantiated.

But the linguistic conception, or the pictorial conception if somehow it could be made to work, would not meet the whole of Forrest's need for uninstantiated structural universals to serve as ersatz possible worlds. It is possible, I take it, that there might be simple natural properties different from any that are instantiated within our world. To cover this 'outer sphere' of possibility, it is not enough to have uninstantiated structural universals that are set-theoretically constructed, or mereologically composed, out of simpler instantiated universals.[23] If he is to cover the full range of possibilities, Forrest needs uninstantiated simples as well; and nothing we can build up out of thisworldly ingredients will help him there.

Only the magical conception could help. It is so far sunk in brute modality that some more wouldn't make matters worse. Let the magician be hanged for a sheep: let him accept uninstantiated structural universals and uninstantiated simples as well, saying that it is yet another brute modal fact that these might have been repeatedly present, and that is why they deserve the name of universals. This position, if only its brute modality were intelligible, would best meet the needs of Forrest's project.

---

23 On inner and outer spheres of possibility, see D. M. Armstrong, 'Metaphysics and Supervenience', *Critica* 14 (1982) pp. 3–17.

4

A Comment on Armstrong and Forrest

The trouble with structural universals is that they afford *prima facie* counterexamples to a twofold principle of uniqueness of composition:

> there is only one mode of composition; and it is such that, for given parts, only one whole is composed of them.

The worse, say I, for structural universals. The worse, say Armstrong and Forrest, for uniqueness of composition.[1] They say so all the more confidently because they think uniqueness of composition threatens not only an outlying province of the theory of universals, but also the heartland – not only structural universals, but also the *structures*, or *states of affairs*, that exist when particulars instantiate universals. If they are right, my bother over structural universals is a sideshow.

I say they are half right. Uniqueness of composition does threaten the structures. In fact, more so even than they say; because we get trouble even if the only universals are monadic, provided that we accept conjunctive structures. Suppose each of two particulars a and b instantiates each of two universals F and G; then it seems that we have

First published in *The Australasian Journal of Philosophy* 64 (1986), pp. 92–93. Reprinted with kind permission from *The Australasian Journal of Philosophy*.

Once more, I have been greatly helped by conversation and correspondence with D. M. Armstrong, John Bigelow, Peter Forrest, and Mark Johnston.

1 D. M. Armstrong, 'In Defence of Structural Universals'; Peter Forrest, 'Neither Magic nor Mereology: A Reply to Lewis'; both in *The Australasian Journal of Philosophy* 64 (1986), pp. 85–91.

two structures (*Fa & Gb*) and (*Ga & Fb*) composed of exactly the same parts, *contra* uniqueness of composition.

But I say the structures are merely a second outlying province, alongside the structural universals. A threat to them is no threat to the heartland. Give away the structures, and we could still do the main business of a theory of universals.[2] We could still say that two particulars have something in common when there is some one universal they both instantiate, and are exactly alike when they instantiate exactly the same universals. (Or, if we also gave away structural universals: . . . when their corresponding parts instantiate exactly the same universals.) Those who wished could still run a relation-of-universals theory of lawhood, though perhaps more in Tooley's style than Armstrong's. The loci of the universals would still mark out the joints in nature.

What could we *not* do, if universals were held but structures were lost? One thing – we could not, without structures, uphold the principle that every truth has a truthmaker. Here is the particular *a*; here is the universal *F*; it is a truth that *a* instantiates *F*. What is the truthmaker for this truth? What is the entity whose very existence is a sufficient condition for *a* to instantiate *F*? The structure *Fa* would have done; for this structure is supposed to exist only if its particular part instantiates its universal part.[3] But if the structure is given away, what other truthmaker may we find? Not *F*, not *a*, nor both together; not their mereological sum; not any set-theoretic construction from them. For all these things would exist just the same, whether *a* instantiated *F* or not. What else? If every truth must have its truthmaker, it is vital to hold onto the structures. If not, not.

---

2 Goodman's principal system in *The Structure of Appearance* is a theory of universals ('qualia') without structures. His nearest thing to a structure is the mereological sum of a colour quale *F* and a place-time *a*. But this cannot be what Armstrong and Forrest call a 'structure' or a 'state of affairs' because it would exist whether or not colour *F* occurs at place-time *a*.

3 That's why it's no good to say that the structure *Fa* is the ordered pair of *F* and *a*, and that such a pair is called a 'structure' iff its second term instantiates its first. That way, what depends on whether *a* instantiates *F* is not whether the thing exists, but just whether it deserves a name. A pair that exists regardless, never mind what name it might deserve, won't do for a truthmaker.

Suppose the leading rivals to a theory of universals – resemblance or natural-class nominalism, sparse trope theory – were somehow out of the running. Set aside the issue of structural universals. Then we're left with a stark clash of principles: a truthmaker for every truth, versus uniqueness of composition. If that's the choice we face, I say it's no contest. I expect Armstrong and Forrest would say the same. But there I fear our agreement gives out.

5

Extrinsic properties

I

Some properties of things are entirely *intrinsic*, or *internal*, to the things that have them: shape, charge, internal structure. Other properties are not entirely intrinsic: being a brother, being in debt, being within three miles of Carfax, thinking of Vienna. These properties are at least partly *extrinsic*, or *relational*. Properties may be more or less extrinsic; being a brother has more of an admixture of intrinsic structure than being a sibling does, yet both are extrinsic.

A sentence or statement or proposition that ascribes intrinsic properties to something is entirely about that thing; whereas an ascription of extrinsic properties to something is not entirely about that thing, though it may well be about some larger whole which includes that thing as part. A thing has its intrinsic properties in virtue of the way that thing itself, and nothing else, is. Not so for extrinsic properties, though a thing may well have these in virtue of the way some larger whole is. The intrinsic properties of something depend only on that thing; whereas the extrinsic properties of something may depend, wholly or partly, on something else. If something has an intrinsic prop-

First published in *Philosophical Studies* 44 (1983), pp. 197–200. Copyright © 1983 by D. Reidel Publishing Company, Dordrecht-Holland. Reprinted with kind permission from Kluwer Academic Publishers.

I thank Gilbert Harman, Frank Jackson, Mark Johnston, and Donald Morrison for comments.

erty, then so does any perfect duplicate of that thing; whereas duplicates situated in different surroundings will differ in their extrinsic properties.

The circles close. Two things are perfect duplicates iff they have the very same intrinsic properties. The way something is is given by the totality of its intrinsic properties. To depend on something is to depend on the way that thing is. And a sentence or statement or proposition is entirely about something iff the intrinsic properties of that thing suffice to settle its truth value. We have a tight little family of interdefinables.

What to do? (1) We could Quine the lot, give over the entire family as unintelligible and dispensable. That would be absurd. (2) We could take one or another member of the family, it scarcely matters which, as primitive. That would be quite acceptable, I think, but disappointing. Or (3) we could somehow break in from outside. That would be best.

II

Jaegwon Kim ([2], pp. 59–60), elaborating a suggestion of R. M. Chisholm ([1], p. 127), has proposed a chain of definitions that would indeed, if successful, break into the family.

> D1 (Chisholm): G is *rooted outside times at which it is had* = df
> Necessarily for any object x and any time t, x has the property G at t only if x exists at some time before or after t.

> D2 (Kim): G is *rooted outside the objects that have it* = df
> Necessarily any object x has G only if some contingent object wholly distinct from x exists.

('Wholly distinct' means more than 'nonidentical'; an object's proper parts are neither identical with it nor wholly distinct from it. 'Contingent' is included lest the existence of necessary beings such as the numbers interfere.)

D3 (Kim):   G is *internal* = df

> G is neither rooted outside times at which it is had nor outside the objects that have it.

We can simplify. Let us suppose that things are divisible into temporal segments, and that possession of properties by things at times amounts to possession of properties by things that may be temporal segments of other things. Then if G is rooted outside times at which it is had, also it is rooted outside the objects that have it, so we can drop the first half of the *definiens* in D3. Substituting D2 for the second half and driving in the negation, we get

D4   G is *internal* = df

> Possibly some object *x* has G although no contingent object wholly distinct from *x* exists.

Consider two properties, *accompaniment* and *loneliness*: something is *accompanied* iff it coexists with some wholly distinct contingent object, *lonely* iff not. Kim's idea, in a nutshell, is that extrinsic properties are those that imply accompaniment, whereas intrinsic properties are compatible with loneliness. (One property implies another iff it is impossible to have the first without the second; two properties are compatible iff it is possible to have both.) Indeed, accompaniment is an extrinsic property *par excellence*, with no admixture whatever of the intrinsic. And any property that implies it is likewise extrinsic – you can't wipe out the extrinsic information about accompaniment just by adding *more* information. Further, any intrinsic property is indeed compatible with loneliness – anything shares its intrinsic properties with a lonely duplicate, most likely at another possible world. So far, so good.

III

But the failure of Kim's proposal should now be plain to see. Loneliness is just as extrinsic as accompaniment, yet certainly it does not imply accompaniment and certainly it is compatible with itself. If something is lonely – the cosmos, or some lesser otherwordly thing – its loneliness remains unrooted.

We have seen two kinds of extrinsic properties. Kim has defined the *positive extrinsic properties*, as we may call them: accompaniment, and all other properties that imply it. We can with equal ease define the *negative extrinsic properties*: loneliness, and all other properties that imply it. But those are not all. Consider the disjunctive property of either being lonely or else coexisting with exactly six pigs (wholly distinct from oneself). This too is extrinsic; but it is not positive intrinsic in view of the first disjunct, and it is not negative extrinsic in view of the second. It is the disjunction of a negative extrinsic and a positive extrinsic, but in its mixed way it is still extrinsic. Likewise, consider the property of being the fattest pig; it is extrinsic, but it is neither positive nor negative extrinsic.

A property differs between duplicates iff its negation does so as well; so the extrinsic properties are closed under negation. The example just considered suggests that we also have closure under disjunction – our disjunction of extrinsic properties was itself extrinsic. And we might also expect closure of the extrinsic properties under converse implication: how can an intrinsic property imply an extrinsic one? So we might hope to build on Kim's proposal, making it the basis for an inductive definition that would cover all the extrinsic properties, leaving the (more important) intrinsic properties as residue.

No hope: a class of properties containing accompaniment closed under negation and disjunction and converse implication would be the class of *all* properties. To show that squareness is extrinsic, for instance, we could use our supposed closure principles as follows. Accompaniment is extrinsic; then so is loneliness; then so are squareness-and-accompaniment and squareness-and-loneliness, which imply accompaniment and loneliness respectively; then so is squareness, which is the disjunction of squareness-and-accompaniment and squareness-and-loneliness. Our closure principles cannot all be right. In fact, two out of three are wrong. Closure under disjunction is refuted by the example just considered. Closure under converse implication also fails: squareness is intrinsic, but implies squareness-or-accompaniment; and the latter is extrinsic, since it can differ between duplicates. (This much is true: an intrinsic property cannot imply an *unconditionally* extrinsic property, that being a property such that whenever something has it, some perfect duplicate of that thing lacks it.)

Kim has come tantalizingly close. Almost any extrinsic property that a sensible person would ever mention is positive extrinsic. Nevertheless, I conjecture that there is no way to enlarge the opening made by Chisholm and Kim, and if we still want to break in we had best try another window.

BIBLIOGRAPHY

[1] R. M. Chisholm: 1976, *Person and Object* (Open Court, La Salle, Illinois).
[2] Jaegwon Kim:1982, 'Psychophysical supervenience', *Philosophical Studies* 41, pp. 51–70.

6

Defining 'intrinsic'

WITH RAE LANGTON

I. KIM AND LEWIS

Jaegwon Kim defined an *intrinsic* property, in effect, as a property that could belong to something that did not coexist with any contingent object wholly distinct from itself.[1] Call such an object *lonely* or *unaccompanied*; and call an object *accompanied* iff it does coexist with some contingent object wholly distinct from itself. So an intrinsic property in the sense of Kim's definition is a property compatible with loneliness; in other words, a property that does not imply accompaniment.[2]

First published in *Philosophy and Phenomenological Research* 58 (1998), 333–345. Reprinted with kind permission from Rae Langton and from *Philosophy and Phenomenological Research*.

We thank C. A. J. Coady, Allen Hazen, Richard Holton, Peter Menzies, George Molnar, Denis Robinson, Barry Taylor, and those who discussed this paper when it was presented at the 1996 Australasian Association of Philosophy conference. We also thank the Boyce Gibson Memorial Library. One author owes a particular debt to Lloyd Humberstone, who prompted her interest in contemporary (as opposed to eighteenth century) work on the metaphysics of intrinsic properties. Preliminary versions of some of the ideas in the present paper were raised in Langton's 'Defining "Intrinsic"', Appendix 2 of *Kantian Humility*, Princeton University Doctoral Dissertation, 1995. They are applied to Kant in the dissertation, and in a book, tentatively titled *Kantian Humility*, Oxford University Press (forthcoming, 1998).

1 Jaegwon Kim, 'Psychophysical Supervenience', *Philosophical Studies* 41 (1982), 51–70.

2 This way of putting it simplifies Kim's formulation by foisting on him a view he is not in fact committed to: the view that things that persist through time consist of

David Lewis objected that loneliness itself is a property that could belong to something lonely, yet it is not an intrinsic property. He concluded that Kim's proposal failed. He also conjectured that nothing resembling Kim's definition would work, and if we want to define 'intrinsic' we had best try something altogether different.[3]

II. A KIM-STYLE DEFINITION

That sweepingly negative judgement was premature. Though Kim's definition does indeed fail, a definition in much the same style may succeed.

First step. One intuitive idea is that an intrinsic property can be had by a thing whether it is lonely or whether it is accompanied. It is compatible with either; it implies neither.

Second step. Another intuitive idea is that, although an intrinsic property is compatible with loneliness, a thing's being lonely is not what makes the thing have that property. Lacking the property also is compatible with loneliness. And likewise with accompaniment: if a property is intrinsic, being accompanied is not what makes something have that property. Lacking the property also is compatible with accompaniment.

Putting the first and second steps together, we have that all four cases are possible. A lonely thing can have the property, a lonely thing can lack the property, an accompanied thing can have the property, an accompanied thing can lack the property. For short:

wholly distinct temporal parts at different times. Given that view, one way for you-now to be accompanied is for you to persist through time, so that you-now coexist with your past or future temporal parts. But Kim himself remains neutral about the metaphysics of temporal parts; so what he actually says is as follows. Property G is *rooted outside the time at which it is had* iff, necessarily, for any object *x* and time *t*, *x* has G at *t* only if *x* exists at some time before or after *t*; G is *rooted outside the things that have it* iff, necessarily, any object *x* has G only if some contingent object wholly distinct from *x* exists; G is *intrinsic* – Kim's term is 'internal' – iff G is neither rooted outside times at which it is had nor outside the things that have it. We shall ignore this complication henceforth.

3 David Lewis, 'Extrinsic Properties', *Philosophical Studies* 44 (1983), 197–200 (reprinted in this volume as Chapter 5).

117

having or lacking the property is *independent* of accompaniment or loneliness.

So can we define an intrinsic property as one that is independent in this way? Subject to some qualifications, yes; but not in full generality.

A first qualification is that the proposed definition, and likewise all that follows, is to be understood as restricted to pure, or qualitative, properties – as opposed to impure, or haecceitistic, properties. There may be impure extrinsic properties, such as the property of voting for Howard (as opposed to the pure extrinsic property of voting for someone). There may be impure intrinsic properties, such as the property of being Howard, or having Howard's nose as a proper part (as opposed to the pure intrinsic property of having a nose as a proper part).[4] These impure properties are had only by Howard, and not by Howard's duplicates, or even (perhaps) his counterparts. Our proposal is offered as a way of distinguishing amongst the pure, or qualitative properties, those which are intrinsic, and those which are extrinsic. Impure properties are set aside as falling outside the scope of the present discussion. To be sure, we might eventually wish to classify impure properties also as intrinsic or extrinsic. But that is a task for another occasion.

III. THE PROBLEM OF DISJUNCTIVE PROPERTIES

Our proposed definition, as it stands, plainly does not work for disjunctive properties. Consider the disjunctive property of being either

4 Pure and impure relational properties are described in E. J. Khamara, 'Indiscernibles and the Absolute Theory of Space and Time', *Studia Leibnitiana* 20 (1988), 140–159. The notion of pure and impure intrinsic properties, by analogy with Khamara's distinction, was raised by Rae Langton (in conversation) and discussed by Humberstone in 'Intrinsic/Extrinsic', *Synthese* 108 (1996), 205–267 (accepted for publication in 1992), and in Langton's *Kantian Humility* (Princeton University Doctoral Dissertation, 1995). The notion of an 'interior property' attributed by Humberstone to J. M. Dunn includes both impure and pure intrinsic properties (J. M. Dunn, 'Relevant Predication 2: Intrinsic Properties and Internal Relations', *Philosophical Studies* 60 (1990), 177–206). Humberstone distinguishes the family of duplication-related concepts of intrinsicness from the interiority conception, and from a notion he calls non-relationality of properties.

cubical and lonely or else non-cubical and accompanied. This property surely is not intrinsic. Yet having or lacking it is independent of accompaniment or loneliness: all four cases are possible.

So we require a second qualification: our definition should be deemed to fall silent about disjunctive properties. All it does is to divide non-disjunctive intrinsic properties from non-disjunctive extrinsic properties.

(The same goes for any definition that selects some one or two or three of the four cases, and says that a property is intrinsic iff all the selected cases are possible. Again, the property of being cubical and lonely or else non-cubical and accompanied will be misclassified as intrinsic.)

If a property is independent of accompaniment or loneliness, its negation also is independent. Yet if a property is intrinsic, so is its negation; and if a property is not intrinsic, neither is its negation. So we would expect trouble with negations of disjunctive properties. The property of being neither cubical and lonely nor non-cubical and accompanied is independent of accompaniment or loneliness: all four cases are possible. Yet it is not intrinsic. So the definition proposed so far fails in this case too.[5]

What is a disjunctive property? Not just any property that can be expressed as a disjunction! Any property at all can be expressed as a disjunction: something is G iff either it is G-and-H or else it is G-and-not-H. But we think most philosophers will be willing to help themselves to some version or other of the distinction between 'natural' and 'unnatural' properties. Given that distinction, we can go on to capture our intuition that some properties are 'disjunctive' in a way that other properties are not.

Some of us will help ourselves to some sort of primitive notion of naturalness of properties. Others will accept an ontology of sparse universals, or of sparse tropes, that has a built-in distinction between natural properties and other properties. Still others will wish to

---

5 A neater example is due to Peter Vallentyne ('Intrinsic Properties Defined', *Philosophical Studies* 88 (1997), 209–19): the property of being the only red thing. This is the negation of the disjunctive property of being either non-red or else both red and accompanied by another red thing.

characterize the natural properties as those that play some interesting special role in our thinking – but for our present purposes, even this vegetarian metaphysics will suffice. One way or another, most of us will be prepared to grant such a distinction.[6] Here we must say farewell to those who will not make so free, and carry on without them.

What matters for now is not how we begin, but how we continue. Given some or other notion of natural properties, let us define the *disjunctive* properties as those properties that can be expressed by a disjunction of (conjunctions of)[7] natural properties; but that are not themselves natural properties. (Or, if naturalness admits of degrees, they are much less natural than the disjuncts in terms of which they can be expressed.) That done, we can cash in our previous partial success, as follows.

Third step: the *basic intrinsic* properties are those properties that are (1) independent of accompaniment or loneliness; (2) not disjunctive properties; and (3) not negations of disjunctive properties.

The basic intrinsic properties are some, but not all, of the intrinsic properties. Other intrinsic properties include disjunctions or conjunctions of basic intrinsic properties; and, indeed, arbitrarily complicated, even infinitely complicated, truth-functional compounds of basic intrinsic properties.

IV. DUPLICATION

Now we pause to recall a familiar pair of definitions. Two things (actual or possible) are (intrinsic) *duplicates* iff they have exactly the same intrinsic properties. (That is: iff all and only the intrinsic properties of one are intrinsic properties of the other.). *Intrinsic properties,*

---

6 See *inter alia* David Lewis, 'New Work for a Theory of Universals', *Australasian Journal of Philosophy* 61 (1983), 343–377 (reprinted in this volume as Chapter 1); David Lewis, 'Against Structural Universals', *Australasian Journal of Philosophy* 64 (1986), 25–46 (reprinted in this volume as Chapter 3), especially p. 26; Barry Taylor, 'On Natural Properties in Metaphysics', *Mind* 102 (1993), 81–100; Mary Kathryn McGowan, *Realism or Non-Realism: Undecidable in Theory, Decidable in Practice* (Princeton University Doctoral Dissertation, 1996).

7 The point of the parenthetical insertion is to remain neutral on the question whether all conjunctions of natural properties are themselves natural.

on the other hand, are those properties that never can differ between duplicates. A tight little circle – and, like all circles of interdefinition, useless by itself. But if we can reach one of the interdefined pair, then we have them both.

And we can. For how could two things differ in their disjunctive properties if they differed not at all in their non-disjunctive properties? And that goes for their disjunctive and non-disjunctive intrinsic properties as it does for their disjunctive and non-disjunctive properties in general. Likewise for all other forms of truth-functional combination, even infinitely complicated forms of truth-functional combination. So we have this:

Fourth step: two things are (intrinsic) *duplicates* iff they have exactly the same basic intrinsic properties.

Fifth step: a property is *intrinsic* iff it never can differ between duplicates; iff whenever two things (actual or possible) are duplicates, either both of them have the property or both of them lack it.

So our definitional circle has opened out into a little spiral. Those intrinsic properties that were left out at the third step, for instance because they were disjunctive, are admitted at the fifth step. The basic intrinsic properties afford a basis upon which all the intrinsic properties supervene. We have our definition.

V. THE PROBLEM OF STRONG LAWS

The modal status of laws of nature has become a matter of controversy. Some deny that laws are mere regularities; rather, laws are said to be regularities that hold by necessity.[8] In other words, it is impossible for them to have counterinstances. But independence of accompaniment or loneliness is a modal notion. If laws are strong, maybe fewer properties than we think will turn out to be independent of accompaniment or loneliness. Then must we conclude that fewer properties than we think are intrinsic?

Suppose, for instance, that the only way that the laws permit for a

8 See, for instance, Sydney Shoemaker, 'Causality and Properties' in *Time and Cause*, ed. Peter van Inwagen (Reidel, 1980); Chris Swoyer, 'The Nature of Natural Laws', *Australasian Journal of Philosophy* 60 (1982), 203–223.

star to be stretched out into an ellipsoid is for it to orbit around another massive star, and undergo distortion by the tidal effects of its companion. The property of being an ellipsoidal star would seem offhand to be an intrinsic property. In fact, it would seem to be a basic intrinsic property. However, this property is incompatible – nomologically incompatible – with loneliness.

But isn't that the wrong sort of incompatibility? – Not if laws are strong! In that case, if an ellipsoidal lonely star is nomologically impossible, it is impossible *simpliciter*. That would mean that the property of being an ellipsoidal star is not a basic intrinsic property – indeed, not any kind of intrinsic property – after all!

Some friends of strong laws may agree: they may say that our intuitions of what is intrinsic are made for a loose and separate world, and it is only to be expected that a world of necessary connections will defy these intuitions.

Well, that is one option. But there is another, perhaps better, alternative. If a theory of strong laws is to be credible, it had better provide not only a sense of 'possible' in which violations of laws are impossible, but also another sense in which violations of laws are possible. Perhaps that second sense cannot be provided. In that case the doctrine of strong laws is not credible enough to deserve consideration. Or perhaps that second sense can somehow be provided. (Friends of strong laws might think it a hoked-up, artificial sense.[9] But no harm done, provided they acknowledge the possibility of lonely ellipsoidal stars, or whatnot, in some sense or other.) If so it is this sense of possibility, whatever it may be, that a friend of strong laws should use in defining 'intrinsic'.

9 They might say that it is a matter of truth in all not-quite-literally-possible world-stories; or that it should be explained in terms of what possible worlds there are according to a certain Humean fiction. On fictionalist treatments of possibility, see Gideon Rosen, 'Modal Fictionalism', *Mind* 99 (1990), 327–354, and 'Modal Fictionalism Fixed', *Analysis* 55 (1995), 67–73; and for yet another slightly artificial sense in which violations of strong laws may count as possible, see Denis Robinson, 'Epiphenomenalism, Laws and Properties', *Philosophical Studies* 69 (1993), p. 31. And in working out these hoked-up possibilities, they had better heed Allen Hazen's warning not to do so in a way that makes the definition circular, by using a principle of recombination stated in terms of intrinsic properties.

The doctrine that God exists necessarily is problematic in a similar way to the doctrine of strong laws. Suppose it to be true. The property of being divinely created turns out, surprisingly, to be a basic intrinsic property. How so? – Surely this property requires accompaniment by a divine creator, wherefore it is a property incompatible with loneliness. – No. An accompanied thing, we said, coexists with a contingent object distinct from itself. So accompaniment by necessarily existing God does not count.

What to do? If we change the definition of accompaniment by striking out the word 'contingent', it will turn out that if anything at all exists necessarily, whether it be God or the number 17, then loneliness is impossible, so no property at all is compatible with loneliness. That cure only makes matters worse.

Or we might accept the conclusion that if God exists necessarily, then the property of being divinely created is intrinsic; and we might deem this conclusion to be a swift *reductio ad absurdum* against the idea of God's necessary existence. Altogether too swift! Or we might accept the bankruptcy of intuition in the face of divine mysteries.

Perhaps a better alternative is again to distinguish senses of necessity. Perhaps God's existence may be supposed to be necessary in some sense. Yet in a second sense, it still might be contingent. (We could expect disagreement about which sense is straightforward and which sense is artificial.) A conviction that the property of being divinely created is not intrinsic would then be evidence, for those of us who are prepared to take the supposition of God's necessary existence seriously, that it is the second sense and not the first that should be used in defining 'intrinsic'.

VI. THE STATUS OF DISPOSITIONS

Some authors take for granted that dispositional properties, such as fragility, should turn out to be intrinsic. Others are equally sure they are extrinsic. Where do we stand?

The answer implicit in our definition is: it depends. We remain neutral (here) between rival theories about what it means to be a law of nature. Different theories of lawhood will yield different answers about whether dispositions are intrinsic in the sense of the definition. A satisfactory situation, we think.

Let us assume that a disposition (or at least, any disposition that will concern us here) obtains in virtue of an intrinsic basis together with the laws of nature. Then whether the disposition is intrinsic boils down to whether the property of being subject to so-and-so laws is intrinsic. We have three cases.[10]

Case 1. The laws are necessary, in whatever sense should be used in defining 'intrinsic'. Then the property of being subject to so-and-so laws is automatically intrinsic. (See Section VII.) Dispositions are likewise intrinsic.

Case 2. The laws are contingent, in whatever is the appropriate sense; and further, the laws to which something is subject can vary independently of whether that thing is accompanied or lonely. Then being subject to so-and-so laws will presumably turn out to be a basic intrinsic property.

Case 3. The laws are contingent; but the property of being subject to so-and-so laws (or perhaps the conjunction of that property with some aspect of intrinsic character) is not independent of accompaniment or loneliness. Suppose, for instance, that laws are regularities that hold throughout a large and diverse cosmos. Then a lonely thing (unless it were itself of cosmic size) would be subject to no laws, for lack of a cosmos to serve as lawmaker. Or suppose that laws of nature are divine decrees, but that the law-making gods are lowly gods and exist contingently. Then a lonely thing, unaccompanied by a law-making god (and not itself a god) would again be subject to no laws. Under either of these suppositions, something unaccompanied by a lawmaker would be subject to no laws. So dispositions would in this case be extrinsic.

Those who take for granted that dispositions are intrinsic may just be dismissing Case 3 out of hand. Or they may instead have a concept of intrinsic properties that is best captured not by our definition but by a version amended so as to ensure that dispositions (with intrinsic bases) will count as intrinsic, no matter what the correct metaphysical

10 Ignoring the possibility that not all laws have the same status.

theory of lawhood may be.[11]   Likewise, those who take for granted
that dispositions are extrinsic may just be dismissing Cases 1 and 2. Or
they may instead have a concept of intrinsic properties that is best
captured not by our definition but by a version amended so as to ensure
that dispositions will count as extrinsic, no matter what the correct
theory of lawhood may be.[12]

VII. CONSEQUENCES OF OUR DEFINITION

A property which necessarily belongs to everything never differs between any two things; *a fortiori* it never differs between duplicates.
Therefore the necessary property (or, if you prefer to individuate properties more finely than by necessary coextensiveness, *any* necessary
property) turns out to be intrinsic under our definition. Likewise, the
(or any) impossible property turns out to be intrinsic.

Here is another way to make the point: necessary and impossible
properties supervene on the basic intrinsic properties in the trivial way
that non-contingent matters supervene on any basis whatever. There
can be no difference in the supervenient without a difference in the
basis, because there can be no difference in the supervenient at all.

Is this consequence acceptable? – We think so. True, the distinction
between intrinsic and extrinsic is of interest mostly when applied to
contingent properties: that is, properties that are neither necessary nor

11 Amended as follows: at the fifth step, after saying what it is for two things to be
duplicates, end by saying that a property is intrinsic iff it never can differ between
duplicates *provided that these duplicates are subject to the same laws*. Here we have
adapted a suggestion put forward by Lloyd Humberstone in 'Intrinsic/Extrinsic',
which in turn is an adaptation of a notion he finds in Kim's informal discussion,
'Psychophysical Supervenience', pp. 66–68. (Humberstone offers a nomologically
sensitive notion of intrinsicness, according to which something is nomologically
intrinsic – 'Kim+-intrinsic', in his terms – iff duplicates in worlds with the same
laws never differ with respect to it.)

12 Amended as follows: wherever 'lonely' appears in the first and second steps of our
definition, put instead 'lonely *and lawless*', where 'lawless' means 'subject to no
laws'. (We might need to resort to some hoked-up sense of possibility to ensure
that lonely and lawless things are possible.) Here we have adapted a suggestion put
forward in Vallentyne, 'Intrinsic Properties Defined'.

impossible. But it is harmless to apply it more widely. True, necessary or impossible properties can be specified in ways that make gratuitous reference to extraneous things – but the same is true of all properties. (As witness the property of being cubical and either adjacent to a sphere or not adjacent to a sphere.)

As already noted, the basic intrinsic properties are some, but not all, of the intrinsic properties. Intrinsic properties that are disjunctive, or that are negations of disjunctive properties, are not basic intrinsic. We have just seen that non-contingent properties also are intrinsic, but of course they are not basic intrinsic. (A property that cannot be lacked at all cannot be lacked by lonely or by accompanied things; one that cannot be had at all cannot be had by lonely or by accompanied things.) But are these the only cases in which the intrinsic properties outrun the basic intrinsic properties? – Our answer is a qualified 'yes'.

Suppose we assume that every accompanied thing has a lonely duplicate, and every lonely thing has an accompanied duplicate. (Here we are speaking of possible things that may or may not be actual.) That assumption may be controversial: on the one hand, it is part of an attractive combinatorial conception of possibility;[13] but for that very reason it will be open to doubt from friends of strong laws, unless they devise a special sense in which violations of strong laws are 'possible'.

Without that assumption, we cannot answer the question before us. Making the assumption, we answer the question as follows. If a property is contingent, not disjunctive, not the negation of a disjunctive property, and intrinsic, then it is basic intrinsic.

Since the property is contingent, some possible thing x has it and some possible thing y lacks it. By our assumption about duplication, x has a duplicate x' which is lonely iff x is accompanied. Since the property is intrinsic and never differs between duplicates, x' also has it. Likewise y has a duplicate y' which is lonely iff y is accompanied, and y' also lacks the property. So the

---

13 Such as that advanced on pp. 87–92 of David Lewis, *On the Plurality of Worlds* (Blackwell, 1986); or in D. M. Armstrong, *A Combinatorial Theory of Possibility* (Cambridge University Press, 1989).

property is independent of accompaniment or loneliness. Therefore it is basic intrinsic. QED.

Recall our starting point: loneliness itself is a property compatible with loneliness, hence intrinsic according to Kim's definition; yet Lewis judged loneliness not to be intrinsic. We would want our definition to classify loneliness, and likewise accompaniment, as extrinsic properties. And so it does. (At least, given our assumption that every accompanied thing has a lonely duplicate, and every lonely thing has an accompanied duplicate.) For loneliness and accompaniment are not basic intrinsic properties; they are not disjunctive properties or negations thereof; and they are contingent properties.

The same goes (subject to the obvious provisos) for properties that imply accompaniment or loneliness: the property of being an accompanied cube, the property of being a lonely sphere, the property of being a daughter, the property of being an entire cosmos are all of them extrinsic. So far, no surprises and no problems.

Other examples are more questionable: ontological categories, posited by contentious metaphysical systems, which may (or may not) be reserved for accompanied entities. Could there be a change without something to undergo that change? If not, and if the change and the changing thing are counted as distinct coexisting entities, then the property of being a change is a property that implies accompaniment. Likewise *mutatis mutandis* for the category of events more generally; for the category of immanent universals;[14] and for the category of states of affairs.[15]

A straightforward option is to follow wherever our definition may lead. That would mean deciding to say, for instance, that the property of being a change was extrinsic – and so likewise was any more specific property of being so-and-so sort of change. But mightn't we want to classify properties of changes in a way that conflicts with that decision? Some changes are sudden, others are gradual; some changes are foreseen, others are unexpected. Wouldn't we want to say that the prop-

---

14 See D. M. Armstrong, *Universals and Scientific Realism* (Cambridge University Press, 1978).

15 See D. M. Armstrong, *A World of States of Affairs* (Cambridge University Press, 1966).

erty of being a sudden change, unlike the property of being a foreseen change, is an *intrinsic* property of changes? But then we had better not also say that the property of being so-and-so sort of change always counts as *extrinsic*.

A timid option is to limit the scope of our definition, declaring that it is meant to apply only to properties of things, not to properties of entities in other categories. That would keep us safe from misclassification, at the cost of cutting us off from some applications of the intrinsic/extrinsic distinction. (Think, for instance, of those familiar discussions in philosophy of mind that attempt to delineate the intrinsic from the extrinsic aspects of brain events. Well lost? – We doubt it.)

A laborious option might be to tinker with the notion of distinctness. When something changes, the thing and the change coexist, and in some sense these are two wholly distinct entities. But perhaps there is room for another, more relaxed sense in which the thing and its change do *not* count as distinct. In that relaxed sense, a sudden change to something in an otherwise empty universe could count as lonely, even though it remains true that the change and the changing thing coexist. We get the desired result that being sudden qualifies as an intrinsic property of changes. A foreseen change, however, could not possibly count as lonely even in the relaxed sense.

What makes this option laborious is that the work of tinkering with the notion of distinctness may have to be done over, category by category and metaphysical system by metaphysical system. A tall order! Nevertheless, probably the best alternative.

All the more so, because there is another side to the problem – a difficulty that the other options fail to address. Unless somehow we can block the conclusion that a changing thing and its changes are distinct coexisting entities, not only does it turn out that the changes are accompanied by the thing, but also that the thing is accompanied by its changes. Then a changing thing cannot be lonely; so the property of changing is not basic intrinsic, and presumably not intrinsic at all! Never mind what we do or do not want to say about the properties of changes; the trouble now is that we are misclassifying a property of ordinary things. The laborious option offers a remedy. The straightforward option and the timid option do not.

VIII. RELATIONS

Relations, like properties, can be classified as intrinsic or extrinsic. Consider, for example, the case of a two-place relation. (The case of a more-then-two-place relation is similar. The case of a one-place relation is just the case of a property.)

The ordered pair of x and y is *accompanied* iff it coexists with some contingent object wholly distinct both from x and from y. (Equivalently, wholly distinct from the mereological sum of x and y, assuming that they have a sum.) Otherwise the pair is *lonely*. A relation is *independent* of accompaniment or loneliness iff all four cases are possible: a lonely pair can stand in the relation, a lonely pair can fail to stand in the relation, an accompanied pair can stand in the relation, an accompanied pair can fail to stand in the relation.

For relations, as for properties, we distinguish pure from impure (qualitative from haecceitistic) relations, and we set aside the latter. We also distinguish natural from unnatural relations; that enables us to distinguish disjunctive relations from others. Now, the *basic intrinsic relations* are those (pure) relations that are (1) independent of accompaniment or loneliness; (2) not disjunctive relations; (3) not negations of disjunctive relations. Two ordered pairs are *duplicates* iff they stand in exactly the same basic intrinsic relations. A relation is *intrinsic* iff it never can differ between duplicate pairs.

So far, just a transposition of what we already said about properties. But we end with a distinction that has no parallel in the case of properties. Some relations are *internal*: they supervene on the intrinsic properties of their relata. A relation of match in intrinsic respects, for example congruence of shape, is an internal relation. A spatiotemporal distance relation is an intrinsic relation (unless nature holds surprises), but not an internal relation. The relation of aunt to niece is not an intrinsic relation at all.[16]

---

16 Beware: our use of the term 'internal relation' is not to be conflated with that of the British Idealists. For a different terminology, see Lewis, 'New Work for a Theory of Universals', 356 (fn. 16): a relation 'intrinsic to its relata' versus a relation 'intrinsic to its pairs'.

We can show that the internal relations are some, but perhaps not all, of the intrinsic relations.

> If x and x' are duplicates, and so are y and y', it follows that x stands to y in exactly the same internal relations as x' stands to y'. Yet it does not follow that the pair of x and y and the pair of x' and y' are duplicate pairs; so it does not follow that x and y stand in all the same intrinsic relations. Suppose, on the other hand, that the pair of x and y and the pair of x' and y' are duplicate pairs: they stand in all the same intrinsic relations. Then x and x' have the same basic intrinsic properties, and so likewise do y and y'. Suppose, for instance, that x has basic intrinsic property F. Let R be the relation that anything having F stands in to everything, and anything else stands in to nothing. R is not a disjunctive relation or the negation of a disjunctive relation; since F is independent of accompaniment and loneliness, so is R; so R is a basic intrinsic relation; so R is an intrinsic relation. Since x has F, x stands in R to y; so x' stands in R to y'; so x' also has F. Likewise for all other basic intrinsic properties of x, x', y, and y'. So the two duplicate pairs stand in the same internal relations. Since internal relations never can differ between duplicate pairs, they are intrinsic relations. QED.

IX. LEWIS

When Lewis objected to Kim's definitions of 'intrinsic' and advised that we should try something completely different, the line he took was as follows.[17] Having become persuaded by D. M. Armstrong that we should be willing to help ourselves to a distinction between natural properties and other properties, he put forward the hypothesis that all perfectly natural properties are intrinsic; and further, that two things are duplicates iff they have exactly the same perfectly natural properties. Then he said (just as we have) that a property is intrinsic iff it never can differ between duplicates – and he was done.

That definition is simpler than our present one. So far as we can

---

17 David Lewis, 'New Work for a Theory of Universals', pp. 355–357.

see, it does not conflict with our present one. What's wrong with it? True, Lewis had to help himself to a distinction between natural properties and others – but so did we.

Reply: Lewis's burden of commitments was, nevertheless, much heavier than ours. All we need is enough of a distinction to sort out the disjunctive properties from the rest. We need not insist that it makes sense to single out a class of *perfectly* natural properties, as opposed to a larger class of *natural-enough* properties; or that the members of our élite class will all, without exception, strike us as intrinsic; or that the élite class will serve as a basis on which the complete qualitative character of everything there is, and everything there could have been, supervenes. You can believe all that if you like. Indeed, Lewis still does believe all that. But for present purposes, at least, we can get by with much less; and if we get by with much less, we have a definition we can offer to philosophers more risk-averse than Lewis.

X. VALLENTYNE

Peter Vallentyne considered the definition of an intrinsic property as a property independent of accompaniment or loneliness, and rejected it for the reasons we have considered.[18] He then turned in a different direction.

Vallentyne helps himself to the notion of a duplicate, and considers in particular the lonely duplicates of things. He says, in effect,[19] that G is an intrinsic property iff G never can differ between a thing and a lonely duplicate of that thing.

This is not far away from something familiar: the half of the tight little circle that we've already seen which says that an intrinsic property is one that never can differ between duplicates.

18 Vallentyne, 'Intrinsic Properties Defined'. Vallentyne's work was independent of ours and approximately simultaneous.
19 This is a simplification of Vallentyne's actual formulation. Further complications arise because (1) Vallentyne, like Kim, remains neutral about the metaphysics of temporal parts; (2) his definition covers impure as well as pure properties; and (3) he uses a version of the 'lonely and lawless' amendment considered in Section VI (note 12) in order to classify 'law-constituted' properties – e.g. dispositions – as extrinsic.

The restriction to the case where one of the duplicates is lonely makes no difference, provided we may assume that everything has a lonely duplicate.

> Suppose G never can differ between duplicates at all. *A fortiori,* G never can differ between a thing and its lonely duplicate. Conversely, suppose G never can differ between a thing and its lonely duplicate. Let x and y be duplicates. We have assumed that there exists a lonely duplicate of x, call it z. By transitivity of duplication, z is a duplicate also of y. *Ex hypothesi* G does not differ between x and z, or between y and z. So G does not differ between x and y. QED.

You might think the definitional circle between 'intrinsic' and 'duplicate' is too tight to be enlightening; or you might think it's worth something. We think it's worth something, but we think a definition that starts at a greater distance from its target is worth more. But, either way, Vallentyne's new twist on the tight circle – his attention to the special case of the lonely duplicate – seems not to make much difference. So, while we don't suggest that Vallentyne's definition fails to work, it seems to us that our rival definition has something more to offer.

7

Finkish dispositions

I. THE CONDITIONAL ANALYSIS REFUTED

The analysis stated. All of us used to think, and many of us still think, that statements about how a thing is disposed to respond to stimuli can be analysed straightforwardly in terms of counterfactual conditionals. A fragile thing is one that would break if struck; an irascible man is one who would become angry if provoked; and so on. In general, we can state the *simple conditional analysis* thus:

> Something *x* is disposed at time *t* to give response *r* to stimulus *s* iff, if *x* were to undergo stimulus *s* at time *t*, *x* would give response *r*.

Simple indeed – but false. The simple conditional analysis has been decisively refuted by C. B. Martin. The refutation has long been a matter of folklore – I myself learned of it from Ian Hunt in 1971 – but now it has belatedly appeared in print.[1]

First published in *The Philosophical Quarterly* 47 (1997), pp. 143–158. Reprinted with kind permission from Blackwell Publishers.

Thanks are due to C. B. Martin, Allen Hazen, Daniel Nolan, Barry Taylor, and others; and to the Boyce Gibson Memorial Library and Ormond College.

1 C. B. Martin, 'Dispositions and Conditionals', *The Philosophical Quarterly*, 44 (1994), pp. 1–8. See also R. K. Shope, 'The Conditional Fallacy in Contemporary Philosophy', *Journal of Philosophy*, 75 (1978), pp. 397–413; M. Johnston, 'How to Speak of the Colors', *Philosophical Studies*, 68 (1992), pp. 221–63.

How a disposition can be finkish. Dispositions come and go, and we can cause them to come and go. Glass-blowers learn to anneal a newly made joint so as to make it less fragile. Annoyances can make a man irascible; peace and quiet can soothe him again.

Anything can cause anything; so stimulus *s* itself might chance to be the very thing that would cause the disposition to give response *r* to stimulus *s* to go away. If it went away quickly enough, it would not be manifested. In this way it could be false that if *x* were to undergo *s, x* would give response *r*. And yet, so long as *s* does not come along, *x* retains its disposition. Such a disposition, which would straight away vanish if put to the test, is called *finkish*. A finkishly fragile thing is fragile, sure enough, so long as it is not struck. But if it were struck, it would straight away cease to be fragile, and it would not break.

Any finkish disposition is a counter-example to the simple conditional analysis. The thing is disposed to give response *r* to stimulus *s*; it is not true that if it were to undergo *s*, it would give response *r*. The analysandum is true, the alleged analysans is false.

How a lack of a disposition can be finkish. Suppose instead that we have something that is not yet disposed to give *r* in response to *s*. It might gain that disposition; and *s* itself might be the very thing that would cause it to gain that disposition. If the disposition were gained quickly enough, while *s* was still present, it would at once be manifested. So the counterfactual analysans is true: if the thing were to undergo *s*, it would give response *r*. And yet, so long as *s* does not come along, the dispositional analysandum is false: the thing has not yet gained the disposition to give response *r* to *s*. This time, it is the lack of the disposition that is finkish, but again we have a counter-example to the simple conditional analysis.

Dispositions with finkish partners. Dispositions, as Martin has often emphasized, can come in pairs: *x* is disposed to respond to the presence of *y*, and *y* is disposed to respond to the presence of *x*, by a response *r* given jointly by *x* and *y* together.[2] In a nice case, where the simple conditional analysis works, we can express this by a counterfactual: if

2 See, e.g., C. B. Martin, 'How It Is: Entities, Absences and Voids', *Australasian Journal of Philosophy*, 74 (1996), pp. 62ff.

x and y were to come into one another's presence, they would jointly give response r.

(Or, more generally: if x and y were to enter into such and such a relationship. . . . But let us stick to the case where the relationship is a matter of proximity.)

For example, I and a certain disc are so disposed that if I and it came together, it would cause in me a sensation of yellow. We could say that it is disposed to influence me; or that I am disposed to respond to it. Or both. Or we could say that the two-part system consisting of me and the disc is disposed to respond to the coming together of its parts. In the nice case, where the simple conditional analysis works, it does not matter which we say.

But in a finkish case, perhaps the coming together of me and the disc would alter my dispositions, or the disc's dispositions, or both, so that if I and it came together, there would be no sensation of yellow. The disposition of the two-part system to respond to the coming together of its parts is finkish in just the way we have already considered.

Nothing new yet. But suppose we want to speak not only about the dispositions of the two-part system but also about the dispositions of the two parts, of me and of the disc. It might be that the coming together would alter my dispositions, but would have no effect on the disc's dispositions. Then my disposition to respond to the disc would be finkish, but the disc's disposition to influence me would not be.

Yet if the disc's disposition is not finkish (that is, if it is not itself a counter-example to the simple conditional analysis) why would it not be manifested? Because it is a disposition to influence me-as-I-*would*-be-if-I-had-not-lost-my-own-finkish-disposition; and that is not how I would be if I and the disc came together. Because of the finkishness of my disposition, the unfinkish disposition of the disc can have no occasion to be manifested.

Saul Kripke has imagined a special shade of yellow, 'killer yellow', which, thanks to some quirk of our neural wiring, would instantly kill anyone who set eyes on it.[3] If what I have just said is

3 The example occurs in unpublished lectures. I am obliged to note that I am not reporting the whole of what he said in those lectures.

right, then, whatever else may fairly be said against a dispositional theory of colours, the case of killer yellow does not suffice as a refutation.

Resisting the refutation: a dilemma about timing? Philosophers being what they are, not everyone will find Martin's refutation of the simple conditional analysis immediately convincing.

One line of resistance begins with a dilemma about timing. A thing might have a finkish disposition to give response r to stimulus s. Since the disposition is finkish, s would cause it to go away. But would it go away instantly?

If no, there would be a little time after the advent of s and before the disposition goes away. During this little time, before the disposition goes away, we would have s and we would still have the disposition. Then would we not have r after all? Then is not the conditional analysans true despite the finkishness of the disposition?

If yes, on the other hand, the case seems to involve a kind of instantaneous causation that is contrary to the normal ways of the world. The resister may protest with some justice that the case is fantastic, that we are not entitled to firm linguistic intuitions about such far-fetched cases, and accordingly that the case is not a convincing refutation.

We might reply by proposing a case in which the disposition would be gone by the time s arrived, but not by means of instantaneous causation. Rather, the finkishly disposed thing would somehow see s coming. Some precursor of s would cause both s and the loss of the disposition.

But then the resister can insist that the counterfactual analysans, if properly interpreted, is true after all. If we counterfactually suppose that s happens at time t, and we hold fixed the actual course of events before t, our supposition does not include s's precursor. Then neither does it include any side-effects of s's precursor, such as the loss of the disposition. Under the supposition of s without s's precursor, r would have followed. It is a familiar point that backtracking counterfactual reasoning, which runs from a counterfactually supposed event to the causal antecedents it would have to have had, is sometimes out of place. The resister need only insist that the counterfactuals whereby we analyse dispositions must not be back-trackers.[4]

Our best hope for an uncontroversial case of a finkish disposition (though I myself also accept the controversial cases that work by instantaneous causation) will be to return to the first horn of the resister's dilemma. That means that s would arrive at least a short time before the disposition went away. Does it really follow that we would have r? Not necessarily. Sometimes it takes some time for a disposition to do its work. When stimulus s arrives and the disposition is present, some process begins. (It might be a process of accumulation: of charge, of neurotransmitter, of tiny cracks, of vexation, etc.) When the process reaches completion, then that is, or that causes, response r. But if the disposition went away part-way through, the process would be aborted. In such a case, the disposition to produce r can be finkish, without any need either for instantaneous causation or for backtracking. (However, the disposition to begin the process is not finkish.) So the resister's dilemma about timing is answered, and the refutation of the simple conditional analysis is unscathed.

Martin's principal example in 'Dispositions and Conditionals' is an 'electro-fink': a machine connected to a wire that makes the wire instantly become live if touched by a conductor; or, if operating on a 'reverse cycle', makes the wire instantly cease to be live if touched by a conductor. It is instructive to see how to amend this example so that it withstands the resister's misgivings. (a) We remove Martin's stipulation that the electro-fink reacts instantaneously. Quickly is good enough. Then the electro-fink on a reverse cycle need not be anything more remarkable than a (sensitive and fast-acting) circuit-breaker. (b) We respecify the effect to which the wire is finkishly disposed not as any flow of electrical current but as flow of a certain wattage for a certain duration – as it might be, enough for electrocution. This is a process that can be aborted by breaking the circuit part-way through.

Resisting the refutation: a compound disposition? A different line of resistance suggests that if something is finkishly disposed to give response

4 See my 'Counterfactual Dependence and Time's Arrow', *Noûs*, 13 (1979), pp. 455–76.

r to stimulus *s*, what it really has is a compound disposition. It has a state that at least resembles a disposition to give response *r* to *s*. Our resister, since he accepts the simple conditional analysis, will think it inaccurate to call this state a disposition. (I shall signal his terminological scruples with inverted commas.) At any rate, this first 'disposition' is embedded in a second disposition. The thing is disposed to lose the first 'disposition' in response to *s*.

Now the resister is struck by the difference between the first 'disposition' all by itself and the first 'disposition' when it is embedded in the second. He implores us not to be over-impressed by such similarities as there are, and instead to heed the difference the second disposition makes to the overall dispositional character of the thing. When we say that the thing is disposed to give *r* in response to *s*, he thinks we are misled by thinking of the first 'disposition' in abstraction from the second.

Well, that may be so, or it may not, in the sort of case the resister has in mind. (I myself think it is not so.) Be that as it may, there is a different sort of case. It may be that the thing would lose the first 'disposition' in response to *s*, but *not* because of any second disposition of that thing; rather because of something wholly extrinsic.

A sorcerer takes a liking to a fragile glass, one that is a perfect intrinsic duplicate of all the other fragile glasses off the same production line. He does nothing at all to change the dispositional character of his glass. He only watches and waits, resolved that if ever his glass is struck, then, quick as a flash, he will cast a spell that changes the glass, renders it no longer fragile, and thereby aborts the process of breaking. So his finkishly fragile glass would not break if struck – but no thanks to any protective disposition of the glass itself. Thanks, instead, to a disposition of the sorcerer.

I have replied to the resister by wielding an assumption that dispositions are an intrinsic matter. (Except perhaps in so far as they depend on the laws of nature. I myself would wish to insist on that exception, but this is a controversial matter that need not be considered now.) That is: if two things (actual or merely possible) are exact intrinsic duplicates (and if they are subject to the same laws of nature) then they are disposed alike. I have used this premise twice over. Suppose the sorcerer's protected glass and another, unprotected, glass off the same production line are intrinsic duplicates (and both subject to the actual laws of nature). Then they are disposed alike. Certainly the unprotected glass is disposed to break if struck; therefore so is the sorcerer's glass. Certainly the unprotected glass is not disposed to lose its fragility if struck; therefore neither is the sorcerer's glass.

I do not deny that the simple conditional analysis enjoys some plausibility. But so does the principle that dispositions are an intrinsic matter. The case of the sorcerer sets up a tug-of-war between conflicting attractions, and to me it seems clear that the simple conditional analysis has the weaker pull.

At least in such cases, Martin's refutation succeeds. I myself think it succeeds in other cases as well. But to refute an analysis, one counter-example is all we need.

Whither? Once we scrap the simple conditional analysis, what should we say about dispositions? Martin's own response is radical: a theory of irreducible dispositionality. Properties are Janus-faced: each of them has, inseparably, a qualitative (or 'categorical') and a dispositional aspect. Since dispositionality is irreducible, it is not to be explained in terms of the causal and nomological roles of properties, but rather *vice versa*.[5]

Those who are disappointed with the usual menu of theories of lawhood and causation might do well to try out this new approach. But those of us whose inclinations are more Fabian than revolutionary, and who still back one or another of the usual approaches to lawhood and causation, may well suspect that Martin has over-reacted. If what we want is not a new theory of everything, but only a new analysis of dispositions that gets right what the simple conditional analysis got wrong, the thing to try first is a not-quite-so-simple conditional analysis. Rather than starting with irreducible dispositionality, as Martin does, we shall start with fairly widely shared ideas about properties, causation, lawhood and counterfactuals; and on this foundation we shall hope to build a reformed conditional analysis of dispositions.

5 See Martin, 'How It Is: Entities, Absences and Voids' pp. 62ff.; also his 'Power for Realists', in J. Bacon, K. Campbell and L. Reinhardt (eds), *Ontology, Causality and Mind* (Cambridge UP, 1993), and elsewhere.

II. A REFORMED CONDITIONAL ANALYSIS

Causal Bases. Suppose that a certain glass is (non-finkishly) fragile; and it is struck; and so it breaks. The breaking presumably was caused; and caused jointly by the striking and by some property B of the glass. We call this property B, a property which would join with striking to cause breaking, a *causal basis* for the fragility of the glass.

Three comments. (a) Different fragile things may have different causal bases for their fragility. (b) Strictly speaking, it is the having of the property that does the causing: a particular event, or perhaps a state of affairs. To speak of the property itself as a cause is elliptical. (c) What causes what depends on the laws of nature. If lawhood is a contingent matter, as many but not all of us think it is, then it is also a contingent matter which properties can and which cannot serve as causal bases for fragility.

Prior, Pargetter and Jackson have argued convincingly for the thesis that all dispositions must have causal bases.[6] Let us assume this. Or at any rate, let us agree to set aside baseless dispositions, if such there be. Our goal, for now, is a reformed conditional analysis of based dispositions – including finkish ones.

(Prior *et al.* argue from a simple conditional analysis of dispositions. But that flaw in their argument is not a serious one. Though wrong as an analysis, the simple conditional analysis remains true as a rough and ready generalization: fragile things that are struck do for the most part break, and those that are unstruck would for the most part break if they were struck. So, despite the possibility of finkish fragility, still for the most part we must posit causes for the breakings that fragile things do or would undergo.)

A finkish disposition is a disposition with a finkish base. The fink-

6 E. W. Prior, R. Pargetter and F. Jackson, 'Three Theses about Dispositions', *American Philosophical Quarterly*, 19 (1982), pp. 251–3. Earlier discussions of dispositions and their causal bases include W. V. Quine, *Word and Object* (MIT Press, 1960), pp. 222–6; D. M. Armstrong, *A Materialist Theory of the Mind* (London: Routledge & Kegan Paul, 1968), pp. 85–8, and *Belief, Truth and Knowledge* (Cambridge UP, 1973), pp. 11–16; J. L. Mackie, *Truth, Probability, and Paradox* (Oxford UP, 1973), pp. 129–48, and 'Dispositions, Grounds, and Causes', *Synthese*, 34 (1977), pp. 361–70.

ishly fragile glass has a property B that would join with striking to cause breaking; and yet the glass would not break if struck. Because if the glass were struck, straight away it would lose the property B. And it would lose B soon enough to abort the process of breaking.

Then is it true to say, as I did, that B 'would join with striking to cause breaking'? Yes and no. What I meant, when I said that, was that if the glass were struck and retained B, then B together with the striking would cause breaking. That much is true. And yet it is also true that if the glass were struck it would not retain B. Thus the possibility of finkishness rests on a logical peculiarity of counterfactuals: their 'variable strictness'.[7] It can happen that two counterfactuals

If it were that p, it would be that not-q
If it were that p and q, it would be that r

are true together, and that the truth of the second is not merely vacuous truth. Because the first counterfactual is true, the supposition that p and q is more far-fetched, more 'remote from actuality', than the supposition just that p. But we are not forbidden to entertain a supposition merely because it is comparatively far-fetched. Variable strictness means that some entertainable suppositions are more far-fetched than others.

The finkish lack of a disposition works in a parallel way. The glass has no causal basis for fragility, therefore it is not fragile. Yet it would break if struck, Because, if it were struck, it would straight away gain some property B that would serve as a causal basis for fragility. And B would arrive in time (though maybe only just in time) to join with the striking to cause the glass to break.

(But will not the striking be over and done with by the time B arrives? Not necessarily. And even if it is, B could join with after-effects of the striking to cause the breaking. Then the striking would still be a cause of the breaking via a causal chain passing through the after-effects.)

Once we appreciate that finkishness pertains, in the first instance,

---

7 R. Stalnaker, 'A Theory of Conditionals', in N. Rescher (ed.), *Studies in Logical Theory* (Oxford: Basil Blackwell, 1968); D. Lewis, *Counterfactuals* (Oxford: Basil Blackwell, 1973).

to particular causal bases and to lacks of particular causal bases, we are in a position to describe a variety of finkishness that has so far escaped our notice. Suppose that B_1 and B_2 are two alternative causal bases for fragility. As it actually is, the glass has B_1 and lacks B_2. But if it were struck, it would undergo a swap: straight away it would lose the property B_1 and gain the property B_2. It finkishly has one basis for fragility and it finkishly lacks another. Yet it is not finkishly fragile, at least not in the sense of being a counter-example to the simple conditional analysis. It is fragile thanks to the basis B_1. If struck, it would be fragile thanks instead to the substitute basis B_2. If struck, therefore, it would break. But its breaking if struck would not be a manifestation of the fragility it has when not struck, because if it were struck it would come to be fragile in a different way.

We need to add something to our characterization of finkish fragility, so as to distinguish it from the different situation just considered. As follows: the finkishly fragile glass has a property B that would join with striking to cause breaking, yet the glass would not break if struck. Because if it were struck, it would lose B, *and it would not gain any substitute basis for fragility*.

Towards an analysis: beginning. Once we have accepted the thesis that all dispositions must have causal bases, it is an easy step to conjoin the converse thesis and to say, for instance, that something is fragile if and only if it has some causal basis for fragility. That biconditional, generalized and spelt out, shall be our reformed analysis of dispositions. In saying what it means for a property to be a causal basis for fragility, or whatever, we shall need a counterfactual conditional. But the conditional part of our reformed analysis will come at the end. Before that, we need a beginning and a middle.

The beginning of any analysis is an analysandum. Ours shall be as follows:

Something x is disposed at time t to give response r to stimulus s iff . . .

The noteworthy thing about our analysandum is what it is *not*. Our plan is to answer one question without getting entangled in another. The question we want to answer is 'What is it to *have* such and such a disposition (as it might be, the disposition to break if struck)?'. The question we want to leave unsettled is 'What *is* a disposition?'.

Once we accept that a disposition must have a causal basis, we might choose to say, as Armstrong has done, that the disposition *is* its causal basis. That choice has the advantage of delivering a straightforward account of the role of dispositions in causal explanation: the fragility of the glass, along with the striking, are the causes that jointly cause the breaking. On the other hand, that choice has the drawback that what we would offhand think was *one* disposition, fragility, turns out to be different properties in different possible cases – and, very likely, in different actual cases.[8]

Or we might instead choose to say, as Prior and her allies have done, that the disposition is the second-order property of having some suitable causal basis or other.[9] That way, fragility is indeed a single property common to all fragile things, actual or merely possible. However, the drawback of this choice is that if fragility is the second-order property, it is far from clear how it plays a role in causal explanation. When the struck glass breaks, do we want to say that the breaking is caused *both* by the second-order property which is the fragility *and* by whatever first-order property is the causal basis for the fragility in that particular case? It is not a case of overdetermination, after all! But neither should we want to say, as Prior *et al.* do, that fragility is causally impotent.

If forced to choose, I would side with Prior against Armstrong; and I would dodge the overdetermination-or-impotence issue by appeal to some fancy and contentious metaphysics. (Thus. Let us speak of the *relata* of the causal relation as 'events', whether or not that is altogether appropriate as a matter of ordinary language. Sometimes an event, in this sense, is a having of a certain property by a certain thing.[10] Now we can say that just one event joins with the striking to cause the breaking, so there is no overdetermination. This one event is a having

---

8 Armstrong, *Belief, Truth and Knowledge* pp. 14–16.

9 'Three Theses about Dispositions' pp. 253–6; E. Prior, *Dispositions* (Aberdeen UP, 1985), pp. 82–95.

10 For details, see my 'Events', in D. Lewis, *Philosophical Papers*, Vol. II (Oxford UP, 1986).

of the causal basis. But also, perhaps in a different sense, this same event is a having of the second-order property. Two different properties are had in the same single event. So the second-order property is not impotent.) This may work, but it is complicated and contentious and best avoided for as long as possible. Our choice of an analysandum is meant to allow us to remain neutral in the disagreement between Armstrong and Prior. When a glass is fragile, it has two properties. It has some first-order property which is a causal basis for fragility; it also has the second-order property of having some causal basis for fragility or other. We need not say which of these two properties of the glass is its fragility.[11]

If we remain neutral in the disagreement between Armstrong and Prior, not only do we refuse to say which properties are dispositional; equally, we refuse to say which properties are *non*-dispositional, or 'categorical'. So we would be unwise to speak, as many do, of 'categorical bases'. Because if we then saw fit to go Armstrong's way, and to identify the disposition itself with its causal basis (in a particular case), we would end up claiming to identify dispositional with non-dispositional properties, and claiming that dispositions are their own categorical bases! Rather than risk such confusion, we do better to eschew the alleged distinction between dispositional and 'categorical' properties altogether.

Our chosen analysandum has another advantage: generality. Suppose instead that we had taken some particular example of a dispositional concept: the concept of a poison, say, or the concept of fragility or the concept of a lethal virus. A dispositional concept is the concept of being disposed to give such and such response to such and such stimulus. So the first problem we face in analysing any particular dispositional concept, before we can turn to the more general questions that our particular example was meant to illustrate, is the problem of specifying the stimulus and the response correctly.

11 S. Mumford, in 'Conditionals, Functional Essences and Martin on Dispositions', *The Philosophical Quarterly*, 46 (1996), pp. 86–92, gives a reply to Martin which agrees to a considerable extent with mine, but which is built upon an answer to the very question that I have taken care to bypass, namely, the question of what dispositions are.

We might offhand define a poison as a substance that is disposed to cause death if ingested. But that is rough: the specifications both of the response and of the stimulus stand in need of various corrections. To take just one of the latter corrections: we should really say 'if ingested without its antidote'. Yet the need for this correction to the analysis of 'poison' teaches no lesson about the analysis of dispositionality in general.

(Some, for instance Johnston,[12] might doubt the need for the correction. They say that a disposition may be masked by something that prevents the response even when both the stimulus and the causal basis are present; in this way, we get failures of the conditional analysis even when the causal basis is not finkish. One who is prepared to speak of masking might stay with the simple definition of a poison as a substance disposed to cause death if ingested, but might say as well that the disposition of poisons to kill is masked by antidotes. Perhaps we have no substantive issue here, but only a difference between styles of book-keeping. But if so, I think the masker's style is less advantageous than it may seem. For even if we say that the poison has the disposition spelt out in the simple definition, and we say as well that this disposition is masked by antidotes, do we not still want to say that the poison has the further disposition spelt out in the complicated corrected definition?)

Or, to take fragility: we have said so far, and we shall go on saying, when greater precision is not required, that being fragile means being disposed to break if struck. But what of this story (due, near enough, to Daniel Nolan)? When a styrofoam dish is struck, it makes a distinctive sound. When the Hater of Styrofoam hears this sound, he comes and tears the dish apart by brute force. So, when the Hater is within earshot, styrofoam dishes are disposed to end up broken if struck. However, there is a certain direct and standard process whereby fragile things most often (actually, nowadays, and hereabouts) break when struck, and the styrofoam dishes in the story are not at all disposed to undergo that process.[13] Are they fragile? To say so would be at best a misleading truth, and at worst an outright falsehood; and I

12 'How to Speak of the Colors' p. 233.
13 Cf. A. D. Smith, 'Dispositional Properties', *Mind*, 86 (1977), p. 444.

have no idea which. However, my purpose in raising this question was *not* to answer it, but rather to insist that it is merely the question of which response-specification is built into the particular dispositional concept of fragility. Once again, it affords no lesson about dispositionality in general.

To show this, I turn to a case that goes differently. A certain virus is disposed to cause those who become infected with it to end up dead before their time, but *not* to undergo the direct and standard process whereby lethal viruses mostly kill their victims. For this virus does not itself interfere with any of the processes that constitute life. Rather, it interferes with the victim's defences against *other* pathogens – whereupon those *other* pathogens, like the Hater of Styrofoam, do the dirty work. Do we call this a lethal virus? Of course we do. After all, my story of the virus is not just another philosophical fantasy! It is the true story of HIV, slightly simplified.

We should not think, therefore, that dispositional concepts generally have built-in response-specifications requiring a direct and standard process. The concept of fragility does. (Though whether it is built in as a matter of truth-conditions or as a matter of implicature remains unclear.) The concept of a lethal virus does not.

Towards an analysis: middle. We begin our analysans with a restricted existential quantifier over properties:

iff, for some suitable property B that x has at t . . .

'Suitable', of course, is a mere place-holder. We want to restrict the quantification to properties that can serve as causal bases for a disposition.

We need to require that B is a property (a having of) which can cause something. But we shall provide for this later, in the conditional part of the analysis: we shall say counterfactually what B would cause. So it is unnecessary to add a requirement of causal potency at this point as well.

Some would deny that negative properties, such as the absence of force or fear or food, can do any causing. Should we then impose a restriction that properties suitable as causal bases for dispositions must be entirely positive (whatever that means)? No. For everyone agrees that negative properties make some sort of difference to what happens, and the difference they make is causal. Martin puts the point thus: 'Absences and voids are causally *relevant* but not causally *operative*'.[14] I myself would draw no such distinction between 'causation' and 'causal relevance'. But if others can make good on this supposed distinction, let them by all means help themselves to it. Anyhow, call it what you will, what matters is that we must not omit the causal difference-making of negative properties from the causal roles of bases for dispositions. Therefore we want no restriction to positive properties.

What we do need to require is that B is an intrinsic property of x. Earlier, we considered and accepted a principle that dispositions are an intrinsic matter. If causal bases could be extrinsic then it could happen, contrary to that principle, that two intrinsic duplicates (subject to the same laws of nature) were differently disposed, because of some difference in their extrinsic causal bases.

We illustrated the principle that dispositions are an intrinsic matter by the case of the sorcerer and his protected glass. But to illustrate the principle further, and to placate those who will not be convinced by fantastic examples, I offer the case of Willie. Willie is a dangerous man to mess with. Why so? Willie is a weakling and a pacifist. But Willie has a big brother – a very big brother – who is neither a weakling nor a pacifist. Willie has the extrinsic property of being protected by such a brother; and it is Willie's having this extrinsic property that would cause anyone who messed about with Willie to come to grief. If we allowed extrinsic properties to serve as causal bases of dispositions, we would have to say that Willie's *own* disposition makes him a dangerous man to mess about with. But we very much do not want to say that. We want to say instead that the disposition that protects Willie is a disposition of Willie's brother. And the reason why is that the disposition's causal basis is an intrinsic property of Willie's brother.

If we insist that dispositions must have intrinsic causal bases, we run a risk of surprises. It just might turn out, for example, that electrons are not after all disposed to repel one another. Because it just might turn out that negative charge, the causal basis of the repulsion, was an extrinsic property involving the state of the surrounding aether. How

14 'How It Is: Entities, Absences and Voids' p. 64.

147

bad would that be? Not so bad, I think, that we ought to buy immunity from such surprises at the cost of saying the wrong thing about dangerous Willie.

Towards an analysis: end. Now at last we reach the conditional part of our reformed conditional analysis, the counterfactual which says that property B is a causal basis for x's disposition to give response r to stimulus s. We shall proceed by successive approximations; asterisks will mark attempts due for subsequent rejection.

Even if B is finkish and would go away in response to s, the counterfactual supposition we want to consider is that s arrives and B nevertheless remains. How long? Long enough to finish the job of causing r, however long that job may take.

* . . . for some time t' after t, if x were to undergo stimulus s at time t and retain property B until t', x would give response r.

The quantificational prefix and the antecedent are now in final form, but the consequent still will not do.

For all that the analysans in its present form tells us, x might finkishly lack fragility: it might be that x would break if struck, but no thanks to any disposition that x already had when unstruck. Yet our quantified counterfactual might come out true. B might be some property entirely unconnected with the breaking: x's colour, say. Or B might be connected in the wrong way with the breaking: logically instead of causally. For instance, B might be the property of either being unstruck or breaking (provided we understand the first disjunct as well as the second in a way that makes it intrinsic). To exclude such inappropriate choices of B, we amend the consequent:

* . . . s and x's having of B would jointly cause x to give response r.

(In case we have chosen to circumvent the alleged impotence of the second-order property in the way considered earlier, we had better say that 'x's having of B' here is to be understood in the sense in which an event is a having of the causal basis, not the different sense in which that same event is a having of the second-order property.)

There is one more problem. (Martin pointed it out to me. At least,

I think this is the problem he had in mind.) It involves what we might call a finkish partial lack of a causal basis. The glass has property B but it lacks property B'. B and B' together would constitute a causal basis for breaking if struck; that is, striking and having B and having B' would together cause breaking. B alone is not a causal basis: striking and having B would not suffice to cause breaking. But the lack of B' is a finkish lack. If the glass were struck, straight away it would gain B'; and in addition it would retain B; and so it would break. And B, together with the striking, would be a cause of the breaking. Not, indeed, the complete cause; but a part of the cause is still a cause, so our analysans in its present form is satisfied. And yet because of the lack of B' it seems false that the unstruck glass is fragile. In short, the problem of finkish lacks has reappeared within our conditional analysis of what it is to be a causal basis.

The solution is to make one final amendment to the consequent of our counterfactual. We have the notion of a complete cause of an effect. (Mill called it the 'whole cause'. I use a different term to mark that we need not be committed to Mill's own analysis.) We can introduce a restriction of that notion: a cause complete in so far as havings of properties intrinsic to x are concerned, though perhaps omitting some events extrinsic to x. For short, 'an x-*complete* cause'. In the example just considered, the striking plus x's having of B would indeed be a cause of the breaking, but not an x-complete cause. So our amended consequent is:

> . . . s and x's having of B would jointly be an x-complete cause of x's giving response r.

Putting all the bits together, our reformed conditional analysis runs as follows:

> Something x is disposed at time t to give response r to stimulus s iff, for some intrinsic property B that x has at t, for some time t' after t, if x were to undergo stimulus s at time t and retain property B until t', s and x's having of B would jointly be an x-complete cause of x's giving response r.

An unlovely mouthful! But I think there is reason to hope that it will do the job.

Being oppositely disposed. A surprising, but unobjectionable, consequence of our reformed conditional analysis is that the same thing, at the same time, may be disposed in two opposite ways: as it might be, to break if struck and also not to break if struck. Of course, one of the two opposite dispositions will have to be finkish. Further, it will have to be the kind of finkish disposition that involves a compound disposition rather than an extrinsic intervention. That may not be the best kind for convincing the resister, but I myself still think it is one possible kind of finkish disposition.

The finkishly fragile glass has intrinsic properties B and B^*. B is an x-complete causal basis for breaking if struck; B^* is an x-complete causal basis for losing B if struck, and also for not breaking if struck. Thanks to B, the glass is finkishly disposed to break if struck. Yet thanks to B^* it also is non-finkishly disposed not to break if struck.

An unsatisfactory reformulation. Given that dispositions must have causal bases, and given that causal bases must be intrinsic, we might hope to stay closer to the simple conditional analysis. How about this, for instance?

> The glass is fragile iff, if it were struck and its intrinsic character were unchanged, it would break.

Martin has warned us that it will not help just to insert a *'ceteris paribus'* into the simple conditional analysis, because when the time comes to say explicitly what is to be held fixed, we shall want to say that it is the dispositional character of the glass that is to be held fixed – and if we say that, our conditional analysis of dispositions becomes circular.[15] But that was not what we said – rather we said that the intrinsic character was to be held fixed. So Martin's warning does not apply. (Or not unless intrinsic character must somehow be analysed in terms of dispositions, which seems unlikely.)

Holding fixed the intrinsic character means holding fixed all the intrinsic causal bases (and all the lacks thereof) which underlie the dispositions (and lacks of dispositions) of the glass. That would solve the problem of finkishness.

15 'Dispositions and Conditionals' pp. 5–6.

But the solution does not work, because holding fixed the intrinsic character of the glass means holding fixed altogether too much. If the glass were struck and its intrinsic character were unchanged, it would indeed retain the intrinsic causal basis of its fragility. But also it would be not at all deformed, not at all compressed, not at all afflicted with vibrations or shock waves, etc. So it would *not* break.

What it would do is astonish a sufficiently knowledgeable observer. We can agree that the glass does have a disposition to astonish such an observer – an extremely finkish disposition, with the entire intrinsic character of the glass as its causal basis. That is not the only disposition the glass has for responding to being struck; and not the most noteworthy disposition. Yet it is this disposition, and not any opposite disposition, that our present proposal deigns to notice.

8

Noneism or allism?

Some few entities – present, actual, particular, spatiotemporal, material, well-bounded things – exist uncontroversially. Scarcely any philosopher denies them. Other alleged entities are controversial: some say they exist, some say they do not. These controversial entities include past and future things, the dead who have ceased to be and those who are not yet even conceived; unactualized possibilia; universals, numbers, and classes; and Meinongian objects, incomplete or inconsistent or both. An expansive friend of the entities who says that all these entities exist may be called an *allist*. A tough desert-dweller who says that none of them exist may be called a *noneist*. In between come most of us, the pickers and choosers, *some-but-only-someists*.

Richard Routley declares himself a noneist.[1] If we may take him at his word, he holds that none of the controversial entities exist. But may we take him at his word?

Sometimes it is wrong to take a philosopher at his word when he

First published in *Mind* 99 (1990), pp. 23–31. Reprinted by permission of Oxford University Press.

I am indebted to Mark Hinchliff, William Lycan, Ken Perszyk, and others for valuable comments; and to Harvard University for research support under a Santayana Fellowship.

1 Richard Routley, *Exploring Meinong's Jungle and Beyond: An Investigation of Noneism and the Theory of Items* (Australian National University, 1980). For short: *Jungle*. Routley, as he then was, is now Richard Sylvan, but I shall refer to him by the name under which the book was written.

tells us what he believes to exist. For if we differ with the philosopher on some point of semantics, then we must make allowance for that difference if we want to report his position in our own words, in indirect quotation. Example. If someone seemingly tells us that God exists, and then goes on to tell us that 'God' denotes the evolutionary-historical process that has brought us into being, and if we ourselves think that this evolutionary-historical process is far from deserving the name he gives it, then we should count him an atheist. We may report that he says the words 'God exists', but we would be wrong to say that he says *that* God exists. (Or at least we would be wrong to say it without immediate qualification.[2]) He believes in something that he thinks deserves the name 'God'. But if we are right and he is wrong about what it takes to deserve the name, then he does not believe in anything that would in fact deserve that name, and we would be wrong to say otherwise.

Second example. Unless we can agree that a congeries of human and divine ideas could deserve the name 'tree in the quad', we ought not to report that Berkeley holds that the tree in the quad exists, no matter how much Berkeley himself may boast of his adherence to common opinion. Third example. If I analyse propositions as classes of possible worlds, and if Plantinga takes it to be wholly obvious (though not *obviously* obvious!) that no class could deserve the name of 'proposition', then I must grant that he makes no mistake when he reports me, by his own lights, as denying the existence of propositions.[3] Or rather, no *new* mistake – his premiss about what it takes to deserve the name 'proposition', say I, is mistake enough. Fourth and fifth examples. I say that a behaviourist denies the existence of experience, even if he himself says he does no such thing; likewise a qualia freak might say that I, as a materialist, also deny the existence of experience. Both of us are within our rights, and so is the behaviourist in his self-description, given our respective premisses. The only difference is that, as we would all three agree, one of us is proceeding from true premisses

2 Gordon Kaufman, *Theology for a Nuclear Age* (Manchester University Press, 1985); cited in Alvin Plantinga, 'Two Concepts of Modality', *Philosophical Perspectives*, 1987, pp. 189–231.

3 Plantinga, op. cit.

about what it takes to deserve the name 'experience' and the other two are not.[4]

The lesson is that whether 'we' may take a philospher at his word depends crucially on who 'we' are, and what philosophical premisses we ourselves argue from. That is distressing. It would be nice to arrive at a non-partisan consensus about what the several philosophical parties say, before we go on to take sides in the argument. And it would be nice to do this in our own words, translating all parties into a common language, rather than by the brute force of direct quotation. We can go some distance by giving the utmost benefit of doubt. We should be at least as generous as conscience will allow in letting things bear names we think they do not very well deserve, especially when we report a position according to which there is no better deserver of the name to be had. But there is a limit to generosity. When we must quietly go along with (what we take to be) someone's mis-speaking in order to give a non-partisan report of his position, the price is too high. For then the advantage of common language is already forsaken.

With Routley likewise there is a semantic difference between him and some of the rest of us, though this time it concerns not the deserving of names but rather the idioms of quantification. So when I ask whether we may take Routley at his word when he declares himself a noneist, again the answer will depend on who 'we' are. Routley sees himself as defying an established orthodoxy; and I am prepared to appoint myself spokesman for the orthodoxy he defies. Or at least for those among the orthodox, if any, who will accept me as their spokesman. (For the solidarity of the Northern establishment is less formidable when viewed from the inside.)

We of the establishment think that there is only one kind of quantification. The several idioms of what we call 'existential' quantification are entirely synonymous and interchangeable. It does not matter whether you say 'Some things are donkeys' or 'There are donkeys' or 'Donkeys exist' – you mean exactly the same thing whichever way you say it. The same goes for more vexed cases: it does not matter whether you say 'Some famous fictional detective uses cocaine', 'There

---

4 Here I am indebted to conversation with Saul Kripke.

is a famous fictional detective who uses cocaine', or 'A famous cocaine-using fictional detective exists' – whether true or whether false, all three statements stand or fall together.

We grant, of course, that often the idioms of quantification are tacitly restricted. They may be restricted, for instance, to salient and well-bounded things, as opposed to gerrymandered chunks of stuff; or to spatiotemporal, material things; or to the here and now; or (in my own opinion) to the here and now and actual; or in ever so many other ways. We gather from context what restrictions are in force, guided by our presumption that what a speaker says is meant to make sense.[5] But we do not think the several idioms correspond in any permanent way to several alternative restrictions. 'Some', 'there are', and 'exist' can all alike be used to quantify unrestrictedly over absolutely everything; or they can all alike bear any of many restrictions.

Routley disagrees. He thinks there are two different kinds of quantification. There is 'existential' quantification rightly so-called, or existentially *loaded* quantification; and there is existentially *neutral* 'particular' quantification (*Jungle*, pp. 174–80 and elsewhere). 'Exist' is the word reserved for loaded quantification, whereas 'there are' and 'some' may be used neutrally. Neutral quantification is weaker than loaded quantification: when φs exist it follows that some things are φs, but not conversely. In fact, loaded quantification is simply a restriction of neutral quantification: φs exist iff some things are φs and exist. And *y exists* iff there exists some x such that $x = y$.

Thus Routley is ready to say 'Some things do not exist'. This is no contradiction, according to him, so long as the 'some' is neutral and the 'exist' is loaded. Whereas if we of the orthodox party said the same words, we would mean something like 'For some x, it is not the case that for some y, $y = x$', or 'There is x such that there is no y such that $y = x$', or 'There exists x, such that there does not exist y such that $y = x$' with the same sort of quantification both times. These three sentences are contradictory, as much by Routley's lights as by ours.

---

5 Tacit restrictions on the idioms of quantification are thus a component of 'conversational score' governed largely by a 'rule of accommodation'. See 'Scorekeeping in a Language Game', in David Lewis, *Philosophical Papers*, vol. I (Oxford University Press, 1983).

When Routley declares himself a noneist, his quantifiers are loaded: none[6] of the controversial entities *exist*. When his quantifiers are neutral, however, he becomes a kind of allist: *there are* all those controversial entities. Or rather, there are all those 'items'; for Routley takes 'entity' to be another existentially loaded term. Some items are past, future, unactualized; some items are universals, numbers, classes; some are incomplete Meinongian objects, and some are inconsistent; but none of all these interesting items *exists*. Speaking loadedly, he is an uncompromising desert-dweller. Speaking neutrally, he relishes 'the beauty and complexity, richness and value of a jungle' full of all the varied items any philosopher could wish (*Jungle*, reverse of the frontispiece).

Which is he really: noneist or allist? His own words do not answer the question what *we* ought to say in reporting his position. He has his two kinds of quantification, the neutral and the loaded; we of the establishment have only one kind. Which of his two corresponds to our one? How should we translate his idioms of quantification into ours? We have two main hypotheses. (1) Perhaps it is Routley's loaded quantification that translates into our one quantification. Under that translation, he holds (as we and he both would say it) that none of the controversial items exists. Then indeed we should take him at his word and call him a noneist. Or (2) perhaps instead it is Routley's neutral quantification that translates into our one quantification. Under that translation he holds (as we would say it though he would not) that all the controversial items exist. That makes him no true noneist, but rather an allist.

Why this fuss over translation? Routley writes in English, after all. Is he not the final authority on his own position? Should we not translate him homophonically? No. He is the final authority on *his* position, but not on *ours*. Therefore he does not have the final word either on how his position should be expressed in our language, or on how ours should be expressed in his. Nor do we. There is no authoritative final word; we can only seek the translation that makes him

---

6 Well, almost none. 'The account of existence given is an almost minimal one. . . . The only controversial objects admitted . . . are microentities and complexes and aggregates' (*Jungle*, p. 755).

make sense to us, and us to him. And whatever presumption there may be in favour of homophonic translation, we cannot translate him altogether homophonically if he sees a distinction where we see none. If we translate idioms of quantification that are not synonymous for him into idioms that are synonymous for us, we make hash of what he is saying, as surely as if we translated all his idioms of quantification by the very same one of ours. This third hypothesis, that our one kind of quantification is *both* of his, amounts to the assumption that despite what he thinks, his two are synonymous. Homophonically translated, Routley incessantly contradicts himself: when he says 'Some things are ϕs but they don't exist' he means what we would mean by 'Some things are ϕs and it is not so that some things are ϕs' or by 'ϕs exist and it is not so that ϕs exist'. To impute contradiction gratuitously is to mistranslate.

(Is it so even in Routley's case? After all, Routley does not shun contradiction as we do: 'The consistency of the world . . . is not at all easy, and perhaps impossible, to establish in a non-question begging way. . . . Good arguments in favour of the consistency assumption, as distinct from prejudice, are hard to come by' (*Jungle*, p. 913). If he is prepared to embrace some contradictions, is it so bad to impute to him others? Might we interpret Routley as holding that some things exist paradoxically, they exist and also do not exist, whereas other things exist unparadoxically; and that neutral quantification differs from loaded quantification because the former is quantification over all things that exist whereas the latter is restricted to things that exist unparadoxically? This is the position we would impute by homophonic translation. It is a position not without interest, though like all positions that embrace paradox it is necessarily and certainly false. But surely it is a misinterpretation. Not because we may never impute contradictions to Routley – translating an explicit friend of contradiction is indeed a special case – but simply because there is, so far as I know, no textual evidence in its favour. Surely if Routley saw his distinction between neutral and loaded quantification as something to be explained in terms of true contradictions he would not hesitate to tell us so.)

A fourth hypothesis is that our one kind of quantification is neither of Routley's two, but something else again. I can see no possible advantage in this alternative and shall pursue it no further. So we are back to the two main hypotheses. Is our one quantification the same as (1) Routley's loaded quantification, or is it (2) Routley's neutral quantification?

Routley takes the first hypothesis for granted. He assumes it is orthodox to take all quantification as loaded, heretical to insist as he does that there is neutral quantification as well. When we use the several idioms of quantification interchangeably – as he knows that we do, at least in our theoretical moments – he thinks that is because we are giving all of them, even 'some', an existential loading (*Jungle*, pp. 427–30).

Under the hypothesis that our one quantification is his loaded quantification, Routley may fault us in several ways. (Not to mention the ways having to do with disagreements not part of the present discussion.) For one thing, because we have no understanding of how existentially neutral quantification is possible – and to that charge, *if* the present hypothesis be granted, we may unabashedly plead guilty. Also, because most of us – the some-but-only-someists – are extravagant in our imputations of existence. Finally, because even so we cripple ourselves in our theorizing by declining to quantify in any way over all the items that, according to Routley speaking neutrally, there really are.

In return, under the present hypothesis, we fault him in one big way: he purports to quantify without quantifying. For when he quantifies neutrally he is not quantifying in the one and only way there is to quantify, since *ex hypothesi* the one way is the loaded way. This we find altogether unintelligible.[7] Now Routley may unabashedly plead guilty to the charge of being beyond our dogma-blinded understanding. And there we reach a standoff.

---

7 See, for instance, William Lycan, 'The Trouble With Possible Worlds' in Michael J. Loux (ed.), *The Possible and the Actual* (Cornell University Prss, 1979), p. 290: 'I have to take my place among those who find *Relentlessly* (i.e. *genuinely* or *primitively*) Meinongian quantification simply unintelligible. . . . I am not expressing any tendentious philosophical *qualm*. I mean that I really cannot understand Relentlessly Meinongian quantification at all; to me it is *literally* gibberish or mere noise.'

We might think that when Routley quantifies without quantifying, he is engaging in some sort of *simulated* quantification. That is something we can understand, and often even accept. Substitutionalists simulate quantification over fictional characters by quantifying for real over fictional names. Bogus Meinong simulates quantification over Meinongian objects, including the incomplete and inconsistent ones, by quantifying for real over property bundles (such as the bundle of goldenness and mountainhood, or the bundle of roundness and squareness).[8] Morton shows how we might simulate quantification over composite entities by infinitely long blocks of genuine quantifiers over simples.[9] Pluralists like Black and Armstrong simulate quantification over classes of individuals by means of irreducibly plural quantification over the individuals themselves.[10] Sturch simulates quantification over (what he takes to be) non-existent Australians by putting genuine quantifiers within the scope of a modifier 'in Australia' which looks as if it merely restricts the quantifier but really functions as a negation symbol.[11] Likewise Prior and Fine simulate quantification over past or future or unactualized things by quantifying within the scope of tense

8 Bogus Meinong, invented (but not under that name) by Terence Parsons, is an orthodox figure who has found a way to speak more or less as Meinong does by quantifying over property bundles and getting it up to look as if he is quantifying over Meinongian objects that instantiate the bundles. See Parsons, 'A Prolegomenon to Meinongian Semantics', *Journal of Philosophy*, 1974, pp. 561–80. Note well: Bogus Meinong is *not* Meinong, or Parsons, or Meinong as he struck Parsons. His role is just to prove the consistency of (one form of) genuine Meinongianism. For he speaks enough as the Meinongians do that if they fell into contradiction, so would he; and yet his position, however deceptively presented, is just an innocent theory of property bundles, which we of the establishment would presume to be consistent.

9 Adam Morton, 'Complex Individuals and Multigrade Relations', *Noûs*, 1975, pp. 309–18.

10 Max Black, 'The Elusiveness of Sets', *Review of Metaphysics*, 1971, pp. 614–36; D. M. Armstrong, *Universals and Scientific Realism*, vol. I (Cambridge University Press, 1978), pp. 32–4. For further discussion of plural quantification, but without any suggestion that it ought to be used to explain away quantification over classes of individuals, see George Boolos, 'To Be is To Be a Value of a Variable (or To Be Some Values of Some Variables)', *Journal of Philosophy*, 1984, pp. 430–49; and 'Nominalist Platonism', *Philosophical Review*, 1985, pp. 327–44.

11 'Report on "WHY?" Competition – Problem No. 1', *Why?*, June, 1958, pp. 2–5.

and modal operators.[12] There are many ways to simulate quantification, and thereby quantify without quantifying. We might find Routley's neutral quantification intelligible enough if it turned out to be just another of these exercises in deceptive simulation. Is it? No; there is no textual evidence in favour.[13] And if it were, he would have no reason to present himself as a heretic. For he himself would agree with us, in the end, that there was really only one sort of genuine quantification.

Under the second of our main hypotheses – that being the hypothesis that our one quantification corresponds not to Routley's 'loaded' quantification but rather to his 'existentially neutral' quantification – we get quite a different picture of the relationship between Routley's position and our orthodoxy. Disagreement remains. But Routley's heresy becomes more intelligible from the standpoint of orthodoxy and, reciprocally, orthodoxy becomes more intelligible from Routley's standpoint. In so far as mutual intelligibility is a desideratum for translation, that makes the second hypothesis better than the first. Therefore I say that the second hypothesis is the right way for us to understand Routley, and the right way for us to report his position in indirect quotation. We go wrong if we take him altogether at his word, and overlook that his meaning of 'existence' might not be the same as ours, just as we go wrong in taking Berkeley altogether at his word when he says 'The tree in the quad exists'.

I also say – though I say it hesitantly, lest my advice be found impertinent – that Routley ought to understand us according to the second hypothesis. He should not say that we dogmatically reject neutral quantification, but instead that we dogmatically reject loaded quantification. He should not say that we impose existential loading on 'some' and 'there are', but rather that we *un*load 'exist' itself. He should say that we outdo him in noneism: we never affirm the existence of *anything*, not the controversial items and not the uncontrov-

---

12 See Fine's 'Postscript' to A. N. Prior and Kit Fine, *Worlds, Times and Selves* (Duckworth, 1977), especially pp. 142–5.

13 And see *Jungle*, p. 81, against a substitutional interpretation; p. 879 against an interpretation in terms of Bogus-Meinongian surrogates.

ersial ones either. Of course we say the words 'donkeys exist', and some of us say 'numbers exist too', but he should understand that by these words we do not mean what he would mean. We talk of our 'existential commitments', and many of us try to cut these down in order to dodge questions about the nature of what we are committed to. But all the while, we are talking only of our neutral-quantificational commitments – the counterpart for us of Routley's own neutral-quantificational commitment to the whole beautiful jungle. Our main fault, he should say, is that we are blind to the distinction between what exists and what does not; and a lesser fault is that we cripple ourselves by our unwise cutting-down of neutral-quantificational commitments.

And what should we say of him, under the second hypothesis? Not that he purports to quantify without quantifying. Not that he denies the existence of some of the items he quantifies over. No; he quantifies just as we do; over everything; that is (as we would say) over everything that exists. We should have no problem understanding his neutral quantification. We may indeed look askance at the extent of his existential commitments – for, despite what he tells us, he is an allist. He affirms the existence of all the controversial entities (as we may call them). He does not join us when we dodge questions about some of these alleged entities by denying that they exist.

Like us, Routley sometimes restricts his quantifiers. When he restricts them to, say, trees, we have no problem understanding him, because we too distinguish trees from non-trees. (We might have a harder time of it if we had to apply the distinction to such Meinongian objects as the tree that is not a tree. But it is unlikely that a Meinongian would be stumped by this problem.) And if he restricts his quantifiers to present things, or to non-numbers, or to individuals, . . . we still have no problem, because again we understand and accept the distinctions whereby he restricts. Maybe not perfectly, but well enough; and in so far as we do not, we should not call the kettle black.

But when Routley 'loads' his quantifiers, he restricts them to the entities which, he says, 'exist'. And then we do not understand, because we ourselves make no such distinction among the entities. If 'existence' is what he thinks it is – a distinction among the items we are committed to – then we dispense with existence.[14] Our main complaint against Routley is that he sees a distinction that is not really there.

Under the second hypothesis, the issue is squarely joined. He says we are blind, we say he is hallucinating. The meaning of quantification *per se* does not enter into it.

The picture is still none too irenic. But our desideratum for translation was not reconciliation, just mutual intelligibility. And there the second hypothesis does better than the first. Difficult though it may be for us to understand how Routley sees a distinction that is not there, and difficult though it may be for him to understand our supposed blindness, a disagreement over whether some alleged distinction is genuine is at least a familiar and intelligible *sort* of disagreement. The same would not be true of the supposed disagreement over ways of quantifying.

At this point you might surmise that the distinction Routley has in mind is genuine, and what is more that we accept it no less than he does. It is just that he calls it the distinction between what 'exists' and what does not; whereas we call it the distinction between present, actual, particular, spatiotemporal things and all the rest. (He may join us in giving it the latter name, though we will not join him in giving it the former.) For does he not say that it is exactly the present, actual, . . . things that 'exist'? – He does. But plainly he takes that to be a highly controversial substantive thesis, not a trivial matter of definition. This hypothesis is altogether too irenic. Or rather, it is one-sidedly irenic: it squares Routley's position on loaded and neutral quantification with orthodoxy, but at the cost of making nonsense of Routley's evident conviction that his position is deeply opposed to orthodoxy. To suppose that Routley mistakes mere terminological difference for profound philosophical disagreement is to accuse him of stupidity far beyond belief.

In short: we dispense with existence – but heed what this means and what it does not. Of course we do not dispense with the word 'exist' as one of our pronunciations for the quantifier. Neither do we

14 In the way explained in Donald C. Williams, 'Dispensing with Existence', *Journal of Philosophy*, 1962, pp. 748–63.

dispense with a trivially universal predicate of existence, automatically satisfied by absolutely everything.[15] But if 'existence' is understood so that it can be a substantive thesis that only some of the things there are exist – or, for that matter, so that it can be a substantive thesis that everying exists – we will have none of it.

15 It might be a queer predicate, though, in the same way that 'selfidentical' and 'proper class' and Routley's 'item' are queer predicates: it might have no extension. For the extension of a predicate is supposed to be the set, or at least the class, of all its satisfiers. But if there are things that cannot be members of any class, and if some such things are among the satisfiers of a predicate, then that predicate has no extension.

9

Many, but almost one

Think of a cloud – just one cloud, and around it clear blue sky. Seen from the ground, the cloud may seem to have a sharp boundary. Not so. The cloud is a swarm of water droplets. At the outskirts of the cloud the density of the droplets falls off. Eventually they are so few and far between that we may hesitate to say that the outlying droplets are still part of the cloud at all; perhaps we might better say only that they are near the cloud. But the transition is gradual. Many surfaces are equally good candidates to be the boundary of the cloud. Therefore many aggregates of droplets, some more inclusive and some less inclusive (and some inclusive in different ways than others), are equally good candidates to be the cloud. Since they have equal claim, how can we say that the cloud is one of these aggregates rather than another? But if all of them count as clouds, then we have many clouds rather than one. And if none of them count, each one being ruled out because of the competition from the others, then we have no cloud. How is it, then, that we have just one cloud? And yet we do.

This is Unger's (1980) 'problem of the many'. Once noticed, we can see that it is everywhere, for all things are swarms of particles.

First published in Keith Campbell, John Bacon, and Lloyd Reinhardt (eds.), *Ontology, Causality, and Mind: Essays on the Philosophy of D. M. Armstrong* (Cambridge, Cambridge University Press, 1993. © 1993 by Cambridge University Press. Reprinted with the permission of Cambridge University Press.

There are always outlying particles, questionably parts of the thing, not definitely included and not definitely not included. So there are always many aggregates, differing by a little bit here and a little bit there, with equal claim to be the thing. We have many things or we have none, but anyway not the one thing we thought we had. That is absurd.

Think of a rusty nail, and the gradual transition from steel, to steel with bits of rust scattered through, to rust adhering to the nail, to rust merely resting on the nail. Or think of a cathode, and its departing electrons. Or think of anything that undergoes evaporation or erosion or abrasion. Or think of yourself, or any organism, with parts that gradually come loose in metabolism or excretion or perspiration or shedding of dead skin. In each case, a thing has questionable parts, and therefore is subject to the problem of the many.

If, as I think, things perdure through time by having temporal parts, then questionable temporal parts add to the problem of the many. If a person comes into existence gradually (whether over weeks or over years or over nanoseconds doesn't matter for our present purpose) then there are questionable temporal parts at the beginning of every human life. Likewise at the end, even in the most sudden death imaginable. Do you think you are one person? – No, there are many aggregates of temporal parts, differing just a little at the ends, with equal claim to count as persons, and equal claim to count as you. Are all those equally good claims good enough? If so, you are many. If not, you are none. Either way we get the wrong answer. For undeniably you are one.

If, as some think but I do not,[1] ordinary things extend through other possible worlds, then the problem of the many takes on still another dimension. Here in this world we have a ship, the *Enigma*; there in another world is a ship built at about the same time, to plans that are nearly the same but not quite, using many of the same planks and some that are not the same. It is questionable whether the ship in that other world is *Enigma* herself, or just a substitute. If *Enigma* is a thing that extends through worlds, then the question is whether *Enigma* includes as a part what's in that other world. We have two versions of *Enigma*, one that includes this questionable other-worldly

1 See Lewis (1986a, pp. 210–20).

part and one that excludes it. They have equal claim to count as ships, and equal claim to count as *Enigma*. We have two ships, coinciding in this world but differing in their full extent. Or else we have none; but anyway not the one ship we thought we had.

THE PARADOX OF 1001 CATS

Cat Tibbles is alone on the mat. Tibbles has hairs $h_1, h_2, \ldots, h_{1000}$. Let c be Tibbles including all these hairs; let c_1 be all of Tibbles except for h_1; and similarly for $c_2, \ldots, c_{1000}$. Each of these c's is a cat. So instead of one cat on the mat, Tibbles, we have at least 1001 cats – which is absurd. This is P. T. Geach's (1980, pp. 215–16) paradox of 1001 cats.

Why should we think that each c_n is a cat? Because, says Geach, 'c_n would clearly be a cat were the hair h_n plucked out, and we cannot reasonably suppose that plucking out a hair *generates* a cat, so c_n must already have been a cat' (p. 215). This need not convince us. We can reply that plucking out h_n turns c_n from a mere proper part of cat Tibbles into the whole of a cat. No new cat is generated, since the cat that c_n becomes the whole of is none other than Tibbles. Nor do c_n and Tibbles ever become identical *simpliciter* – of course not, since what's true about c_n's past still differs from what's true about Tibbles's past. Rather, c_n becomes the whole of cat Tibbles in the sense that c_n's post-plucking temporal part is identical with Tibbles's post-plucking temporal part. So far, so good; except for those, like Geach, who reject the idea of temporal parts. The rest of us have no paradox yet.

But suppose it is spring, and Tibbles is shedding. When a cat sheds, the hairs do not come popping off; they become gradually looser, until finally they are held in place only by the hairs around them. By the end of this gradual process, the loose hairs are no longer parts of the cat. Sometime before the end, they are questionable parts: not definitely still parts of the cat, not definitely not. Suppose each of $h_1, h_2, \ldots, h_{1000}$ is at this questionable stage. Now indeed all of $c_1, c_2, \ldots, c_{1000}$, and also c which includes all the questionable hairs, have equal claim to be a cat, and equal claim to be Tibbles. So now we have 1001 cats. (Indeed, we have many more than that. For instance there is the cat that includes all but the four hairs h_6, h_{408}, h_{882}, and h_{907}.) The paradox of 1001 cats, insofar as it is a real paradox, is another instance of Unger's problem of the many.

To deny that there are many cats on the mat, we must either deny that the many are cats, or else deny that the cats are many. We may solve the paradox by finding a way to disqualify candidates for cathood: there are the many, sure enough, but the many are not all cats. At most one of them is. Perhaps the true cat is one of the many; or perhaps it is something else altogether, and none of the many are cats. Or else, if we grant that all the candidates are truly cats, we must find a way to say that these cats are not truly different from one another. I think both alternatives lead to successful solutions, but we shall see some unsuccessful solutions as well.

TWO SOLUTIONS BY DISQUALIFICATION: NONE OF THE MANY ARE CATS

We could try saying that not one of the c's is a cat; they are many, sure enough, but not many cats. Tibbles, the only genuine cat on the mat, is something else, different from all of them.

One way to disqualify the many is to invoke the alleged distinction between things and the parcels of matter that constitute them. We could try saying that the c's are not cats. Rather, they are cat-constituting parcels of matter. Tibbles is the cat that each of them constitutes.[2]

This dualism of things and their constituters is unparsimonious and unnecessary. It was invented to solve a certain problem, but a better solution to that problem lies elsewhere, as follows. We know that the matter of a thing may exist before and after the thing does; and we know that a thing may gain and lose matter while it still exists, as a cat does, or a wave or a flame. The dualists conclude that the matter is not the thing; constitution is not identity; there are things, there are the parcels of matter that temporarily constitute those things; these are items of two different categories, related by the special relation of

2 This is the solution advanced in Lowe (1982).

constitution. We must agree, at least, that the temporally extended thing is not the temporally extended parcel of matter that temporarily constitutes that thing. But constitution may be identity, all the same, if it is identity between temporal parts. If some matter constitutes a cat for one minute, then a minute-long temporal segment of the cat is identical to a minute-long temporal segment of the matter. The cat consists entirely of the matter that constitutes it, in this sense: The whole of the cat, throughout the time it lives, consists entirely of temporal segments of various parcels of matter. At any moment, if we disregard everything not located at that moment, the cat and the matter that then constitutes it are identical.[3] So only those who reject the notion of temporal parts have any need for the dualism of things and constituters. But suppose we accept it all the same. At best, this just transforms the paradox of 1001 cats into the paradox of 1001 cat-constituters. Is that an improvement? We all thought there was only one cat on the mat. After distinguishing Tibbles from her constituter, would we not still want to think there was only one cat-constituter on the mat?

Further, even granted that Tibbles has many constituters, I still question whether Tibbles is the only cat present. The constituters are cat-like in size, shape, weight, inner structure, and motion. They vibrate and set the air in motion – in short, they purr (especially when you pat them). Any way a cat can be at a moment, cat-constituters also can be; anything a cat can do at a moment, cat-constituters also can do. They are all too cat-like not to be cats. Indeed, they may have unfeline pasts and futures, but that doesn't show that they are never cats; it only shows that they do not remain cats for very long. Now we have the paradox of 1002 cats: Tibbles the constituted cat, and also the 1001 all-too-feline cat-constituters. Nothing has been gained.

3 The dualism of things and their constituters is also meant to solve a modal problem: Even at one moment, the thing might have been made of different matter, so what might have been true of it differs from what might have been true of its matter, so constitution cannot be identity. This problem too has a better solution. We should allow that what is true of a given thing at a given world is a vague and inconstant matter. Conflicting answers, equally correct, may be evoked by different ways of referring to the same thing, e.g., as cat or as cat-constituter. My counterpart theory affords this desirable inconstancy; many rival theories do also. See Lewis (1986a, pp. 248–63).

I conclude that invoking the dualism of cats and cat-constituters to solve the paradox of 1001 cats does not succeed.

A different way to disqualify the many appeals to a doctrine of vagueness in nature. We could try saying that cat Tibbles is a vague object, and that the *c*'s are not cats but rather alternative precisifications of a cat.

In one way, at least, this solution works better than the one before. This time, I cannot complain that at best we only transform the paradox of 1001 cats into the paradox of 1001 cat-precisifications, because that is no paradox. If indeed there are vague objects and precisifications, it is only to be expected that one vague object will have many precisifications.

If the proposal is meant to solve our paradox, it must be meant as serious metaphysics. It cannot just be a way of saying 'in the material mode' that the words 'Tibbles' and 'cat' are vague, and that this vagueness makes it indefinite just which hairs are part of the cat Tibbles. Rather, the idea must be that material objects come in two varieties, vague and precise; cats are vague, the *c*'s are precise, and that is why none of the *c*'s is a cat.

This new dualism of vague objects and their precisifications is, again, unparsimonious and unnecessary. The problem it was made to solve might better be solved another way. It is absurd to think that we have decided to apply the name 'Tibbles' to a certain precisely delimited object; or that we have decided to apply the term 'cat' to each of certain precisely delimited objects. But we needn't conclude that these words must rather apply to certain *im*precisely delimited, vague objects. Instead we should conclude that we never quite made up our minds just what these words apply to. We have made up our minds that 'Tibbles' is to name one or another Tibbles-precisification, but we never decided just which one; we decided that 'cat' was to apply to some and only some cat-precisifications, but again we never decided just which ones. (Nor did we ever decide just which things our new-found terms 'Tibbles-precisification' and 'cat-precisification' were to apply to.) It was very sensible of us not to decide. We probably couldn't have done it if we'd tried; and even if we could have, doing it would have been useless folly.

Semantic indecision will suffice to explain the phenomenon of vagueness.[4] We need no vague objects.

Further, I doubt that I have any correct conception of a vague object. How, for instance, shall I think of an object that is vague in its spatial extent? The closest I can come is to superimpose three pictures. There is the *multiplicity* picture, in which the vague object gives way to its many precisifications, and the vagueness of the object gives way to differences between precisifications. There is the *ignorance* picture, in which the object has some definite but secret extent. And there is the *fadeaway* picture, in which the presence of the object admits of degree, in much the way that the presence of a spot of illumination admits of degree, and the degree diminishes as a function of the distance from the region where the object is most intensely present. None of the three pictures is right. Each one in its own way replaces the alleged vagueness of the object by precision. But if I cannot think of a vague object except by juggling these mistaken pictures, I have no correct conception.[5]

I can complain as before that we end up with a paradox of 1002 cats: Tibbles the vague cat, and also the 1001 precise cats. Once again,

---

4 Provided that there exist the many precisifications for us to be undecided between. If you deny this, you will indeed have need of vague objects. See van Inwagen (1990, pp. 213–83).

5 I grant that the hypothesis of vague objects, for all its faults, can at least be made consistent. If there are vague objects, no doubt they sometimes stand in relations of 'vague identity' to one another. We might think that when a and b are vaguely identical vague objects, the identity statement $a = b$ suffers a truth-value gap; but in fact this conception of vague identity belongs to the theory of vagueness as semantic indecision. As Gareth Evans showed, it doesn't mix with the idea that vague identity is due to vagueness in nature. For if a and b are vaguely identical, they differ in respect of vague identity to a; but nothing, however peculiar it may be, differs in any way from itself; so the identity $a = b$ is definitely false. See Evans (1978). (Evans's too-concise paper invites misunderstanding, but his own testimony confirms my interpretation. See Lewis 1988.) To get a consistent theory of vague objects, different from the bastard theory that is Evans's target, we must disconnect 'vague identity' from truth-value gaps in identity statements. Even if $a = b$ is definitely false, a and b can still be 'vaguely identical' in the sense of sharing some but not all of their precisifications.

the cat-precisifications are all too cat-like. More so than the cat-constituters, in fact: The precisifications are cat-like not just in what they can do and how they can be at a moment, but also over time. They would make good pets – especially since 1001 of them will not eat you out of house and home!

Don't say that the precisifications cannot be cats because cats cannot be precise objects. Surely there could be cats in a world where nature is so much less gradual that the problem of the many goes away. It could happen that cats have no questionable parts at all, neither spatial nor temporal. (In this world, when cats shed in the spring, the hairs *do* come popping off.) So it is at least possible that cat-like precise objects are genuine cats. If so, how can the presence of one vague cat spoil their cathood?

I conclude that invoking the dualism of vague objects and their precisifications to solve the paradox of 1001 cats does not succeed.

A BETTER SOLUTION BY DISQUALIFICATION: ONE OF THE MANY IS A CAT

Since all of the many are so cat-like, there is only one credible way to deny that all of them are cats. When is something very cat-like, yet not a cat? – When it is just a little less than a whole cat, almost all of a cat with just one little bit left out. Or when it is just a little more than a cat, a cat plus a little something extra. Or when it is both a little more and a little less.

Suppose we say that one of our many is exactly a cat, no more and no less; and that each of the rest is disqualified because it is a little less than a cat, or a little more, or both more and less. This invokes no unparsimonious and unnecessary dualisms; it disqualifies all but one of the many without denying that they are very cat-like; it leaves us with just one cat. All very satisfactory.

The trouble, so it seems, is that there is no saying which one is a cat. That is left altogether arbitrary. Settling it takes a semantic decision, and that is the decision we never made (and shouldn't have made, and maybe couldn't have made). No secret fact could answer the question, for we never decided how the answer would depend on secret facts.

Which one deserves the name 'cat' is up to us. If we decline to settle the question, nothing else will settle it for us.[6]

We cannot deny the arbitrariness. What we can deny, though, is that it is trouble. What shall we do, if semantic indecision is inescapable, and yet we wish to carry on talking? The answer, surely, is to exploit the fact that very often our unmade semantic decisions don't matter. Often, what you want to say will be true under all different ways of making the unmade decision. Then if you say it, even if by choice or by necessity you leave the decision forever unmade, you still speak truthfully. It makes no difference just what you meant, what you say is true regardless. And if it makes no difference just what you meant, likewise it makes no difference that you never made up your mind just what to mean. You say that a famous architect designed Fred's house; it never crossed your mind to think whether by 'house' you meant something that did or that didn't include the attached garage; neither does some established convention or secret fact decide the issue; no matter, you knew that what you said was true either way.

This plan for coping with semantic indecision is van Fraassen's (1966) method of *supervaluations*. Call a sentence *super-true* if and only if it is true under all ways of making the unmade semantic decisions; *super-false* if and only if it is false under all ways of making those decisions; and if it is true under some ways and false under others, then it suffers a super-truth-value gap. Super-truth, with respect to a language interpreted in an imperfectly decisive way, replaces truth *simpliciter* as the goal of a cooperative speaker attempting to impart information. We can put it another way: Whatever it is that we do to determine the 'intended' interpretation of our language determines not one interpretation but a range of interpretations. (The range depends on context, and is itself somewhat indeterminate.) What we try for, in imparting information, is truth of what we say under all the intended interpretations.

6 I do not think reference is entirely up to our choice. Some things are by their nature more eligible than others to be referents or objects of thought, and when we do nothing to settle the contest in favour of the less eligible, then the more eligible wins by default; see Lewis (1984). That's no help here: nature is gradual, no handy joint in nature picks out one of the c's from all the rest.

Each intended interpretation of our language puts one of the cat-candidates on the mat into the extension of the word 'cat', and excludes all the rest. Likewise each intended interpretation picks out one cat-candidate, the same one, as the referent of 'Tibbles'. Therefore it is super-true that there is just one cat, Tibbles, on the mat. Because it is super-true, you are entitled to affirm it. And so you may say what you want to say: there is one cat. That is how the method of super-valuations solves the paradox of 1001 cats.

Objection. Just one of the candidates is a cat, no more and no less. But don't try to say which one it is. Nothing you might say would be super-true. For it is exactly this semantic decision that remains unmade; it is exactly in this respect that the intended interpretations differ. Although it is super-true that something is a cat on the mat, there is nothing such that it is super-true of it that *it* is a cat on the mat. (It's like the old puzzle: I owe you a horse, but there's no horse such that I owe you that horse.) This is peculiar.

Reply. So it is. But once you know the reason why, you can learn to accept it.

Objection.[7] Supervaluationism works too well: it stops us from ever stating the problem in the first place. The problem supposedly was that all the many candidates had equal claim to cathood. But under the supervaluationist rule, that may not be said. For under any one way of making the unmade decision, one candidate is picked as a cat. So under any one way of making the decision, the candidates do *not* have equal claim. What's true under all ways of making the decision is super-true. So what's super-true, and what we should have said, is that the candidates do *not* have equal claim. Then what's the problem? And yet the problem was stated. So supervaluationism is mistaken.

Reply. What's mistaken is a fanatical supervaluationism, which automatically applies the supervaluationist rule to any statement whatever, never mind that the statement makes no sense that way. The rule

---

7 Here I'm indebted to remarks of Saul Kripke many years ago. At his request, I note that what I have written here may not correspond exactly to the whole of what he said on that occasion.

should instead be taken as a defeasible presumption. What defeats it, sometimes, is the cardinal principle of pragmatics: The right way to take what is said, if at all possible, is the way that makes sense of the message. Since the supervaluationist rule would have made hash of our statement of the problem, straightway the rule was suspended. We are good at making these accommodations; we don't even notice when we do it. Under the supervaluationist rule, it's right to say that there's only one cat, and so the candidates have unequal claim. Suspending the rule, it's right to say that the candidates have equal claim, and that all of them alike are not definitely not cats. Suspending the rule, it's even right to say that they are all cats! Is this capitulation to the paradox? – No; it's no harm to admit that in *some* sense there are many cats. What's intolerable is to be without any good and natural sense in which there is only one cat.

Objection.[8] The supervaluationist's notion of indeterminate reference is conceptually derivative from the prior notion of reference *simpliciter*. But if the problem of the many is everywhere, and semantic indecision is inescapable, then reference *simpliciter* never happens. To the extent that we gain concepts by 'fixing the reference' on actual examples, we are in no position to have the concept of reference. Then neither are we in a position to have the derivative concept of indeterminate reference due to semantic indecision.

Reply. We don't need actual examples to have the concept. We have plenty of imaginary examples of reference *simpliciter*, uncomplicated by semantic indecision. These examples are set in sharper worlds than ours: worlds where clouds have no outlying droplets, where cats shed their hairs instantaneously, and so on. When we picked up the concept of reference, in childhood, we probably took for granted that our own world was sharp in just that way. (When not puzzling over the problem of the many, maybe we half-believe it still.) We fixed the reference of 'reference' on these imaginary examples in the sharp world we thought we lived in – and if any theory of reference says that cannot be done, so much the worse for it.

---

8 Here I'm indebted to Andrew Strauss (personal communication, 1989).

I conclude that the supervaluationist solution to the paradox of 1001 cats, and to the problem of the many generally, is successful. But is it the only successful solution? – I think not. I turn now to the other sort of solution: the kind which concedes that the many are cats, but seeks to deny that the cats are really many.

RELATIVE IDENTITY: THE MANY ARE NOT DIFFERENT CATS

Geach himself favours one such solution. The paradox of 1001 cats serves as a showcase for his doctrine of relative identity.

> Everything falls into place if we realize that the number of cats on the mat is the number of *different* cats on the mat; and c_{13}, c_{279}, and c are not three different cats, they are one and the same cat. Though none of these 1001 lumps of feline tissue is the same lump of feline tissue as another, each is the same cat as any other: each of them, then, is a cat, but there is only one cat on the mat, and our original story stands. . . . The price to pay is that we must regard '——— —is the same cat as———' as expressing only a certain equivalence relation, not an absolute identity restricted to cats; but this price, I have elsewhere argued, must be paid anyhow, for there is no such absolute identity as logicians have assumed. (1980, p. 216)

'Same cat' is a relation of partial indiscernibility, restricted to respects of comparison somehow associated with the term 'cat', and discernibility by just a few hairs doesn't count. 'Same lump of feline tissue' is a different relation of partial indiscernibility, and a more discerning one.

I agree that sometimes we say 'same', and mean by it not 'absolute identity' but just some relation of partial indiscernibility. I also agree that sometimes we count by relations of partial indiscernibility. As I once wrote:

> If an infirm man wishes to know how many roads he must cross to reach his destination, I will count by identity-along-his-path rather than by identity. By crossing the Chester A. Arthur Parkway and Route 137 at the brief stretch where they have merged, he can cross both by crossing only one road. (1976, p. 27)

I'll happily add that for that brief stretch, the two roads are the same. But though I don't object to this positive part of Geach's view, it doesn't ring true to apply it as he does to the case of the cats.

If you ask me to say whether c_{13}, c_{279}, and c are the same or different, I may indeed be of two minds about how to answer. I might say they're different – after all, I know how they differ! Or I might say they're the same, because the difference is negligible, so I duly ignore it. (Not easy to do while attending to the example as I now am; if I attend to my ignoring of something, *ipso facto* I no longer ignore it.) But if you add the noun phrase, either 'same cat' or 'same lump of feline tissue', it seems to me that I am no less hesitant than before. Just as I was of two minds about 'same', so I am still of two minds about 'same cat' and 'same lump of feline tissue'.

Other cases are different. If you ask me 'same or different?' when you hold Monday's *Melbourne Age* in one hand and Tuesday's *Age* in the other, or when you hold one Monday *Age* in each hand, again I won't know how to answer. But if you ask me 'same or different newspaper?' or 'same or different issue?' or 'same or different copy?' then I'll know just what to say. We can dispute his explanation of what happens, but at least the phenomenon happens exactly as Geach says it does. Not so, I think, for the case of 'same cat' versus 'same lump'.

Something else is lacking in Geach's solution. In other cases where it comes natural to count by a relation other than identity, it seems that identity itself – 'absolute identity' – is not far away. Local identity, as between the Arthur Parkway and Route 137 for the stretch where they have merged, is identity *simpliciter* of spatial parts. Likewise temporary identity, as between a thing and the matter that temporarily constitutes it, is identity *simpliciter* of temporal parts. Qualitative identity is identity *simpliciter* of qualitative character. The newspaper that Monday's *Age* is an issue of and the newspaper that Tuesday's *Age* is an issue of are identical *simpliciter;* likewise my copy and your copy of Monday's *Age* are copies of the identical issue. But Geach never tells us what the 'same cat' relation has to do with identity *simpliciter*.

He wouldn't, of course, because he thinks 'there is no such absolute identity as logicians have assumed'. (Nor would he accept all my examples above; certainly not the one about temporary identity and identity of temporal parts.) But Geach's case against absolute identity is unconvincing. It seems to come down to a challenge: If Geach is determined to construe all that I say in terms of relations of partial indiscernibility, is there any way I can stop him? Can I *force* him to understand? (What's more, can I do it with one hand tied behind my back? Can I do it, for instance, without ever using the second-order quantification that Geach (1967) also challenges?) I suppose not. But I don't see why that should make me doubt that I know the difference between identity and indiscernibility.

We have the concept of identity, *pace* Geach; and if we are to justify denying that the cats are many, we need to show that they are inter-related by a relation closely akin to identity itself. Geach has not shown this, and wouldn't wish to show it. Nevertheless it can be shown, as we shall soon see. But at that point we shall have a solution that by-passes Geach's doctrine of relative identity altogether.

PARTIAL IDENTITY: THE MANY ARE ALMOST ONE

What is the opposite of identity? *Non*-identity, we'd offhand say. Anything is identical to itself; otherwise we have two 'different' things, two 'distinct' things; that is, two non-identical things. Of course it's true that things are either identical or non-identical, and never both. But the real opposite of identity is distinctness: not distinctness in the sense of non-identity, but rather distinctness in the sense of non-overlap (what is called 'disjointness' in the jargon of those who reserve 'distinct' to mean 'non-identical'). We have a spectrum of cases. At one end we find the complete identity of a thing with itself: it and itself are entirely identical, not at all distinct. At the opposite end we find the case of two things that are entirely distinct: They have no part in common. In between we find all the cases of partial overlap: things with parts in common and other parts not in common. (Sometimes one of the overlappers is part of the other, sometimes not.) The things are not entirely identical, not entirely distinct, but some of each. They are partially identical, partially distinct. There may be more overlap or less. Some cases are close to the distinctness end of the spectrum: Siamese twins who share only a finger are almost completely distinct, but not quite. Other cases are close to the identity end. For instance, any two of our cat candidates overlap almost completely. They differ by only a few hairs. They are not quite completely identical, but they are almost completely identical and very far from completely distinct.

It's strange how philosophers have fixed their attention on one end of the spectrum and forgotten how we ordinarily think of identity and distinctness. You'd think the philosophers of common sense and ordinary language would have set us right long ago, but in fact it was Armstrong (1978, Vol. 2, pp. 37–8) who did the job. Overshadowed though it is by Armstrong's still more noteworthy accomplishments, this service still deserves our attention and gratitude.

Assume our cat-candidates are genuine cats. (Set aside, for now, the supervaluationist solution.) Then, strictly speaking, the cats are many. No two of them are completely identical. But any two of them are almost completely identical; their differences are negligible, as I said before. We have many cats, each one almost identical to all the rest.

Remember how we translate statements of number into the language of identity and quantification. 'There is one cat on the mat' becomes 'For some x, x is a cat on the mat, and every cat on the mat is identical to x'. That's false, if we take 'identical' to express the complete and strict identity that lies at the end of the spectrum. But the very extensive overlap of the cats does approximate to complete identity. So what's true is that for some x, x is a cat on the mat, and every cat on the mat is almost identical to x. In this way, the statement that there is one cat on the mat is almost true. The cats are many, but almost one. By a blameless approximation, we may say simply that there is one cat on the mat. Is that true? – Sometimes we'll insist on stricter standards, sometimes we'll be ambivalent, but for most contexts it's true enough. Thus the idea of partial and approximate identity affords another solution to the paradox of 1001 cats.

The added noun phrase has nothing to do with it. Because of their extensive overlap, the many are almost the same cat; they are almost the same lump of feline tissue; and so on for any other noun phrase that applies to them all. Further, the relation of almost-identity, closely akin to the complete identity that we call identity *simpliciter*, is not a relation of partial indiscernibility. Of course we can expect almost-identical things to be very similar in a great many ways: size, shape, location, weight, purring, behaviour, not to mention relational properties like location and ownership. But it is hard to think of any very salient respect in which almost-identical things are guaranteed to be entirely indiscernible. Finally, the relation of almost-identity, in other words extensive overlap, is not in general an equivalence relation. Many steps of almost-identity can take us from one thing to another thing that is entirely distinct from the first. We may hope that almost-identity, when restricted to the many cats as they actually are, will be an equivalence relation; but even that is not entirely guaranteed. It depends on the extent to which the cats differ, and on the threshold for almost-identity (and both of these are matters that we will, very sensibly, leave undecided). What this solution has in common with Geach's is just that we count the cats by a relation other than strict, 'absolute' identity. Beyond that, the theories differ greatly.[9]

ONE SOLUTION TOO MANY?

We find ourselves with two solutions, and that is one more than we needed. Shall we now choose between the way of supervaluation and the way of partial identity? I think not. We might better combine them. We shall see how each can assist the other.

Here is how to combine them. In the first place, there are two kinds of intended interpretations of our language. Given many almost-identical cat-candidates, some will put every (good enough) candidate into the extension of 'cat'; others will put exactly one. Context will favour one sort of interpretation or the other, though not every context will settle the matter. Sometimes, especially in our offhand and unphilosophical moments, context will favour the second, one-cat sort of interpretation; and then the supervaluation rule, with nothing to defeat it, will entitle us to say that there is only one cat. But sometimes,

9 There is another way we sometimes count by a relation other than strict identity. You draw two diagonals in a square; you ask me how many triangles; I say there are four; you deride me for ignoring the four large triangles and counting only the small ones. But the joke is on you. For I was within my rights as a speaker of ordinary language, and you couldn't see it because you insisted on counting by strict identity. I meant that, for some w, x, y, z, (1) w, x, y, and z are triangles; (2) w and x are distinct, and . . . and so are y and z (six clauses); and (3) for any triangle t, either t and w are not distinct, or . . . or t and z are not distinct (four clauses). And by 'distinct' I meant non-overlap rather than non-identity, so what I said was true.

for instance when we have been explicitly attending to the many candidates and noting that they are equally cat-like, context will favour the first, many-cat sort of interpretation. (If we start with one-cat interpretations, and we say things that the supervaluation rule would make hash of, not only is the rule suspended but also the many-cat interpretations come into play.) But even then, we still want some good sense in which there is just one cat (though we may want a way to say the opposite as well). That is what almost-identity offers.

This is one way that almost-identity helps a combined solution. It is still there even when we discuss the paradox of 1001 cats, and we explicitly choose to say that the many are all cats, and we thereby make the supervaluation solution go away.

Perhaps it helps in another way too. The supervaluation rule is more natural in some applications than in others. For instance it seems artificial to apply it to a case of unrelated homonyms. 'You said you were going to the bank. Is that true? No worries, you bank at the ANZ, it's right down by the river, so what you said was true either way!' – I don't think such a response is utterly forbidden, but it's peculiar in a way that other applications of the supervaluation rule are not. The two interpretations of 'bank' are so different that presumably you did make up your mind which one you meant. So the means for coping with semantic indecision are out of place. The supervaluation rule comes natural only when the alternative interpretations don't differ too much. If they are one-cat interpretations that differ only by picking almost-identical cats, that's one way for them not to differ much.

How, on the other hand, do supervaluations help the combined solution? Why not let almost-identity do the whole job?

For one thing, not every case of the problem of the many is like the paradox of 1001 cats. The almost-identity solution won't always work well.[10] We've touched on one atypical case already: if not a problem of the many, at least a problem of two. Fred's house taken as including the garage, and taken as not including the garage, have equal claim to be his house. The claim had better be good enough, else he has no house. So Fred has two houses. No! We've already seen how

10 Here I'm indebted to Phillip Bricker (personal communication, 1990).

to solve this problem by the method of supervaluations. (If that seemed good to you, it shows that the difference between the interpretations was not yet enough to make the supervaluation rule artificial.) But although the two house-candidates overlap very substantially, having all but the garage in common, they do not overlap nearly as extensively as the cats do. Though they are closer to the identity end of the spectrum than the distinctness end, we cannot really say they're almost identical. So likewise we cannot say that the two houses are almost one.

For another thing, take a statement different from the statements of identity and number that have concerned us so far. Introduce a definite description: 'The cat on the mat includes hair h_{17}'. The obvious response to this statement, I suppose, is that it is gappy. It has no definite truth-value, or no definite super-truth-value, as the case may be. But how can we get that answer if we decide that all the cat-candidates are cats, forsake supervaluations, and ask almost-identity to do the whole job? We might subject the definite description to Russellian translation:

(R1) There is something that is identical to all and only cats on the mat, and that includes h_{17}.

Or equivalently:

(R2) Something is identical to all and only cats on the mat, and every cat on the mat includes h_{17}.

Both these translations come out false, because nothing is strictly identical to all and only cats on the mat. That's not the answer we wanted. So we might relax 'identical' to 'almost identical'. When we do, the translations are no longer equivalent: (R1)-relaxed is true, (R2)-relaxed is false. Maybe we're in a state of semantic indecision between (R1)-relaxed and (R2)-relaxed; if so, we could apply the supervaluation rule to get the desired gappiness. Or we might apply the supervaluation rule more directly. Different one-cat interpretations pick out different things as the cat, some that include h_{17} and some that don't. Under any particular one-cat interpretation the Russellian translations are again equivalent, and different one-cat interpretations give them different truth values; so the translations, and likewise the original sentence, suffer super-truth-value gaps. Or more simply, different one-cat interpretations differ in the referent of 'the cat'; some of these referents satisfy 'includes h_{17}' and some don't, so again we get a super-truth-value gap. Whichever way we go, supervaluations give us the gappiness we want. It's hard to see how else to get it.

REFERENCES

Armstrong, D. M. 1978. *Universals and Scientific Realism*, 2 vols. (Cambridge University Press).

Evans, Gareth. 1978. 'Can There be Vague Objects?', *Analysis* 38: 208. Reprinted in *Collected Papers* (Oxford University Press, 1985).

Geach, P. T. 1967. 'Identity', *Review of Metaphysics* 21: 3–12. Reprinted in *Logic Matters* (Oxford: Blackwell, 1972), pp. 238–47.

1980. *Reference and Generality*, 3rd ed. (Ithaca, NY: Cornell University Press).

Lewis, David. 1976. 'Survival and Identity'. In *The Identities of Persons*, ed. Amélie Rorty (Berkeley: University of California Press), pp. 17–40. Reprinted in Lewis, *Philosophical Papers*, vol. 1 (Oxford University Press, 1983), pp. 55–72.

1984. 'Putnam's Paradox', *Australasian Journal of Philosophy* 62: 221–36 (reprinted in this volume as Chapter 2).

1986a. *On the Plurality of Worlds* (Oxford: Blackwell).

1988. 'Vague Identity: Evans Misunderstood', *Analysis* 48: 128–30.

Lowe, E. J. 1982. 'The Paradox of the 1,001 Cats', *Analysis* 42: 27–30.

Unger, Peter. 1980. 'The Problem of the Many', *Midwest Studies in Philosophy* 5: 411–67.

van Fraassen, Bas C. 1966. 'Singular Terms, Truth-Value Gaps, and Free Logic', *Journal of Philosophy* 63: 481–95.

van Inwagen, Peter. 1990. *Material Beings* (Ithaca, NY: Cornell University Press).

10

Casati and Varzi on holes

WITH STEPHANIE LEWIS

Roberto Casati and Achille Varzi, *Holes and Other Superficialities,* MIT Press, Bradford Books, 1994.

Argle. I've said it before and I'll say it again: all things are material. Either holes are somehow material, or else there are no such things. Maybe a hole is the material hole-lining that, as we so misleadingly say, "surrounds" the hole; or else whatever ostensible reference we make to holes is secretly some other sort of language-game altogether, or it's fictitious reference, or it's just plain mistaken.

Bargle. You're ready to say *anything,* aren't you, so long as it isn't plain common sense. Of course what's true is that holes are *im*material entities. – But what do these fellows think?

Casati and Varzi. Exactly so, Bargle: holes are immaterial entities. As Tucholsky put it: a hole *is,* where something *isn't.*

Argle. If there were no matter at all, there'd be one big hole?

Casati and Varzi. No; a hole is always a hole *in* something: a cavity in the cheese, a hollow in a glass bottle, a tunnel through rock. A hole requires a host; and these hosts are material. (Normally, anyway; a hole in the electromagnetic field might be a region where the field vector is uniformly zero. Let's ignore these special cases here.) No matter, no

First published in *The Philosophical Review*, 105 (1996), 77–79. Copyright 1996 Cornell University. Reprinted with kind permission from Stephanie Lewis and the publisher of *The Philosophical Review*.

hosts; no hosts; no holes. Holes are *dependent* entities: they exist in virtue of the arrangement of matter.

Bargle. Right! And the hole is immaterial through and through, and the host is material; and besides, the hole is where the host isn't. So the host and the hole are entirely distinct – the clearest case ever of necessary connection between distinct existences. And there's another of Argle's prejudices punctured!

Argle. Right! The hole is redundant: it supervenes upon the arrangement of matter. So it is no genuine addition to reality; it is nothing over and above the matter it supervenes on. Its being – if being it be – must *not* be taken with ontological seriousness![1]

Casati and Varzi. Steady on. These are deep matters, and there's a lot we can say without becoming embroiled in them. Whether or not the dependence of holes upon matter means what either one of you thinks it means, at least it does mean that hole-statements are true or false in virtue of the arrangement of matter. While we do have a view about the nature of holes – we endorse Bargle's common sense, we reject the alternatives Argle has on offer – it scarcely matters. Take some hole-statements: that a hole is present in a certain material host; or that it is one or another kind of hole, cavity or tunnel or hollow or whatever; or that one hole is part of another; or that the same hole that was here yesterday is here today, though expanded or even shifted; or instead that there's a new and different hole; or. . . . It's the arrangement of matter that makes these statements true or false. You, Bargle, will agree with us that the hole-statements depend for their truth upon the holes, which in turn depend for their existence upon the arrangement of matter; whereas Argle will think that the truth of the hole-statements somehow depends more directly upon the arrangement of matter; but, either way, *our* job is to say how the truth of the hole-statements depends upon the arrangement of matter. And about that, we have quite a lot to say.

1 Evidently Argle is a student of D. M. Armstrong, "Metaphysics and Supervenience," *Critica* 14 (1982): 3–18.

Argle and Bargle. You do indeed. We're impressed. But we do have a few questions for you. Take your taxonomy of holes, and stick to the simplest cases. There are cavities, with no entrance from the outside; hollows, with one entrance; tunnels, with two or more entrances . . .

Casati and Varzi. And depressions: holes that are like hollows except that their entrances begin gradually, without a sharp edge to demarcate the surface inside the hole from the surface outside.

Bargle. Yes – for instance a test tube with a lip hosts a depression, whereas one without a lip hosts a hollow. That's our problem. On page 6, you "distinguish three basic kinds of holes"; but on page 40 it's four. We think you had it right the first time. Why do you divide hollows from depressions by whether there's a demarcating edge, when you don't divide other holes on the same principle? Some tunnels have entrances like the entrances of depressions, whereas others have entrances like the entrances of hollows . . .

Argle. . . . And even a single tunnel might have one kind of entrance at one end and the other at the other; or, if it's a branching tunnel, two entrances of one kind and six of the other.

Bargle. And even a cavity might have a sharp edge dividing part of its inner surface from another part.

Argle. What happens when you fill a hole? No hole any more, right?

Casati and Varzi. That depends. In the first place, you might fill it incompletely, leaving a cavity. In the second place, you might leave a crack where the surface of the hole used to be – a thin hole, maybe even a mere two-dimensional hole, but still a hole. But most important, you might fill it with the wrong sort of matter. A hole in the ground, filled with air or water, is still a hole. A hole in wood, filled with hardened putty, is still a hole.

Argle. For short: a hole filled seamlessly goes away, a hole filled not seamlessly is still there but it has stuff in it. But what if the host itself is none too seamless? Consider a hollow in a pile of miscellaneous rubbish. Fill the hollow with more miscellaneous rubbish. Plenty of inhomogeneity, plenty of cracks, plenty of cavities and hollows and tunnels; but the big hole you filled is gone without a trace.

Bargle. That's part of a bigger problem. You have foremost in mind the case of a hole hosted by homogeneous and cohesive matter. But not all holes are hosted by homogeneous and cohesive matter. In fact, when you think of it microscopically, there's no such thing as homogeneous matter — not in our world, anyway. And cohesiveness is very much a matter of degree.

Argle. Can you have a hole in a big dense swarm of bees?

Bargle. Can you have a hole in a stream of oncoming traffic? If not, how can you ever turn onto a busy road?

Argle. Perhaps some holes are strictly and literally holes, whereas others are holes by courtesy: holes by some sort of metaphorical extension from the case where the host is homogeneous and cohesive. But where do you draw the line?

Bargle. Last question. Why did you call hole-linings *Ludovician* holes? That's what *Argle* thinks holes are. But who appointed *him* the spokesman for our authors?

11

Rearrangement of particles: Reply to Lowe

I. BACKGROUND

Ordinary things, for instance we ourselves, undeniably persist through time. As we persist, we change. And not just in extrinsic ways, as when a child was born elsewhere and I became an uncle. We also change in our own intrinsic character, in the way we ourselves are, apart from our relationships to anything else. When I sit I'm bent, when I stand I'm straight. When I change my shape, that isn't a matter of my changing relationship to other things, or my relationship to other changing things. *I* do the changing, all by myself. Or so it seems. What happens must be possible. But how? Nothing can have the two incompatible shapes, bent and straight. How does having them at different times help? In *On the Plurality of Worlds* (Blackwell, 1986; henceforth *PoW*), p. 204, I listed three solutions, and said that only the third was tenable.

The first solution is that the 'properties' are really relations to times. That lets us say that things persist by *enduring*: the one thing is present at different times; and not mere temporal parts of it, different parts at different times, but *all* of it, wholly present at each of the times. The whole of me stands in the bent-at relation to some times and the straight-at relation to others. I complained that shapes are

First published in *Analysis* 48 (1988), pp. 65–72.

I thank Donald Baxter, Sally Haslanger, Mark Hinchliff, and especially Mark Johnston for helpful discussion.

properties, not relations. No doubt a friend of the first solution will draw a distinction that he will *call* the distinction between matters of one's own intrinsic character and matters of one's relationships: having a shape will go on one side, being an uncle on the other. But call it what he will, his account reveals that really he treats shape, no less than unclehood, as a matter of relations. In this account, nothing just has a shape *simpliciter*. The temporary 'intrinsic properties' of things, so understood, do not deserve the name. This solution amounts to a denial that things really do have temporary intrinsics, and therefore is untenable.[1]

The second solution says that there is only one genuine time, the present. Intrinsic properties are genuine properties, and a thing can have them *simpliciter*, without regard to any relationships to anything else. However, the only intrinsic properties it has *simpliciter* are the properties it has *now*. What passes for persistence and change, on this solution, does not really involve other times. Rather, there are 'abstract' ersatz times, to go with the one 'concrete' genuine time. These represent, or misrepresent, the present. If I am bent now, and straight later, there is an abstract misrepresentation of the present according to which I am straight. 'Persistence' and 'change', so understood, do not deserve their names. This solution amounts to a denial of persistence and change, and therefore is untenable.[2]

---

1 The first solution has an 'adverbial' variant, defended in Sally Haslanger, *Change, Persistence, and Possibility* (Ph.D. dissertation, University of California, Berkeley, 1985); and, at least as a possibility, in Mark Johnston, 'Is There a Problem About Persistence?', *Aristotelian Society Supplementary Volume* 61 (1987), pp. 107–35. The adverbial variant avoids my complaint that shapes are not relations. It puts the relationality not in the shapes themselves but in the having of them: there is a three-place relation of instantiation, this relation holds between me and bentness and some times, and it holds between me and straightness and other times. I ask: what does standing in some relation to straightness have to do with just plain being straight? And the variant still claims that to be shaped is to stand in relations to other things, *inter alia* to times. I say it still amounts to a denial that things have temporary intrinsics.

2 The second solution also has an 'adverbial' variant, defended in discussion by Mark Hinchliff. It omits or plays down the ersatz times. Instead, temporal modifiers introduce relations of things to properties. If I am now bent, bent is just the way I am; whereas if I will be straight later, I stand in some relation to straightness which does not involve any having *simpliciter* of straightness by anything. Change between two

The third solution, the tenable one, is that incompatible temporary intrinsic properties do not all belong to the same thing. A persisting thing *perdures*. It consists of temporal parts, or *stages*, different ones at different times, which differ in their intrinsic properties. When I sit and then stand, bent stages are followed by straight stages. Each stage has its shape *simpliciter*. Shape is truly intrinsic.

To be sure, my shapes belong in the first instance to my stages, and in a derivative, relational way to the whole of me. Persisting thing x is bent at time t iff some stage of x is at t and is bent. What distinguishes the first solution from the third is not that the third does away with shape-at-a-time relations. Rather, it is that the first has wrongly done away with shapes as intrinsic properties that can be had *simpliciter*.

Imagine trying to draw a picture of two different times, t_1 when I sit and t_2 when I stand. You draw two circles, overlapping because I exist at both times so you want to draw me in the intersection. But then you have to draw me bent and also straight, which you can't do; and if *per impossibile* you could, you still wouldn't have done anything to connect the bentness to t_1 and the straightness to t_2 instead of *vice versa*. What to do? The first solution says to draw the circles overlapping, draw me in the intersection as a mere dot or shapeless blob, draw a line labelled 'bent-at' from me to the t_1 circle, and a line labelled 'straight-at' from me to the t_2 circle. A queer way to draw a shape! The second solution says to draw only the t_1 circle, and in it draw me bent; and then draw not another circle but an abstract misrepresenter saying that I'm straight. The third solution says to draw two *non*overlapping circles, in the t_1 circle draw me bent, in the t_2 circle draw me straight, and then draw a connexion to indicate that the bent me plus the straight me add up to a single person.

times, one of them the present, is the modified-having of a property incompatible with a property the thing simply has. Change between two non-present times is modified-having of two incompatible properties. But the modified-having itself goes on in the present. I ask again: what does standing in some relation to straightness have to do with just plain being straight? And the variant still denies that 'persistence' and 'change' involve any genuine times except the present. I say it still amounts to a denial of persistence and change.

II. LOWE'S FOURTH SOLUTION

In his 'Lewis on Perdurance Versus Endurance' (*Analysis* 47.3, June 1987, pp. 152–54), E. J. Lowe agrees that we need a solution, and joins me in rejecting the first and second solutions. But he rejects the third solution as well. He finds it 'scarcely intelligible' to say that things like people or puddles, as opposed to events or processes, have temporal parts. I disagree; but won't repeat here what I have said elsewhere about the intelligibility of temporal parts.[3] Lowe does find perdurance intelligible enough to be denied, and deny it he does.[4] After rejecting all three solutions, Lowe is urgently in need of a fourth.

I too would welcome a fourth solution, but for quite a different reason. If the third solution alone is tenable, then our common-sense belief in persisting things commits us implicitly to perdurance – and this despite the fact that some of us firmly reject the notion of temporal parts (except of events or processes) and many more have never heard of it! It would be better not to impute such surprising commitments to common sense, but only the plain commitment that things do somehow persist, never mind exactly how they do it.[5] If we had two tenable solutions – some sort of endurance theory, as well as the perdurance theory – to suspend judgement between, then such restraint would be feasible as well as sensible. Then we could leave the question of endurance versus perdurance forever unsettled, or perhaps settle it by finding out which coheres better with total science. At any rate we could *not* settle it 'philosophically', by

---

3 In my *Philosophical Papers*, Volume I (Oxford University Press, 1983), pp. 76–7.

4 It is odd that when Lowe denies perdurance, he does not embrace endurance. I should have thought it automatic that if a persisting thing is present at a time, and not just partly present, then it must be wholly present. Lowe doesn't say why he finds 'wholly present at a time' problematic. Maybe he thinks the phrase carries a presupposition that the thing has, or at least is of a kind to have, temporal parts. I intend no such presupposition. If you think it is there, let it hereby be suspended. Then we may carry on saying that a thing 'endures' if it persists without having temporal parts; *a fortiori* if it persists and is of such a kind that it cannot intelligibly have temporal parts.

5 Here I follow the lead of Johnston, op. cit.

drawing out unsuspected consequences of common-sense intuitions. But if we're stuck with the third solution alone, restraint is beyond our reach.

Here is Lowe's fourth solution. Science teaches that things consist of particles. A change of shape for the thing, for instance for me when I sit and then stand, is a rearrangement of its particles. (Likewise for other intrinsic changes, for instance in my temperature or neural activity.) When the particles are rearranged, they undergo a change in their relations to one another; but no change in their intrinsic properties. In fact, it seems likely that fundamental particles *never* change their intrinsic properties. An electron or a quark has a certain charge, rest mass, and so on; all constant, from the creation of the particle to its destruction, no matter how the particle may move around and change its relations to other particles. There is no problem of intrinsic change for particles, if they have no temporary intrinsics. Particles, at least, may safely be supposed to endure; and larger things consist of these enduring particles, undergoing rearrangement but no intrinsic change.[6]

III. FIRST OBJECTION, AND A REPLY

It may be true that particles have no temporary intrinsics. But it is far from certain, and far from necessary. Lowe's solution is at risk from scientific surprises. He might read in tomorrow's paper that the charges of electrons and quarks are not constant after all. They undergo fluctuations too small to detect with yesterday's instruments. If so, must Lowe conclude, after all, that there is no way he can

---

6 I wrote concerning 'fundamental particles *or momentary slices thereof*' (italics added) that 'maybe these things have no accidental intrinsic properties' and hence 'we would not face a problem of accidental intrinsics' for them (*PoW*, p. 205). Lowe cites this as conceding the point he needs; which is peculiar, because accidental intrinsics are not the same thing as temporary intrinsics. For instance a particle might well have the shape of its entire spatiotemporal trajectory as an *accidental*, but certainly not *temporary*, intrinsic property – wherefore my italicized phrase.

No harm done. Though the two hypotheses are independent, it is at least as probable that particles lack temporary intrinsics as it is that they, or their slices, lack accidental intrinsics.

persist? So it seems; because his solution to the problem of his own intrinsic change requires him to consist of particles not subject to intrinsic change.

Likewise, Lowe's solution makes no sense of counterfactual suppositions about persisting people in a world where particles fluctuate in charge. Such a world is possible – at any rate, counterfactual suppositions about it are intelligible – even if it contravenes the actual laws of nature. It doesn't matter whether the otherworldly fluctuating particles are genuine electrons and quarks, so long as some things made of these particles are genuine people – which they well might be.

I offer Lowe this reply. In the case of ordinary large things, such as ourselves, we are entitled to firm intuitions about what should count as just the way the thing itself is, and not at all a matter of relationships. For instance, we should be firm in resisting the idea that our shapes are really relations to times. But it is otherwise for the 'properties' of particles; even for the most familiar ones, charge and rest mass, let alone the new-found 'spins' and 'flavours' and 'colours'. It is up for grabs whether these are as intrinsic as we offhand think. Lacking close acquaintance with the submicroscopic realm, we should be open-minded. If charge turns out to fluctuate, and if our only solution to the problem of persistence requires that particles never undergo intrinsic change, that might be reason enough to conclude that charge – unlike shape! – is really a relation to times. Or if we suppose counterfactually that charge fluctuates, we might insist on making it part of the supposition that charge is not, after all, an intrinsic property.

IV. SECOND OBJECTION, AND A REPLY

Even if the problem of temporary intrinsic *properties* goes away, for particles at least, there is still a problem of temporary intrinsic *relations*.[7]

7 It corresponds to the problem of accidental external relations noted in *PoW*, pp. 205–6, just after the 'concession' Lowe cited. 'External' relations, in one sense of the term, are those intrinsic relations that do not merely supervene on the intrinsic characters of their *relata*.

Exactly as some properties are just a matter of how the thing itself is, without regard to any relationship to any second thing, so some relations are just a matter of how two things are *vis-à-vis* one another, without regard to any relationship to any third thing. The relation is intrinsic to the pair of *relata*. The ever-changing distances of particles from one another seem to be temporary intrinsic relations. Rearrangement of particles poses the same old problem of temporary intrinsics, except that now it is a problem about intrinsic relations rather than intrinsic properties. How can the same two things stand in different, incompatible intrinsic relations? How can the same two particles have two different distances? How does it help that they have them at different times?

We have three solutions, as before. First solution: particles have their temporary distances by standing in different relationships to different times. They endure, so whatever relations they enter into must be relations of the entire enduring particle. But there is no such thing as being a certain distance apart *simpliciter*. Instead there are three-place distance-at-a-time relations. This solution is untenable because it amounts to a denial that distances are intrinsic relations. Second solution: there is only one genuine time, the present, and the only distance there is between two particles is their distance *now*. What passes for persistence and change is the abstract misrepresentation of this one time, according to which the two particles exist and have some different distance. This solution is untenable because it amounts to a denial of persistence and change. Third solution: the particles perdure, and it is in the first instance their temporal parts that are various distances apart. Lowe will reject this as 'scarcely intelligible'. Properties or relations, it's all the same problem. What has Lowe gained?

Try again drawing the circles for t_1 and t_2, overlapping now because a certain two particles exist at both times and so you want to draw them in the intersection. They've undergone rearrangement, as particles often do. You have to draw them at two different distances apart, which you can't do; and if *per impossibile* you could, you still wouldn't have done anything to connect one distance to t_1 and the other to t_2 instead of *vice versa*. What to do?

I offer Lowe this reply. Suppose he is prepared to accept a substantival theory of spacetime, and one that distinguishes occupants of spacetime from the regions of spacetime they occupy. It might be nicer to stay neutral, but if Lowe has the problem about persistence that he thinks he has, a solution would be worth the commitment. Then for each particle, there is a spacetime region that is its trajectory. Lowe might grant that a spacetime region has temporal parts: it is like an event or process, unlike a person or puddle or particle. Suppose (for convenience only) that the particles are point-sized; then the smallest temporal parts of their trajectories are spacetime points. An enduring particle is wholly present at each point on its trajectory. Distances are intrinsic relations, sure enough; but of points, not particles. When two points are a certain distance apart, that's just a matter of how the two points are *vis-à-vis* one another, regardless of any relationship to any third thing. Enduring particles have their distances in a derivative and relational way: particles x and y are one metre apart at t iff points p and q are one metre apart, p and q are at t, p is one of the points where x is, and q is one of the points where y is. So in the first instance it is the trajectories that undergo rearrangement. They change their distances from one another in the unproblematic fashion of perdurers. Their different temporal parts, at different times, are at different distances. The particles undergo rearrangement vicariously: their trajectories do it for them. All the particle has to do is to occupy each point of its trajectory. That requires no change in intrinsic relations. The particle need only bear the same intrinsic relation of occupancy to each of many points.

Draw the circles overlapping; put the particles themselves in the intersection; but put all the spacetime points which the particles occupy outside the intersection, some in the t_1 circle and some in the t_2 circle. Draw lines of occupancy from the particles to their points.

This might be acceptable, as a last resort, if we had eliminated the alternatives. It is peculiar to say that the particle is only indirectly involved in its own relationships of distance; but at least these turn out to be proper intrinsic relationships of *something*, and what's more, something intimately associated with the particle. What makes this picture of endurance barely acceptable is that it has so much *per*durance mixed in.

Waive the first two objections. Give Lowe enduring particles, and their rearrangement. I want to ask: what has this to do with *me?* My particles endure, but what do I do?

A strange worry. Surely I am nothing over and above my particles: I am them, they are me. The 'are' of composition is just the plural of the 'is' of identity. So if it's settled what they do, there can't be any further question what I do. You might as well say: I know all about the life of Cicero, now what about Tully?

I can agree to this, or near enough; but Lowe can't. Strictly speaking, of course, neither of us can say that I am my particles. If I were, I would exist whenever they do; but I don't. My beginning was a rearrangement of preexisting particles; my end will be a rearrangement of particles that will exist afterward. Further, I eat and excrete; so I cannot be identical both to the particles I was composed of yesterday and to those I am composed of today. But for me, as a perdurance theorist, the correction is close at hand. I consist of temporal segments of particles. So what's true to say, by way of identifying myself with my particles, is that I am my particle-segments. But for Lowe, who rejects particle-segments, this correction will be 'scarcely intelligible'. I think he has no other way to make sense of saying that I just *am* my particles. Composition as identity is not for him.

He will need, instead, to understand composition as a one–many relation of things that are in no sense identical. (It will be a temporary intrinsic relation, and so will give him a new problem of temporary intrinsics.) The relation of me to my particles is an interesting and intimate one, no doubt. But if it is not identity, then to say that my particles endure is simply not to address the question whether *I* endure; and how, if I do endure, I manage to undergo intrinsic change. What my particles do is, strictly speaking, irrelevant. Lowe has not offered any fourth solution, satisfactory or otherwise, to the problem of my intrinsic change. Rather, he has changed the subject.

12

Armstrong on combinatorial possibility

D. M. Armstrong, *A Combinatorial Theory of Possibility*,
Cambridge University Press, 1989.

TWO UNFAMILIAR QUESTIONS, JOINTLY ANSWERED

Later we shall see how Armstrong answers some familiar questions
about the metaphysics of modality. But the core of his theory lies
elsewhere. He raises two *un*familiar questions, and answers them
jointly as follows.

(1) What is the range of different possibilities? – The range of all recombinations of actually instantiated universals.
(2) What does it take to make a possibility statement true? – The
universals thus recombined.

ARMSTRONG'S COMBINATORIALISM:
THE POSITIVE SIDE

The range-of-possibilities question is everyone's question. It can be
framed in different ways to suit different views about the nature of
possibilities; and no matter how we frame it, we can, if we like, borrow

First published in *The Australasian Journal of Philosophy* 70 (1992), pp. 211–224. Reprinted with kind permission from *The Australasian Journal of Philosophy*.

Armstrong's answer. We can say that for any way of recombining all or some of the universals that are found within our actual world, there is another 'concrete' world wherein these constituents are thus recombined; or there is an 'abstract' ersatz world that represents these universals as being thus recombined; or it is primitively possible, without benefit of any entities to play the role of possible worlds, that they might have been thus recombined.

If we like, we can say positively, as Armstrong (almost) does, that no recombination is excluded: there are no exclusions or necessary connections between genuine, distinct universals. Roughly, anything can coexist with anything, and anything can fail to coexist with anything.

It does seem that we have mutually exclusive properties, gamuts of alternative determinates of the same determinable. If we are to follow Armstrong, we must diagnose any such case in one of three ways. (1) The exclusive properties may not be genuine universals: for instance, when F excludes non-F. A genuine universal must be quite specific, else its miscellaneous instances could not plausibly be thought to have some one thing in common. It's unlikely that F and non-F both would qualify. Or (2) the exclusive properties may be genuine universals that are not wholly distinct: conjunctive or structural universals, built up somehow out of simpler universals, with common constituents. Shapes are mutually exclusive, for instance, and shapes are structural if anything is. Armstrong suggests that more cases of exclusion could be treated in the same way: colours, for instance, if colours are really structural properties of the coloured surface. Or mass, if we identify being five kilograms with the structural property of consisting of five distinct one-kilogram parts. (But here I see a problem. Armstrong's explanation of why different mass properties are exclusive, pp. 78–79, seems to presuppose that a whole cannot share a universal with its own part. Why not? If something has a mass of five kilograms by consisting of five one-kilogram parts, how does that prevent it from also having a mass of one kilogram?) Or (3) the exclusion may be not an absolutely necessary exclusion, but a merely lawful exclusion. Suppose that unit positive and negative charge really are as simple as current theory says they are. Then Armstrong's combinatorialism decrees that it is possible *simpliciter* that a single particle might have both charges at once; but if this possibility violates the contingent laws of nature, that might be exclusion enough.

It is essential to have the third diagnosis available. Else we run the risk that metaphysics may force us to posit hidden structure where science discerns none. We might indeed discover that charge was a matter of hidden structure, but we have no business discovering it by philosophy! But when we look up Armstrong's account of exclusion laws in *What is a Law of Nature?* (Cambridge: Cambridge University Press, 1983), pp. 143–146, we hit trouble. He says, for good reasons that I won't repeat here, that exclusion laws are derived laws. A law that no F is a G must be a consequence of some positive law that every F is an H, where H excludes G. And the exclusion between H and G is not a further law, on pain of regress; it is an absolutely necessary exclusion. Further, we cannot assume that the excluder H is a structural universal, on pain, again, of letting philosophy dictate to science. In short: since combinatorialism disallows necessary exclusion between distinct universals, it must allow exclusion laws as a substitute; but exclusion laws turn out to depend on necessary exclusion! The problem for Armstrong is urgent. I shall return to it later, and offer at least the beginning of a solution.

COMBINATORIALISM: THE NEGATIVE SIDE

The other side of Armstrong's combinatorialism is the thesis that re-combination gives all the possibilities there are. There is no 'outer sphere' of possibilities wherein are found new and different universals, alien to the actual world. There could not, for instance, have been some extra fundamental properties of fundamental particles.

Surely it is possible in *some* sense that there might have been alien universals. That is not to be denied. What may be up for grabs, though, is whether to reclassify such outer-sphere possibilities as merely doxastic (or epistemic) possibilities. When we think some long sentence in a logic exercise 'might' be true, when really it is contradictory, ignorance masquerades as contingency; and to follow Armstrong, we must say the same about our offhand impression that there 'might' have been universals different from all the ones there actually are. It matters little whether we call an outer-sphere possibility a genuine possibility, or whether we call it a merely doxastic possibility instead. What's in a name? What does matter, though, is that we must have a serious theory of these outer-sphere whatchamacallums, alongside our combinatorial theory of the inner sphere. And here Armstrong still owes us something. His section on doxastically possible worlds (pp. 73–76) doesn't help, because it mostly concerns the doxastic possibilities that arise if we take universals to be wholly distinct when really they are not. That is a different case. He does say (p. 73) that alien universals 'fit smoothly into the present account of doxastically possible worlds' but doesn't really explain how. We must still await his developed theory of the outer sphere.

WHAT IS THERE TO RECOMBINE?

Almost anyone could be some kind of combinatorialist. But Armstrong's own brand of combinatorialism depends heavily upon his account of the constitution of this world – *the* world, if he is right, the one and only world. What possibilities we get by recombining the elements of the world depends on what those elements are. If we think the elements are point particles, we can use recombination to generate all manner of weird and wonderful rearrangements of particles, but we cannot get new kinds of particles. We can combine the head and neck of an emu with the body of a kangaroo, but not the mass of an electron with the charge of a quark. (We might still think such novel particles were possible, but not in virtue of any principle of recombination.) Whereas if we think with Armstrong that even the smallest particles are 'layer-cakes' made of a particular substratum plus several universals, one for mass and one for charge and so on, then indeed we can get new kinds of particles by recombining the layers of the cake.

For Armstrong, the world is made of universals and 'thin' particulars, always bound together into states of affairs. A state of affairs Fa exists if particular a instantiates universal F. (Likewise for dyadic, triadic, . . . universals, if there are any.) 'Thick' particulars, ordinary things like dogs and shoes, consist of states of affairs. The most inclusive of these things, consisting of all the states of affairs there are, is the world. Outside it there is nothing.

To me, it is mysterious how a state of affairs is made out of its particular and universal constituents. We may not think of it as the composition of a whole out of its parts: first, because different states of affairs may have the very same constituents; and second, because the existence of the constituents by no means entails the existence of the state of affairs. It is some sort of unmereological composition, and to my mind, that is a contradiction in terms. In any case the universals, just as if they were literally parts of the world, are the elements available for recombination.

Why just the universals? Why not the universals and particulars both, since both are equal partners in making a state of affairs? As an opening move, Armstrong presents the system of Brian Skyrms' 'Tractarian Nominalism' (reprinted as an appendix), which does indeed apply recombination to the universals and particulars both. But Armstrong revises this bit by bit, and soon arrives at a combinatorialism of universals alone. The particulars ('thin' particulars) are still there, but they function only as interchangeable hooks whereby universals are fastened together in patterns of coinstantiation. For Armstrong, what identifies a possibility is just the pattern in which universals are hooked together, it makes no difference which hooks are used to do the fastening. The possibility Fa & Ga & Fb & aRb is no different from Fb & Gb & Fc & bRc. Armstrong rejects haecceitistic differences between possibilities. In Carnap's terms, his possibilities are given by structure-descriptions, not state-descriptions.

Further, Armstrong's combinatorialism of universals alone is not limited by the actual supply of hooks. Universals are repeatable, and some ways of recombining them involve more extensive repetition than actually happens. Maybe the world is finite in extent and detail, but could have been infinite; maybe it is infinite, but could have had a greater infinite size. A world with more particulars than there actually are seems perfectly possible. Yet it cannot be made just by hanging the universals differently on the same old hooks, if there are not enough hooks to go around. To ensure that a bigger world is possible. Armstrong must admit the possibility of additional hooks.

Armstrong departs in one more way from the simple combinatorialism of 'Tractarian Nominalism'. Once we might have thought that *Hydrogen atom* was a simple universal instantiated by homogeneous blobs of matter; but no, it is a structural universal instantiated by composites of an electron orbiting a proton. We might have thought next that *Proton* was simple; but no, it is a structural universal instantiated by triplets of quarks. Maybe *Quark* is simple; or maybe the simples are still a few levels further down. Or maybe not; maybe the world is infinitely complex. Maybe there are no simples, and all universals are structures built out of simpler universals. Armstrong will not rule out this hypothesis of infinite complexity *a priori*. In case it is true, the recombination of universals that generates alternative possibilities must always be recombination of structural universals. But in that case the universals being recombined are not wholly distinct, as simples would be, so there may be necessary exclusions or connections between them. If *Hydrogen atom* and *Helium atom* were simples, combinatorialism would have to insist that there might have been an atom that was both at once. ('Might' in the sense of absolute possibility, not in the sense of conformity to the laws of nature.) But since they are structural universals, with some of the same simpler universals as shared constituents, they are entitled to be incompatible – as, of course, they are. Structural universals may also be involved in necessary connections: whenever something instantiates *Helium atom*, there must be a part of it that instantiates *Neutron*. We may still hope that unconstrained recombination will reappear when we reach the ultimate simples out of which all these structural universals are constructed – but not if it's structures all the way down.

(The building of structural universals out of simpler universals is no less mysterious than the building of states of affairs. When Armstrong says that *Hydrogen atom* and *Helium atom* are allowed to be incompatible because they are not wholly distinct, I think he relies on an illicit assimilation of unmereological 'composition' to composition rightly so called. But I've said my say 'Against Structural Universals' elsewhere, *Australasian Journal of Philosophy* 64 (1986) pp. 25–46, (reprinted in this volume as Chapter 3), and needn't repeat it here.)

THE DEMAND FOR TRUTH-MAKERS

Armstrong's other central question, what makes possibility statements true, is by no means everyone's question. It presupposes Armstrong's principle that every truth must have a truth-maker: for any true contingent statement, there is some entity whose existence entails that statement. The existence of certain universals entails the truth of any possibility statement that says how those universals might have been recombined. (Since those universals might not have been instantiated, and if so would not have existed, the possibility statement is indeed contingent. If there had been fewer universals to recombine, there would have been fewer possibilities. What is actual, namely a certain roster of universals, might have been impossible. Hence Armstrong's modal logic is S4, without the 'Brouwersche Axiom'.) The existence of the recombinable universals is enough to make the possibility statement true, because no restrictions of exclusion (well, almost none) need to be satisfied. And nothing less will make it true, because there are no possibilities that involve alien universals found nowhere in actuality.

We can scarcely exaggerate the importance of the demand for truthmakers throughout Armstrong's writings; but unfortunately he takes it so much for granted that we may find it hard to recognise when his arguments are premised on it. (It would be a helpful thing for him to give it a much fuller and more explicit discussion.) For instance, consider one part of Armstrong's attack on the 'Ostrich Nominalism' of Quine, Devitt, and many more of us. The Ostrich says 'there are no universals but the proposition that *a* is *F* is perfectly all right as it is'; he 'sees no need for any reductive analyses' of the schema of predication; he thereby dodges a compulsory question (*Universals and Scientific Realism*, Cambridge: Cambridge University Press, 1978, vol. I, pp. 16–17). He 'gives the predicate what has been said to be the privilege of the harlot: power without responsibility. The predicate is informative, it makes a vital contribution to telling us what is the case, the world is different if it is different, yet ontologically it is supposed not to commit us. Nice work: if you can get it.' ('Against "Ostrich" Nominalism', *Pacific Philosophical Quarterly* 61 (1980) p. 443.) What is going on here? When I first read these passages, the best explanation I could find was that Armstrong demanded that we do away with all unanalysed predication. That seemed strange. Because not only the Ostrich, but also Armstrong's own theory, and all the rival theories that Armstrong deems to be wrong but not evasive, must resort to primitive predication sooner or later. Everyone knows that a chain of definitions cannot, without circularity, go on forever. There will always be primitives. So what is *really* going on? I suggest that Armstrong has an unfamiliar notion of analysis. Analysis is not, primarily, a quest for definitions. Rather, it is a quest for truth-makers. The 'harlot's privilege' is not the privilege of using undefined terms. It is the privilege of truth without benefit of truth-makers. The Ostrich should be redefined more generally as one who can't see why true predications have to have truth-makers. Then he needn't be an Ostrich *Nominalist* (as Armstrong says, p. 41). If I were committed to universals myself, I would be an *Ostrich Realist*: I would think it was just true, without benefit of truth-makers, that a particular instantiates a universal.

Or consider Armstrong's idea of a supervenient free lunch (ch. 8, and many other recent writings). If the S's supervene on the R's, in the sense that the existence of the R's entails the existence of the S's, then the S's are a 'free lunch'; they are redundant, given the R's; they are no real addition to our ontology. Why not? After all, Armstrong is not denying that the S's really do exist. He isn't saying, as a Meinongian might, that they are some of the things there are of which we may truly say that there are no such things; or, as a Quinean might, that in saying they exist we are indulging in a misleading *façon de parler*. Nor does he mean that each of the S's is identical to an R. Nor does he mean that each S is composed of R's; a mereological free lunch is only one kind of supervenient free lunch among others. Then what does he mean? I submit that, just as he has an unfamiliar notion of analysis, so he has an unfamiliar notion of ontology. *Pace* Quine, his question is not: what is there? But rather: what does it take to provide truth-makers for all the truths? That way, it makes perfect sense to say that supervenient entities add nothing to our ontology. A supervenient entity is still an entity, but it is altogether superfluous as a truth-maker. If the existence of some R's entails the existence of a certain S which in turn entails the truth of a certain statement, then those R's, taken together, already make the statement true.

It's easy to believe that *some* truths have truth-makers, for instance the existential truth that there are dogs. Dog Harry suffices to make it true. (At least, provided he is essentially a dog, and so could not have existed without a dog existing. That is no problem for Armstrong, since he thinks that at least the thickest version of Harry is essentially a dog; see p. 52.) Dog Milo also suffices to make it true; and so does any other dog.

Other truths are existential truths more or less thinly disguised, for instance the truth that I am an uncle. A disjunction has a truth-maker if either disjunct has one. And we could go on. But should we agree with Armstrong that *every* truth (every contingent truth) has a truth-maker? I think not.

How about negative existential truths? It seems, offhand, that they are true not because things of some kind *do* exist, but rather because counterexamples *don't* exist. They are true for lack of false-makers. Why defy this first impression?

(Don't say: 'Aha! It's a *lack* that makes it true.' The noun is a happenstance of idiom, and to say that a negative existential is true for lack of false-makers is the same as to say that it's true because there aren't any false-makers. The demand for truth-makers might lead one into ontological seriousness about lacks, but not *vice versa*.)

And how about predications? They seem, for the most part, to be true not because of *whether* things are, but because of *how* things are. (Exceptions: those that are equivalent to existentials or negative existentials, as predications of unclehood or bachelorhood are; and those that predicate an essential property.) Even if we grant that ways to be are entities – universals, or properties in some other sense – still the predication is true not in virtue of the mere existence of the thing and the property. It's true just because the thing instantiates the property. So says the Ostrich; why isn't he right?

We've already met Armstrong's truth-makers for predications: the states of affairs. The existence of the state of affairs composed unmereologically out of a and F entails that a is F. Whether states of affairs are crucial to the theory of universals, as Armstrong thinks, or a gratuitous and mysterious addition, as I think, depends on whether he's right that they're needed to do a job of truth-making.

Armstrong's truth-makers for negative existentials first appear in this book (pp. 92–97). Suppose Bruce, Bruce, Bruce, Bruce, and Michael are the entire department. Then there is a relation of *totality* that the aggregate A (or maybe the class) of the Bruces and Michael bears to the property M of being a member of the department; and if that aggregate does bear that relation to that property, then there can be no other members of the department. We may suppose that the relation of totality is a genuine universal T (a dyadic universal, and second-order in its second argument place, being a relation to a property). Then when T is instantiated by A and M, we have a state of affairs $T(A,M)$: a *totality fact*. Its existence entails the negative existential truth that there are no other members of the department, and so is the desired truth-maker. In a similar way, Armstrong appeals to totality facts as truth-makers for negated predications. Suppose universals G and H comprise the entire nature of a; we have a totality fact that relates the aggregate of G and H to the property of being a property of a; the existence of this totality fact entails that a is not also F. Or suppose that Fa, Gb, and aRb are all the (first-order) states of affairs there are; we have a totality fact that relates Fa & Gb & aRb to the property of being a (first-order) state of affairs. The existence of this totality fact entails several negated predications: b is not F, a is not G, and b does not bear R to a. It also entails negative existentials: there are no monadic universals except F and G, no dyadic universals except R, no triadic universals at all; and there are no (first-order) states of affairs except for the given three. Thus the totality fact serves as a truth-maker for several negative truths.

(We may look askance at such properties as being a member of the department, being a property of a, or being a state of affairs. What are these things doing in Armstrong's system? He wouldn't take them to be genuine universals! His answer is that they get in as supervenient free lunches. Insubstantial though these lunches may be, evidently they are good enough to be constituents of states of affairs.)

Totality facts break the rules of combinatorialism. The idea was that anything can coexist with anything, yet these totality facts have as their very *raison d'être* to refuse to coexist with other facts. But sometimes a specialist in exceptional exclusions may come in handy. Recall our problem about exclusion laws: to get them, we needed some absolutely necessary exclusions. And now we have some. Given a universal F, let us use the totality relation to construct a relational property TF, the property of *having F as total nature*. Something instantiates TF iff it instantiates F (and TF) and nothing else. TF does look like a candidate for a genuine universal: its instances are not at all miscellaneous. A state of affairs *TFa* is a totality fact; *pace* combinatorialism, it excludes all other states of affairs involving the particular *a*, for instance *Ga*. Now suppose we have a positive law that every *F* is a *TF*. Then we have the derived exclusion law that no *F* is a *G*. Unfortunately, we have more besides: the derived law is that *F* excludes *all* other universals. Maybe laws involving totality facts could also be made to yield less peculiar, weaker exclusion laws. But I have no space here to discuss how this might be attempted.

TRUTH AND BEING

It is plain to see how much damage Armstrong's demand for truth-makers has done to his combinatorialism. The intuitive price is very high – and all for nothing if, as I think, the demand for truth-makers is wrong in the first place. Yet it is not altogether wrong. I think it is an over-reaction to something right and important and under-appreciated. What's right, roughly speaking, is that truths must have *things* as their subject matter.

The special case of a negative existential is the exception that proves the rule. Exactly because there are no things of the appropriate sort, very little is true about them. The whole truth about arctic penguins is: there aren't any. Whereas the whole truth about antarctic penguins would fill many a book. Indeed, a subject matter can be empty: That's one way for it to be – just one way. But a subject matter can be non-empty in ever so many different ways.

To be less rough, I borrow a slogan from John Bigelow: 'Truth is supervenient on being'. (*The Reality of Numbers*, Oxford: Oxford University Press, 1988, pp. 132–133 and 158–159.) As an Ostrich – a matter on which Bigelow is of two minds – I want to construe 'being' broadly: it covers not only *whether* things are, but also *how* they are. Then the slogan means that no two possibilities can differ about what's true unless they also differ in what things there are, or in how they are. In saying just this much, we do not join Armstrong in demanding truth-makers for negative existentials, or for all predications. Yet I think we do justice to the insight behind his demand: truths are about things, they don't float in a void. The slogan must be rightly construed. 'How things are' must not be taken to cover just any old condition that things satisfy, on pain of trivialization. As often happens, the thought we want is out of reach so long as we burden ourselves with an egalitarian theory of properties. Given Armstrong's sparse theory of universals, 'how things are' could be taken to mean 'which genuine universals things instantiate'. In his 'Real Possibilities', *Philosophical Studies* 53 (1988) pp. 37–64, Bigelow speaks of 'what things there are and how they are arranged'; he surely doesn't mean that truth supervenes on spatiotemporal arrangement alone, but he might well mean 'what particulars and universals there are and how they are arranged into a pattern of coinstantiation'. For myself, since I remain uncommitted about universals, I would prefer a more neutral formulation: truth is supervenient on what things there are and which perfectly natural properties and relations they instantiate.

All too often, philosophical positions posit truths that fail to supervene on being. Consider phenomenalism, with its brute counterfactual truths about nonexistent experience. Armstrong has told us how Charlie Martin long ago persuaded him to smell a rat. ('C. B. Martin, Counterfactuals, Causality, and Conditionals', in John Heil (ed.), *Cause, Mind and Reality: Essays Honouring C. B Martin*, Dordrecht: Kluwer, 1989.) Right! But the way Martin explained the bad smell, namely as the stink of truths without truth-makers, cast suspicion not only on the ratty counterfactuals that well deserved it, but also on innocent negative existentials and predications. By all means find something wrong with phenomenalist counterfactuals. But if my denial that there are arctic penguins is likewise true without benefit of any truth-maker, true just because there aren't any arctic penguins to make it false, then is it really a companion in guilt?

Other philosophical positions that fall victim to the principle that truth is supervenient on being (*a fortiori* to the demand for truth-makers) include Ryleanism, with its brute counterfactuals about nonexistent behaviour. Also, Prior's presentism, which says that although there is nothing outside the present, yet there are past-tensed and future-tensed truths that do not supervene on the present, and hence do not supervene on being. Also, the view that the distinction between laws of nature and accidental regularities is primitive, supervening neither on patterns in the array of particular fact nor on relations of universals. Exercise: find more.

Besides his questions about the range of possibilities and the truth-makers for possibility statements, Armstrong addresses other questions more familiar to metaphysicians of modality.

(3) Do we need any primitive modal concepts? – No.
(4) What do we quantify over in quantifying over possibilities? If there are three ways events might possibly go, what are there three of? – Nothing.

PRIMITIVE MODALITY

Armstrong specifies, clearly and in detail, just when a recombination of universals into a pattern of coinstantiation – in other words, a con-junctive state of affairs – is possible. If the universals that enter into it are distinct, and if it includes no totality facts or laws, the necessary and sufficient condition for its possibility is that the universals in ques-tion must exist. If it does include totality facts that break the rules of combinatorialism, there is another necessary condition: the exclusions imposed by the totality facts must be respected. If it includes laws, there is yet another necessary condition: if we have a state of affairs $N(F, G)$ that makes it a law that all Fs are Gs, and a state of affairs Fa, we must have Ga as well. (Unless $N(F, G)$ is defeated by some over-riding law; see *What is a Law of Nature?* pp. 147–150.) And if the universals in question are not wholly distinct, we must analyse them into simpler universals until we reach distinctness, and then apply the conditions as above. That is the whole story; and nowhere does any modal primitive appear. We need no extra clause to say, for instance, that the universals involved are compatible; because for Armstrong distinct universals are always compatible. (With an exception for to-tality facts, but that can be mentioned by name.) So we need no prim-itive notion of compatibility. Nor must we amend the conditions of possibility to say that there are *or might be* such-and-such universals; for Armstrong, the only universals there might be are the ones there are. So far, so good.

But when we speak of whether it is possible that————, we will seldom fill the blank with an explicit description of some recombination of universals. Suppose we fill it instead with 'a donkey talks'. Elsewhere, I've argued that this example poses a problem for any theory that treats possibilities as story-like: as composed of sentences (or of representations in a system analogous to language, or of propositions). Suppose the sentences describe just the basic structure of the world – the arrangement of particles, or the pattern of coinstantiation of genuine universals, or whatever – and say nothing explicit about such supervenient features as talkers and donkeys. Then it is possible that a donkey talks iff some such story S *implicitly represents* that a donkey talks. And what does that mean? We don't know any recipe for a talking donkey in terms of elements of the basic structure; and if we did, we still wouldn't know it *a priori* and so wouldn't be entitled to build it into our analyses. Armstrong agrees (pp. 101–102). All we can say is that S implicitly represents that a donkey talks iff, necessarily, S is true only if a donkey talks. And here we resort to unanalysed necessity.

(It won't help to switch to stories in a richer language, which do explicitly address the question whether a donkey talks. For then we'd have to restrict ourselves to consistent stories; that is, to stories in which what is implicitly represented in the chapter about the basic structure of the world agrees with what is explicit in the chapter about talking donkeys.)

Armstrong's states of affairs look like sentences, sometimes short and sometimes long conjunctions, about the basic structure of the world. So I used to think he faced the problem of implicit representation and couldn't get rid of primitive modality. But I was forgetting his doctrine of thick particulars. Armstrong's world of states of affairs is a world of facts *and* a world of things, because the things are themselves made out of facts. Dog Harry, taken as a thick particular, is a big conjunctive state of affairs. And so would a talking donkey be, if there were one. States of affairs are sentence-like, sure enough, but they're thing-like as well. So Armstrong has a way around my problem. He can say that a world, taken as a big state of affairs, implicitly represents that a donkey talks iff part of it is a talking donkey. No unanalysed modality there!

So far, all's well; but we shall return to the issue of primitive modality later.

According to Armstrong, other possible worlds, and unactualized possible individuals, just don't exist. They are fictions. (That is why he cannot say that the truth-makers for possibility-statements are the possibilities themselves.) We often say that useful idealizations, like frictionless planes and ideal gasses, are nonexistent fictions. These things are unactualized possible individuals, and Armstrong's plan is simply to say the same about *possibilia* in general.

To call a possible world fictitious is to say that it does not exist, but does exist according to some fiction. So we must ask: what fiction? A fictionalist has two alternatives. There could be many little fictions of one world each; or one big fiction of many worlds.

The immediate problem with the many-fiction alternative is that the many fictions don't exist. Nobody has even once told a fully detailed story about what goes on in an alternative world (except maybe for stories of very simple worlds). Still less have our busy authors given us the countless such stories that we need. The world-stories are no less fictitious than the worlds themselves.

A remedy is to say that all the world-stories exist as mathematical representations – set-theoretical models, sets of sentences, or whatnot. This is the theory I have called 'linguistic ersatzism'. I have asked how alien universals can be unambiguously represented using the resources of this world; but Armstrong needn't worry about that, so long as he ignores the outer sphere. I have asked how to distinguish consistent from inconsistent representations; but combinatorialism gives an answer to that, provided the representations represent only the recombination of universals and say nothing explicit about whether there are talking donkeys. Further, Armstrong argues that the resources of this world afford a naturalistic foundation for all of set-theoretical mathematics. (See ch. 9. I will not discuss this chapter. It is tangential to the rest of the book, and it may in part be superseded by Armstrong, 'Classes are States of Affairs', *Mind* 100 (1991) pp. 189–200.) If that is right, he has all the mathematical modelling clay he needs to represent the worlds of the inner sphere.

It is hard to see why Armstrong should not be a naturalistic ersatzer. He says that 'if this could be done satisfactorily, it would be a particularly economical solution' (p. 31). But he says no more; and instead goes on to consider and reject *non*-naturalistic ersatzism, in which the representing entities are actual but 'abstract', causally inert and outside of space and time. Later, after explicitly mentioning mathematical constructions, he says 'My quarrel with the ersatzer is perhaps not very deep . . . But the quarrel is real. Mere representations of possibilities . . . are not to be identified with the possibilities that we seek to represent' (p. 41). Agreed. There are 'constructivist' philosophers who treat the real world as if it were a story, full of features that are artifacts freely put in by the author. Armstrong will have none of that, of course. An ersatzer who treated all the worlds as constructed representations, the real one along with the rest, would be travelling in unwelcome company. But most ersatzers nowadays take good care to distinguish their world-stories from worlds. They would never confuse this world itself with the true one among all the world-stories. It's not wrong to treat a story as if it were a story!

If we abandon ersatzism, there is another way to rescue the many fictions of one world each. The problem is that these many untold stories are themselves fictitious. We can grant the point, and go for a *compound fictionalism*. If a novel concerns the life of a story-teller, there may be stories that exist according to that novel but do not really exist: fictitious fictions. And there may be things that, according to the novel, exist according to these stories; but do not exist according to the novel itself; and do not exist. So we could have one big (fantastic!) fiction according to which all the little fictions of one world each do exist. So then a possible world would be doubly fictitious, something that exists according to a fiction that exists according to another fiction. This is the solution Armstrong adopts.

Compound fictionalism is clumsy. We see just how clumsy it is if we consider not a plain possibility statement, but rather a numerical possibility statement. Suppose we say that a certain course of events, say the break-up of the Soviet Union, might unfold in three quite different ways. It's not that three quite different possible worlds exist. It's not that according to some fiction, there is some other fiction according to which three such worlds exist. What's true, rather, is that according to one 'outer' fiction, three 'inner' fictions exist; and according to the outer fiction, it's true according to the first inner fiction

211

that the break-up happens in one way; and according to the outer fiction, it's true according to the second inner fiction that the break-up happens in quite another way; and according to the outer fiction, it's true according to the third inner fiction that the break-up happens in another way still. (And if you think this isn't bad enough yet, note how I've been fudging by appearing to quantify over 'ways', whatever those are. That would need cleaning up, somehow, in a correct compound-fictionalist translation.) I don't say this is unacceptable; I do say that it should move Armstrong to see if he can patch up his quarrel with naturalistic ersatzism.

MANY-WORLDS FICTIONALISM

Armstrong might abandon the many fictions of one world each, and go instead for the one big fiction of many worlds. This would lead to a position that houses his combinatorialism within the sort of 'modal fictionalism' considered by Gideon Rosen (in his excellent article of that name, *Mind* 99 (1990) pp. 327–354). Does a fiction exist according to which there exist many 'concrete' worlds? Yes, if indeed it is a fiction – I wrote it myself. We could join that fiction of the plurality of worlds with Armstrong's doctrine that a world is a world of particulars and universals bound together in states of affairs; and we could strike out the part about the alien universals and the worlds of the outer sphere; and we could add that the worlds are subject to Armstrong's form of the principle of recombination. Consider it done. Then Armstrong could say that possible worlds exist according to this one big fiction of many worlds. And he could say, as Rosen does, that it is possible that there are blue swans iff, according to that big fiction, together with its factual background, at least one world has blue swans in it. In general, this many-worlds modal fictionalism borrows its analyses from the many-worlds theory of modality, and consequently shares many of its advantages.

The main cost, as Rosen says, is that we need the primitive notion of truth according to a fiction. Indeed, any version of fictionalism needs this notion: not only the one big fiction of many worlds, but also the many little fictions of one world each and the big fiction of many little fictions. The notion is modal: it is the notion of being implied by, being implicitly represented by, the fiction. Or worse, in case we are dealing with impossible fictions, it is hyperintensional. However thing-like Armstrong's states of affairs may be, fictions about states of affairs are story-like and not thing-like. So I fear that by going fictionalist, Armstrong has brought back the problem of implicit representation and the need for primitive modality – or worse.

But even setting that aside, all is not rosy. Many-worlds fictionalism is close enough to the many-worlds theory to share not only its advantages but its problems. One problem for the many-world theory is that the many worlds may appear to be parts of one big divided actuality, rather than alternative possibilities. I think this is a spoils-to-the-victor issue: if you accept the many-worlds theory on other grounds, as I do, you should denounce that appearance as an illusion; whereas if you reject the many-worlds theory on other grounds, as Armstrong does, you should take the appearance at face value, as Armstrong does. That is why Armstrong rejects many-worlds fictionalism. 'The trouble with this idea is that the fiction would be a fiction of a monstrously swollen actuality. But the merely possible worlds are *alternative* to the actual world' (p. 50). I reply that in dealing with a fiction, we ought to suspend disbelief. One thing true according to the fiction – Armstrong needn't agree that it is true *simpliciter* – is that the many worlds are not all actual.

There is a better reason why Armstrong should reject many-worlds factionalism. It shares another of the many-world theory's problems: the problem of demarcation. If there are many worlds, where does one leave off and another begin? (No problem for the many fictions of one world each, because different worlds are creatures of different fictions.) Armstrong rejects demarcation by spatiotemporal isolation. He thinks it possible that a single world might contain spatiotemporally isolated 'island universes' (p. 16). How else can he solve the demarcation problem? For him it would be a problem about what's true in the fiction, not about what's true; but no less of a problem for that.

(The intuitive case that island universes are possible has been much strengthened by a recent argument in John Bigelow and Robert Pargetter, 'Beyond the Blank Stare', *Theoria* 53 (1987), pp. 97–114. First, mightn't there be a world of *almost* isolated island universes, linked only by a few short-lived wormholes? And mightn't the presence of the wormholes depend on what happens in the islands? And then wouldn't it be true that if the goings-on in the islands had been just a little different, there wouldn't have been any wormholes? Then wouldn't there have been a world of altogether isolated islands?)

Armstrong does have another solution available for the demarcation problem, but it's a solution that brings new trouble. The world – or *a* world, according to the fiction of many worlds – is a world of states of affairs; and it includes a fact of totality. If many worlds coexist, as the fiction says they do, they are demarcated by their facts of totality. If there is a fact of totality for the conjunctive state of affairs *Fa* & *Gb* & *aRb*, but also there is a state of affairs *Ga*, the latter state of affairs must belong to a different world. It cannot be part of a world whose totality fact excludes it. But this shows that the fiction of many worlds, understood Armstrong's way, is an *impossible* fiction. (The many-worlds theory itself, if burdened with Armstrong's doctrine of totality facts, would be inconsistent outright.) The fiction says that states of affairs somehow manage to coexist with totality facts that ought to exclude them. Maybe there are ways to say what's true according to an impossible fiction; maybe that's a problem we must solve anyway to handle other cases; but maybe solutions that apply to other cases won't carry over to this case. Anyhow, it's a most unwelcome complication. It's a good reason why Armstrong should choose compound fictionalism, as he did, or else naturalistic ersatzism.

CONCLUSION

By now it will be evident that Armstrong's position on possibility is important and attractive and worthy of very serious attention. His book presents it admirably.

13

A world of truthmakers?

D. M. Armstrong, *A World of States of Affairs*,
Cambridge University Press, 1996.

Suppose we have a thing *A* and a property *F*, and *A* has *F*. But suppose
that *A* has *F* contingently: *A* could have lacked the property *F* even
though *A* existed, even though *F* existed, or even though both existed
together. And suppose that *F* is an intrinsic property: when something
has *F*, that is entirely a matter of the nature of that thing itself, not at
all a matter of its relations to other things. (Fill in an example if you
like; but beware lest your example raise irrelevant questions about
whether the property you chose really is a property in the fullest sense
of the word, and whether it really is intrinsic.)

If we believe Armstrong, there must then exist a second thing, *B*.
B is entirely distinct from *A*, and from *F*, and so from both together;
yet *B*'s existence is necessarily connected to whether or not *A* has *F*.
Necessarily, if *A* has *F*, as it does, then *B* must exist; necessarily, if *A*
had lacked *F*, as it might have done, then *B* could not have existed.

That is the central thesis of Armstrong's book. It is strange. If two
things are entirely distinct, as *A* and *B* have been said to be, we want
to say that questions about the existence and intrinsic nature of one
are independent of questions about the existence and intrinsic nature
of the other. Since Melbourne and Sydney are entirely distinct, Mel-

First published (under an altered title) in *The Times Literary Supplement* 4950 (February
13, 1998) p. 30. Reprinted with kind permission from *The Times Literary Supplement*.

bourne could exist without Sydney, or Sydney without Melbourne, or both of them could exist together, or neither. Possibility is 'combinatorial': there are two possibilities for whether or not Melbourne exists, two possibilities for whether or not Sydney exists, and either of the two possibilities for Melbourne can be combined with either of the two possibilities for Sydney. Likewise, possibilities about the intrinsic natures of distinct things are independent: Melbourne could be flat and Sydney could be hilly, or Sydney could be flat and Melbourne hilly, or both could be flat, or both could be hilly. And, likewise, whether Melbourne is flat or hilly is independent of whether Sydney does or does not exist: again, four different cases are possible. Or so we would all think. But how boldly we should extrapolate the lesson of such examples is a disputed matter.

To be sure, the laws of nature establish connections between the existence and the intrinsic natures of distinct things. But Armstrong's necessary connection between A and B is not a merely lawful connection. Armstrong agrees (though not everyone does) that the laws of nature might have been different; indeed, that there might have been no laws at all. But even then, so Armstrong thinks, it still would have been necessary – necessary in the strongest sense of the word – that B exists if and only if A has F.

Why should anyone believe such a thing? There is a good reason and there is a bad reason. It is the good reason that guides Armstrong. But it is the bad reason that may, all too easily, persuade his readers to drop their guard.

Let us consider the bad reason first. I introduced Armstrong's thesis in a deliberately abstruse and alienating way, refusing to reveal the name that he gives to the thing B whose existence is necessarily connected to whether or not A has F. Now I shall tell you: he says that B is the 'state of affairs of A's having F'. So his thesis is that, necessarily, the state of affairs of A's having F exists if and only if A has F. Said that way, it suddenly sounds not at all hard to believe – rather, it sounds like the merest truism.

Our teachers used to warn us, rather too often and rather too stridently, not to be bewitched by language. They told us, in particular, to beware of 'pseudo-reference': not to be taken in by phrases that superficially resemble referring terms, but that actually play some quite

216

different role in the game of language. The menace of pseudo-reference may be less widespread than we once feared, but that is not to say that it never happens at all. Maybe 'the state of affairs of A's having F' is a pseudo-referring term. Maybe it does not refer to anything at all, so *a fortiori* it does not refer to anything B that stands in remarkable necessary connections to the intrinsic nature of something entirely distinct from itself. In that case, saying 'the state of affairs of A's having F exists' might be nothing more than a long-winded way of saying that A has F. Then our 'mere truism' would indeed be true; and our comfort in assenting to it would be well explained. But then we would be much mistaken if we read that comfortable pseudo-referential truism in an ontologically serious way, falsely imputing a reference where in fact there is none. By all means assent to the comfortable truism; but unless we can rule out the hypothesis of pseudo-reference, assent to the truism gives us no reason to believe that there exists something B whose existence is necessarily connected to whether A has F.

So much for the bad reason to believe Armstrong's thesis. Now for the good reason, which is Armstrong's own reason. It has nothing at all to do with our offhand assent to the comfortable truism. (Except for this: thanks to the truism, if indeed there were something B whose existence was necessarily connected to whether A had F, then 'the state of affairs of A's having F' would be an apt name to confer on B; and accordingly, it is the name Armstrong has chosen. But the availability of an apt name is no proof that there exists something that deserves that name.)

To understand the good reason, we turn to the topic of truth. Statements divide into truths and falsehoods. Some of the truths are necessary truths; set those aside. The rest of the truths are contingent: they are truths that might have been false. Now ask: when a statement S is (contingently) true, *what makes it true*? It wouldn't seem right to say: 'Well, S just *is* true, and that's all there is to it'. Rather, we want to say that its truth is a relational property. The world – the totality of all the entities there actually are – makes S true. Or rather, since few truths purport to describe the entire world, some part of the world makes S true. Somewhere within the world, S has a 'truthmaker'. Something E exists such that, necessarily, if E exists then S is true. (Or perhaps several things exist, any one of which would have sufficed to make S true. Each and every cat – at least if it is a cat essentially – is a truthmaker for the statement that something is a cat.)

Armstrong, along with his one-time colleague C. B. Martin, was a pioneer in demanding explicitly that truths must have truthmakers; and in castigating philosophical systems that failed to satisfy this demand. Think, for instance, of a metaphysic that reduces the material world to J. S. Mill's 'permanent possibilities of sensation': what, if not the *un*reduced material world beyond the door, could be the truthmaker for a truth about what sensations would have followed the sensation of opening the door? The point seems well taken, at least so far as this example goes. But why stop there?

Some truths are predications: truths about the properties had by things, in particular about the intrinsic properties contingently had by things. Take the statement that thing A has property F. If it is true, as we supposed it to be, and if we accept Armstrong's general demand that truths must have truthmakers, then this truth must have a truthmaker. Its truthmaker is what Armstrong calls a 'state of affairs'. Others might call it a 'fact'. But this word is to be shunned, because it means sometimes a truth, sometimes a truthmaker; sometimes that which might have existed and been a falsehood, sometimes that which would not have existed at all. Call it what you will, a truthmaker for this predication would be something B such that, necessarily, if B exists, then the statement that A has F is true. In other words, such that, necessarily, if B exists, then A has F. And now we are most of the way to Armstrong's thesis.

Why does the truthmaker B have to be wholly distinct from A and from F? Indeed, couldn't it just consist of A plus F? – No; because then B would automatically exist if A and F did. But we stipulated that F was to be a contingent property of A; so it has to be possible for A not to have F even though A and F both exist. (Or could B consist of some parts of A and F? – No, for much the same reason.) Armstrong does indeed call A and F the 'constituents' of the state of affairs B. But that terminology is safe only if we resist all temptation to read 'constituent' literally as a synonym for 'part'.[1]

1 [Added 1998] Beware: my terminology differs from Armstrong's. The way that

Or might there be just some part of B, call it B^-, that is entirely distinct from A and F? Then A and F and B^- jointly would do the job of truthmaking. That hypothesis provides a truthmaker. But now B^-, rather than the whole of B, is involved in a strange necessary connection between distinct things: necessarily, given that A and F exist, B^- exists if and only if A has F. Nothing is gained, simplicity is lost. Or might there be two redundant truthmakers, B_1 and B_2, either one of which would have sufficed to make it true that A has F? Or might it have been possible for something else, B_3, to have done the truthmaking, if only B_3 had existed? Then our necessary connection between distinct things takes this form: necessarily, there exists either B_1 or B_2 or B_3 if and only if A has F. Again: nothing gained, simplicity lost.

In short, the good reason to believe Armstrong's thesis is that it affords the simplest way, if not quite the only way, of providing truthmakers for predications. If we do not satisfy the demand for truthmakers, there will be nothing much we can say about why these contingent truths are true. We shall just have to say: the statement that A has F is true because A has F. It's so because it's so. It just is. How bad would that be? Would it be just as bad as a parallel throwing-up-of-hands in the case of the alleged truths about permanent possibilities of sensation?

On the other hand, how bad would it be to abandon combinatorialism about possibility, and posit necessary connections between distinct things? That is the price we pay for uncompromising adherence to the demand for truthmakers. Because, sadly, the demand for truthmakers just *is* a demand for necessary connections.

Another instance of the conflict between combinatorialism and the demand for truthmakers appears when we ask what the truthmaker is for a (contingent) denial of existence: the statement, say, that there are

Armstrong's states of affairs are built out of their constituents is in some ways analogous and in other ways disanalogous to mereological composition. He calls it 'unmereological composition'; whereas I reserve the word 'composition' exclusively for mereological composition. Likewise, Armstrong says that states of affairs and their constituents are mereologically distinct, but unmereologically not distinct; whereas I give the word 'distinct' an exclusively mereological sense, so that states of affairs and their constituents are said to be distinct *simpliciter*.

no arctic penguins. The truthmaker for that truth would have to be something that could not possibly coexist with an arctic penguin. Armstrong's world of states of affairs provides a suitable candidate for the job. But do we want there to be any such thing? – Not if we believe, as combinatorialists, that anything can coexist with anything. Worse still, suppose we were such wholehearted combinatorialists as to think it possible that there might have been absolutely nothing at all. It would then have been true that there was nothing. Would there have been a truthmaker for this truth? – If so, there would have been something, and not rather nothing. Contradiction.

One principle or the other has to be compromised. Stick to the demand for truthmakers and compromise combinatorialism, and you will be led to Armstrong's world of states of affairs, or to something very like it. (Armstrong's book is exemplary in the justice it does to nearby alternatives to his own system.) You can hold on, as Armstrong does, to a limited version of combinatorialism which pertains only to the independence of distinct states of affairs. But you cannot hold on to the sort of combinatorialism which is denied by the necessary connection between B and the intrinsic character of A, nor can you accept any combinatorial argument for the possibility that nothing exists.

Stick to uncompromising combinatorialism, and deny that predications need truthmakers, and you will have no good reason to believe in states of affairs at all, still less to believe any of what Armstrong says about them. Some other aspects of Amstrong's system are nevertheless left standing: most importantly, his distinctive conception of (fundamental) properties as contingently existing beings with multiple locations in space and time.

The need to choose between combinatorialism and truthmaking is not widely acknowledged. But it is a real fork in the road: both directions beckon, but we cannot take both. Thanks to Armstrong's excellent book, we know much better than before what lies ahead if we choose truthmaking and forsake combinatorialism.

14

Maudlin and modal mystery

Tim Maudlin claims to derive a contradiction from my account of possible worlds.[1] But the principle that plays the crucial role in Maudlin's refutation is not mine. Maudlin credits it rather to Aristotle.[2] On the one occasion when I considered something resembling Maudlin's Aristotelian principle, I took a dim view of it, saying that if it had the power to support a certain conclusion, then it could equally well support an incompatible conclusion.[3] If the combination of my account of possible worlds with Maudlin's Greek gift turns out to be contradictory, that should come as no surprise.

Here, stated more generally than Maudlin states it, is how the refutation works. Let T be some theory about the nature and structure of modal reality. (It need not be a modal realist theory.) Let T treat some questions about modal reality as mysteries. In other words, T is incomplete: for some statement, M, about modal reality, neither M nor not-M is a theorem of T. Let T treat all statements about modal reality as non-contingent: if any such statement is possibly true, then it is true *simpliciter*. And, finally, let T contain the Aristotelian principle:

First published in *The Australasian Journal of Philosophy* 74 (1996), pp. 683–684. Reprinted with kind permission from *The Australasian Journal of Philosophy*.

1 'On the Impossibility of David Lewis' Modal Realism', *Australasian Journal of Philosophy* 74 (1996) pp. 671–682.
2 At the end of his paper, Maudlin does indeed liken me to an ancient Greek. But the Greek mentioned is not Aristotle.
3 See my 'Anselm and Actuality', *Noûs* 4 (1970) pp. 175–188, esp. pp. 182–183.

whatever cannot be refuted in T is possibly true. Now we are in trouble. M cannot be refuted in T, else not-M would be a theorem. Likewise not-M cannot be refuted in T, else M would be a theorem. So, by the Aristotelian principle, both M and not-M are possibly true. Both of them, being statements about modal reality, are non-contingent. So both of them are true *simpliciter*: a contradiction. T's agnosticism about M has been its downfall – together, of course, with T's acceptance of the Aristotelian principle. Beware of Greeks bearing gifts!

Here is a second version: instead of taking the contradictories M and not-M, we suppose that T is agnostic between several contraries M_1, M_2, . . . ; and we use the Aristotelian principle to show that each of these contraries is true. Here is a third version: first we use the Aristotelian principle to show that a disjunction of some of the contraries, M_2-or-M_3-or . . . , is true. Then we note that if the disjunction is true, some particular disjunct must be true. Then we use the Aristotelian principle again to show that some different one of the contrary disjuncts is true. This third version is the form that Maudlin's refutation actually takes, but that makes it unnecessarily complicated. His choice of a modal mystery is the question whether there are indiscernible possible worlds, and if so how many of them there are. But that is inessential. Any question on which T remains agnostic would serve as well.

Maudlin's presentation is further complicated by a certain elasticity in the formulation of the Aristotelian principle: 'that which . . . , being assumed, results in nothing impossible' is possible.[4] How shall we understand 'results' and 'impossible'? If we read 'results' simply as 'strictly implies', and 'impossible' simply as 'impossible', then indeed the Aristotelian principle will be 'tautologous' and 'unobjectionable', as Maudlin says it is. (And besides, it will stand some chance of being what Aristotle himself had in mind.) But then, since it makes no mention at all of theory T, it will not yield inferences premised on T's agnosticism. So it will not serve the needs of Maudlin's refutation.

---

4 *Prior Analytics* 32a19. My ellipsis effects a conversion from Aristotelian terminology, in which what is necessary is not called 'possible', to modern terminology. Maudlin at one point replaces 'results' by 'entails'.

Suppose, for instance, that although T has nothing to say about the question one way or the other, M is in fact false. M is non-contingent, so it is not only false but impossible. So M *does* result in something impossible – namely, M itself – and the Aristotelian principle as we have so far interpreted it is powerless to prove that M is possibly true.

If instead we read 'results' as 'results by theory T' and 'impossible' as 'contradicting theory T' (or if we read them respectively as 'results by logic alone' and 'contradicting T', or if we read them respectively as 'results by theory T' and 'contradictory by logic alone') then we have an Aristotelian principle that will meet Maudlin's needs, but will no longer be tautologous or unobjectionable.

Read one way, the Aristotelian principle is powerless to do much of anything. Read another way, it has the power to engender contradiction not only in my own, admittedly controversial theory of modal reality, but in all manner of theories of modal reality. One way, it is useless; the other way, worse than useless. Away with it!

15

Humean Supervenience debugged

Years ago, I wrote that much of my work could be seen in hindsight as a campaign on behalf of "Humean Supervenience": the thesis that the whole truth about a world like ours supervenes on the spatiotemporal distribution of local qualities (1986, pp. ix–xvi). I thought this campaign had been mostly successful. Despite some unfinished business with causation, especially the problem presented in Menzies (1989), I think so still. But I wrote that "There is one big bad bug: chance. It is here, and here alone, that I fear defeat" (1986, p. xiv). I think I can say at last how to beat the bug. But first I'll have to take a lot of time reviewing old ground. I'll reintroduce Humean Supervenience, with some afterthoughts. I'll say what a Humean analysis of chance might look like. I'll say why Humean analyses of chance are in bad trouble, and why unHumean analyses are not an acceptable refuge. I'll give the beginning of a solution to the problem that plagues Humean analyses, and I'll say why that beginning is not good enough. And then I'll come at last to the good news: thanks to a suggestion by Michael Thau, I think I know how to complete the solution. The resulting rescue of Humean chance won't give us all we might wish, but I think it gives us enough.

So the key idea in this paper is Thau's. I thank him for kindly

First published in *Mind* 103 (1994), pp. 473–490. Reprinted by permission of Oxford University Press.

Thanks, above all, to Michael Thau and Ned Hall; and to many others who have helped me by discussions of this material.

permitting me to use it here in my own way. But it can be used in other ways as well. Thau himself has not joined my campaign on behalf of Humean Supervenience. But there are other theses about chance, weaker and less contentious than Humean Supervenience itself, that are bitten by their own versions of the big bad bug. As Thau (1994) explains in his companion paper, his idea can be used also in defence of those weaker theses.

1. HUMEAN SUPERVENIENCE

To begin, we may be certain *a priori* that any contingent truth whatever is made true, somehow, by the pattern of instantiation of fundamental properties and relations by particular things. In Bigelow's phrase, truth is supervenient on being (1988, pp. 132–3 and 158–9). If two possible worlds are discernible in any way at all, it must be because they differ in what things there are in them, or in how those things are. And "how things are" is fully given by the fundamental, perfectly natural, properties and relations that those things instantiate.

From this starting point, we can go on to add various further theses about the basis on which all else supervenes. As an anti-haecceitist, I myself would drop the "what things there are" clause; I claim that all contingent truth supervenes just on the pattern of coinstantiation, never mind which particular hooks the properties and relations are hanging on. (On my view, the hooks are never identical from one world to another, but that by itself doesn't make the worlds discernible.) Some will wish to add that the fundamental properties and relations are Armstrong's immanent universals; or maybe that they are Williams's families of exactly resembling tropes. And we may reasonably hope that physics – present-day physics, or anyway some not-too-distant improvement thereof – will give us the inventory of all the perfectly natural properties and relations that ever appear in this world.

Humean Supervenience is yet another speculative addition to the thesis that truth supervenes on being. It says that in a world like ours, the fundamental relations are exactly the spatiotemporal relations: distance relations, both spacelike and timelike, and perhaps also occupancy relations between point-sized things and spacetime points. And it says that in a world like ours, the fundamental properties are local qualities: perfectly natural intrinsic properties of points, or of point-sized occupants of points. Therefore it says that all else supervenes on the spatiotemporal arrangement of local qualities throughout all of history, past and present and future.

The picture is inspired by classical physics. Humean Supervenience doesn't actually say that physics is right about what local qualities there are, but that's the case to keep in mind. But if we keep physics in mind, we'd better remember that physics isn't really classical. For instance, a rival picture inspired by waves in state-space might say that many fundamental properties are instantiated not at points but at point-tuples (Forrest 1988, p. 155). The point of defending Humean Supervenience is not to support reactionary physics, but rather to resist philosophical arguments that there are more things in heaven and earth than physics has dreamt of. Therefore if I defend the *philosophical* tenability of Humean Supervenience, that defence can doubtless be adapted to whatever better supervenience thesis may emerge from better physics.

Even classical electromagnetism raises a question for Humean Supervenience as I stated it. Denis Robinson (1989) has asked: is a vector field an arrangement of local qualities? I said qualities were intrinsic; that means they can never differ between duplicates; and I would have said offhand that two things can be duplicates even if they point in different directions. Maybe this last opinion should be reconsidered, so that vector-valued magnitudes may count as intrinsic properties. What else could they be? Any attempt to reconstrue them as relational properties seems seriously artificial.

Humean Supervenience is meant to be contingent: it says that among *worlds like ours*, no two differ without difference in the arrangement of qualities. But when is a world like ours? I used to say: when it's a world of the "inner sphere", free of fundamental properties or relations that are alien to our world. Sally Haslanger (1994) has shown that this answer probably won't do. One lesson of the Armstrong (1980)[1]

---

1 This paper was presented at the 1976 conference of the Australasian Association of Philosophy.

spinning sphere (also known as the Kripke[2] spinning disk) is that one way to get a difference between worlds with the exact same arrangement of local qualities is to have things that are bilocated in spacetime. Take two worlds containing spheres of homogeneous matter, unlike the particulate matter of our world; in one world the sphere spins and in the other it doesn't; but the arrangement of local qualities is just the same. These are worlds in which things persist through time not by consisting of distinct temporal parts, but rather by bilocation in space-time: persisting things are wholly present in their entirety at different times. The difference between the spinning and the stationary spheres is a difference in the pattern of bilocation. No worries for Humean Supervenience, so I thought: I believe that ours is a temporal-parts-world, therefore neither of the worlds in the story is a world like ours. But why assume that things that indulge in bilocation must differ in their fundamental nature from things that don't? Why think that if ours is a temporal-parts-world, then otherworldly bilocated things must have properties alien to our world? No good reason, I fear. Haslanger's point seems well taken. I still want to insist that if ours is a temporal-parts-world, then bilocation-worlds don't count as "worlds like ours", but I think I must abandon my former reason why not.

2. SYMMETRY AND FREQUENCY

Chance is objective single-case probability: for instance, the 50% probability that a certain particular tritium atom will decay sometime in the next 12.26 years. Chance is not the same thing as degree of belief, or *credence* as I'll call it; chance is neither anyone's actual credence nor the credence warranted by our total available evidence. If there were no believers, or if our total evidence came from misleadingly unrepresentative samples, that wouldn't affect chance in any way.

Nevertheless, the chance of decay is connected as follows to credence: if a rational believer knew that the chance of decay was 50%, then almost no matter what else he might or might not know as well, he would believe to degree 50% that decay was going to occur. *Almost*

2 Saul Kripke, "Identity Through Time", presented at the 1979 conference of the American Philosophical Association, Eastern Division, and elsewhere.

no matter; because if he had reliable news from the future about whether decay would occur, then of course that news would legitimately affect his credence.

This connection between chance and credence is an instance of what I call the *Principal Principle* (Lewis 1980).[3] We shall see much more of it as we go on, both as the key to our concept of chance and as an obstacle to Humean analyses.

If Humean Supervenience is true, then contingent truths about chance are in the same boat as all other contingent truths: they must be made true, somehow, by the spatiotemporal arrangement of local qualities. How might this be? Any satisfactory answer must meet a severe test. The Principal Principle requires that the chancemaking pattern in the arrangement of qualities must be something that would, if known, correspondingly constrain rational credence. Whatever makes it true that the chance of decay is 50% must also, if known, make it rational to believe to degree 50% that decay will occur.

In simple cases, two candidates for chancemakers come to mind: symmetries and frequencies. Take symmetries first. Suppose a drunkard is wandering through a maze of T-junctions, and at each junction we can find nothing that looks like a relevant difference between the case that he turns left and the case that he turns right. We could well understand if rational credence had to treat the cases alike, for lack of a relevant difference. If the symmetry is something that would, if known, constrain credence, then it is suitable to serve as a chancemaker. In short, Humean chances might be based on a principle of indifference.

We know, of course, that an unrestricted principle of indifference is inconsistent. If we define partitions of alternative cases by means of ingeniously hoked-up properties, we can get the principle to say almost anything we like. But let us assume, as we should and as we already have done, that we can somehow distinguish natural properties from hoked-up gerrymanders. And let us apply the principle only to natural partitions. We still have no guarantee that we will get univocal answers, but we no longer know that we will not.

So far, so good; but I still I have two reservations about symmetries as chance-makers. For one thing, there is no reason to think we have

---

3 Reprinted with added postscripts in Lewis (1986). See also Mellor (1971).

symmetries to underlie all the chance phenomena we think there are. It would be nice to think that each tritium atom contains a tiny drunkard in a maze of symmetrical T-junctions, and the atom decays when its drunkard finds his way out. But this is sheer fantasy. So far as we know, nothing remotely like it is true.

More important, symmetries are only defeasible constrainers of rational credence. Therefore they can be only defeasible chancemakers. The symmetry of the T-junctions would no longer require 50–50 division of credence if we also knew that, despite this symmetry, the drunkards turn right nine times out of ten. Now we do have a relevant difference between left and right turns. Frequencies can defeat symmetries. And when symmetries are undefeated, that is because the frequencies are such as not to defeat them. So now it looks as if frequencies are the real chancemakers.

A frequency is the right sort of thing to be a Humean chancemaker: it is a pattern in the spatiotemporal arrangement of qualities. And we can well understand how frequencies, if known, could constrain rational credence. So far, so good. The simplest frequency analysis of single-case chance will just say that the chance of a given outcome in a given case equals the frequency of similar outcomes in all cases of exactly the same kind.

Again, this would be worse than useless if we couldn't distinguish natural from gerrymandered kinds; again, we could get the analysis to yield almost any answer we liked. But we can distinguish. (If we could not, puzzles about chance would be the least of our worries.) Further, nature has been kind to us. Large chance systems seem to be put together out of many copies of very small chance systems; and very small chance systems often do come in enormous classes of exact copies. You see one tritium atom, you've seen them all.

In some cases, I think this simple frequency analysis is near enough right. But it has its limits, and even when it works well, I'd like to see it subsumed under something more general. It is only plausible when we do have the enormous classes of exact copies. Tritium atoms are abundant; not so for atoms of unobtainium[346]. It's hard to make the stuff; in fact in all of space and time, past present and future, there only ever exist two Un[346] atoms: one with a lifetime of 4.8 microseconds, as chance would have it; the other with a lifetime of 6.1 microseconds.

So exactly half of all Un^{346} atoms decay in 4.8 microseconds. What does this frequency make true concerning the half-life of Un^{346}, in other words concerning the chance that an atom of it will decay in a given time? Next to nothing, I should think.

Further, consider unobtainium^{349}. This isotope is even harder to make, and in fact there is not one atom of it in all of space and time. Its frequency of decay in a given time is undefined: $0/0$. If there's any truth about its chance of decay, this undefined frequency cannot be the truthmaker.

The problem of unobtainium, in both versions, may set us thinking of frequencies not in our actual world, but rather in counterfactual situations where unobtainium is abundant. (Maybe even infinitely abundant, but let's ignore the issues that will raise.) I think that's a blind alley. Different abundant-unobtainium worlds will have different decay frequencies; to ask what the frequency would be if unobtainium were abundant, we have to select those of the abundant-unobtainium worlds that are closest to actuality. Suppose indeed that we have the same decay frequency in all these worlds. I ask: what makes them closest? It must be something X that just these abundant-unobtainium worlds, some of the ones with the right decay frequency, have in common with our actual world. But then it is X, here in our actual world where unobtainium is scarce or absent, that is the real chance-maker. The abundant-unobtainium worlds that also have X are just a sideshow.

Another well-known problem for simple frequentism: if spacetime is finite and chance systems get only just so small, then all frequencies are rational numbers. Yet the great majority of real numbers are irrational, and we have no pre-philosophical reason to doubt that chances in a finite world can take irrational values.

The answer to our problems about unobtanium lies in remembering that single-case chances follow from general probabilistic laws of nature. (At least, the ones we know about do; and I think it's a spoils-to-the-victor question whether the same goes in general. The analysis I shall put forward can't handle lawless chances, and I take that to be no problem.) There are general laws of radioactive decay that apply to all atoms. These laws yield the chance of decay in a given time, and hence the half-life, as a function of the nuclear structure of the atom in question. (Or rather, they would yield the chance but for the intractability of the required calculation.) Unobtainium atoms have their chances of decay not in virtue of decay frequencies for unobtainium, but rather in virtue of these general laws. The appeal to laws also solves our problem about irrational values. Whether or not the world is finite, there is no reason why the function of nuclear structure that is built into the law can only yield rational values.

In general, probabilistic laws yield history-to-chance conditionals. For any given moment, these conditionals tell us the chance distribution over alternative future histories from that moment on, as a function of the previous history of particular facts up to and including that moment. The historical antecedents are of course given by the arrangement of qualities. The laws do the rest.

So the appeal to laws just postpones our problem. What pattern in the arrangement of qualities makes the chances? In part, features of history up to the moment in question. For the rest, it is the pattern that makes the probabilistic laws, whatever that is. So now we must turn to a Humean analysis of laws, and see whether we can extend that to cover probabilistic laws. I think we can.

3. THE BEST-SYSTEM ANALYSIS OF LAW

Ramsey once thought that laws were "consequences of those propositions which we should take as axioms if we knew everything and organized it as simply as possible in a deductive system" (1990, p. 150).[4] I trust that by "it" he meant not everything, but only as much of everything as admits of simple organization; else everything would count as a law. I would expand Ramsey's idea thus (see Lewis 1973, p. 73). Take all deductive systems whose theorems are true. Some are simpler, better systematized than others. Some are stronger, more informative, than others. These virtues compete: an uninformative system can be very simple, an unsystematized compendium of miscellaneous information can be very informative. The best system is the one that strikes as good a balance as truth will allow between simplicity and strength. How good a balance that is will depend on

4 Here I quote Ramsey's later summary of his former view.

how kind nature is. A regularity is a law iff it is a theorem of the best system.

Some familiar complaints seem to me question-begging. (See Armstrong (1983, pp. 40–59); van Fraassen (1989, pp. 45–51). If you're prepared to agree that theorems of the best system are rightly called laws, presumably you'll also want to say that they underlie causal explanations; that they support counterfactuals; that they are not mere coincidences; that they and their consequences are in some good sense necessary; and that they may be confirmed by their instances. If not, not. It's a standoff – spoils to the victor. Other complaints are more worrisome. Like any regularity theory, the best-system analysis says that laws hold in virtue of patterns spread over all of space and time. If laws underlie causation, that means that we are wrong if we think, for instance, that the causal roles of my brain states here and now are an entirely local matter. That's an unpleasant surprise, but I'm prepared to bite the bullet.

The worst problem about the best-system analysis is that when we ask where the standards of simplicity and strength and balance come from, the answer may seem to be that they come from us. Now, some ratbag idealist might say that if we don't like the misfortunes that the laws of nature visit upon us, we can change the laws – in fact, we can make them always have been different – just by changing the way we think! (Talk about the power of positive thinking.) It would be very bad if my analysis endorsed such lunacy. I used to think rigidification came to the rescue: in talking about what the laws would be if we changed our thinking, we use not our hypothetical new standards of simplicity and strength and balance, but rather our actual and present standards. But now I think that is a cosmetic remedy only. It doesn't make the problem go away, it only makes it harder to state.

The real answer lies elsewhere: if nature is kind to us, the problem needn't arise. I suppose our standards of simplicity and strength and balance are only partly a matter of psychology. It's not because of how we happen to think that a linear function is simpler than a quartic or a step function; it's not because of how we happen to think that a shorter alternation of prenex quantifiers is simpler than a longer one; and so on. Maybe some of the exchange rates between aspects of simplicity, etc., are a psychological matter, but not just anything goes.

If nature is kind, the best system will be *robustly* best – so far ahead of its rivals that it will come out first under any standards of simplicity and strength and balance. We have no guarantee that nature is kind in this way, but no evidence that it isn't. It's a reasonable hope. Perhaps we presuppose it in our thinking about law. I can admit that *if* nature were unkind, and *if* disagreeing rival systems were running neck-and-neck, than lawhood might be a psychological matter, and that would be very peculiar. I can even concede that in that case the theorems of the barely-best system would not very well deserve the name of laws. But I'd blame the trouble on unkind nature, not on the analysis; and I suggest we not cross these bridges unless we come to them.

(Likewise for the threat that two very different systems are tied for best. (See Armstrong (1983, pp. 70–71); van Fraassen (1989, pp. 48–49).) I used to say that the laws are then the theorems common to both systems, which could leave us with next to no laws. Now I'll admit that in this unfortunate case there would be no very good deservers of the name of laws. But what of it? We haven't the slightest reason to think the case really arises.)

The best-system analysis is Humean. The arrangement of qualities provides the candidate true systems, and considerations of simplicity and strength and balance do the rest.

But so far, we don't have probabilistic laws. If chances were somehow given, we could just include them in the subject matter of the competing true systems, and go on as before.[5] But chances are not yet given. We decided that the chance-making patterns in the arrangement of qualities had to include the lawmaking patterns for the probabilistic laws that determine the chances in all the different cases.

4. THE BEST-SYSTEM ANALYSIS OF LAW AND CHANCE TOGETHER

So we modify the best-system analysis to make it deliver the chances and the laws that govern them in one package deal. Consider deductive

---

5 Well, not quite as before: we'd have to impose constraints that would, for instance, disqualify a system according to which some law had once had some chance of not being true. See Lewis (1986, pp. 124–8).

systems that pertain not only to what happens in history, but also to what the chances are of various outcomes in various situations – for instance, the decay probabilities for atoms of various isotopes. Require these systems to be true in what they say about history. We cannot yet require them to be true in what they say about chance, because we have yet to say what chance means; our systems are as yet not fully interpreted. Require also that these systems aren't in the business of guessing the outcomes of what, by their own lights, are chance events: they never say that A without also saying that A never had any chance of not coming about.

As before, some systems will be simpler than others. Almost as before, some will be stronger than others: some will say either what will happen or what the chances will be when situations of a certain kind arise, whereas others will fall silent both about the outcomes and about the chances. And further, some will fit the actual course of history better than others. That is, the chance of that course of history will be higher according to some systems than according to others. (Though it may well turn out that no otherwise satisfactory system makes the chance of the actual course of history very high; for this chance will come out as a product of chances for astronomically many chance events.) Insofar as a system falls silent, of course it fits whatever happens.

The virtues of simplicity, strength, and fit trade off. The best system is the system that gets the best balance of all three. As before, the laws are those regularities that are theorems of the best system. But now some of the laws are probabilistic. So now we can analyse chance: the chances are what the probabilistic laws of the best system say they are. (See Lewis (1986, pp. 128–9).)

As before, we may reasonably hope that the best system is very far ahead of the rest; and very robustly ahead, so that the winner of the race does not depend on how we happen to weigh the various desiderata. How well the laws and chances deserve their names should depend on how kind nature has been in providing a decisive front runner. The prospect is best if the chance events are not too few and not too miscellaneous.

In the simplest case, the best-system analysis reduces to frequentism. Suppose that all chance events – more precisely, all events that the leading candidates for best system would deem to be chancy – fall into one large and homogeneous class. To fall silent about the chances of these events would cost too much in strength. To subdivide the class and assign different chances to different cases would cost too much in simplicity. To assign equal single-case chances that differed from the actual frequency of the outcomes would cost too much in fit. For we get the best fit by equating the chances to the frequency; and the larger the class is, the more decisively is this so.

But suppose the class is not so very large; and suppose the frequency is very close to some especially simple value – say, 50–50. Then the system that assigns uniform chances of 50% exactly gains in simplicity at not too much cost in fit. The decisive front-runner might therefore be a system that rounds off the actual frequency.

Or suppose the class is not so very homogeneous. It divides, in virtue of not-too-gruesome classifications, into a few large subclasses that exhibit different frequencies of outcomes. (To take an extreme case, a class of Js that are 50% Ks might exhibit a regular alternation in time: K, not-K, K, not-K,. . . .) Then a system that assigns unequal chances in different subclasses will gain greatly in fit at not too much cost in simplicity.

Or suppose the class is inhomogeneous in a different way. Each member is associated with some value of a continuously variable magnitude M. (In an extreme case, no two members have exactly the same value of M.) If we divide into as many subclasses as there are values of M, the subclasses will be too numerous for simplicity and too small for the frequencies in them to mean much. Instead, the best system will contain a functional law whereby chance depends on the value of M in that particular case. Different candidate systems will use different functions. Some functions, for instance a constant function, will go too far in gaining simplicity at the expense of fit. Others will do the opposite. We may hope that some function – and hence the system that employs it – will be just right, and hence the decisive front runner.

In this last case, and others that combine several of the complications we've considered, frequentism has been left behind altogether. That's how we can get decay chances for Un^{346}, and even for Un^{349}, in virtue of chancemaking patterns that don't involve decay frequencies for unobtainium itself.

235

Despite appearances and the odd metaphor, this is not epistemology! You're welcome to spot an analogy, but I insist that I am not talking about how evidence determines what's reasonable to believe about laws and chances. Rather, I'm talking about how nature – the Humean arrangement of qualities – determines what's true about the laws and chances. Whether there are any believers living in the lawful and chancy world has nothing to do with it.

It is this best-system analysis of law and chance together that I've wanted to believe for many years. Until very recently, I thought I knew a decisive reason why it couldn't be true. Hence my lamentation about the big bad bug. But now that Michael Thau has shown me the way out, I can endorse the best-system analysis with a clear conscience.

5. UNDERMINING

The big bad bug bites a range of different Humean analyses of chance. Simple frequentism falls in that range; so does the best-system analysis. Let's suppose that we have a Humean analysis which says that present chances supervene upon the whole of history, future as well as present and past; but not upon the past and present alone. That's so if present chances are given by frequencies throughout all of time. That's so also if present chances are given by probabilistic laws, plus present conditions to which those laws are applicable, and if those laws obtain in virtue of the fit of candidate systems to the whole of history.

Then different alternative future histories would determine different present chances. (Else the future would be irrelevant, and present chances would be determined by the past and present alone.) And let's suppose, further, that the differences between these alternative futures are differences in the outcomes of present or future chance events. Then each of these futures will have some non-zero present chance of coming about.

Let F be some particular one of these alternative futures: one that determines different present chances than the actual future does. F will not come about, since it differs from the actual future. But there is some present chance of F. That is, there is some present chance that events would go in such a way as to complete a chancemaking pattern that would make the present chances different from what they actually are. The present chances *undermine* themselves.

For instance, there is some minute present chance that far more tritium atoms will exist in the future than have existed hitherto, and each one of them will decay in only a few minutes. If this unlikely future came to pass, presumably it would complete a chancemaking pattern on which the half-life of tritium would be very much less than the actual 12.26 years. Certainly that's so under simple frequentism, and most likely it's so under the best-system analysis as well. Could it come to pass, given the present chances? Well, yes and no. It could, in the sense that there's non-zero present chance of it. It couldn't, in the sense that its coming to pass contradicts the truth about present chances. If it came to pass, the truth about present chances would be different. Although there is a certain chance that this future will come about, there is no chance that it will come about while still having the same present chance it actually has. It's not that if this future came about, the truth about the present would change retrospectively. Rather, it would never have been what it actually is, and would always have been something different.

This undermining is certainly very peculiar. But I think that, so far, it is no worse than peculiar. I would not join Bigelow, Collins, and Pargetter (1993, pp. 443–62) when they intuit a "basic chance principle" to exclude it outright. For I think the only basic principle we have about chance, the principle that tells us all we know, is the Principal Principle. And at first sight the Principal Principle says nothing against undermining. It concerns, rather, the connection between chance and credence.

But look again, and it seems that the Principal Principle does rule out undermining. It was this discovery that led me to despair of a Humean analysis of chance. (See Lewis 1986, pp. xiv – xvii, 111–3, 130.)

Now is the time to take a closer look at what the Principle says.[6] Above, I applied it to the case of someone who knows the chances, but that is a special case. The general case involves not knowledge but

---

6 I have simplified my formulation in (1980) by combining the propositions there called X and E.

conditioning. Take some particular time – I'll call it "the present", but in fact it could be any time. Let C be a rational credence function for someone whose evidence is limited to the past and present – that is, for anyone who doesn't have access to some very remarkable channels of information. Let P be the function that gives the present chances of all propositions. Let A be any proposition. Let E be any proposition that satisfies two conditions. First, it specifies the present chance of A, in accordance with the function P. Second, it contains no "inadmissible" information about future history; that is, it does not give any information about how chance events in the present and future will turn out. (We don't assume that E is known; that extra assumption would yield the special case considered earlier.) Then the Principal Principle is the equation

$$C(A/E) = P(A).$$

Now take A to be F, our alternative future history that would yield present chances different from the actual ones; and let E be the whole truth about the present chances as they actually are. We recall that F had some present chance of coming about, so by the Principal Principle, $C(F/E) \neq 0$. But F is inconsistent with E, so $C(F/E) = 0$. Contradiction. I could tolerate undermining as merely peculiar. But not contradiction!

6. NO REFUGE

It is because the chancemaking pattern lies partly in the future that we have some chance of getting a future that would undermine present chances. This problem would go away if we could assume that the chancemaking pattern lay entirely in the past. That would be so if all of our history-to-chance conditionals, which specify exactly what chances would follow any given initial segment of history, were necessarily true. (See Lewis 1980, final section.)

We dare not assume this. First, because of the problem of the early moment. There might be a beginning of time; or at least a beginning of the part of time in which certain kinds of chancy phenomena go on. What could make the chances at a moment not long after the beginning? (Or at the beginning itself?) There's not much room for any sort of chancemaking pattern in the time before this early moment. To the extent that chancemaking patterns are just frequencies in large and uniform classes, the problem is that the relevant classes, if confined to the time before the early moment, may be ridiculously small. But the problem won't go away if instead we take the different sort of chancemaking pattern envisaged by the best-system analysis.

Second, because of the problem of fluctuation. We usually think that there are laws, and hence regularities, of uniform chances. All tritium atoms throughout space and time have precisely the same chance of decaying in a given period. But the different atoms are preceded by different initial segments of history, and it is not to be expected that the different chancemaking patterns in these different segments will all make precisely the same chance of decay.

(Taking these two problems together, we get what I'll call the problem of drift. For simple frequentism, it goes as follows. Suppose that early on, Js divide about 50–50 between Ks and not-Ks, but so far there haven't been many Js altogether. Then we should expect that there might chance to be a run of Ks, or not-Ks, that would significantly raise, or lower, the chance that the next J would be a K. Such a run might perpetuate itself, with the result that the chance of a J being a K would drift almost to one, or zero, and remain there for a long time after. But we do not at all expect the chances in radioactive decay, say, to undergo any such drift.)

At this point, my opponents will doubtless say that I have done their work for them. I have refuted the position I wanted to hold. It only remains for me to concede defeat, and agree that the chancemakers are not, after all, patterns in the arrangement of qualities. They are something else altogether: special chancemaking relations of universals, primitive facts about chance, or what have you. (See Armstrong (1980, pp. 128–36); Tooley (1987, pp. 142–60).)

But I think there is no refuge here. Be my guest – posit all the primitive unHumean whatnots you like. (I only ask that your alleged truths should supervene on being.) But play fair in naming your whatnots. Don't call any alleged feature of reality "chance" unless you've already shown that you have something, knowledge of which could constrain rational credence. I think I see, dimly but well enough, how knowledge of frequencies and symmetries and best systems could constrain rational credence. I don't begin to see, for instance, how knowledge that two universals stand in a certain special relation $N*$ could constrain rational credence about the future coinstantiation of those universals.[7]

Unless, of course, you can convince me first that this special relation is a chancemaking relation: that the fact that $N*$ (J,K) makes it so, for instance, that each J has 50% chance of being K. But you can't just tell me so. You have to show me. Only if I already see – dimly will do! – how knowing the fact that $N*$ (J,K) should make me believe to degree 50% that the next J will be a K, will I agree that the $N*$ relation deserves the name of chancemaker that you have given it.

The same complaint applies, by the way, to theories that qualify technically as Humean because the special primitive chancemaking whatnots they posit are said to be qualities instantiated at points. Again, I can only agree that the whatnots deserve the name of chancemakers if I can already see, disregarding the names they allegedly deserve, how knowledge of them constrains rational credence in accordance with the Principal Principle.

7. THE BEGINNING OF A SOLUTION

Our problem, where F is an unactualized future that would undermine the actual present chances given by E, is that $C(F/E) = 0$ because F and E are inconsistent, but $C(F/E) \neq 0$ by the Principal Principle because E specifies that F has non-zero chance of coming about. If that use of the Principal Principle is fallacious, the contradiction goes away. We're left with nothing worse than peculiar undermining.

But that use of the Principal Principle *is* fallacious, if indeed the present chances are made by a pattern that extends into the future. Then E bears inadmissible information about future history: it excludes the future F, and it likewise excludes all other futures that would undermine the present chances given by E. Since E is inadmissible, the Principal Principle does not apply. The fatal move that led from Humeanism to contradiction is no better than the obvious blunder:

7 Thanks here to Alex Byrne.

C(the coin will fall heads/it is fair and will fall heads in 99 of the next 100 tosses) $= \frac{1}{2}$

or even

C(the coin will fall heads/it is fair and it will fall heads) $= \frac{1}{2}$.

Victory! – Another such victory and I am undone. What we have just seen is that if chancemaking patterns extend into the future, then *any* use of the Principal Principle is fallacious. For *any* proposition that bears information about present chances thereby bears information about future history. The Principal Principle never applies; and yet without it I deny that we have any handle at all on the concept of chance.

I saw this, but I didn't dare to believe my eyes. I wrote

If anyone wants to defend the best-system theory of laws and chances . . . I suppose the right move would be to cripple the Principal Principle by declaring that information about the chances at a time is not, in general, admissible at that time; and hence that hypothetical information about chances, which can join with admissible historical information to imply chances at a time, is likewise inadmissible. The reason would be that, under the proposed analysis of chances, information about present chances is a disguised form of inadmissible information about future history – to some extent, it reveals the outcomes of matters that are presently chancy. That crippling stops all versions of our *reductio*. . . . I think the cost is excessive; in ordinary calculations with chances, it seems intuitively right to rely on this . . . information. So, much as I would like to use the best-system approach in defence of Humean supervenience, I cannot support this way out of our difficulty. (1986, pp. 130–1)

If I'd seen more clearly, I could have put the core of my *reductio* like this. According to the best-system analysis, information about present chances is inadmissible, because it reveals future history. But this information is not inadmissible, as witness the way it figures in everyday reasoning about chance and credence. Contradiction.

8. THE SOLUTION COMPLETED

Now we're ready at last to hear from Thau. As follows.

First, admissibility admits of degree. A proposition E may be imperfectly admissible because it reveals something or other about future history; and yet it may be very nearly admissible, because it reveals so little as to make a negligible impact on rational credence.

Second, degrees of admissibility are a relative matter. The imperfectly admissible E may carry lots of inadmissible information that is relevant to whether B, but very little that is relevant to whether A.

Third, near-admissibility may be good enough. If E specifies that the present chance of A is $P(A)$, and if E is nearly admissible relative to A, then the conclusion that $C(A/E = P(A)$ will hold, if not exactly, at least to a very good approximation. If information about present chances is never perfectly admissible, then the Principal Principle never can apply strictly. But the Principle applied loosely will very often come very close, so our ordinary reasoning about chance and credence will be unimpaired. Only a few peculiar applications will be so badly crippled that they cannot be regained even as approximations.

And one of these applications that cannot be regained will be the one that figured in our reductio. If F is a future that would undermine the chances specified in E, then, relative to F, E is as inadmissible as it could possibly be. For E flatly contradicts F. Our use of the Principal Principle to conclude that $C(F/E)$ is non-zero was neither strictly nor loosely correct. Hence it no longer stands in the way of the correct conclusion that $C(F/E) = 0$.

9. CORRECTING THE PRINCIPAL PRINCIPLE

We face a question. If the old Principal Principle applies only as an approximation, what is it an approximation to? How, exactly, is chance related to credence? Can we find a new, corrected Principal Principle that works exactly when the old one works only approximately?

Here I shall present only a special case of the correction I favour, applicable only to a special case of the old Principal Principle. (However, the old Principle in full generality follows from the special case; and in parallel fashion, a new general Principal Principle follows from the corrected treatment of the special case.) Ned Hall and I proposed the same correction independently. In his companion paper (1994), he gives a much fuller discussion of the correction, its motivation, and its consequences. To reach the special case I want to present,[8] we consider a certain very informative proposition, as follows. Let H_{tw} be the proposition giving the complete history of world w up to, and including, time t – as it might be, the actual world up to the present. Let T_w be the complete theory of chance for world w – a proposition giving all the probabilistic laws, and therefore all the true history-to-chance conditionals, that hold at w. And let P_{tw} be the chance distribution at time t and world w. If T_w were admissible, then the conjunction $H_{tw}T_w$ also would be admissible. Further, it would specify the chance (at t, at w) of any proposition A. So we could put it for E in the old Principal Principle. Dropping the subscripts henceforth by way of abbreviation, we would have:

$$\text{(OP)} \qquad C(A/HT) = P(A).$$

The correction I favour is to replace (OP) by this new version:

$$\text{(NP)} \qquad C(A/HT) = P(A/T).$$

If T were perfectly admissible, then (OP) would be correctly derived as an instance of the old Principal Principle. If so, then also the change from old to new would be no change at all. For in that case, we would have $P(T) = 1$. (Proof: for A in (OP), put T itself.) Hence we would have $P(A) = P(A/T)$, making (OP) and (NP) equivalent.

But if, as the Humean thinks, there are undermining futures with non-zero present chance that make T false, then T rules out these undermining futures. If so, then, T and HT are not perfectly admissible; (OP) is not correctly derived; the old Principal Principle cannot be applied to determine $C(A/HT)$; $P(T) \neq 1$; and, exceptional cases aside, it will turn out that $P(A) \neq P(A/T)$. If so, then I say we should accept (NP) as our new, corrected Principal Principle. We should abandon (OP) except insofar as it is a convenient approximation to (NP).

By conditionalising credence or chance on T, we ignore undermining futures. The trouble with (OP) is that on the left-hand side we do conditionalise on T, but on the right-hand side we don't. No

---

8 It is this special case that appears as "the Principal Principle Reformulated" in Lewis (1980).

harm would come of this discrepancy if there weren't any undermining futures to worry about. But if there are, then it is only to be expected that the discrepancy will cause trouble. We've already seen the trouble: taking A as an undermining future F, $C(F/HT) = 0$, but $P(F) \neq 0$. To remove the discrepancy, we conditionalise the right-hand side as well as the left: $P(F/T) = 0$, so all's well. The Principal Principle, thus corrected, no longer stands in the way of Humean Supervenience. By my lights as a Humean, that is reason enough to correct it. In his companion paper, Hall argues that we have other good reasons as well.

In formulating (OP) and (NP), we didn't mention admissibility or near-admissibility. Rather, we fixed on the particular propositions H and T, noting only in passing that H is uncontroversially admissible while T's admissibility is questionable. But we can regain contact with Thau's lesson about imperfect and relative admissibility, as follows. Define the *admissibility quotient* of T (and of HT), relative to A, as the quotient $P(A/T)/P(A)$. Then (OP) is a good approximation just to the extent that the admissibility quotient is close to one. (Or if $P(A/T)$ and $P(A)$ are both zero, making the quotient undefined. Let us ignore this case.) We have perfect admissibility when the quotient is one exactly; that's so just when A and T are probabilistically independent with respect to P. T is perfectly admissible relative to A if (but not only if) A is any proposition that is entirely about past and present history. For instance, T is perfectly admissible relative to H.

If, on the other hand, A is an undermining future that contradicts T, then the admissibility quotient is zero, and (OP) is not at all a good approximation to (NP).

More commonplace applications of the Principal Principle, where A typically concerns a small sample from a big population, are quite another story: we can expect an admissibility quotient very close to one. Here's an easy example. Hitherto, exactly ⅔ of Js have been Ks; and we know somehow, that there are 10,002 more Js still to come. Our complete theory of chance, T, says that every J, anywhere and anywhen, has ⅔ chance of being a K. Simple frequentism – a simplistic form of Humeanism, but good enough for a toy example – says that T holds iff exactly ⅔ of all Js are Ks. Equivalently, given what we know about the past: iff ⅔ of the future Js are Ks. Now let A say that three out of the next four *J*s will be *K*s. It is a routine matter to calculate the admissibility quotient of *T* with respect to *A*.[9] It turns out to be about 1.00015. So this time, though (OP) is not exactly right, it is indeed a very good approximation. If our example had concerned the next four *J*s from a population of astronomical size, the approximation would have been much better still.

10. AGAINST PERFECTIONISM

Our new version of the Principal Principle is better by Humean lights; but for myself, I still find the old one more intuitive. (Once we return to the general case, the new version gets quite messy.[10]) So I still say that the old Principle is "the key to our concept of chance". And yet it's only approximately right, and that only sometimes. Chance can be defined as that feature of Reality that obeys the old Principle, yet chance doesn't quite obey it! Isn't this incoherent?

Not at all. Let's put it this way. A feature of Reality deserves the

9    $P(A) = \left(\dfrac{2}{3}\right)^4$; $P(A/T) = \dfrac{P(AT)}{P(T)} = \dfrac{P(A)\left(\dfrac{2}{3}\right)^{6665}\left(\dfrac{1}{3}\right)^{3333}\left(\dfrac{9998!}{6665!\,3333!}\right)}{\left(\dfrac{2}{3}\right)^{6668}\left(\dfrac{1}{3}\right)^{3334}\left(\dfrac{10002!}{6668!\,3334!}\right)}$

When we divide out to obtain $P(A/T)/P(A)$, most terms cancel and we are left with a product of a few fractions. The number of these fractions is the sample size, 4, and each of them differs from one by something of the order of the reciprocal of the population of future *J*s, 10,002.

10   Here is how we regain generality. By probability theory, including a suitable form of additivity – as it might be, a principle of infinite additivity of infinitesimal quantities in a suitable non-standard model – we find that $C(A/E)$ equals the $C(-/E)$-expectation of the quantity whose value at each world w is $C(A/EH_{tw}T_w)$. Assuming that proposition E is entirely about history up to t and chances at t, we find that whenever $C(-/E)$ assigns w positive credence, $EH_{tw}T_w$ simplifies to $H_{tw}T_w$. So according to (OP), $C(A/E)$ is the $C(-/E)$-expectation of the quantity whose value at each w is $P_{tw}(A)$; whereas according to (NP), it is the $C(-/E)$-expectation of the quantity whose value at each w is $P_{tw}(A/T_w)$. Assuming further that E specifies the chance at t of A, so that $P_{tw}(A)$ has a constant value at all E-worlds, we find that the expectation of chance derived from (OP) just equals this same value. Sad to say, the parallel expression derived from (NP) remains unsimplified.

name of chance to the extent that it occupies the definitive role of chance; and occupying the role means obeying the old Principle, applied as if information about present chances, and the complete theory of chance, were perfectly admissible. Because of undermining, nothing perfectly occupies the role, so nothing perfectly deserves the name. But near enough is good enough. If nature is kind to us, the chances ascribed by the probabilistic laws of the best system will obey the old Principle to a very good approximation in commonplace applications. They will thereby occupy the chance-role well enough to deserve the name. To deny that they are *really* chances would be just silly.

It's an old story. Maybe nothing could perfectly deserve the name "sensation" unless it were infallibly introspectible; or the name "simultaneity" unless it were a frame-independent equivalence relation; or the name "value" unless it couldn't possibly fail to attract anyone who was well acquainted with it. If so, then there are no perfect deservers of these names to be had. But it would be silly to lose our Moorings and deny that there existed any such things as sensations, simultaneity, and values. In each case, an imperfect candidate may deserve the name quite well enough.

REFERENCES

Armstrong, D. M. 1980: "Identity Through Time", in Peter van Inwagen, ed., *Time and Cause: Essays Presented to Richard Taylor*. Dordrecht: Reidel.
———1983: *What is a Law of Nature?*. Cambridge: Cambridge University Press.
Bigelow, John 1988: *The Reality of Numbers*. Oxford: Oxford University Press.
Bigelow, John, Collins, John, and Pargetter, Robert 1993: "The Big Bad Bug: What are the Humean's Chances?". *British Journal of Philosophy of Science*, 44, pp. 443–62.
Forrest, Peter 1988: *Quantum Metaphysics*. Oxford: Blackwell.
Hall, Ned 1994: "Correcting the Guide to Objective Chance". *Mind*, 103, pp. 505–18.
Haslanger, Sally (1994): "Humean Supervenience and Enduring Things". *Australasian Journal of Philosophy*, 72, pp. 339–59.
Lewis, David 1973: *Counterfactuals*. Oxford: Blackwell.
———1980: "A Subjectivist's Guide to Objective Chance", in Richard C. Jeffrey, ed., *Studies in Inductive Logic and Probability*, vol. II. Berkeley: University of California. Reprinted with added postscripts in Lewis 1986, pp. 83–132.
———1986: *Philosophical Papers*, vol. II. Oxford: Oxford University Press.

Mellor, D. H. 1971: *The Matter of Chance*. Cambridge: Cambridge University Press.

Menzies, Peter 1989: "Probabilistic Causation and Causal Processes: A Critique of Lewis". *Philosophy of Science*, 56, pp. 642–63.

Ramsey, F. P. 1990: *Philosophical Papers*. Cambridge: Cambridge University Press.

Robinson, Denis 1989: "Matter, Motion and Humean Supervenience". *Australasian Journal of Philosophy*, 67, pp. 394–409.

Thau, Michael 1994: "Undermining and Admissibility". *Mind*, 103, pp. 491–503.

Tooley, Michael 1987: *Causation: A Realist Approach*. Oxford: Oxford University Press.

van Fraassen, Bas 1989: *Laws and Symmetry*. Oxford: Oxford University Press.

16

Psychophysical and theoretical identifications

Psychophysical identity theorists often say that the identifications they anticipate between mental and neural states are essentially like various uncontroversial theoretical identifications: the identification of water with H$_2$O, of light with electromagnetic radiation, and so on. Such theoretical identifications are usually described as pieces of voluntary theorizing, as follows. Theoretical advances make it possible to simplify total science by positing bridge laws identifying some of the entities discussed in one theory with entities discussed in another theory. In the name of parsimony, we posit those bridge laws forthwith. Identifications are made, not found.

In 'An Argument for the Identity Theory',[1] I claimed that this was a bad picture of psychophysical identification, since a suitable physiological theory could *imply* psychophysical identities — not merely make it reasonable to posit them for the sake of parsimony. The implication was as follows:

Mental state M = the occupant of causal role R (by definition of M).

First published in *The Australasian Journal of Philosophy* 50 (1972), 249–258. Reprinted with kind permission from *The Australasian Journal of Philosophy*.

Previous versions of this paper were presented at a conference on Philosophical Problems of Psychology held at Honolulu in March, 1968; at the annual meeting of the Australasian Association of Philosophy held at Brisbane in August, 1971; and at various university colloquia.

1 *Journal of Philosophy*, **63** (1966): 17–25.

Neural state N = the occupant of causal role R (by the physiological theory).

∴ Mental state M = neural state N (by transitivity of =).

If the meanings of the names of mental states were really such as to provide the first premise, and if the advance of physiology were such as to provide the second premise, then the conclusion would follow. Physiology and the meanings of words would leave us no choice but to make the psychophysical identification.

In this sequel, I shall uphold the view that psychophysical identifications thus described would be like theoretical identifications, though they would not fit the usual account thereof. For the usual account, I claim, is wrong; theoretical identifications *in general* are implied by the theories that make them possible – not posited independently. This follows from a general hypothesis about the meanings of theoretical terms: that they are definable functionally, by reference to causal roles.[2] Applied to common-sense psychology – folk science rather than professional science, but a theory nonetheless – we get the hypothesis of my previous paper[3] that a mental state M (say, an experience) is definable as the occupant of a certain causal role R – that is, as the state, of whatever sort, that is causally connected in specified ways to sensory stimuli, motor responses, and other mental states.

First, I consider an example of theoretical identification chosen to be remote from past philosophizing; then I give my general account of the meanings of theoretical terms and the nature of theoretical identifications; finally I return to the case of psychophysical identity.

I

We are assembled in the drawing room of the country house; the detective reconstructs the crime. That is, he proposes a *theory* designed

2 See my 'How to Define Theoretical Terms', *Journal of Philosophy*, **67** (1970): 427–446.

3 Since advocated also by D. M. Armstrong, in *A Materialist Theory of the Mind* (New York: Humanities Press, 1968). He expresses it thus: 'The concept of a mental state is primarily the concept of a state of the person apt for bringing about a certain sort of behaviour [and secondarily also, in some cases] apt for being brought about by a certain sort of stimulus', p. 82.

to be the best explanation of phenomena we have observed: the death of Mr. Body, the blood on the wallpaper, the silence of the dog in the night, the clock seventeen minutes fast, and so on. He launches into his story:

X, Y and Z conspired to murder Mr. Body. Seventeen years ago, in the gold fields of Uganda, X was Body's partner . . . Last week, Y and Z conferred in a bar in Reading . . . Tuesday night at 11:17, Y went to the attic and set a time bomb . . . Seventeen minutes later, X met Z in the billiard room and gave him the lead pipe . . . Just when the bomb went off in the attic, X fired three shots into the study through the French windows . . .

And so it goes: a long story. Let us pretend that it is a single long conjunctive sentence.

The story contains the three names 'X', 'Y' and 'Z'. The detective uses these new terms without explanation, as though we knew what they meant. But we do not. We never used them before, at least not in the senses they bear in the present context. All we know about their meanings is what we gradually gather from the story itself. Call these *theoretical terms (T-terms* for short) because they are introduced by a theory. Call the rest of the terms in the story *O-terms.* These are all the *other* terms except the T-terms; they are all the *old, original* terms we understood before the theory was proposed. We could call them our 'pre-theoretical' terms. But 'O' does *not* stand for 'observational'. Not all the O-terms are observational terms, whatever those may be. They are just any old terms. If part of the story was mathematical – if it included a calculation of the trajectory that took the second bullet to the chandelier without breaking the vase – then some of the O-terms will be mathematical. If the story says that something happened because of something else, then the O-terms will include the intensional connective 'because', or the operator 'it is a law that', or something of the sort.

Nor do the theoretical terms name some sort of peculiar theoretical, unobservable, semi-fictitious entities. The story makes plain that they name *people.* Not theoretical people, different somehow from ordinary, observational people – just people!

On my account, the detective plunged right into his story, using 'X', 'Y' and 'Z' as if they were names with understood denotation. It would have made little difference if he had started, instead, with initial existential quantifiers: 'There exist X, Y and Z such that . . .' and then told the story. In that case, the terms 'X', 'Y' and 'Z' would have been bound variables rather than T-terms. But the story would have had the same explanatory power. The second version of the story, with the T-terms turned into variables bound by existential quantifiers, is the Ramsey sentence of the first. Bear in mind, as evidence for what is to come, how little difference the initial quantifiers seem to make to the detective's assertion.

Suppose that after we have heard the detective's story, we learn that it is true of a certain three people: Plum, Peacock and Mustard. If we put the name 'Plum' in place of 'X', 'Peacock' in place of 'Y', and 'Mustard' in place of 'Z' throughout, we get a true story about the doings of those three people. We will say that Plum, Peacock and Mustard together *realize* (or are a *realization* of) the detective's theory.

We may also find out that the story is not true of any other triple.[4] Put in any three names that do not name Plum, Peacock and Mustard (in that order) and the story we get is false. We will say that Plum, Peacock and Mustard *uniquely realize* (are the *unique realization* of) the theory.

We might learn both of these facts. (The detective might have known them all along, but held them back to spring his trap; or he, like us, might learn them only after his story had been told.) And if we did, we would surely conclude that X, Y and Z in the story were Plum, Peacock and Mustard. I maintain that we would be compelled so to conclude, given the senses borne by the terms 'X', 'Y' and 'Z' in virtue of the way the detective introduced them in his theorizing, and given our information about Plum, Peacock and Mustard.

In telling his story, the detective set forth three roles and said that they were occupied by X, Y and Z. He must have specified the meanings of the three T-terms 'X', 'Y' and 'Z' thereby; for they had meanings afterwards, they had none before, and nothing else was done to give them meanings. They were introduced by an implicit functional

---

4 The story itself might imply this. If, for instance, the story said 'X saw Y give Z the candlestick while the three of them were alone in the billiard room at 9:17', then the story could not possibly be true of more than one triple.

definition, being reserved to name the occupants of the three roles. When we find out who are the occupants of the three roles, we find out who are X, Y and Z. Here is our theoretical identification.

In saying that the roles were occupied by X, Y and Z, the detective implied that they were occupied. That is, his theory implied its Ramsey sentence. That seems right; if we learnt that no triple realized the story, or even came close, we would have to conclude that the story was false. We would also have to deny that the names 'X', 'Y' and 'Z' named anything; for they were introduced as names for the occupants of roles that turned out to be unoccupied.

I also claim that the detective implied that the roles were uniquely occupied, when he reserved names for their occupants and proceeded as if those names had been given definite referents. Suppose we learnt that two different triples realized the theory: Plum, Peacock, Mustard; and Green, White, Scarlet. (Or the two different triples might overlap: Plum, Peacock, Mustard; and Green, Peacock, Scarlet.) I think we would be most inclined to say that the story was false, and that the names 'X', 'Y' and 'Z' did not name anything. They were introduced as names for the occupants of certain roles; but there is no such thing as *the* occupant of a doubly occupied role, so there is nothing suitable for them to name.

If, as I claim, the T-terms are definable as naming the first, second, and third components of the unique triple that realizes the story, then the T-terms can be treated like definite descriptions. If the story is uniquely realized, they name what they ought to name; if the story is unrealized or multiply realized, they are like improper descriptions. If too many triples realize the story, 'X' is like 'the moon of Mars'; if too few triples – none – realize the story, 'X' is like 'the moon of Venus'. Improper descriptions are not meaningless. Hilary Putnam has objected that on this sort of account of theoretical terms, the theoretical terms of a falsified theory come out meaningless.[5] But they do not, if theoretical terms of unrealized theories are like improper descriptions. 'The moon of Mars' and 'The moon of Venus' do not (in any normal way) name anything here in our actual world; but they are not

---

5 'What Theories Are Not', in Nagel, Suppes and Tarski eds., *Logic, Methodology and Philosophy of Science* (Stanford University Press, 1962): 247.

meaningless, because we know very well what they name in certain alternative possible worlds. Similarly, we know what 'X' names in any world where the detective's theory is true, whether or not our actual world is such a world.

A complication: what if the theorizing detective has made one little mistake? He should have said that Y went to the attic at 11:37, not 11:17. The story as told is unrealized, true of no one. But another story is realized, indeed uniquely realized: the story we get by deleting or correcting the little mistake. We can say that the story as told is *nearly realized*, has a unique *near-realization*. (The notion of a near-realization is hard to analyze, but easy to understand.) In this case the T-terms ought to name the components of the near-realization. More generally: they should name the components of the nearest realization of the theory, provided there is a unique nearest realization and it is near enough. Only if the story comes nowhere near to being realized, or if there are two equally near nearest realizations, should we resort to treating the T-terms like improper descriptions. But let us set aside this complication for the sake of simplicity, though we know well that scientific theories are often nearly realized but rarely realized, and that theoretical reduction is usually blended with revision of the reduced theory.

This completes our example. It may seem atypical: the T-terms are names, not predicates or functors. But that is of no importance. It is a popular exercise to recast a language so that its nonlogical vocabulary consists entirely of predicates; but it is just as easy to recast a language so that its nonlogical vocabulary consists entirely of names (provided that the logical vocabulary includes a copula). These names, of course, may purport to name individuals, sets, attributes, species, states, functions, relations, magnitudes, phenomena or what have you; but they are still names. Assume this done, so that we may replace all T-terms by variables of the same sort.

II

We now proceed to a general account of the functional definability of T-terms and the nature of theoretical identification. Suppose we have a new theory, T, introducing the new terms $t_1 \ldots t_n$. These are our T-terms. (Let them be names.) Every other term in our vocabulary, therefore, is an O-term. The theory T is presented in a sentence called the *postulate* of T. Assume this is a single sentence, perhaps a long conjunction. It says of the entities – states, magnitudes, species, or whatever – named by the T-terms that they occupy certain *causal roles*; that they stand in specified causal (and other) relations to entities named by O-terms, and to one another. We write the postulate thus:[6]

$$T[t].$$

Replacing the T-terms uniformly by free variables $x_1 \ldots x_n$, we get a formula in which only O-terms appear:

$$T[x].$$

Any n-tuple of entities which satisfies this formula is a realization of the theory T. Prefixing existential quantifiers, we get the *Ramsey sentence* of T, which says that T has at least one realization:

$$\exists x\, T[x].$$

We can also write a *modified Ramsey sentence* which says that T has a unique realization:[7]

$$\exists_1 x\, T[x].$$

The Ramsey sentence has exactly the same O-content as the postulate of T; any sentence free of T-terms follows logically from one if and only if it follows from the other.[8] The modified Ramsey sentence has slightly more O-content. I claim that this surplus O-content does belong to the theory T – there are more theorems of T than follow

6 Notation: boldface names and variables denote n-tuples; the corresponding subscripted names and variables denote components of n-tuples. For instance, t is $<t_1 \ldots t_n>$. This notation is easily dispensable, and hence carries no ontic commitment to n-tuples.

7 That is, $\exists y \forall x(T[x] \equiv y = x)$. Note that $\exists_1 x_1 \ldots \exists_1 x_n\, T[x]$ does not imply $\exists_1 x\, T[x]$, and does not say that T is uniquely realized.

8 On the assumptions – reasonable for the postulate of a scientific theory – that the T-terms occur purely referentially in the postulate, and in such a way that the postulate is false if any of them are denotationless. We shall make these assumptions henceforth.

logically from the postulate alone. For in presenting the postulate as if the T-terms have been well-defined thereby, the theorist has implicitly asserted that T is uniquely realized.

We can write the *Carnap sentence* of T: the conditional of the Ramsey sentence and the postulate, which says that if T is realized, then the T-terms name the components of some realization of T:

$$\exists \mathbf{x}\ T[\mathbf{x}] \supset T[\mathbf{t}].$$

Carnap has suggested this sentence as a meaning postulate for T[9] but if we want T-terms of unrealized or multiply realized theories to have the status of improper descriptions, our meaning postulates should instead be a *modified Carnap sentence*, this conditional with our modified Ramsey sentence as antecedent:

$$\exists_1 \mathbf{x}\ T[\mathbf{x}] \supset T[\mathbf{t}],$$

together with another conditional to cover the remaining cases:[10]

$$\sim \exists_1 \mathbf{x}\ T[\mathbf{x}] \supset \mathbf{t} = \star.$$

This pair of meaning postulates is logically equivalent[11] to a sentence which explicitly defines the T-terms by means of O-terms:

$$\mathbf{t} = \imath \mathbf{x}\ T[\mathbf{x}].$$

This is what I have called functional definition. The T-terms have been defined as the occupants of the causal roles specified by the theory T; as *the* entities, whatever those may be, that bear certain causal relations to one another and to the referents of the O-terms.

<hr/>

9 Most recently in *Philosophical Foundations of Physics* (New York: Basic Books, 1966): 265–274. Carnap, of course, has in mind the case in which the O-terms belong to an observation language.

10 $\mathbf{t} = \star$ means that each t_i is denotationless. Let $*$ be some chosen necessarily denotationless name; then $\star$ is $<* \ldots *>$ and $\mathbf{t} = \star$ is equivalent to the conjunction of all the identities $t_i = *$.

11 Given a theory of descriptions which makes an identity true whenever both its terms have the status of improper descriptions, false whenever one term has that status and the other does not. This might best be the theory of descriptions in Dana Scott, 'Existence and Description in Formal Logic', in R. Schoenman, ed., *Bertrand Russell: Philosopher of the Century* (London: Allen & Unwin, 1967).

If I am right, T-terms are eliminable – we can always replace them by their definientia. Of course, this is not to say that theories are fictions, or that theories are uninterpreted formal abacuses, or that theoretical entities are unreal. Quite the opposite! Because we understand the O-terms, and we can define the T-terms from them, theories are fully meaningful; we have reason to think a good theory true; and if a theory is true, then whatever exists according to the theory really *does* exist.

I said that there are more theorems of T than follow logically from the postulate alone. More precisely: the theorems of T are just those sentences which follow from the postulate together with the corresponding functional definition of the T-terms. For that definition, I claim, is given implicitly when the postulate is presented as bestowing meanings on the T-terms introduced in it.

It may happen, after the introduction of the T-terms, that we come to believe of a certain n-tuple of entities, specified otherwise than as the entities that realize T, that they do realize T. That is, we may come to accept a sentence

$$T[\mathbf{r}]$$

where $r_1 \ldots r_n$ are either O-terms or theoretical terms of some other theory, introduced into our language independently of $t_1 \ldots t_n$. This sentence, which we may call a *weak reduction premise* for T, is free of T-terms. Our acceptance of it might have nothing to do with our previous acceptance of T. We might accept it as part of some new theory; or we might believe it as part of our miscellaneous, unsystematized general knowledge. Yet having accepted it, for whatever reason, we are logically compelled to make theoretical identifications. The reduction premise, together with the functional definition of the T-terms and the postulate of T, logically implies the identity:

$$\mathbf{t} = \mathbf{r}.$$

In other words, the postulate and the weak reduction premise definitionally imply the identities $t_i = r_i$.

Or we might somehow come to believe of a certain n-tuple of entities that they *uniquely* realize T; that is, to accept a sentence

$$\forall \mathbf{x}(T[\mathbf{x}] \equiv \mathbf{x} = \mathbf{r})$$

where $r_1 \ldots r_n$ are as above. We may call this a *strong reduction premise* for T, since it definitionally implies the theoretical identifications by itself, without the aid of the postulate of T. The strong reduction premise logically implies the identity

$$\mathbf{r} = \imath \mathbf{x} T[\mathbf{x}]$$

which, together with the functional definition of the T-terms, implies the identities $t_i = r_i$ by transitivity of identity.

These theoretical identifications are not voluntary posits, made in the name of parsimony; they are deductive inferences. According to their definitions, the T-terms name the occupants of the causal roles specified by the theory T. According to the weak reduction premise and T, or the strong reduction premise by itself, the occupants of those causal roles turn out to be the referents of $r_1 \ldots r_n$. Therefore, those are the entities named by the T-terms. That is how we inferred that X, Y and Z were Plum, Peacock and Mustard; and that, I suggest, is how we make theoretical identifications in general.

III

And that is how, someday, we will infer that[12] the mental states M_1, $M_2, \ldots$ are the neural states $N_1, N_2, \ldots$.

Think of common-sense psychology as a term-introducing scientific theory, though one invented long before there was any such institution as professional science. Collect all the platitudes you can think of regarding the causal relations of mental states, sensory stimuli, and motor responses. Perhaps we can think of them as having the form:

When someone is in so-and-so combination of mental states and receives sensory stimuli of so-and-so kind, he tends with so-and-

---

12 In general, or in the case of a given species, or in the case of a given person. It might turn out that the causal roles definitive of mental states are occupied by different neural (or other) states in different organisms. See my discussion of Hilary Putnam 'Psychological Predicates' in *Journal of Philosophy*, **66** (1969): 23–25.

so probability to be caused thereby to go into so-and-so mental states and produce so-and-so motor responses.

Add also all the platitudes to the effect that one mental state falls under another – 'toothache is a kind of pain', and the like. Perhaps there are platitudes of other forms as well. Include only platitudes which are common knowledge among us – everyone knows them, everyone knows that everyone else knows them, and so on. For the meanings of our words are common knowledge, and I am going to claim that names of mental states derive their meaning from these platitudes.

Form the conjunction of these platitudes; or better, form a cluster of them – a disjunction of all conjunctions of *most* of them. (That way it will not matter if a few are wrong.) This is the postulate of our term-introducing theory. The names of mental states are the T-terms.[13] The O-terms used to introduce them must be sufficient for speaking of stimuli and responses, and for speaking of causal relations among these and states of unspecified nature.

From the postulate, form the definition of the T-terms; it defines the mental states by reference to their causal relations to stimuli, responses, and each other. When we learn what sort of states occupy those causal roles definitive of the mental states, we will learn what states the mental states are – exactly as we found out who X was when we found out that Plum was the man who occupied a certain role, and exactly as we found out what light was when we found that electromagnetic radiation was the phenomenon that occupied a certain role.

Imagine our ancestors first speaking only of external things, stimuli, and responses – and perhaps producing what we, but not they, may call *Äusserungen* of mental states – until some genius invented the the-

---

13 It may be objected that the number of mental states is infinite, or at least enormous; for instance, there are as many states of belief as there are propositions to be believed. But it would be better to say that there is one state of belief, and it is a relational state, relating people to propositions. (Similarly, centigrade temperature is a relational state, relating objects to numbers.) The platitudes involving belief would, of course, contain universally quantified proposition-variables. Likewise for other mental states with intentional objects.

ory of mental states, with its newly introduced T-terms, to explain the regularities among stimuli and responses. But that did not happen. Our common-sense psychology was never a newly invented term-introducing scientific theory – not even of prehistoric folk-science. The story that mental terms were introduced as theoretical terms is a myth.

It is, in fact, Sellars' myth of our Rylean ancestors.[14] And though it is a myth, it may be a good myth or a bad one. It is a good myth if our names of mental states do in fact mean just what they would mean if the myth were true.[15] I adopt the working hypothesis that it is a good myth. This hypothesis can be tested, in principle, in whatever way any hypothesis about the conventional meanings of our words can be tested. I have not tested it; but I offer one item of evidence. Many philosophers have found Rylean behaviorism at least plausible; more have found watered down, 'criteriological' behaviorism plausible. There is a strong odor of analyticity about the platitudes of common-sense psychology. The myth explains the odor of analyticity and the plausibility of behaviorism. If the names of mental states are like theoretical terms, they name nothing unless the theory (the cluster of platitudes) is more or less true. Hence it is analytic that *either* pain, etc., do not exist *or* most of our platitudes about them are true. If this

14 Wilfrid Sellars, 'Empiricism and the Philosophy of Mind', in Feigl and Scriven, eds., *Minnesota Studies in the Philosophy of Science*, I (University of Minnesota Press, 1956): 309–320.

15 Two myths which cannot both be true together can nevertheless both be good together. Part of my myth says that names of color-sensations were T-terms, introduced using names of colors as O-terms. If this is a good myth, we should be able to define 'sensation of red' roughly as 'that state apt for being brought about by the presence of something red (before one's open eyes, in good light, etc.)'. A second myth says that names of colors were T-terms introduced using names of color-sensations as O-terms. If this second myth is good, we should be able to define 'red' roughly as 'that property of things apt for bringing about the sensation of red'. The two myths could not both be true, for which came first: names of color-sensations or of colors? But they could both be good. We could have a circle in which colors are correctly defined in terms of sensations and sensations are correctly defined in terms of colors. We could not discover the meanings *both* of names of colors and of names of color-sensations just by looking at the circle of correct definitions, but so what?

seems analytic to you, you should accept the myth, and be prepared for psychophysical identifications.

The hypothesis that names of mental states are like functionally defined theoretical terms solves a familiar problem about mental explanations. How can my behavior be explained by an explanans consisting of nothing but particular-fact premises about my present state of mind? Where are the covering laws? The solution is that the requisite covering laws are implied by the particular-fact premises. Ascriptions to me of various particular beliefs and desires, say, cannot be true if there are no such states as belief and desire; cannot be true, that is, unless the causal roles definitive of belief and desire are occupied. But these roles can only be occupied by states causally related in the proper lawful way to behavior.

Formally, suppose we have a mental explanation of behavior as follows.

$$\frac{C_1[\mathbf{t}],\ C_2[\mathbf{t}],\ \ldots}{E}$$

Here E describes the behavior to be explained; $C_1[\mathbf{t}]$, $C_2[\mathbf{t}]$, ... are particular-fact premises describing the agent's state of mind at the time. Various of the mental terms $t_1 \ldots t_n$ appear in these premises, in such a way that the premises would be false if the terms named nothing. Now let $L_1[\mathbf{t}]$, $L_2[\mathbf{t}]$, ... be the platitudinous purported causal laws whereby – according to the myth – the mental terms were introduced. Ignoring clustering for simplicity, we may take the term-introducing postulate to be the conjunction of these. Then our explanation may be rewritten:

$$\frac{\exists_1\mathbf{x}\left(\begin{array}{l} L_1[\mathbf{x}]\,\&\,L_2[\mathbf{x}]\,\&\,\ldots\,\& \\ C_1[\mathbf{x}]\,\&\,C_2[\mathbf{x}]\,\&\,\ldots \end{array}\right)}{E}$$

The new explanans is a definitional consequence of the original one. In the expanded version, however, laws appear explicitly alongside the particular-fact premises. We have, so to speak, an existential generalization of an ordinary covering-law explanation.[16]

The causal definability of mental terms has been thought to contradict the necessary infallibility of introspection.[17] Pain is one state; belief that one is in pain is another. (Confusingly, either of the two may be called 'awareness of pain'.) Why cannot I believe that I am in pain without being in pain – that is, without being in whatever state it is that occupies so-and-so causal role? Doubtless I am so built that this normally does not happen; but what makes it impossible?

I do not know whether introspection is (in some or all cases) infallible. But if it is, that is no difficulty for me. Here it is important that, on my version of causal definability, the mental terms stand or fall together. If common-sense psychology fails, all of them are alike denotationless.

Suppose that among the platitudes are some to the effect that introspection is reliable: 'belief that one is in pain never occurs unless pain occurs' or the like. Suppose further that these platitudes enter the term-introducing postulate as conjuncts, not as cluster members; and suppose that they are so important that an *n*-tuple that fails to satisfy them perfectly is not even a near-realization of common-sense psychology. (I neither endorse nor repudiate these suppositions.) Then the necessary infallibility of introspection is assured. Two states cannot be pain and belief that one is in pain, respectively (in the case of a given individual or species) if the second *ever* occurs without the first. The state that *usually* occupies the role of belief that one is in pain may, of course, occur without the state that *usually* occupies the role of pain; but in that case (under the suppositions above) the former no longer is the state of belief that one is in pain, and the latter no longer is pain. Indeed, the victim no longer is in any mental state whatever, since his states no longer realize (or nearly realize) common-sense psychology. Therefore it is impossible to believe that one is in pain and not be in pain.

---

16 See 'How to Define Theoretical Terms': 440–441.

17 By Armstrong, in *A Materialist Theory of the Mind*, pp. 100–113. He finds independent grounds for denying the infallibility of introspection.

17

What experience teaches

EXPERIENCE THE BEST TEACHER

They say that experience is the best teacher, and the classroom is no substitute for Real Life. There's truth to this. If you want to know what some new and different experience is like, you can learn it by going out and really *having* that experience. You can't learn it by being told about the experience, however thorough your lessons may be.

Does this prove much of anything about the metaphysics of mind and the limits of science? I think not.

Example: Skunks and Vegemite I have smelled skunks, so I know what it's like to smell skunks. But skunks live only in some parts of the world, so you may never have smelled a skunk. If you haven't smelled a skunk, then you don't know what it's like. You never will, unless someday you smell a skunk for yourself. On the other hand, you may have tasted Vegemite, that famous Australian substance; and I never have. So you may know what it's like to taste Vegemite. I don't, and unless I taste Vegemite (what, and spoil a good example!), I never will. It won't help at all to take lessons on the chemical composition of

First published in *Proceedings of the Russellian Society* (University of Sydney) 13 (1988), pp. 29–57. Reprinted with kind permission from the Russellian Society.

Part of this paper derives from a lecture at La Trobe University in 1981. I thank La Trobe for support in 1981, Harvard University for support under a Santayana Fellowship in 1988, and Frank Jackson for very helpful discussion.

skunk scent or Vegemite, the physiology of the nostrils or the taste-buds, and the neurophysiology of the sensory nerves and the brain.

Example: The Captive Scientist.[1] Mary, a brilliant scientist, has lived from birth in a cell where everything is black or white. (Even she herself is painted all over.) She views the world on black-and-white television. By television she reads books, she joins in discussion, she watches the results of experiments done under her direction. In this way she becomes the world's leading expert on color and color vision and the brain states produced by exposure to colors. But she doesn't know what it's like to see color. And she never will, unless she escapes from her cell.

Example: The Bat.[2] The bat is an alien creature, with a sonar sense quite unlike any sense of ours. We can never have the experiences of a bat; because we could not become bat-like enough to have those experiences and still be ourselves. We will never know what it's like to be a bat. Not even if we come to know all the facts there are about the bat's behavior and behavioral dispositions, about the bat's physical structure and processes, about the bat's functional organization. Not even if we come to know all the same sort of physical facts about all the other bats, or about other creatures, or about ourselves. Not even if we come to possess all physical facts whatever. Not even if we become able to recognize all the mathematical and logical implications of all these facts, no matter how complicated and how far beyond the reach of finite deduction.

Experience is the best teacher, in this sense: having an experience is the best way or perhaps the only way, of coming to know what that experience is like. No amount of scientific information about the stimuli that produce that experience and the process that goes on in you when you have that experience will enable you to know what it's like to have the experience.

1 See Frank Jackson, "Epiphenomenal qualia," *Philosophical Quarterly* 32 (1982), pp. 127–36; "What Mary didn't know," *Journal of Philosophy* 83 (1986), pp. 291–5.
2 See B. A. Farrell, "Experience," *Mind* 59 (1950), pp. 170–98; and Thomas Nagel, "What is it like to be a bat?" *Philosophical Review* 83 (1974), pp. 435–50, also in Thomas Nagel, *Mortal Questions* (Cambridge: Cambridge University Press, 1979).

Having an experience is surely one good way, and surely the only practical way, of coming to know what that experience is like. Can we say, flatly, that it is the only *possible* way? Probably not. There is a change that takes place in you when you have the experience and thereby come to know what it's like. Perhaps the exact same change could in principle be produced in you by precise neurosurgery, very far beyond the limits of present-day technique. Or it could possibly be produced in you by magic. If we ignore the laws of nature, which are after all contingent, then there is no necessary connection between cause and effect: anything could cause anything. For instance, the casting of a spell could do to you exactly what your first smell of skunk would do. We might quibble about whether a state produced in this artificial fashion would deserve the *name* "knowing what it's like to smell a skunk," but we can imagine that so far as what goes on within you is concerned, it would differ not at all.[3] Just as we can imagine that a spell might produce the same change as a smell, so likewise we can imagine that science lessons might cause that same change. Even that is possible, in the broadest sense of the word. If we ignored all we know about how the world really works, we could not say what might happen to someone if he were taught about the chemistry of scent and the physiology of the nose. There might have been a causal mechanism that transforms science lessons into whatever it is that experience gives us. But there isn't. It is not an absolutely necessary truth that experience is the best teacher about what a new experience is like. It's a contingent truth. But we have good reason to think it's true.

We have good reason to think that something of this kind is true, anyway, but less reason to be sure exactly what. Maybe some way of giving the lessons that hasn't yet been invented, and some way of taking them in that hasn't yet been practiced, could give us a big surprise. Consider sight-reading: a trained musician can read the score and know what it would be like to hear the music. If I'd never heard that some people can sight-read, I would never have thought it hu-

3 See Peter Unger, "On experience and the development of the understanding," *American Philosophical Quarterly* 3 (1966), pp. 1–9.

manly possible. Of course the moral is that new music isn't altogether new – the big new experience is a rearrangement of lots of little old experiences. It just might turn out the same for new smells and tastes *vis-à-vis* old ones; or even for color vision *vis-à-vis* black and white;[4] or even for sonar sense experience *vis-à-vis* the sort we enjoy. The thing we can say with some confidence is that we have no faculty for knowing on the basis of mere science lessons what some *new enough* experience would be like. But how new is "new enough"? – There, we just might be in for surprises.

THREE WAYS TO MISS THE POINT

The First Way. A literalist might see the phrase "know what it's like" and take that to mean: "know what it resembles." Then he might ask: what's so hard about that? Why can't you just be told which experiences resemble one another? You needn't have had the experiences – all you need, to be taught your lessons, is some way of referring to them. You could be told: the smell of skunk somewhat resembles the smell of burning rubber. I have been told: the taste of Vegemite somewhat resembles that of Marmite. Black-and-white Mary might know more than most of us about the resemblances among color-experiences. She might know which ones are spontaneously called "similar" by subjects who have them; which gradual changes from one to another tend to escape notice; which ones get conflated with which in memory; which ones involve roughly the same neurons firing in similar rhythms; and so forth. We could even know what the bat's sonar experiences resemble just by knowing that they do not at all resemble any experiences of humans, but do resemble – as it might be – certain experiences that occur in certain fish. This misses the point. *Pace* the literalist, "know what it's like" does not mean "know what it resembles." The most that's true is that knowing what it resembles *may* help you to know what it's like. If you are taught that experience A resembles B and C closely, D less, E not at all, that will help you know what A is like – *if* you know already what B and C and D and

---

4 For such speculation, see Paul M. Churchland, "Reduction, qualia, and the direct introspection of brain states," *Journal of Philosophy* 82 (1985), pp. 8–28.

E are like. Otherwise, it helps you not at all. I don't know any better what it's like to taste Vegemite when I'm told that it tastes like Marmite, because I don't know what Marmite tastes like either. (Nor do I know any better what Marmite tastes like for being told it tastes like Vegemite.) Maybe Mary knows enough to triangulate each color experience exactly in a network of resemblances, or in many networks of resemblance in different respects, while never knowing what any node of any network is like. Maybe we could do the same for bat experiences. But no amount of information about resemblances, just by itself, does anything to help us know what an experience is like.

The Second Way. In so far as I don't know what it would be like to drive a steam locomotive fast on a cold, stormy night, part of my problem is just that I don't know what experiences I would have. The firebox puts out a lot of heat, especially when the fireman opens the door to throw on more coal; on the other hand, the cab is drafty and gives poor protection from the weather. Would I be too hot or too cold? Or both by turns? Or would it be chilled face and scorched legs? If I knew the answers to such questions, I'd know much better what it would be like to drive the locomotive. So maybe "know what it's like" just means "know what experiences one has." Then again: what's the problem? Why can't you just be told what experiences you would have if, say, you tasted Vegemite? Again, you needn't have had the experiences – all you need, to be taught your lessons, is some way of referring to them. We have ways to refer to experiences we haven't had. We can refer to them in terms of their causes: the experience one has upon tasting Vegemite, the experience one has upon tasting a substance of such-and-such chemical composition. Or we can refer to them in terms of their effects: the experience that just caused Fred to say "Yeeuch!" Or we can refer to them in terms of the physical states of the nervous system that mediate between those causes and effects: the experience one has when one's nerves are firing in such-and-such pattern. (According to some materialists, I myself for one, this means the experience which is identical with such-and-such firing pattern. According to other materialists it means the experience which is re-alized by such-and-such firing pattern. According to many dualists, it means the experience which is merely the lawful companion of such-and-such firing pattern. But whichever it is, we get a way of referring to the experience.) Black-and-white Mary is in a position to refer to color-experiences in all these ways. Therefore you should have no problem in telling her exactly what experiences one has upon seeing the colors. Or rather, your only problem is that you'd be telling her what she knows very well already! In general, to know what is the X is to know that the X is the Y, where it's not too obvious that the X is the Y. (Just knowing that the X is the X won't do, of course, because it is too obvious.) If Mary knows that the experience of seeing green is the experience associated with such-and-such pattern of nerve firings, then she knows the right sort of unobvious identity. So she knows what experience one has upon seeing green.

(Sometimes it's suggested that you need a "rigid designator": you know what is the X by knowing that the X is the Y only if "the Y" is a term whose referent does not depend on any contingent matter of fact. In the first place, this suggestion is false. You can know who is the man on the balcony by knowing that the man on the balcony is the Prime Minister even if neither "the Prime Minister" nor any other phrase available to you rigidly designates the man who is, in fact, the Prime Minister. In the second place, according to one version of Materialism (the one I accept) a description of the form "the state of having nerves firing in such-and-such a pattern" *is* a rigid designator, and what it designates is in fact an experience; and according to another version of Materialism, a description of the form "having some or other state which occupies so-and-so functional role" is a rigid designator of an experience. So even if the false suggestion were granted, still it hasn't been shown, without begging the question against Materialism, that Mary could not know what experience one has upon seeing red.)

Since Mary *does* know what experiences she would have if she saw the colors, but she *doesn't* know what it would be like to see the colors, we'd better conclude that "know what it's like" does not after all mean "know what experiences one has." The locomotive example was misleading. Yes, by learning what experiences the driver would have, I can know what driving the locomotive would be like; but only because I already know what those experiences are like. (It matters that I know what they're like under the appropriate descriptions – as it might be, the description "chilled face and scorched legs." This is something we'll return to later.) Mary may know as well as I do that when the driver leans out into the storm to watch the signals, he will have the experience of seeing sometimes green lights and sometimes red. She knows better than I what experiences he has when signals come into view. She can give many more unobviously equivalent descriptions of those experiences than I can. But knowing what color-experiences the driver has won't help Mary to know what his job is like. It will help me.

The Third Way. Until Mary sees green, here is one thing she will never know: she will never know that she is seeing green. The reason why is just that until she sees green, it will never be true that she is seeing green. Some knowledge is irreducibly egocentric, or *de se*.[5] It is not just knowledge about what goes on in the world; it is knowledge of who and when in the world one is. Knowledge of what goes on in the world will be true alike for all who live in that world; whereas egocentric knowledge may be true for one and false for another, or true for one at one time and false for the same one at another time. Maybe Mary knows in advance, as she plots her escape, that 9 a.m. on the 13th of May, 1997, is the moment when someone previously confined in a black-and-white cell sees color for the first time. But until that moment comes, she will never know that she herself is then seeing color – because she isn't. What isn't true isn't knowledge. This goes as much for egocentric knowledge as for the rest. So only those of whom an egocentric proposition is true can know it, and only at times when it is true of them can they know it. That one is then seeing color is an egocentric proposition. So we've found a proposition which Mary can never know until she sees color – which, as it happens, is the very moment when she will first know what it's like to see color! Have we discovered the reason why experience is the best teacher?

5 See my "Attitudes *de dicto* and *de se*," *Philosophical Review* 88 (1979), pp. 513–43, also in my *Philosophical Papers*, vol. 1 (New York: Oxford University Press, 1983); and Roderick Chisholm, *The First Person: An Essay on Reference and Intentionality* (Minneapolis: University of Minnesota Press, 1981).

And not contingently after all, but as a necessary consequence of the logic of egocentric knowledge?

No; we have two separate phenomena here, and only some bewitchment about the "first-person perspective" could make us miss the difference. In the first place, Mary will probably go on knowing what it's like to see green after she stops knowing the egocentric proposition that she's then seeing green. Since what isn't true isn't known she must stop knowing that proposition the moment she stops seeing green. (Does that only mean that we should have taken a different egocentric proposition: that one *has* seen green? No; for in that case Mary could go on knowing the proposition even after she forgets what it's like to see green, as might happen if she were soon recaptured.) In the second place, Mary might come to know what it's like to see green even if she didn't know the egocentric proposition. She might not have known in advance that her escape route would take her across a green meadow, and it might take her a little while to recognize grass by its shape. So at first she might know only that she was seeing some colors or other, and thereby finding out what some color-experiences or other were like, without being able to put a name either to the colors or to the experiences. She would then know what it was like to see green, though not under that description, indeed not under any description more useful than "the color-experience I'm having now"; but she would not know the egocentric proposition that she is then seeing green, since she wouldn't know which color she was seeing. In the third place, the gaining of egocentric knowledge may have prerequisites that have nothing to do with experience. Just as Mary can't know she's seeing green until she *does* see green, she can't know she's turning 50 until she *does* turn 50. But – I hope! – turning 50 does not involve some special experience. In short, though indeed one can gain egocentric knowledge that one is in some situation only when one is in it, that is not the same as finding out what an experience is like only when one has that experience.

We've just rejected two suggestions that don't work separately, and we may note that they don't work any better when put together. One knows what is the X by knowing that the X is the Y, where the identity is not too obvious; and "the Y" might be an egocentric description. So knowledge that the X is the Y might be irreducibly egocentric knowledge, therefore knowledge that cannot be had until it is true of one that the X is the Y. So one way of knowing what is the X will remain unavailable until it comes true of one that the X is the Y. One way that I could gain an unobvious identity concerning the taste of Vegemite would be for it to come true that the taste of Vegemite was the taste I was having at that very moment – and that would come true at the very moment I tasted Vegemite and found out what it was like! Is this why experience is the best teacher? – No; cases of gaining an unobvious egocentric identity are a dime a dozen, and most of them do not result in finding out what an experience is like. Suppose I plan ahead that I will finally break down and taste Vegemite next Thursday noon. Then on Wednesday noon, if I watch the clock, I first gain the unobvious egocentric knowledge that the taste of Vegemite is the taste I shall be having in exactly 24 hours, and thereby I have a new way of knowing what is the taste of Vegemite. But on Wednesday noon I don't yet know what it's like. Another example: from time to time I find myself next to a Vegemite-taster. On those occasions, and only those, I know what is the taste of Vegemite by knowing that it is the taste being had by the person next to me. But on no such occasion has it ever yet happened that I knew what it was like to taste Vegemite.

THE HYPOTHESIS OF PHENOMENAL INFORMATION

No amount of the physical information that black-and-white Mary gathers could help her know what it was like to see colors; no amount of the physical information that we might gather about bats could help us know what it's like to have their experiences; and likewise in other cases. There is a natural and tempting explanation of why physical information does not help. That is the hypothesis that besides physical information there is an irreducibly different kind of information to be had: *phenomenal information*. The two are independent. Two possible cases might be exactly alike physically, yet differ phenomenally. When we get physical information we narrow down the physical possibilities, and perhaps we narrow them down all the way to one, but we leave open a range of phenomenal possibilities. When we have an experience, on the other hand, we acquire phenomenal information; possibilities previously open are eliminated; and that is what it is to learn what the experience is like.

(Analogy. Suppose the question concerned the location of a point within a certain region of the x-y plane. We might be told that its x-coordinate lies in certain intervals, and outside certain others. We might even get enough of this information to fix the x-coordinate exactly. But no amount of x-information would tell us anything about the y-coordinate; any amount of x-information leaves open all the y-possibilities. But when at last we make a y-measurement, we acquire a new kind of information; possibilities previously open are eliminated; and that is how we learn where the point is in the y-direction.)

What might the subject matter of phenomenal information be? *If* the Hypothesis of Phenomenal Information is true, then you have an easy answer: it is information about experience. More specifically, it is information about a certain part or aspect or feature of experience. But if the Hypothesis is false, then there is still experience (complete with all its parts and aspects and features) and yet no information about experience is phenomenal information. So it cannot be said in a neutral way, without presupposing the Hypothesis, that information about experience is phenomenal information. For if the Hypothesis is false and Materialism is true, it may be that all the information there is about experience is physical information, and can very well be presented in lessons for the inexperienced.

It makes no difference to put some fashionable new phrase in place of "experience." If instead of "experience" you say "raw feel" (or just "feeling"), or "way it feels," or "what it's like," then I submit that you mean nothing different. Is there anything it's like to be this robot? Does this robot have experiences? – I can tell no difference between the new question and the old. Does sunburn feel the same way to you that it does to me? Do we have the same raw feel? Do we have the same experience when sunburned? – Again, same question. "Know the feeling," "know what it's like" – interchangeable. (Except that the former may hint at an alternative to the Hypothesis of Phenomenal Information.) So if the friend of phenomenal information says that its subject matter is raw feels, or ways to feel, or what it's like, then I respond just as I do if he says that the subject matter is experience. Maybe so, *if* the Hypothesis of Phenomenal Information is true; but if the Hypothesis is false and Materialism is true, nevertheless there is still information about raw feels, ways to feel or what it's like; but in that case it is physical information and can be conveyed in lessons.

We might get a candidate for the subject matter of phenomenal information that is not just experience renamed, but is still tendentious. For instance, we might be told that phenomenal information concerns the intrinsic character of experience. A friend of phenomenal information might indeed believe that it reveals certain special, non-physical intrinsic properties of experience. He might even believe that it reveals the existence of some special non-physical thing or process, *all* of whose intrinsic properties are non-physical. But he is by no means alone in saying that experience has an intrinsic character. Plenty of us materialists say so too. We say that a certain color-experience is whatever state occupies a certain functional role. So if the occupant of that role (universally, or in the case of humans, or in the case of certain humans) is a certain pattern of neutral firing, then that pattern of firing *is* the experience (in the case in question). Therefore the intrinsic character of the experience is the intrinsic character of the firing pattern. For instance, a frequency of firing is part of the intrinsic character of the experience. If we materialists are right about what experience is, then black-and-white Mary knows all about the intrinsic character of color-experience; whereas most people who know what color-experience is like remain totally ignorant about its intrinsic character.[6]

To say that phenomenal information concerns "qualia" would be tendentious in much the same way. For how was this notion introduced? Often thus. We are told to imagine someone who, when he sees red things, has just the sort of experiences that we have when we see green things, and vice versa; and we are told to call this a case of "inverted qualia". And then we are told to imagine someone queerer still, who sees red and responds to it appropriately, and indeed has entirely the same functional organization of inner states as we do and yet has no experiences at all; and we are told to call this a case of "absent qualia". Now a friend of phenomenal information might well

6 See Gilbert Harman, "The intrinsic quality of experience," *Philosophical Perspectives* 4 (1990).

think that these deficiencies have something to do with the non-physical subject matter of phenomenal information. But others can understand them otherwise. Some materialists will reject the cases outright, but others, and I for one, will make sense of them as best we can. Maybe the point is that the states that occupy the roles of experiences, and therefore *are* the experiences, in normal people are inverted or absent in victims of inverted or absent qualia. (This presupposes, what might be false, that most people are enough alike). Experience of red – the state that occupies that role in normal people – occurs also in the victim of "inverted qualia," but in him it occupies the role of experience of green; whereas the state that occupies in him the role of experience of red is the state that occupies in normal people the role of experience of green. Experience of red and of green – that is, the occupants of those roles for normal people – do not occur at all in the victim of "absent qualia"; the occupants of those roles for him are states that don't occur at all in the normal. Thus we make good sense of inverted and absent qualia; but in such a way that "qualia" is just the word for role-occupying states taken *per se* rather than *qua* occupants of roles. Qualia, so understood, could not be the subject matter of phenomenal information. Mary knows all about them. We who have them mostly don't.[7]

It is best to rest content with an unhelpful name and a *via negativa*. Stipulate that "the phenomenal aspect of the world" is to name whatever is the subject matter of phenomenal information, if there is any such thing; the phenomenal aspect, if such there be, is that which we can become informed about by having new experiences but never by taking lessons. Having said this, it will be safe to say that information about the phenomenal aspect of the world can only be phenomenal information. But all we really know, after thus closing the circle, is that phenomenal information is supposed to reveal the presence of some sort of non-physical things or processes within experience, or

7 See Ned Block and Jerry A. Fodor, "What psychological states are not," *Philosophical Review* 81 (1972), pp. 159–81, also in Ned Block (ed.), *Readings in Philosophy of Psychology*, vol. I (Cambridge, MA: Harvard University Press, 1980); and my "Mad pain and Martian pain", in *Readings in Philosophy of Psychology*, vol. I, and in my *Philosophical Papers*, vol. I.

else it is supposed to reveal that certain physical things or processes within experience have some sort of non-physical properties.

THE KNOWLEDGE ARGUMENT

If we invoke the Hypothesis of Phenomenal Information to explain why no amount of physical information suffices to teach us what a new experience is like, then we have a powerful argument to refute any materialist theory of the mind. Frank Jackson (see note 1) calls it the "Knowledge Argument." Arguments against one materialist theory or another are never very conclusive. It is always possible to adjust the details. But the Knowledge Argument, if it worked, would directly refute the bare minimum that is common to *all* materialist theories.

It goes as follows. First in a simplified form; afterward we'll do it properly. Minimal Materialism is a supervenience thesis: no difference without physical difference. That is: any two possibilities that are just alike physically are just alike *simpliciter*. If two possibilities are just alike physically, then no physical information can eliminate one but not both of them. If two possibilities are just alike *simpliciter* (if that is possible) then no information whatsoever can eliminate one but not both of them. So if there is a kind of information – namely, phenomenal information – that can eliminate possibilities that any amount of physical information leaves open, then there must be possibilities that are just alike physically, but not just alike *simpliciter*. That is just what minimal Materialism denies.

(Analogy. If two possible locations in our region agree in their x-coordinate, then no amount of x-information can eliminate one but not both. If, *per impossibile*, two possible locations agreed in all their coordinates, then no information whatsoever could eliminate one but not both. So if there is a kind of information – namely, y-information – that can eliminate locations that any amount of x-information leaves open, then there must be locations in the region that agree in their x-coordinate but not in all their coordinates.)

Now to remove the simplification. What we saw so far was the Knowledge Argument against Materialism taken as a necessary truth, applying unrestrictedly to all possible worlds. But we materialists usually think that Materialism is a contingent truth. We grant that there are spooky possible worlds where Materialism is false, but we insist that our actual world isn't one of them. If so, then there might after all be two possibilities that are alike physically but not alike *simpliciter*, but one or both of the two would have to be possibilities where Materialism was false. Spooky worlds could differ with respect to their spooks without differing physically. Our minimal Materialism must be a *restricted* supervenience thesis: within a certain class of worlds, which includes our actual world, there is no difference without physical difference. Within that class, any two possibilities just alike physically are just alike *simpliciter*. But what delineates the relevant class? (It is trivial that our world belongs to *some* class wherein there is no difference without physical difference. That will be so however spooky our world may be. The unit class of our world is one such class, for instance. And so is any class that contains our world, and contains no two physical duplicates.) I think the relevant class should consist of the worlds that have nothing wholly alien to this world. The inhabitants of such a non-alien world could be made from the inhabitants of ours, so to speak, by a process of division and recombination. That will make no wholly different kinds of things, and no wholly different fundamental properties of things.[8] Our restricted materialist supervenience thesis should go as follows: throughout the non-alien worlds, there is no difference without physical difference.

If the Hypothesis of Phenomenal Information be granted, then the Knowledge Argument refutes this restricted supervenience nearly as decisively as it refutes the unrestricted version. Consider a possibility that is eliminated by phenomenal information, but not by any amount of physical information. There are two cases. Maybe this possibility has nothing that is alien to our world. In that case the argument goes as before: actuality and the eliminated possibility are just alike physically, they are not just alike *simpliciter*, furthermore, both of them fall within the restriction to non-alien worlds, so we have a counterexample even

8 See my "New work for a theory of universals," *Australasian Journal of Philosophy* 61 (1983), pp. 343–77 (reprinted in this volume as Chapter 1), especially pp. 361–4. For a different view about how to state minimal Materialism, see Terence Horgan, "Supervenience and microphysics," *Pacific Philosophical Quarterly* 63 (1982), pp. 29–43.

to restricted supervenience. Or maybe instead the eliminated possibility does have something X which is alien to this world – an alien kind of thing, or maybe an alien fundamental property of non-alien things. Then the phenomenal information gained by having a new experience has revealed something negative: at least in part, it is the information that X is *not* present. How can that be? If there is such a thing as phenomenal information, presumably what it reveals is positive: the presence of something hitherto unknown. Not, of course, something alien from actuality itself; but something alien from actuality as it is inadequately represented by the inexperienced and by the materialists. If Mary learns something when she finds out what it's like to see the colors, presumably she learns that there's *more* to the world than she knew before – not *less*. It's easy to think that phenomenal information might eliminate possibilities that are impoverished by comparison with actuality, but that would make a counterexample to the restricted supervenience thesis. To eliminate possibilities without making a counterexample, phenomenal information would have to eliminate possibilities less impoverished than actuality. And how can phenomenal information do that? Compare ordinary perceptual information. Maybe Jean-Paul can just *see* that Pierre is absent from the café, at least if it's a small café. But how can he just see that Pierre is absent from Paris, let alone from the whole of actuality?

(Is there a third case? What if the eliminated possibility is in one respect richer than actuality, in another respect poorer? Suppose the eliminated possibility has X, which is alien from actuality, but also it lacks Y. Then phenomenal information might eliminate it by revealing the actual presence of Y, without having to reveal the actual absence of X – But then I say there ought to be a third possibility, one with neither X nor Y, poorer and in no respect richer than actuality, and again without any physical difference from actuality. For why should taking away X automatically restore Y? Why can't they vary independently?[9] But this third possibility differs *simpliciter* from actuality with-

9 On recombination of possibilities, see my *On the Plurality of Worlds* (Oxford: Blackwell, 1986), pp. 87–92. The present argument may call for a principle that also allows recombination of properties; I now think that would not necessarily require treating properties as non-spatiotemporal parts of their instances. On recombination of prop-

out differing physically. Further, it has nothing alien from actuality. So we regain a counterexample to the restricted supervenience thesis.)

The Knowledge Argument works. There is no way to grant the Hypothesis of Phenomenal Information and still uphold Materialism. Therefore I deny the Hypothesis. I cannot refute it outright. But later I shall argue, first, that it is more peculiar, and therefore less tempting, that it may at first seem; and, second, that we are not forced to accept it, since an alternative hypothesis does justice to the way experience best teaches us what it's like.

THREE MORE WAYS TO MISS THE POINT

The Hypothesis of Phenomenal Information characterizes information in terms of eliminated possibilities. But there are other conceptions of "information." Therefore the Hypothesis has look-alikes: hypotheses which say that experience produces "information" which could not be gained otherwise, but do not characterize this "information" in terms of eliminated possibilities. These look-alikes do not work as premises for the Knowledge Argument. They do not say that phenomenal information eliminates possibilities that differ, but do not differ physically, from uneliminated possibilities. The look-alike hypotheses of phenomenal "information" are consistent with Materialism, and may very well be true. But they don't make the Knowledge Argument go away. Whatever harmless look-alikes may or may not be true, and whatever conception may or may not deserve the name "information," the only way to save Materialism is fix our attention squarely on the genuine Hypothesis of Phenomenal Information, and deny it. To avert our eyes, and attend to something else, is no substitute for that denial.

Might a look-alike help at least to this extent: by giving us something true that well might have been confused with the genuine Hypothesis, thereby explaining how we might have believed the Hypothesis although it was false? I think not. Each of the look-alikes turns out to imply not only that experience can give us "information"

erties, see also D. M. Armstrong, *A Combinatorial Theory of Possibility* (Cambridge: Cambridge University Press, 1989).

that no amount of lessons can give, but also that lessons in Russian can give us "information" that no amount of lessons in English can give (and vice versa). I doubt that any friend of phenomenal information ever thought that the special role of experience in teaching what it's like was on a par with the special role of Russian! I will have to say before I'm done that phenomenal information is an illusion, but I think I must look elsewhere for a credible hypothesis about what sort of illusion it might be.

The Fourth Way. If a hidden camera takes photographs of a room, the film ends up bearing traces of what went on in the room. The traces are distinctive: that is, the details of the traces depend on the details of what went on, and if what went on had been different in any of many ways, the traces would have been correspondingly different. So we can say that the traces bear information, and that he who has the film has the information. That might be said because the traces, plus the way they depend on what went on, suffice to eliminate possibilities; but instead we might say "information" and just mean "distinctive traces." If so, it's certainly true that new experience imparts "information" unlike any that can be gained from lessons. Experience and lessons leave different kinds of traces. That is so whether or not the experience eliminates possibilities that the lessons leave open. It is equally true, of course, that lessons in Russian leave traces unlike any that are left by lessons in English, regardless of whether the lessons cover the same ground and eliminate the same possibilities.

The Fifth Way. When we speak of transmission of "information," we often mean transmission of text. Repositories of "information," such as libraries, are storehouses of text. Whether the text is empty verbiage or highly informative is beside the point. Maybe we too contain information by being storehouses of text. Maybe there is a language of thought, and maybe the way we believe things is to store sentences of this language in some special way, or in some special part of our brains. In that case, we could say that storing away a new sentence was storing away a new piece of "information," whether or not that new piece eliminated any possibilities not already eliminated by the sentences stored previously. Maybe, also, the language of thought is not fixed once and for all, but can gain new words. Maybe, for instance, it borrows words from public language. And maybe, when one has a new experience, that causes one's language of thought to gain a new word which denotes that experience – a word which could not have been added to the language by any other means. If all this is so, then when Mary sees colors, her language of thought gains new words, allowing her to store away new sentences and thereby gain "information." All this about the language of thought, the storing of sentences, and the gaining of words is speculation. But it is plausible speculation, even if no longer the only game in town. If it is all true, then we have another look-alike hypothesis of phenomenal "information." When Mary gains new words and stores new sentences, that is "information" that she never had before, regardless of whether it eliminates any possibilities that she had not eliminated already.

But again, the special role of experience turns out to be on a par with the special role of Russian. If the language of thought picks up new words by borrowing from public language, then lessons in Russian add new words, and result in the storing of new sentences, and thereby impart "information" that never could have been had from lessons in English. (You might say that the new Russian words are mere synonyms of old words, or at least old phrases, that were there already; and synonyms don't count. But no reason has been given why the new inner words created by experience may not also be synonyms of old phrases, perhaps of long descriptions in the language of neurophysiology.)

The Sixth Way. A philosopher who is skeptical about possibility, as so many are, may wish to replace possibilities themselves with linguistic ersatz possibilities: maximal consistent sets of sentences. And he may be content to take "consistent" in a narrowly logical sense, so that a set with "Fred is married" and "Fred is a bachelor" may count as consistent, and only an overt contradiction like "Fred is married" and "Fred is not married" will be ruled out.[10] The ersatz possibilities might also be taken as sets of sentences of the language of thought, if the philosopher believes in it. Then if someone's language of thought gains new words, whether as a result of new experience or as a result of

10 See *On the Plurality of Worlds*, pp. 142–65, on linguistic ersatz possibilities.

being taught in Russian, the ersatz possibilities become richer and more numerous. The sets of sentences that were maximal before are no longer maximal after new words are added. So when Mary sees colors and her language of thought gains new words, there are new ersatz possibilities; and she can straightway eliminate some of them. Suppose she knows beforehand that she is about to see green, and that the experience of seeing green is associated with neural firing pattern F. So when she sees green and gains the new word G for her experience, then straightway there are new, enriched ersatz possibilities with sentences saying that she has G without F, and straightway she knows enough to eliminate these ersatz possibilities. (Even if she does not know beforehand what she is about to see, straightway she can eliminate at least those of her new-found ersatz possibilities with sentences denying that she then has G.) Just as we can characterize information in terms of elimination of possibilities, so we can characterize ersatz "information" in terms of elimination of ersatz "possibilities." So here we have the closest look-alike hypothesis of all, provided that language-of-thoughtism is true. But we still do not have the genuine Hypothesis of Phenomenal Information, since the eliminated ersatz possibility of G without F may not have been a genuine possibility at all. It may have been like the ersatz possibility of married bachelors.

CURIOUSER AND CURIOUSER

The Hypothesis of Phenomenal Information is more peculiar than it may at first seem. For one thing, because it is opposed to more than just Materialism. Some of you may have welcomed the Knowledge Argument because you thought all along that physical information was inadequate to explain the phenomena of mind. You may have been convinced all along that the mind could do things that no physical system could do: bend spoons, invent new jokes, demonstrate the consistency of arithmetic, reduce the wave packet, or what have you. You may have been convinced that the full causal story of how the deeds of mind are accomplished involves the causal interactions not only of material bodies but also of astral bodies; not only the vibrations of the electromagnetic field but also the good or bad vibes of the psionic field; not only protoplasm but ectoplasm. I doubt it, but never mind. It's irrelevant to our topic. The Knowledge Argument is targeted against you no less than it is against Materialism itself.

Let *parapsychology* be the science of all the non-physical things, properties, causal processes, laws of nature, and so forth that may be required to explain the things we do. Let us suppose that we learn ever so much parapsychology. It will make no difference. Black-and-white Mary may study all the parapsychology as well as all the psychophysics of color vision, but she still won't know what it's like. Lessons on the aura of Vegemite will do no more for us than lessons on its chemical composition. And so it goes. Our intuitive starting point wasn't just that *physics* lessons couldn't help the inexperienced to know what it's like. It was that *lessons* couldn't help. If there is such a thing as phenomenal information, it isn't just independent of physical information. It's independent of every sort of information that could be served up in lessons for the inexperienced. For it is supposed to eliminate possibilities that any amount of lessons leave open. Therefore phenomenal information is not just parapsychological information, if such there be. It's something very much stranger.

The genuine Hypothesis of Phenomenal Information, as distinguished from its look-alikes, treats information in terms of the elimination of possibilities. When we lack information, several alternative possibilities are open, when we get the information some of the alternatives are excluded. But a second peculiar thing about phenomenal information is that it resists this treatment. (So does logical or mathematical "information." However, phenomenal information cannot be logical or mathematical, because lessons in logic and mathematics no more teach us what a new experience is like than lessons in physics or parapsychology do.) When someone doesn't know what it's like to have an experience, where are the alternative open possibilities? I cannot present to myself in thought a range of alternative possibilities about what it might be like to taste Vegemite. That is because I cannot imagine either what it *is* like to taste Vegemite, or any alternative way that it *might* be like but in fact isn't. (I could perfectly well imagine that Vegemite tastes just like peanut butter, or something else familiar to me, but let's suppose I've been told authoritatively that this isn't so.) I can't even pose the question that phenomenal information is supposed to answer: is it this way or that? It seems that the alternative possibilities must be unthinkable beforehand; and afterward too, except for the one that turns out to be actualized. I don't say there's anything altogether impossible about a range of unthinkable alternatives; only something peculiar. But it's peculiar enough to suggest that we may somehow have gone astray.

FROM PHENOMENAL TO EPIPHENOMENAL

A third peculiar thing about phenomenal information is that it is strangely isolated from all other sorts of information; and this is so regardless of whether the mind works on physical or parapsychological principles. The phenomenal aspect of the world has nothing to do with explaining why people seemingly talk about the phenomenal aspect of the world. For instance, it plays no part in explaining the movements of the pens of philosophers writing treatises about phenomenal information and the way experience has provided them with it.

When Mary gets out of her black-and-white cell, her jaw drops. She says "At last! So this is what it's like to see colors!" Afterward she does things she couldn't do before, such as recognizing a new sample of the first color she ever saw. She may also do other things she didn't do before: unfortunate things, like writing about phenomenal information and the poverty of Materialism. One might think she said what she said and did what she did because she came to know what it's like to see colors. Not so, if the Hypothesis of Phenomenal Information is right. For suppose the phenomenal aspect of the world had been otherwise, so that she gained different phenomenal information. Or suppose the phenomenal aspect of the world had been absent altogether, as we materialists think it is. Would that have made the slightest difference to what she did or said then or later? I think not. Making a difference to what she does or says means, at least in part, making a difference to the motions of the particles of which she is composed. (Or better: making a difference to the spatiotemporal shape of the wave-function of those particles. But let that pass.) For how could she do or say anything different, if none of her particles moved any differently? But if something non-physical sometimes makes a difference to the motions of physical particles, then physics as we know it is wrong. Not just silent, not just incomplete – wrong. Either the particles are caused to change their motion without benefit of any force, or else there is some extra force that works very differently from the usual four. To believe in the phenomenal aspect of the world, but deny that it is epiphenomenal, is to bet against the truth of physics. Given the success of physics hitherto, and even with due allowance for the foundational ailments of quantum mechanics, such betting is rash! A friend of the phenomenal aspect would be safer to join Jackson in defense of *epiphenomenal* qualia.

But there is more to the case than just an empirical bet in favor of physics. Suppose there is a phenomenal aspect of the world, and suppose it does make some difference to the motions of Mary's jaw or the noises out of her mouth. Then we can describe the phenomenal aspect, if we know enough, in terms of its physical effects. It is that on which physical phenomena depend in such-and-such way. This descriptive handle will enable us to give lessons on it to the inexperienced. But in so far as we can give lessons on it, what we have is just parapsychology. That whereof we cannot learn except by having the experience still eludes us. I do not argue that *everything* about the alleged distinctive subject matter of phenomenal information must be epiphenomenal. Part of it may be parapsychological instead. But I insist that *some* aspect of it must be epiphenomenal.

Suppose that the Hypothesis of Phenomenal Information is true and suppose that V_1 and V_2 are all of the maximally specific phenomenal possibilities concerning what it's like to taste Vegemite; anyone who tastes Vegemite will find out which one obtains, and no one else can. And suppose that P_1 and P_2 are all the maximally specific physical possibilities. (Of course we really need far more than two Ps, and maybe a friend of phenomenal information would want more than two Vs, but absurdly small numbers will do for an example.) Then we have four alternative hypotheses about the causal independence or dependence of the Ps on the Vs. Each one can be expressed as a pair of counterfactual conditionals. Two hypotheses are patterns of dependence.

K_1: if V_1 then P_1, if V_2 then P_2
K_2: if V_1 then P_2, if V_2 then P_1

The other two are patterns of independence.

K_3: if V_1 then P_1, if V_2 then P_1
K_4: if V_1 then P_2, if V_2 then P_2

These dependency hypotheses are, I take it, contingent propositions. They are made true, if they are, by some contingent feature of the world, though it's indeed a vexed question what sort of feature it is.[11] Now we have eight joint possibilities.

$K_1V_1P_1$ $K_3V_1P_1$ $K_3V_2P_1$ $K_2V_2P_1$
$K_2V_1P_2$ $K_4V_1P_2$ $K_4V_2P_2$ $K_1V_2P_2$

Between the four on the top row and the four on the bottom row, there is the physical difference between P_1 and P_2. Between the four on the left and the four on the right, there is the phenomenal difference between V_1 and V_2. And between the four on the edges and the four in the middle there is a parapsychological difference. It is the difference between dependence and independence of the physical on the phenomenal; between efficacy and epiphenomenalism, so far as this one example is concerned. There's nothing ineffable about that. Whether or not you've tasted Vegemite, and whether or not you can conceive of the alleged difference between V_1 and V_2, you can still be told whether the physical difference between P_1 and P_2 does or doesn't depend on some part of the phenomenal aspect of the world.

Lessons can teach the inexperienced which parapsychological possibility obtains, dependence or independence. Let it be dependence: we have either K_1 or K_2. For if we had independence, then already we would have found our epiphenomenal difference: namely, the difference between V_1 and V_2. And lessons can teach the inexperienced which of the two physical possibilities obtains. Without loss of generality let it be P_1. Now two of our original eight joint possibilities remain open: $K_1V_1P_1$ and $K_2V_2P_1$. The difference between those is not at all physical, and not at all parapsychological: it's P_1, and it's

11 On dependency hypotheses, see my "Causal decision theory," *Australasian Journal of Philosophy* 59 (1981), pp. 5–30, reprinted in my *Philosophical Papers*, vol. II (New York: Oxford University Press, 1986).

dependence, in both cases. The difference is entirely phenomenal. And also it is entirely epiphenomenal. Nothing physical, and nothing parapsychological, depends on the difference between $K_1V_1P_1$ and $K_2V_2P_1$. We have the same sort of pattern of dependence either way; it's just that the phenomenal possibilities have been swapped. Whether it's independence or whether it's dependence, therefore, we have found an epiphenomenal part of the phenomenal aspect of the world. It is the residue left behind when we remove the parapsychological part.

Suppose that someday I taste Vegemite, and hold forth about how I know at last what it's like. The sound of my holding forth is a physical effect, part of the realized physical possibility P_1. This physical effect is exactly the same whether it's part of the joint possibility $K_1V_1P_1$ or part of its alternative $K_2V_2P_1$. It may be caused by V_1 in accordance with K_1, or it may instead be caused by V_2 in accordance with K_2, but it's the same either way. So it does not occur because we have K_1V_1 rather than K_2V_2, or vice versa. The alleged difference between these two possibilities does nothing to explain the alleged physical manifestation of my finding out which one of them is realized. It is in that way that the difference is epiphenomenal. That makes it very queer, and repugnant to good sense.

THE ABILITY HYPOTHESIS

So the Hypothesis of Phenomenal Information turns out to be very peculiar indeed. It would be nice, and not only for materialists, if we could reject it. For materialists, it is essential to reject it. And we can. There is an alternative hypothesis about what it is to learn what an experience is like: the *Ability Hypothesis*. Laurence Nemirow summarizes it thus:

some modes of understanding consist, not in the grasping of facts, but in the acquisition of abilities. . . . As for understanding an experience, we may construe that as an ability to place oneself, at will, in a state representative of the experience. I understand the experience of seeing red if I can at will visualize red. Now it is perfectly clear why there must be a special connection between the ability to place oneself in a state representative of a given experience and the point of view of experiencer: exercising the ability just *is* what we call "adopting the point of view of experiencer." . . . We can, then, come to terms with the subjectivity of our understanding of experience without positing subjective facts as the objects of our understanding. This account explains, incidentally, the linguistic incommunicability of our subjective understanding of experience (a phenomenon which might seem to support the hypothesis of subjective facts). The latter is explained as a special case of the linguistic incommunicability of abilities to place oneself at will in a given state, such as the state of having lowered blood pressure, and the state of having wiggling ears.[12]

If you have a new experience, you gain abilities to remember and to imagine. After you taste Vegemite, and you learn what it's like, you can afterward remember the experience you had. By remembering how it once was, you can afterward imagine such an experience. Indeed, even if you eventually forget the occasion itself, you will very likely retain your ability to imagine such an experience.

Further, you gain an ability to recognize the same experience if it comes again. If you taste Vegemite on another day, you will probably know that you have met the taste once before. And if, while tasting Vegemite, you know that it is Vegemite you are tasting, then you will be able to put the name to the experience if you have it again. Or if you are told nothing at the time, but later you somehow know that it is Vegemite that you are then remembering or imagining tasting, again you can put the name to the experience, or to the memory, or to the experience of imagining, if it comes again. Here, the ability you gain is an ability to gain information if given other information. Neverthe-

---

12 Laurence Nemirow, review of Nagel's *Mortal Questions, Philosophical Review* 89 (1980), pp. 475–6. For a fuller statement, see Nemirow, "Physicalism and the cognitive role of acquaintance," in *Mind and Cognition: A Reader*, ed. by W. G. Lycan (Blackwell, 1990) and *Functionalism and the Subjective Quality of Experience* (doctoral dissertation, Stanford, 1979). See also Michael Tye, "The subjective qualities of experience," *Mind* 95 (1986), pp. 1–17.

I should record a disagreement with Nemirow on one very small point. We agree that the phrase "what experience E is like" does not denote some "subjective quality" of E, something which supposedly would be part of the subject matter of the phenomenal information gained by having E. But whereas I have taken the phrase to denote E itself, Nemirow takes it to be a syncategorematic part of the expression "know what experience E is like". See "Physicalism and the cognitive role of acquaintance" section III.

less, the information gained is not phenomenal, and the ability to gain information is not the same thing as information itself.

Earlier, I mentioned "knowing what an experience is like under a description." Now I can say that what I meant by this was having the ability to remember or imagine an experience while also knowing the egocentric proposition that what one is then imagining is the experience of such-and-such description. One might well know what an experience is like under one description, but not under another. One might even know what some experience is like, but not under any description whatever – unless it be some rather trivial description like "that queer taste that I'm imagining right now." That is what would happen if you slipped a dab of Vegemite into my food without telling me what it was: afterward, I would know what it was like to taste Vegemite, but not under that description, and not under any other non-trivial description. It might be suggested that "knowing what it's like to taste Vegemite" really means what I'd call "knowing what it's like to taste Vegemite under the description 'tasting Vegemite'"; and if so, knowing what it's like would involve both ability and information. I disagree. For surely it would make sense to say: "I know this experience well, I've long known what it's like, but only today have I found out that it's the experience of tasting Vegemite." But this verbal question is unimportant. For the information involved in knowing what it's like under a description, and allegedly involved in knowing what it's like, is anyhow not the queer phenomenal information that needs rejecting.

(Is there a problem here for the friend of phenomenal information? Suppose he says that knowing what it's like to taste Vegemite means knowing that the taste of Vegemite has a certain "phenomenal character." This requires putting the name to the taste, so clearly it corresponds to our notion of knowing what it's like to taste Vegemite under the description "tasting Vegemite." But we also have our notion of knowing what it's like *simpliciter*, and what can he offer that corresponds to that? Perhaps he should answer by appeal to a trivial description, as follows: knowing what it's like *simpliciter* means knowing what it's like under the trivial description "taste I'm imagining now," and that means knowing that the taste one is imagining now has a certain phenomenal character.)

As well as gaining the ability to remember and imagine the experience you had, you also gain the ability to imagine related experiences that you never had. After tasting Vegemite, you might for instance become able to imagine tasting Vegemite ice cream. By performing imaginative experiments, you can predict with some confidence what you would do in circumstances that have never arisen – whether you'd ask for a second helping of Vegemite ice cream, for example.

These abilities to remember and imagine and recognize are abilities you cannot gain (unless by super-neurosurgery, or by magic) except by tasting Vegemite and learning what it's like. You can't get them by taking lessons on the physics or the parapsychology of the experience, or even by taking comprehensive lessons that cover the whole of physics and parapsychology. The Ability Hypothesis says that knowing what an experience is like just *is* the possession of these abilities to remember, imagine, and recognize. It isn't the possession of any kind of information, ordinary or peculiar. It isn't knowing that certain possibilities aren't actualized. It isn't knowing-that. It's knowing-how. Therefore it should be no surprise that lessons won't teach you what an experience is like. Lessons impart information; ability is something else. Knowledge-that does not automatically provide know-how.

There are parallel cases. Some know how to wiggle their ears; others don't. If you can't do it, no amount of information will help. Some know how to eat with chopsticks, others don't. Information will help up to a point – for instance, if your trouble is that you hold one chopstick in each hand – but no amount of information, by itself, will bring you to a very high level of know-how. Some know how to recognize a C-38 locomotive by sight, others don't. If you don't, it won't much help if you memorize a detailed geometrical description of its shape, even though that does all the eliminating of possibilities that there is to be done. (Conversely, knowing the shape by sight doesn't enable you to write down the geometrical description.) Information very often contributes to know-how, but often it doesn't contribute enough. That's why music students have to practice.

Know-how is ability. But of course some aspects of ability are in no sense knowledge: strength, sufficient funds. Other aspects of ability are, purely and simply, a matter of information. If you want to know how to open the combination lock on the bank vault, information is all you need. It remains that there are aspects of ability that do *not* consist simply of possession of information, and that we *do* call knowledge. The Ability Hypothesis holds that knowing what an experience is like is that sort of knowledge.

If the Ability Hypothesis is the correct analysis of knowing what an experience is like, then phenomenal information is an illusion. We ought to explain that illusion. It would be feeble, I think, just to say that we're fooled by the ambiguity of the word "know": we confuse ability with information because we confuse knowledge in the sense of knowing-how with knowledge in the sense of knowing-that. There may be two senses of the word "know," but they are well and truly entangled. They mark the two pure endpoints of a range of mixed cases. The usual thing is that we gain information and ability together. If so, it should be no surprise if we apply to pure cases of gaining ability, or to pure cases of gaining information, the same word "know" that we apply to all the mixed cases.

Along with information and ability, acquaintance is a third element of the mixture. If Lloyd George died too soon, there's a sense in which Father never can know him. Information won't do it, even if Father is a most thorough biographer and the archives are very complete. (And the trouble isn't that there's some very special information about someone that you can only get by being in his presence.) Know-how won't do it either, no matter how good Father may be at imagining Lloyd George, seemingly remembering him, and recognizing him. (Father may be able to recognize Lloyd George even if there's no longer any Lloyd George to recognize – if *per impossibile* he did turn up, Father could tell it was him.) Again, what we have is not just a third separate sense of "know." Meeting someone, gaining a lot of information about him that would be hard to gain otherwise, and gaining abilities regarding him usually go together. The pure cases are exceptions.

A friend of phenomenal information will agree, of course, that when we learn what an experience is like, we gain abilities to remember, imagine, and recognize. But he will say that it is because we gain phenomenal information that we gain the abilities. He might even say the same about other cases of gaining know-how: you can recognize the C-38 when you have phenomenal information about what it's like to see that shape, you can eat with chopsticks or wiggle your ears when you gain phenomenal information about the experience of doing so, and so on. What should friends of the Ability Hypothesis make of this? Is he offering a conjecture, which we must reject, about the causal origin of abilities? I think not. He thinks, as we do, that experiences leave distinctive traces in people, and that these traces enable us to do things. Likewise being taught to recognize a C-38 or to eat with chopsticks, or whatever happens on first wiggling the ears, leave traces that enable us to do things afterward. That much is common ground. He also interprets these enabling traces as representations that bear information about their causes. (If the same traces had been caused in some deviant way they might perhaps have carried misinformation.) We might even be able to accept that too. The time for us to quarrel comes only when he says that these traces represent special phenomenal facts, facts which cannot be represented in any other way, and therefore which cannot be taught in physics lessons or even in parapsychology lessons. That is the part, and the *only* part, which we must reject. But that is no part of his psychological story about how we gain abilities. It is just a gratuitous metaphysical gloss on that story.

We say that learning what an experience is like means gaining certain abilities. If the causal basis for those abilities turns out also to be a special kind of representation of some sort of information, so be it. We need only deny that it represents a special kind of information about a special subject matter. Apart from that it's up for grabs what, if anything, it may represent. The details of stimuli: the chemical composition of Vegemite, reflectances of surfaces, the motions of well-handled chopsticks or of ears? The details of inner states produced by those stimuli: patterns of firings of nerves? We could agree to either, so long as we did not confuse 'having information' represented in this special way with having the same information in the form of knowledge or belief. Or we could disagree. Treating the ability-conferring trace as a representation is optional. What's essential is that when we learn what an experience is like by having it, we gain abilities to remember, imagine, and recognize.

18

Reduction of mind

I am a realist and a reductive materialist about mind. I hold that mental states are contingently identical to physical – in particular, neural – states. My position is very like the 'Australian materialism' of Place, Smart, and especially Armstrong. Like Smart and Armstrong, I am an ex-Rylean, and I retain some part of the Rylean legacy. In view of how the term is contested, I do not know whether I am a 'functionalist'.

I. SUPERVENIENCE AND ANALYSIS

My reductionism about mind begins as part of an *a priori* reductionism about everything. This world, or any possible world, consists of things which instantiate fundamental properties and which, in pairs or triples or . . . , instantiate fundamental relations. Few properties are fundamental: the property of being a club or a tub or a pub, for instance, is an unnatural gerrymander, a condition satisfied by miscellaneous things in miscellaneous ways. A fundamental, or 'perfectly natural', property is the extreme opposite. Its instances share exactly some aspect of their

First published in *A Companion to Philosophy of Mind*, ed. by Samuel Guttenplan (Blackwell, 1994). Reprinted with kind permission from Blackwell Publishers.

Thanks to the Boyce Gibson Memorial Library and the philosophy department of Birkbeck College; and to the editor, Ned Block, Alex Byrne, Mark Crimmins, Allen Hazen, Ned Hall, Elijah Millgram, Thomas Nagel, and especially Frank Jackson.

intrinsic nature. Likewise for relations.[1] I hold, as an *a priori* principle, that every contingent truth must be made true, somehow, by the pattern of coinstantiation of fundamental properties and relations. The whole truth about the world, including the mental part of the world, supervenes on this pattern. If two possible worlds were exactly isomorphic in their patterns of coinstantiation of fundamental properties and relations, they would thereby be exactly alike *simpliciter*.[2]

It is a task of physics to provide an inventory of all the fundamental properties and relations that occur in the world. (That's because it is also a task of physics to discover the fundamental laws of nature, and only the fundamental properties and relations may appear in the fundamental laws.[3]) We have no *a priori* guarantee of it, but we may reasonably think that present-day physics already goes a long way toward a complete and correct inventory. Remember that the physical nature of ordinary matter under mild conditions is very well understood.[4] And we may reasonably hope that future physics can finish the job in the same distinctive style. We may think, for instance, that mass and charge are among the fundamental properties; and that whatever fundamental properties remain as yet undiscovered are likewise instantiated by very small things that come in very large classes of exact duplicates. We may further think that the very same fundamental properties and relations, governed by the very same laws, occur in the living and the dead parts of the world, and in the sentient and the insentient parts, and in the clever and the stupid parts. In short: if we optimistically extrapolate the triumph of physics hitherto, we may provisionally accept that all fundamental properties and relations that actually occur are physical. This is the thesis of materialism.

(It was so named when the best physics of the day was the physics

---

1 See David Lewis, 'New Work for a Theory of Universals', *Australasian Journal of Philosophy* 61 (1983), pp. 343–377 (reprinted in this volume as Chapter 1); and David Lewis, *On the Plurality of Worlds* (Blackwell, 1986), pp. 59–69.

2 See David Lewis, 'Critical Notice of D. M. Armstrong, *A Combinatorial Theory of Possibility*', *Australasian Journal of Philosophy* 70 (1992), pp. 211–224 (reprinted in this volume as Chapter 12).

3 Lewis, 'New Work for a Theory of Universals', pp. 365–370.

4 Gerald Feinberg, 'Physics and the Thales Problem', *Journal of Philosophy* 66 (1966), pp. 5–13.

of matter alone. Now our best physics acknowledges other bearers of fundamental properties: parts of pervasive fields, parts of causally active spacetime. But it would be pedantry to change the name on that account, and disown our intellectual ancestors. Or worse, it would be a tacky marketing ploy, akin to British Rail's decree that second class passengers shall now be called 'standard class customers'.)

If materialism is true, as I believe it is, then the *a priori* supervenience of everything upon the pattern of coinstantiation of *fundamental* properties and relations yields an *a posteriori* supervenience of everything upon the pattern of coinstantiation of fundamental *physical* properties and relations. Materialist supervenience should be a contingent matter. To make it so, we supply a restriction that makes reference to actuality. Thus: if two worlds were physically isomorphic, and if no fundamental properties or relations alien to actuality occurred in either world, then these worlds would be exactly alike *simpliciter*. Disregarding alien worlds, the whole truth supervenes upon the physical truth. In particular, the whole mental truth supervenes. So here we have the common core of all materialist theories of the mind.[5]

A materialist who stops here has already said enough to come under formidable attack. An especially well-focused version of the attack comes from Frank Jackson.[6] Mary, confined in a room where all she can see is black or white, studies the physics of colour and colour vision and colour experience (and any other physics you might think relevant) until she knows it all. Then she herself sees colour for the first time, and at last she knows what it's like to see colour. What is this knowledge that Mary has gained? It may seem that she has eliminated some possibilities left open by all her previous knowledge; she has distinguished the actual world from other possible worlds that are exactly like it in all relevant physical respects. But if materialist supervenience is true, this cannot be what has happened.

Materialists have said many things about what does happen in such a case. I myself, following Nemirow, call it a case of know-how: Mary

5 Lewis, 'New Work for a Theory of Universals', pp. 361–365.
6 Frank Jackson, 'Epiphenomenal Qualia', *Philosophical Quarterly* 32 (1982), pp. 127–136.

gains new imaginative abilities.[7] Others have said that Mary gains new relations of acquaintance, or new means of mental representation; or that the change in her is just that she has now seen colour. These suggestions need not be taken as rival alternatives. And much ink has been spent on the question whether these various happenings could in any sense be called the gaining of 'new knowledge', 'new belief', or 'new information'. But for a materialist, the heart of the matter is not what *does* happen but what *doesn't*: Mary does not distinguish the actual world from other worlds that are its physical duplicates but not its duplicates *simpliciter*.

Imagine a grid of a million tiny spots – pixels – each of which can be made light or dark. When some are light and some are dark, they form a picture, replete with interesting intrinsic gestalt properties. The case evokes reductionist comments. Yes, the picture really does exist. Yes, it really does have those gestalt properties. However, the picture and the properties reduce to the arrangement of light and dark pixels. They are nothing over and above the pixels. They make nothing true that is not made true already by the pixels. They could go unmentioned in an inventory of what there is without thereby rendering that inventory incomplete. And so on.

Such comments seem to me obviously right. The picture reduces to the pixels. And that is because the picture supervenes on the pixels: there could be no difference in the picture and its properties without some difference in the arrangement of light and dark pixels. Further, the supervenience is asymmetric: not just any difference in the pixels would matter to the gestalt properties of the picture. And it is supervenience of the large upon the small and many. In such a case, say I, supervenience is reduction. And the materialist supervenience of mind and all else upon the arrangement of atoms in the void – or whatever replaces atoms in the void in true physics – is another such case.

Yet thousands say that what's good about stating materialism in terms of supervenience is that this avoids reductionism! There's no

---

7 Laurence Nemirow, 'Physicalism and the Cognitive Role of Acquaintance' and David Lewis, 'What Experience Teaches', both in *Mind and Cognition: A Reader*, ed. by W. G. Lycan (Blackwell, 1990); the latter is reprinted in this volume as Chapter 17.

hope of settling this disagreement by appeal to some uncontested definition of the term 'reductionism'. Because the term *is* contested, and the aim of some contestants is to see to it that whatever position they may hold, 'reductionism' shall be the name for something else.

At any rate, materialist supervenience means that for anything mental, there are physical conditions that would be sufficient for its presence, and physical conditions that would be sufficient for its absence. (These conditions will include conditions saying that certain inventories are complete: an electron has only so-and-so quantum numbers, for instance, and it responds only to such-and-such forces. But it's fair to call such a condition 'physical', since it answers a kind of question that physics does indeed address.) And no matter how the world may be, provided it is free of fundamental properties or relations alien to actuality, a condition of the one sort or the other will obtain. For all we know so far, the conditions associated with a given mental item might be complicated and miscellaneous – even infinitely complicated and miscellaneous. But so long as we limit ourselves just to the question of how this mental item can find a place in the world of fundamental physics, it is irrelevant how complicated and miscellaneous the conditions might be.

It may seem unsatisfactory that physical conditions should always settle whether the mental item is present or absent. For mightn't that sometimes be a vague question with no determinate answer? A short reply to this objection from vagueness is that if it did show that the mental was irreducible to fundamental physics despite supervenience, it would likewise show that boiling was irreducible to fundamental physics – which is absurd. For it is a vague matter just where simmering leaves off and boiling begins.

A longer reply has three parts. (1) If the physical settles the mental insofar as anything does, we still have materialist supervenience. Part of what it means for two physically isomorphic worlds to be just alike mentally is that any mental indeterminacy in one is exactly matched by mental indeterminacy in the other. (2) Whenever it is a vague question whether some simplistic mental classification applies, it will be determinate that some more subtle classification applies. What's determinate may be not that you do love him or that you don't, but rather that you're in a certain equivocal state of mind that defies easy description. (3) If all indeterminacy is a matter of semantic indecision,[8] then there is no indeterminacy in the things themselves. How could we conjure up some irreducible mental item just by failing to decide exactly which reducible item we're referring to?

It may seem that when supervenience guarantees that there are physical conditions sufficient for the presence or absence of a given mental item, the sufficiency is of the wrong sort. The implication is necessary but not *a priori*. You might want to say, for instance, that black-and-white Mary really did gain new knowledge when she first saw colour; although what she learned followed necessarily from all the physics she knew beforehand, she had remained ignorant because it didn't follow *a priori*.

A short reply to this objection from necessity *a posteriori* is that if it did show that the mental was irreducible to fundamental physics, it would likewise show that boiling was irreducible to fundamental physics – which is absurd. For the identity between boiling and a certain process described in fundamental physical terms is necessary *a posteriori* if anything is.

(A longer reply, following Jackson, is founded upon the 'two-dimensional' analysis of necessity *a posteriori*.[9] Two-dimensionalism says that there is no such thing as a necessary *a posteriori* proposition. However, one single sentence φ may be associated in two different ways with two different propositions, one of them necessary and the other one contingent; and the contingent one can be known only *a posteriori*. Suppose we choose to adopt a conception of meaning under which our conventions of language sometimes fix meanings only as a function of matters of contingent fact – for example, a conception on which the meaning of 'boils' is left dependent on which physical phenomenon turns out to occupy the boiling-role. Then if we interpret a sentence φ using the meanings of its words as fixed in world W_1, we

8 Lewis, *On the Plurality of Worlds*, pp. 212–213.

9 Frank Jackson, 'Armchair Metaphysics', in *Philosophy in Mind*, ed. by J. O'Leary Hawthorne and M. Michael (Kluwer, 1994); Robert Stalnaker, 'Assertion', *Syntax and Semantics* 9 (1978), pp. 315–332; M. K. Davies and I. L. Humberstone, 'Two Notions of Necessity', *Philosophical Studies* 38 (1980), pp. 1–30 ; and Pavel Tichý, 'Kripke on Necessity *A Posteriori*', *Philosophical Studies* 43 (1983), pp. 225–241.

get proposition H_1; using the meanings as fixed in W_2, we get H_2; and so on. Call these the propositions *horizontally expressed* by ϕ at the various worlds; and let H be the proposition horizontally expressed by ϕ at the actual world. The proposition *diagonally expressed* by ϕ is the proposition D that holds at any world W iff the proposition horizontally expressed by ϕ at W is true at W. So if we know D, we know that ϕ horizontally expresses some truth or other, but we may not know which truth. Sentence ϕ is necessary *a posteriori* iff H is necessary but D is knowable only *a posteriori*. Likewise, a proposition P *necessarily implies* that ϕ iff P implies H; but P *a priori implies* that ϕ iff P implies D. Our worry was that when ϕ was about the mind, and P was a premise made true by fundamental physics, P might imply that ϕ necessarily but not *a priori*. But if so, and if you think it matters, just take another proposition Q: let Q be true at exactly those worlds where ϕ horizontally expresses the same proposition H that it actually does. Q is true. Given the materialist supervenience of everything, Q as well as P is made true by fundamental physics. P and Q together imply *a priori* that ϕ. So the gap between physical premises and mental conclusion is closed. Anyone who wants to reopen it – for instance, in order to square materialist supervenience with Mary's supposed ignorance – must somehow show that the two-dimensional analysis of necessity *a posteriori* is inadequate.)

If we limit ourselves to the question how mind finds a place in the world of physics, our work is done. Materialist supervenience offers a full answer. But if we expand our interests a little, we'll see that among the supervenient features of the world, mind must be very exceptional. There are countless such features. In our little toy example of the picture and the pixels, the supervenient properties number 2 to the power: 2 to the millionth power. In the case of materialist supervenience, the number will be far greater. The infinite cardinal beth-3 is a conservative estimate. The vast majority of supervenient features of the world are given only by miscellaneously infinite disjunctions of infinitely complex physical conditions. Therefore they are beyond our power to detect, to name, or to think about one at a time. Mental features of the world, however, are not at all beyond our ken. Finite assemblies of particles – us – can track them. Therefore there must be some sort of simplicity to them. Maybe it will be a subtle sort of simplicity, visible only if you look in just the right way. (Think of the Mandelbrot set: its overwhelming complexity, its short and simple recipe.) But somehow it must be there. Revealing this simplicity is a job for conceptual analysis.

Arbiters of fashion proclaim that analysis is out of date. Yet without it, I see no possible way to establish that any feature of the world does or does not deserve a name drawn from our traditional mental vocabulary. We should repudiate not analysis itself, but only some simplistic goals for it. We should allow for semantic indecision: any interesting analysandum is likely to turn out vague and ambiguous. Often the best that any one analysis can do is to fall safely within the range of indecision. And we should allow for semantic satisficing: analysis may reveal what it would take to deserve a name perfectly, but imperfect deservers of the name may yet deserve it well enough. (And sometimes the perfect case may be impossible.) If so, there is bound to be semantic indecision about how well is well enough.

I offer not analyses, but a recipe for analyses. We have a very extensive shared understanding of how we work mentally. Think of it as a theory: folk psychology. It is common knowledge among us; but it is tacit, as our grammatical knowledge is. We can tell which particular predictions and explanations conform to its principles, but we cannot expound those principles systematically.[10] Folk psychology is a powerful instrument of prediction. We are capable of all sorts of behaviour that would seem bizarre and unintelligible, and this is exactly the behaviour that folk psychology predicts, rightly, will seldom occur. (But we take a special interest in questions that lie beyond the predictive power of folk psychology; wherefore ingrates may fairly complain of a lack of *interesting* predictions!) Folk psychology has evolved through thousands of years of close observation of one another. It is not the last word in psychology, but we should be confident that so far as it goes − and it does go far − it is largely right.

---

10 *Pace* David Lewis, 'Psychophysical and Theoretical Identifications', *Australasian Journal of Philosophy* 50 (1972), pp. 249–258 (reprinted in this volume as Chapter 16), eliciting the general principles of folk psychology is no mere matter of gathering platitudes.

Folk psychology concerns the causal relations of mental states, perceptual stimuli, and behavioural responses. It says how mental states, singly or in combination, are apt for causing behaviour; and it says how mental states are apt to change under the impact of perceptual stimuli and other mental states. Thus it associates with each mental state a typical causal role. Now we have our recipe for analyses. Suppose we've managed to elicit all the tacitly known general principles of folk psychology. Whenever M is a folk-psychological name for a mental state, folk psychology will say that state M typically occupies a certain causal role: call this the M-role. Then we analyse M as meaning 'the state that typically occupies the M-role'. Folk psychology implicitly defines the term M, and we have only to make that definition explicit.

Since the causal roles of mental states involve other mental states, we might fear circularity. The remedy is due in its essentials to Ramsey.[11] Suppose, for instance, that folk psychology had only three names for mental states: L, M, N. We associate with this triplet of names a complex causal role for a triplet of states, including causal relations within the triplet: call this the LMN-role. Folk psychology says that the states L, M, N jointly occupy the LMN-role. That implies that M occupies the derivative role: coming second in a triplet of states that jointly occupy the LMN-role. Taking this as our M-role, we proceed as before. Say that the names L, M, N are *interdefined*. The defining of all three via the LMN-role is a package deal.

We might fear circularity for another reason. The causal roles of mental states involve responses to perceptual stimuli. But the relevant feature of the stimulus will often be some secondary quality – for instance, a colour. We cannot replace the secondary quality with a specification of the stimulus in purely physical terms, on pain of going

11 F. P. Ramsey, 'Theories' in Ramsey, *The Foundations of Mathematics*. (Routledge & Kegan Paul, 1931), pp. 212–236; Rudolf Carnap, 'Replies and Expositions' in *The Philosophy of Rudolf Carnap*, ed. by P. A. Schilpp (Cambridge University Press, 1963), pp. 958–966. See also David Lewis, 'How to Define Theoretical Terms', *Journal of Philosophy* 67 (1970), pp. 427–446, reprinted in Lewis, *Philosophical Papers*, Vol. 1 (Oxford University Press, 1983); and Lewis, 'Psychophysical and Theoretical Identifications'.

beyond what is known to folk psychology. But if we analyse the secondary quality in terms of the distinctive mental states its presence is apt to evoke, we close a definitional circle. So we should take interdefinition further. Let folk psychology include folk psychophysics. This will say, for instance, that the pair of a certain colour and the corresponding sensation jointly occupy a complex causal role that consists in part, but only in part, of the former being apt to cause the latter. Now we have a derivative role associated with the name of the colour, and another associated with the name of the sensation: the role of coming first or coming second, respectively, in a pair that jointly occupies this complex role.

We might worry also about the behaviour that mental states are apt for causing. Often we describe behaviour in a mentally loaded way: as action. To say that you kicked the ball to your teammate is to describe your behaviour. But such a description presupposes a great deal about how your behaviour was meant to serve your desires according to your beliefs; and also about the presence of the ball and the playing surface and the other player, and about the social facts that unite players into teams. More threat of circularity? More need for interdefinition? I don't know how such further interdefinition would work; and anyway, it would be well to call a halt before folk psychology expands into a folk theory of the entire *Lebenswelt*!

Describing the behaviour in purely physical terms – the angle of the knee, the velocity of the foot – would get rid of those presuppositions. But, just as in the case of the stimuli, it would go beyond what is known to folk psychology. Further, these descriptions would never fit the behaviour of space aliens not of humanoid shape; and yet we should not dismiss out of hand the speculation that folk psychology might apply to aliens as well as to ourselves.

Fortunately there is a third way to describe behaviour. When you kicked the ball, your body moved in such a way that *if* you had been on a flat surface in Earth-normal gravity with a suitably placed ball in front of you and a suitably placed teammate some distance away, *then* the impact of your foot upon the ball would have propelled the ball onto a trajectory bringing it within the teammate's reach. That description is available to the folk. They wouldn't give it spontaneously, but they can recognize it as correct. It presupposes nothing about your mental states, not even that you have any; nothing about whether the ball and the playing field and the gravity and the teammate are really there; nothing about your humanoid shape, except that you have some sort of foot. It could just as well describe the behaviour of a mindless mechanical contraption, in the shape of a space alien (with a foot), thrashing about in free fall.

(I don't say that we should really use these 'if – then' descriptions of behaviour. Rather, my point is that their availability shows how to unload the presuppositions from our ordinary descriptions.)

If M means 'the state that typically occupies the M-role' and if that role is only imperfectly occupied, what are we to do? – Satisfice: let the name M go to a state that deserves it imperfectly. And if nothing comes anywhere near occupying the M-role? – Then the name M has no referent. The boundary between the cases is vague. To take an example from a different term-introducing theory, I suppose it to be indeterminate whether 'dephlogisticated air' refers to oxygen or to nothing. But folk psychology is in far better shape than phlogiston theory, despite scare stories to the contrary. We can happily grant that there are no perfect deservers of folk-psychological names, but we shouldn't doubt that there are states that deserve those names well enough.

What to do if the M-role, or the LMN-role, turns out to be doubly occupied? I used to think that in this case too the name M had no referent.[12] But now I think it might be better, sometimes or always, to say that the name turns out to be ambiguous in reference. That follows the lead of Field; and it is consistent with, though not required by, the treatment of Carnap.[13] Note that we face the same choice with phrases like 'the moon of Mars'; and in that case too I'd now lean toward ambiguity of reference rather than lack of it.

My recipe for analyses, like Rylean analytic behaviourism, posits analytic truths that constrain the causal relations of mental states to behaviour. (We have no necessary connections between distinct existences, of course; the necessity is verbal. The state itself could have failed to

---

12 David Lewis, 'How to Define Theoretical Terms' and 'Psychophysical and Theoretical Identifications'.

13 Hartry Field, 'Theory Change and the Indeterminacy of Reference', *Journal of Philosophy* 70 (1973), pp. 462–481; Carnap *loc. cit.*

occupy its causal role, but would thereby have failed to deserve its mental name.) But the constraints are weak enough to be credible. Because the state that typically occupies a role need not occupy it invariably, and also because a state may deserve a name well enough in virtue of a role that it occupies imperfectly, we are safe from the behaviourist's bugbears. We have a place for the resolute deceiver, disposed come what may to behave as if his mental states were other than they really are. We have a place for the total and incurable paralytic with a rich mental life and no behavioural dispositions whatever. We even have a place for a madman whose mental states are causally related to behaviour and stimuli and one another in a totally haywire fashion.[14] And yet not anything goes. At some point – and just where that point comes is a matter of semantic indecision – weird tales of mental states that habitually offend against the principles of folk psychology stop making sense; because at some point the offending states lose all claim to their folk-psychological names. To that extent, analytic behaviourism was right. To quote my closest ally in these matters, ' . . . outward physical behaviour and tendencies to behave do in some way enter into our ordinary concept of mind. Whatever theory of mind is true, it has a debt to pay, and a peace to be made, with behaviourism.'[15]

When we describe mental state M as the occupant of the M-role, that is what Smart calls a topic-neutral description.[16] It says nothing about what sort of state it is that occupies the role. It might be a non-physical or a physical state, and if it is physical it might be a state of neural activity in the brain, or a pattern of currents and charges on a silicon chip, or the jangling of an enormous assemblage of beer cans. What state occupies the M-role and thereby deserves the name M is an *a posteriori* matter. But if materialist supervenience is true, and every

---

14 David Lewis, 'Mad Pain and Martian Pain', in *Readings in Philosophy of Psychology*, Vol. 1, ed. by N. Block (Harvard University Press, 1980), reprinted with postscript in Lewis, *Philosophical Papers*, Vol. 1 (Oxford University Press, 1983).

15 D. M. Armstrong, *A Materialist Theory of Mind* (Routledge & Kegan Paul, 1968), p. 68.

16 J. J. C. Smart, 'Sensations and Brain Processes', *Philosophical Review*, 68 (1959), pp. 141–156.

feature of the world supervenes upon fundamental physics, then the occupant of the role is some physical state or other – because there's nothing else for it to be. We know enough to rule out the chip and the cans, and to support the hypothesis that what occupies the role is some pattern of neural activity. When we know more, we shall know what pattern of neural activity it is. Then we shall have the premises of an argument for psychophysical identification:[17]

mental state M = the occupant of the M-role (by analysis),
physical state P = the occupant of the M-role (by science),
therefore $M = P$.

That's how conceptual analysis can reveal the simple formula – or anyway, the much less than infinitely complicated formula – whereby, when we know enough, we can pick out a mental feature of the world from all the countless other features of the world that likewise supervene on fundamental physics.

The causal-role analyses would still hold even if materialist supervenience failed. They might even still yield psychophysical identifications. Even if we lived in a spook-infested world, it might be physical states that occupied the causal roles (in us, if not in the spooks) and thereby deserved the folk-psychological names. Or it might be nonphysical states that occupied the roles. Then, if we knew enough parapsychology, we would have the premises of an argument for psycho-*non*physical identification.

When our argument delivers an identification $M = P$, the identity is contingent. How so? – All identity is self-identity, and nothing could possibly have failed to be self-identical. But that is not required. It's contingent, and it can only be known *a posteriori*, which physical (or other) states occupy which causal roles. So if M means 'the occupant

17 See David Lewis, 'An Argument for the Identity Theory', *Journal of Philosophy* 63 (1966), pp. 17–25, reprinted with additions in Lewis, *Philosophical Papers*, Vol. 1 (Oxford University Press, 1983); and Lewis, 'Psychophysical and Theoretical Identifications'. See Armstrong, *A Materialist Theory of the Mind*, for an independent and simultaneous presentation of the same position, with a much fuller discussion of what the definitive causal roles might be.

of the M-role' it's contingent which state is the referent of M; it's contingent whether some one state is the common referent of M and P; so it's contingent whether $M = P$ is true.

Kripke vigorously intuits that some names for mental states, in particular 'pain', are rigid designators: that is, it's not contingent what their referents are.[18] I myself intuit no such thing, so the non-rigidity imputed by causal-role analyses troubles me not at all.

Here is an argument that 'pain' is not a rigid designator. Think of some occasion when you were in severe pain, unmistakable and unignorable. All will agree, except for some philosophers and faith healers, that there is a state that actually occupies the pain role (or near enough); that it is called 'pain'; and that you were in it on that occasion. For now, I assume nothing about the nature of this state, or about how it deserves its name. Now consider an unactualized situation in which it is some different state that occupies the pain role in place of the actual occupant; and in which you were in that different state; and which is otherwise as much like the actual situation as possible. Can you distinguish the actual situation from this unactualized alternative? I say not, or not without laborious investigation. But if 'pain' is a rigid designator, then the alternative situation is one in which you were not in pain, so you could distinguish the two very easily. So 'pain' is not a rigid designator.

Philosophical arguments are never incontrovertible – well, hardly ever. Their purpose is to help expound a position, not to coerce agreement. In this case, the controverter might say that if the actual occupant of the pain role is not a physical state, but rather is a special sort of non-physical state, then indeed you can distinguish the two situations. He might join me in saying that this would not be so if the actual occupant of the role were a physical state – else neurophysiology would be easier than it is – and take this together with intuitions of rigidity to yield a *reductio* against materialism. Myself, I don't see how the physical or non-physical nature of the actual occupant of the role has anything to do with whether the two situations can be distinguished. Talk of 'phenomenal character' and the like doesn't help. Either it is loaded with question-begging philosophical doctrine, or else

18 Saul Kripke, *Naming and Necessity* (Blackwell, 1980), pp. 147–148.

it just reiterates the undisputed fact that pain is a kind of experience.[19]

If there is variation across worlds with respect to which states occupy the folk-psychological roles and deserve the folk-psychological names (and if this variation doesn't always require differences in the laws of nature, as presumably it doesn't) then also there can be variations within a single world. For possibility obeys a principle of recombination: roughly, any possible kind of thing can coexist with any other.[20] For all we know, there may be variation even within this world. Maybe there are space aliens, and maybe there will soon be artificial intelligences, in whom the folk-psychological roles are occupied (or near enough) by states very different from any states of a human nervous system. Presumably, at least some folk-psychological roles are occupied in at least some animals, and maybe there is variation across species. There might even be variation within humanity. It depends on the extent to which we are hard-wired, and on the extent of genetic variation in our wiring.

We should beware, however, of finding spurious variation by overlooking common descriptions. Imagine two mechanical calculators that are just alike in design. When they add columns of numbers, the amount carried goes into a register, and the register used for this purpose is selected by throwing a switch. Don't say that the carry-seventeen role is occupied in one machine by a state of register A and in the other by a state of register B. Say instead that in both machines alike the role is occupied by a state of the register selected by the switch. (Equivalently, by a state of a part of the calculator large enough to include the switch and both registers.) If there is a kind of thinking that some of us do in the left side of the brain and others do in the right side, that might be a parallel case.

If M means 'the occupant of the M-role' and there is variation in what occupies the M-role, then our psychophysical identities need to be restricted: not plain $M = P$, but M-in-$K = P$, where K is a kind within which P occupies the M-role. Human pain might be one thing,

---

19 The controverter just imagined would agree with the discussion in Kripke, *Naming and Necessity*, pp. 144–155. But I don't mean to suggest that Kripke would agree with him. At any rate, the words I have put in his mouth are not Kripke's.

20 Lewis, *On the Plurality of Worlds*, pp. 86–92.

Martian pain might be something else.[21] As with contingency, which is variation across worlds, so likewise with variation in a single world: the variability in no way infects the identity relation, but rather concerns the reference of the mental name.

The threat of variation has led many to retreat from 'type–type' to 'token–token' identity. They will not say that $M = P$, where M and P are names for a state that can be common to different things at different times – that is, for a property had by things at times. But they will say that $m = p$, where m and p are mental and physical names for a particular, unrepeatable event. Token–token identities are all very well, in their derivative way, but the flight from type–type identities was quite unnecessary. For our restricted identities, of the form M-in-$K = P$, are still type–type.

But don't we at least have a choice? Couldn't our causal role analyses be recast in terms of the causal roles of tokens, and if they were, would they not then yield token–token identities? After all, the only way for a type to occupy a causal role is through the causes and effects of its tokens. The effects of pain are the effects of pain-events. – I think, following Jackson, Pargetter, and Prior, that this recasting of the analyses would not be easy.[22] There are more causal relations than one. Besides causing, there is preventing. It too may figure in folk-psychological causal roles; for instance, pain tends to prevent undivided attention to anything else. Prevention cannot straightforwardly be treated as a causal relation of tokens, because the prevented tokens do not exist – not in this world, anyway. It is better taken as a relation of types.

If a retreat had been needed, a better retreat would have been to 'subtype–subtype' identity. Let MK name the conjunctive property of being in state M and being of kind K; and likewise for PK. Do we really want psychophysical identities of the form $MK = PK$? – Close, but I think not quite right. For one thing, M-in-K is not the same thing as MK. The former but not the latter can occur also in something that isn't of kind K. For another thing, it is P itself, not PK, that occupies the M-role in things of kind K.

21 Lewis, 'Mad Pain and Martian Pain'.
22 Frank Jackson, Robert Pargetter, and Elizabeth Prior, 'Functionalism and Type-type Identity Theories', *Philosophical Studies* 42 (1982), pp. 209–225.

Non-rigidity means that M is different states in different possible cases; variation would mean that M was different states in different actual cases. But don't we think that there is *one* property of being in the state M – one property that is common to all, actual or possible, of whatever kind, who can truly be said to be in state M? – There is. It is the property such that, for any possible X, X has it just in case X is in the state that occupies the M-role for X's kind at X's world.[23] The gerund 'being in M' can be taken, at least on one good disambiguation, as a rigid designator of this property. However, this property is not the occupant of the M-role. It cannot occupy that or any other causal role because it is excessively disjunctive, and therefore no events are essentially havings of it.[24] To admit it as causally efficacious would lead to absurd double-counting of causes. It would be like saying that the meat fried in Footscray cooked because it had the property of being either fried in Footscray or boiled in Bundoora – only worse, because the disjunction would be much longer and more miscellaneous.

Since the highly disjunctive property of being in M does not occupy the M-role, I say it cannot be the referent of M. Many disagree. They would like it if M turned out to be a rigid designator of a property common to all who are in M. So the property I call 'being in M', they call simply M; and the property that I call M, the occupant of the M-role, they call 'the realisation of M'. They have made the wrong choice, since it is absurd to deny that M itself is causally efficacious. Still, their mistake is superficial. They have the right properties in mind, even if they give them the wrong names.

It is unfortunate that this superficial question has sometimes been taken to mark the boundary of 'functionalism'. Sometimes so and sometimes not – and that's why I have no idea whether I am a functionalist.

Those who take 'pain' to be a rigid designator of the highly disjunctive property will need to controvert my argument that 'pain' is not rigid, and they will not wish to claim that one can distinguish situations in which the pain-role is differently occupied. Instead, they

23 In 'How to Define Theoretical Terms' I called it the 'diagonalized sense' of M.
24 David Lewis, 'Events' in Lewis, *Philosophical Papers*, Vol. 2 (Oxford University Press, 1986).

should controvert the first step, and deny that the actual occupant of the pain-role is called 'pain'. I call that denial a *reductio*.

II. CONTENT

A mind is an organ of representation. Many things are true according to it; that is, they are believed. Or better, they are more or less probable according to it; that is, they are believed or disbelieved to varying degrees. Likewise, many things are desired to varying positive or negative degrees. What is believed, or what is desired, we call the content of belief or desire.

(I think it an open question to what extent other states with content – doubting, wondering, fearing, pretending, . . . – require separate treatment, and to what extent they can be reduced to patterns in belief and desire and contentless feeling. Be that as it may, I shall ignore them here.)

What determines the content of belief and desire? – The occupation of folk-psychological roles by physical states, presumably neural states; and ultimately the pattern of coinstantiation of fundamental physical properties and relations. But to say just that is to say not much. Those who agree with it can, and do, approach the problem of content in very different ways.

I can best present the approach I favour by opposing it to an alternative. A crude sketch will suffice, so in fairness I name my opponent *Strawman*. I doubt there is anyone real who takes exactly the position that Strawman does – but very many are to be found in his near vicinity.

Strawman says that folk psychology says – and truly – that there is a language of thought. It has words, and it has syntactic constructions whereby those words can be combined into sentences. Some of these sentences have a special status. Strawman says they are 'written in the belief box' or 'in the desire box', but even Strawman doesn't take that altogether literally. There are folk-psychological causal roles for the words, for the syntactic constructions, and for the belief and desire boxes. It is by occupying these roles that the occupants deserve their folk-psychological names.

The question what determines content then becomes the question: what determines the semantics of the language of thought? Strawman says that folk psychology specifies the semantic operations that correspond to syntactic constructions such as predication. As for the words, Strawman says that folk psychology includes, in its usual tacit and unsystematic way, a causal theory of reference.[25] There are many relations of acquaintance that connect the mind to things, including properties and relations, in the external world. Some are relations of perceptual acquaintance. Others are less direct: you are acquainted with the thing by being acquainted with its traces. Often, you are acquainted with the thing by way of its *linguistic* traces – that is, you have heard of it by name. Somehow, in virtue of the different causal roles of different words of the language of thought, different words are associated with different relations of acquaintance, which connect them to different external things. Whatever a word is thus connected to is the referent of that word.

Once the words of the language of thought have their referents, the sentences have their meanings. These are structures built up from the referents of the words in a way that mirrors the syntactic construction of the sentences from the words. Take predication – Strawman's favourite example. A word F of your language of thought is connected by one relation of acquaintance to the property of being French. Another word A is connected by another relation of acquaintance to the man André. (The first relation might be linguistic, for instance, and the second perceptual.) The syntactic construction of predication builds a sentence $F(A)$. Its meaning is the ordered pair of the property of being French and André. Such a pair is a 'singular proposition', true just in case its second element instantiates its first. (Other singular propositions are triples, quadruples, . . . , with relations in the first place.) If you have $F(A)$ written in your belief box, you thereby believe that André is French.

Strawman's account of content is sketchy, as I said it would be. Even with help from all his allies, I doubt he will find it easy to fill the gaps. I especially wonder what he can say about how the words get hooked up to the right relations of acquaintance. A causal theory of reference for public language might usefully mention mutual expectations among language-users, intentions to instill beliefs, semantic intentions, or other such instances of mental content. But even if we

25 More or less as in Kripke, *Naming and Necessity*.

309

had corresponding expectations or intentions about our own language of thought, Strawman could not without circularity use them in a general account of mental content.

Suppose, all the same, that Strawman's account could be completed successfully by its own lights. I would still have four objections.

First, I don't believe that folk psychology says there is a language of thought. Rather, I think it is agnostic about how mental representation works – and wisely so.

What is the issue? Of course everybody should agree that the medium of mental representation is somehow analogous to language. A raven is like a writing-desk. Anything can be analogized to anything. And of course nobody thinks the head is full of tiny writing.

A serious issue, and one on which I take folk psychology to be agnostic, concerns the relation between the whole and the parts of a representation. Suppose I have a piece of paper according to which, *inter alia*, Collingwood is east of Fitzroy. Can I tear the paper up so that I get one snippet that has exactly the content that Collingwood is east of Fitzroy, nothing more and nothing less? If the paper is covered with writing, maybe I can; for maybe 'Collingwood is east of Fitzroy' is one of the sentences written there. But if the paper is a map, any snippet according to which Collingwood is east of Fitzroy will be a snippet according to which more is true besides. For instance, I see no way to lose the information that they are adjacent, and that a street runs along the border. And I see no way to lose all information about their size and shape.

(A hologram, or famously a connectionist network, differs even more from a paper covered with writing. If we make a hologram of the map and break it into snippets, detail will be lost in blur. But the arrangement of *all* the suburbs, provided it was shown with sufficient prominence on the original map, will remain to the last.)

Mental representation is language-like to the extent that parts of the content are the content of parts of the representation. If our beliefs are 'a map . . . by which we steer', as Ramsey said,[26] then they are to

26 F. P. Ramsey, 'General Propositions and Causality' in Ramsey, *The Foundations of Mathematics* (Routledge & Kegan Paul, 1931), p. 238.

that extent not language-like. And to that extent, also, it is misleading to speak in the plural of beliefs. What is one belief? No snippet of a map is big enough that, determinately, something is true according to it, and also small enough that, determinately, nothing is true according to any smaller part of it. If mental representation is map-like (let alone if it is hologram-like) then 'beliefs' is a bogus plural. You have beliefs the way you have the blues, or the mumps, or the shivers.

But if mental representation is language-like, one belief is one sentence written in the belief box, so 'beliefs' is a genuine plural. Whether the plural is bogus or genuine is not settled by rules of grammar. Rather, it is an empirical question, and a question that folk psychology leaves open. 'The shivers' might be a parallel case. Is there such a thing as one shiver? – Maybe and maybe not. I don't think one cycle of vibration should be called 'one shiver', but there might be a better candidate. What if one firing of a control neuron would set you shivering for four seconds, and prolonged shivering is caused by this neuron firing every two seconds? If so, I think the shivering set off by one firing could well be called 'one shiver', and then it is right to say that shivering consists of a sequence of overlapping shivers. Under this hypothesis, the plural is genuine. Under other hypotheses, the plural is bogus.

Of course you might say, under the hypothesis that mental representation is map-like, that any proposition true according to the mental map is one belief. Or you might say that the one belief that Collingwood is east of Fitzroy is the highly disjunctive state of having some mental map or other according to which that *inter alia* is true. Say so if you like. But I only insist that if you say either thing, then you may not also assume that 'one belief' is the sort of thing that can occupy a causal role. You may still say ' . . . because he believes that Collingwood is east of Fitzroy', but only if you mean by it ' . . . because he has beliefs' – bogus plural! – 'according to which *inter alia* Collingwood is east of Fitzroy'.

If Strawman heeds the advice of some of his allies, he will respond by changing his position. He will give away conceptual analysis and folk psychology, and market his wares as 'cognitive science'. No problem, then, if the folk are agnostic about the language of thought. Let it be a new hypothesis, advanced because it best ex-

311

plains. . . . What? Well-known facts about belief? – But 'belief' is a folk-psychological name for a kind of state posited by folk psychology. If Strawman leaves all that behind him, where shall he find his evidence? He can never again set up thought experiments and ask us what we want to say about them. That would only elicit our folk-psychological preconceptions. He can make a fresh start if he really wants to – I assume he will not want to – but he cannot have his cake and eat it too.[27]

If Strawman stands his ground, on the other hand, he will insist that folk psychology is far from agnostic about the language of thought. It has plenty to say, after all, about our 'concepts' (or 'ideas') of things. Our concept of a concept, says Strawman, is just our concept of a word of the language of thought. – I doubt it. I haven't much of any concept of Elsternwick. I have little idea what the place looks like, what sort of people live there,. . . . All I know is that there is a place of that name, and roughly where it is. But I *do* have the word. (At least, I have the word 'Elsternwick' of our public language. *If* I have a language of thought, presumably this word has been borrowed into it.) My lack of a concept isn't lack of a word; rather, I lack any very rich cluster of associated descriptions.

Strawman can reply that even if I haven't *much* concept of Elsternwick, still I have enough of one that I can think about Elsternwick (for instance, when I think how little I know about it). It is this minimal concept of a concept, he says, that is our folk-psychological concept of a word of the language of thought. – Yes, I have a concept of Elsternwick in the minimal sense that I have *whatever it takes* to be able to think about it. But must the basis of such an ability, in general or even in this case, be the possession of a word? On that question, the folk and I remain agnostic.

My second objection to Strawman's account is that it delivers only wide content. Which singular propositions you believe depends upon which external things are suitably connected by relations of acquaintance to the words of your language of thought.

Strawman holds that all content is wide because he has learned the

27 See Frank Jackson, 'Armchair Metaphysics'.

lesson of Twin Earth. Recall the example.[28] Oscar the Earthling believes that water often falls from clouds. Twoscar on Twin Earth is in no way acquainted with water, that is, with H_2O. Rather, Twoscar is acquainted with XYZ, a superficially similar liquid that is abundant on Twin Earth, in exactly the way that Oscar is acquainted with H_2O. There is no other relevant difference between Twoscar and Oscar. We are invited to agree that Twoscar does not believe that water falls from clouds, and believes instead that XYZ falls from clouds. Strawman does agree.

And so do I, but with many reservations. For one thing, I think agreement is not compulsory. Like any up-to-date philosopher of 1955, I think that 'water' is a cluster concept. Among the conditions in the cluster are: it is liquid, it is colourless, it is odorless, it supports life. But, *pace* the philosopher of 1955, there is more to the cluster than that. Another condition in the cluster is: it is a natural kind. Another condition is indexical: it is abundant hereabouts. Another is metalinguistic: many call it 'water'. Another is both metalinguistic and indexical: *I* have heard of it under the name 'water'. When we hear that XYZ off on Twin Earth fits many of the conditions in the cluster but not all, we are in a state of semantic indecision about whether it deserves the name 'water'.[29] When in a state of semantic indecision, we are often glad to go either way, and accommodate our own usage temporarily to the whims of our conversational partners.[30] So if some philosopher, call him Schmutnam, invites us to join him in saying that the water on Twin Earth differs in chemical composition from the water here, we will happily follow his lead. And if another philosopher, Putnam (*op. cit.*), invites us to say that the stuff on Twin Earth is not water – and hence that Twoscar does not believe that water falls from clouds – we will just as happily follow his lead. We should have

28 Hilary Putnam, 'The Meaning of "Meaning' ", in *Language, Mind and Knowledge*, ed. by K. Gunderson (University of Minnesota Press, 1975), pp. 139–142.

29 Peter Unger, *Philosophical Relativity* (University of Minnesota Press, 1984), pp. 79–104. But while I agree with Unger about what happens in various cases, I don't endorse all the morals he draws.

30 David Lewis, 'Scorekeeping in a Language Game', *Journal of Philosophical Logic* 8 (1979), pp. 339–359, reprinted in Lewis, *Philosophical Papers*, Vol. 1 (Oxford University Press, 1983).

followed Putnam's lead only for the duration of that conversation, then lapsed back into our accommodating state of indecision. But, sad to say, we thought that instead of playing along with a whim, we were settling a question once and for all. And so we came away lastingly misled.

The example half succeeds. It is not compulsory, but certainly it is permissible, to say that Oscar does believe that water falls from clouds and differently acquainted Twoscar does not. Therefore wide content does serve a purpose. It enters into the analysis of some sentences that are about belief, or at least partly about belief; or at least it does so under some permissible disambiguations of these sentences.

Other examples are similar. Twoscar is acquainted with molybdenum as Oscar is with aluminium; with a disease of bone as Oscar is with a disease of joints; with spy robots as Oscar is with cats; and so on. It seems to matter little whether Twoscar is our neighbour, or whether he lives on a remote planet, or whether he lives in a different possible world. In each case we find that the difference in what Twoscar and Oscar are acquainted with makes a difference to the truth value, under some disambiguation, of some sentences that are at least partly about belief. But that is all we find. There is nothing here to support Strawman's thesis that wide content is the only kind of content; or that it is in any way preeminent or basic.

We should not jump to the conclusion that just any belief sentence is susceptible to Twin Earth examples. Oscar thinks that square pegs don't fit round holes; I don't think you can tell an even halfway convincing story of how Twoscar, just by being differently acquainted, fails to think so too. Oscar believes there's a famous sea-side place called 'Blackpool'; so does differently acquainted Twoscar, though of course it may not be Blackpool – not *our* Blackpool – that he has in mind. Oscar believes that the stuff he has heard of under the name 'water' falls from clouds. So does Twoscar – and so does Twoscar even if you alter not only his acquaintance with water but also his relations of acquaintance to other things as well. You know the recipe for Twin-Earth examples. You can follow it in these cases too. But what you get falls flat even as an example of how content is sometimes wide, let alone as evidence that content is always wide.

The famous brain in a bottle is your exact duplicate with respect to brain states and their typical causal roles; but is acquainted only with aspects of the computer that fabricates its virtual reality. You and the brain share no objects of acquaintance. So, according to Strawman, you and the brain share no common beliefs whatever.

Newborn Swampman, just this moment formed by an unlikely chance assembly of atoms, also is your exact duplicate with respect *inter alia* to brain states and their typical causal roles.[31] But so far, he hasn't had time to become acquainted with much of anything. Therefore, according to Strawman, he believes not much of anything.

Strawman and his allies may think that we have here two remarkable philosophical discoveries. I think, rather, that Strawman's thesis that all content is wide has here met with a twofold *reductio ad absurdum*. Granted, the brain in a bottle shares no wide content of belief with you. Granted, Swampman has no wide content of belief at all. Yet there must be some good sense in which both the brain and Swampman are your mental twins; some good sense in which they believe just what you do. (And in our less extreme cases, there must be some good sense in which Twoscar believes just what Oscar does.) Strawman's position is unacceptable. Not because it posits wide content; but because it omits narrow content, content independent of what one is acquainted with. It omits the sort of content that you and the brain and Swampman, and likewise Oscar and Twoscar, have in common.

(Narrow content is independent of what you are acquainted with, but that does not mean that it is altogether intrinsic to you. For it still depends on the causal roles of your brain states; causation depends on the laws of nature; and if some sort of regularity theory of lawhood is true, living under such-and-such laws is not intrinsic to you. Further, it is the *typical* causal roles of your brain states that matter. But you may be an atypical member of your kind; hence what is typical of your kind is not intrinsic to you. So I can say only this: if X and Y are intrinsic duplicates, and if they live under the same laws of nature, and if they are the same in kind, then they must be exactly alike in narrow content.)

In insisting on the existence of narrow content, I am not guided by

---

31 Donald Davidson, 'Knowing One's Own Mind', *Proceedings and Addresses of the American Philosophical Association* 60 (1987), pp. 441–458.

any preconception about what sort of properties may figure in causal explanation, or in truly scientific explanation. I dare say the fundamental laws of physics must concern perfectly natural, intrinsic properties. But that's irrelevant, since causal and scientific explanation seldom consists in subsumption under these fundamental laws. Rather, it is a matter of giving information about how things are caused.[32] Such information can come in many forms, both within science and without, and there is no reason to proscribe extrinsic classifications. (Lynne Baker told me a nice example: the science of economics is all about extrinsic properties like poverty and debt. Yet there is nothing wrong, and nothing unscientific, in saying that Fred stays poor because of his burden of debt.)

I am guided, rather, by my tacit mastery of the principles of folk psychology. I said: Oscar believes that the stuff he has heard of under the name 'water' falls from clouds; and so does Twoscar. (And so do you, and so does the brain in a bottle, and so does Swampman.) These are ordinary folk-psychological belief sentences; but narrow ones, as witness the fact that they are not susceptible to Twin-Earth examples.

This narrow content is content, rightly so-called: something is true according to the belief-system in question. The content is true on condition that the stuff the believer has heard of under the name 'water' does indeed fall from clouds; otherwise false. It is not 'purely syntactic content' – something I take to be a contradiction in terms. Nor is it a mere function that delivers genuine content as output when given circumstances of acquaintance as input. Nor is it merely phenomenalistic content, restricted in subject matter to the believer's experience.

However, it is not content that can be given by a singular proposition, and that leads to my third objection against Strawman's account.

Strawman's singular propositions suffice to specify which things have which properties. If all else supervenes upon the pattern of coinstantiation of fundamental properties, that in turn will suffice to specify

---

32 David Lewis, 'Causal Explanation', in Lewis, *Philosophical Papers*, Vol. 2 (Oxford University Press, 1986).

the way the world is. But much of the content of our knowledge and belief is *de se*: it concerns not the world but oneself.[33] However much I may know about the things that make up the world, their properties and their arrangement, it is something extra to know which one of all these things is *me*. This *de se* knowledge, whereby I locate myself in the world and self-ascribe the properties I think myself to possess, is not knowledge of how the world is. Its content cannot be captured by singular propositions. What singular proposition is expressed when I say, or I think, 'I am DL'? – Just the proposition that DL = DL. And when I self-ascribe the property *F*? – Just the proposition that DL is *F*. But I can know these propositions without knowing who I am, or whether I am *F*. (And you can know them too.) Strawman's only recourse is to say that *de se* knowledge is characterized not by its *de se* content but some other way – and if he says that, he confesses that his account of content is inadequate.

Belief that falls short of knowledge can likewise have *de se* content. If you take *your*self to be DL, your false belief and my true belief have their *de se* content in common. Desire also has *de se* content. If you desire to be *F* and I believe myself to be *F*, again the two attitudes have their *de se* content in common.

There is also tensed content. The world is spread out over many times; but we can have knowledge, or belief or desire, about which of these times is now. Again, this is not knowledge of how the whole spread-out world is. It is something extra. Some would speak of content *de se et nunc*, but I would subsume *de nunc* under *de se*. For I think we persist through time by consisting of many time-slices, or momentary selves; and in the last analysis, it is these momentary selves that do our thinking. So when I think 'It's now time for lunch', that's one of my momentary selves self-ascribing *de se* the property of being located at lunchtime.

33 John Perry, 'Frege on Demonstratives', *Philosophical Review* 86 (1977), pp. 474–497; David Lewis, 'Attitudes *De Dicto* and *De Se*', *Philosophical Review* 88 (1979), pp. 513–543, reprinted with postscripts in Lewis, *Philosophical Papers*, Vol. 1 (Oxford University Press, 1983); and Roderick Chisholm, 'The Indirect Reflexive' in *Intention and Intentionality: Essays in Honour of G. E. M. Anscombe*, ed. by C. Diamond and J. Teichman (Harvester, 1979).

The 'propositions', if we may call them that, which make up *de se* content are true or false not absolutely, as singular propositions are, but relative to a subject. (Or to a subject at a time, if you don't believe in momentary selves.) The content of my knowledge *de se* that I am DL is something that is true for me but not for you. Its linguistic expression requires a first-person pronoun, or some equivalent device. We could call it an 'egocentric proposition' (or 'egocentric and tensed'). Or we can simply identify it with the property that I self-ascribe: the property of being DL. Likewise the *de se* content of my belief that I have *F* is just the property *F* itself; the *de se* content of my belief that it's lunchtime is the property (possessed not by the whole of me but by some of my momentary selves) of being located at lunch-time; and so on. A *de se* self-ascription of a property is true just on condition that the self-ascriber possesses the self-ascribed property.

(May I say, then, that *de se* belief has 'truth conditions'? Not if Strawman has his way. He goes in for terminological piracy. He transforms one term after another into a mere synonym for 'singular proposition'. He has taken 'object of thought'. He has taken 'content'. He has taken 'proposition'. He is well on the way to taking 'truth condition'. When he has taken all the terms for his own, dissident thoughts will be unsayable.)

Since Strawman has no place for *de se* content, it makes sense that he overlooks narrow content as well. For narrow content is very often *de se*. To revisit our previous example: Oscar self-ascribes having heard, under the name 'water', of a liquid that falls from clouds. He also self-ascribes the property of being at a place (and time) in the vicinity of which the most abundant liquid is one that falls from clouds. Differently acquainted Twoscar self-ascribes these same two properties, and in this way Oscar and Twoscar share the same *de se* narrow content of belief.

On my own view, it is just such *de se* narrow content that underlies wide content. The semantics of the alleged language of thought needn't enter into it. To the extent that language enters my story at all, it is not by way of language of thought, but rather by way of thought about language – about the ordinary public language, whereby, for instance, Oscar heard of something under the name 'water'.

Here is one recipe: if *R* is a relation of acquaintance, and subject *S* self-ascribes being R-acquainted uniquely with something that has property F (the narrow part), and if S is R-acquainted uniquely with A (the wide part), S thereby widely believes the singular proposition that A has F.[34] There are variants on the recipe. Our example of French André was a case in which property F as well as individual A enters indirectly as an object of acquaintance; we must of course let in cases where the property F gives way to a relation with two or more *relata*; maybe sometimes we should drop the qualification 'uniquely'; and maybe sometimes the relation R is not, or not entirely, a matter of acquaintance. But in every case, wide belief in a singular proposition derives from narrow *de se* self-ascription plus facts about what the subject is related to.

Often we know a lot about which singular propositions someone believes in this wide and derivative way; but we know less about *how* – in virtue of just which self-ascriptions and relations of acquaintance – he believes those singular propositions. So it's no surprise to find that our ordinary-language belief sentences often seem to be ascriptions of wide content. Often; but not always. In these last few paragraphs, I've been talking about *de se* narrow content, and I've been talking about it in plain English. (Such bits of jargon as I used were first explained in plain English.)

There are still other dimensions to the semantic complexity and the multifarious ambiguity of ordinary-language belief sentences. Think of the belief sentences that show up as test cases in articles advocating one semantic analysis or another. I *always* want to say: 'in a sense that's true, in a sense false'. One complication is that we get direct-quotational effects even in what is ostensibly indirect quotation.[35] An example: Fred knows perfectly well that the house he lives in is made of wood, but Fred also thinks that 'abode' is the English word for a house made of mud-brick. 'Fred believes that he has an abode – yes or no?' In at least some contexts (this isn't one of them) I'd be prepared to insist on 'no'. Wouldn't you? Moral: if you hope to understand the folk psychology of belief by studying the linguistic phenomenology of ordinary belief sentences, you're in for big trouble.

---

34 Lewis, 'Attitudes *De Dicto* and *De Se*', pp. 538–543.

35 See Steven Rieber, 'A Test for Quotation', *Philosophical Studies* 68 (1992), pp. 83–94.

I've said that narrow content is very often *de se*, but by resorting to a cheap trick I can change 'often' to 'always'. Take an apparent exception: the narrow belief that square pegs won't fit in round holes. Take this to be the *de se* self-ascription of the property of inhabiting a world wherein square pegs won't fit in round holes. A peculiar property, since either all the inhabitants of a world share it or else none do; and, like many other self-ascribed properties, very far from fundamental; but in a broad enough sense of the word, a property all the same. Likewise you can self-ascribe the property of inhabiting a world where there's a famous sea-side place called 'Blackpool'. And so on, until all narrow content has been included as *de se*. Hoky, but maybe worthwhile for the sake of uniform treatment.

My final objection is that Strawman ignores large parts of the folk psychology of belief and desire: the parts that characterize aspects of our rationality. Folk psychology says that a system of beliefs and desires tends to cause behaviour that serves the subject's desires according to his beliefs. Folk psychology says that beliefs change constantly under the impact of perceptual evidence: we keep picking up new beliefs, mostly true, about our perceptual surroundings; whereupon our other beliefs (and our instrumental desires) change to cohere with these new beliefs. Folk psychology sets presumptive limits to what basic desires we can have or lack: *de gustibus non disputandum*, but still a bedrock craving for a saucer of mud would be unintelligible.[36] Likewise it sets limits to our sense of plausibility: which hypotheses we find credible prior to evidence, hence which hypotheses are easily confirmed when their predictions come true. And it sets presumptive limits on what our contents of belief and desire can be. Self-ascribed properties may be 'far from fundamental', I said − but not *too* far. Especially gruesome gerrymanders are *prima facie* ineligible to be contents of belief and desire.[37] In short, folk psychology says that we make sense. It credits us with a modicum of rationality in our acting, believing, and desiring.

36 G. E. M. Anscombe, *Intention* (Blackwell, 1958), pp. 69–71.
37 See Lewis, 'New Work for a Theory of Universals', pp. 370–377; Lewis, *On the Plurality of Worlds*, pp. 38–39 and 105–108.

(Beware. 'Rationality' is an elastic word, and here I've stretched it to cover a lot. If you'd rather use it more narrowly – just for the serving of desires according to beliefs, say – no harm done. So long as you don't just ignore the several other departments of rationality that I listed, it doesn't matter what you call them.)

If mental states are to be analysed as occupants of folk-psychological roles, and if the folk psychology of belief and desire has a lot to say about rationality, and if what it says is framed in terms of content, then it seems that constraints of rationality are constitutive of content. Yet Strawman's account of content makes no place for constitutive rationality. Why not?

Perhaps Strawman thought, wisely, that it would be better to say too little than too much. It wouldn't do to conclude that, as a matter of analytic necessity, anyone who can be said to have beliefs and desires at all must be an ideally rational *homo economicus*! Our rationality is very imperfect, Strawman knows it, and he knows that the folk know it too. Of course we overlook options and hypotheses, we practice inference to the third-best explanation, we engage in doublethink, and so on, and on, and on.

But there is no cause for alarm. Folk psychology can be taken as a theory of imperfect, near-enough rationality, yet such rationality as it does affirm can still be constitutive. And even if folk psychology did set too high a standard – even if, to take the worst case, it were a theory of ideal rationality – still an imperfect but near-enough occupant of a folk-psychological role could thereby be an imperfect but near-enough deserver of a folk-psychological name. Remember also that the *typical* occupant of a role needn't occupy it in every case. In short, constitutive rationality leaves plenty of room for human folly.

(I think that systematic theories of ideal rationality – decision theory, for instance, and the theory of learning from experience by conditionalizing a subjective probability distribution – are severely idealized versions of parts of folk psychology. They are founded upon our tacit knowledge of folk psychology, elicited in the guise of 'intuition'. But folk psychology also supplies the grains of salt to be applied to these idealizations. Sometimes it supplies complementary pairs of opposite idealizations: a quantitative theory of subjective probabilities and utilities precise to however many decimal places, and alongside it a non-quantitative theory of beliefs and desires that don't admit of degree at all.)

Constitutive rationality is part of the legacy of behaviourism, and that is a second reason why Strawman mistrusts it. A behaviourist analysis might say, roughly, that a subject's beliefs and desires are those beliefs and desires, attribution of which would best make sense of how the subject is disposed to behave, and of how his changing behavioural dispositions depend on the changing perceptible features of his surroundings. But Strawman is a robust realist about beliefs and desires. He takes them to be genuine inner states, and causes of behaviour. He won't like an analysis that dispenses with efficacious inner states in favour of mere patterns of dispositions. Still less would he like it if the behaviourist went on to say that attributions of belief and desire governed by constitutive rationality were instrumentally useful, or warranted by rules of assertability, but not straightforwardly true.

I applaud these misgivings. I too am a robust realist about beliefs and desires. (About whole systems of beliefs and desires, anyway, though maybe not about all the little snippets – the sentences written in the belief and desire boxes – of which these systems may or may not be composed.) But I say the proper remedy is not to shun constitutive rationality, but to apply it differently. The behaviourist applies it directly to the subject; I say we should apply it to the subject's inner state. The behaviourist says that the subject *has* that system of beliefs and desires that best makes sense of how the subject is disposed to behave. Whereas I'd say that the inner state *is* that system of beliefs and desires that best makes sense of the behaviour which that state is apt for causing in subjects. Thus I'd use constitutive rationality not to dispense with causally efficacious inner states, but rather to define their content.

A third reason why Strawman shuns constitutive rationality is that sometimes it needs be be applied not to the singular propositions that are the wide content of belief and desire, but instead to the underlying *de se* narrow content. The furniture of the *Lebenswelt* which presents us with our problems of decision and learning consists, in the first instance, of objects given *qua* objects of acquaintance, and individuated by acquaintance.[38] That is a matter of narrow content. If you are lucky, and you're never wrong or uncertain about whether you're really R-acquainted with something, and you're never wrong or uncertain about whether the thing you're R_1-acquainted with is or isn't the same as the thing you're R_2-acquainted with, then we can talk about your beliefs and desires entirely in terms of wide content. We can safely let things *simpliciter* stand in for things-*qua*-objects-of-acquaintance. But if you're not so lucky, that won't work. Take unlucky Pierre.[39] He self-ascribes being R_1-acquainted with a pretty city and being R_2-acquainted with an ugly city. But in fact he is R_1-acquainted and R_2-acquainted with the same city, London. Thereby he believes both that London is pretty and that London is ugly. (Kripke derives this conclusion from certain premises, but I find the conclusion at least as obvious as the premises.) I take this to be a conflict in wide content: Pierre widely believes two singular propositions that predicate conflicting properties of the same thing. Folk psychology says that by careful attention we can detect and eliminate conflicts in our beliefs – especially if we're good at logic, as Pierre is. But plainly that was never meant to apply to Pierre's conflict of singular propositions. Mere thought can't save him. What he needs is the information *de se* that he is R_1-acquainted and R_2-acquainted with the very same thing.[40]

And suppose Pierre believes that by boarding the bus before him, he can be taken to London for a week of sight-seeing. Would boarding that bus serve his desires according to his beliefs? – It helps not at all to know that he widely believes both that London is pretty and that London is ugly. What does help is the information already given about his narrow self-ascriptions, plus one further thing: he also self-ascribes

38 See Jaakko Hintikka, 'Knowledge by Acquaintance – Individuation by Acquaintance' in *Bertrand Russell: A Collection of Critical Essays*, ed. by D. Pears (Doubleday, 1972); David Lewis, 'Individuation by Acquaintance and by Stipulation', *Philosophical Review* 92 (1983), pp. 3–32 (reprinted in this volume as Chapter 22).

39 Saul Kripke, 'A Puzzle about Belief' in *Meaning and Use*, ed. Avishai Margalit (Dordrecht: Reidel, 1979).

40 David Lewis, 'What Puzzling Pierre Does Not Believe', *Australasian Journal of Philosophy* 59 (1981), pp. 283–289 (reprinted in this volume as Chapter 24).

having a bus before him that would take him to the place he is R_1-acquainted with.[41,42]

This completes my list of objections against Strawman's program for explaining content. Doubtless you can think of ever so many ways of amending Strawman's theses to get around my objections. Some lists of amendments would take us to the positions really held by real people. Of course I can't show that no version of Strawman-amended can work. But for myself, I pin my hopes on a more radical reversal of Strawman's position.

With Strawman for a foil, my own approach can be summed up quickly. The contentful unit is the entire system of beliefs and desires. (Maybe it divides up into contentful snippets, maybe not.) That system is an inner state that typically causes behaviour, and changes under the impact of perception (and also spontaneously). Its content is defined, insofar as it is defined at all, by constitutive rationality on the basis of its typical causal role. This content is in the first instance narrow and *de se* (or *de se et nunc* if you'd rather steer clear of momentary selves). Wide content is derivative, a product of narrow content and relationships of acquaintance with external things.

---

41 See Lewis, *On the Plurality of Worlds*, p. 58.

42 On constitutive rationality, see Robert Stalnaker, *Inquiry* (MIT Press, 1984), pp. 1–42; David Lewis, 'Radical Interpretation', *Synthese* 23 (1974), pp. 331–44, reprinted with postscripts in Lewis, *Philosophical Papers*, Vol. 1 (Oxford University Press, 1983); and Lewis, *On the Plurality of Worlds*, pp. 27–40. But see 'Radical Interpretation' with caution: it began as a conversation with Donald Davidson, and I went rather too far in granting undisputed common ground. (1) I gave an important place to the subject Karl's beliefs as expressed in Karl's own language; that certainly suggests language-of-thought-ism, though I hope I committed myself to nothing more than the safe thesis that Karl's medium of mental representation is *somehow* analogous to language. (2) I was too individualistic: I ignored the possibility that deviant Karl might believe something in virtue of the causal role of his inner state not in Karl himself but in others who are more typical members of Karl's kind. (3) I had not yet come to appreciate the role of *de se* content. Also see *On the Plurality of Worlds*, with caution: besides endorsing constitutive rationality, I also stated it within a controversial framework of realism about unactualized *possibilia*. I still think that's a good way to state it; but I never said it was the only way. Constitutive rationality and realism about *possibilia* needn't be a package deal!

19

Should a materialist believe in qualia?

Should a materialist believe in qualia? Yes and no. 'Qualia' is a name for the occupants of a certain functional role that is spelled out in our tacitly known folk psychology. If materialism is true, there are no perfect occupants of the role, and hence no perfect deservers of the name. But in all probability there are imperfect occupants of the role, imperfect deservers of the name. Good enough deservers of the name? May they just be called 'qualia'? I say yes.

But I take this to be a case of semantic indecision. There is no settled answer to the question 'how good is good enough?'. In part, maybe, it is a political question. The foe (or friend) of materialism who wants to make it out to be something radical and bizarre is entitled to say that materialist 'qualia' are bogus, ersatz qualia; whereas a conservative materialist like me may say with equal right that qualia exist but are not quite as we take them to be.[1]

First published in *The Australasian Journal of Philosophy* 73 (1995), pp. 140–144. Reprinted with kind permission from *The Australasian Journal of Philosophy*.

I thank Robert M. Adams, D. M. Armstrong, Mark Johnston, and an anonymous reader for the *Australasian Journal of Philosophy*.

I dedicate this paper gratefully to Jerome Shaffer, my first teacher in philosophy, on the occasion of his retirement.

1 This is a reply, *inter alia*, to Robert M. Adams, 'Flavors, Colors, and God', in his *The Virtue of Faith and Other Essays in Philosophical Theology* (Oxford: Oxford University Press, 1987) pp. 243–262. Adams argues that 'it is a theoretical advantage of theism that it makes possible a [theological] explanation' of the correlation of qualia and physical states (p. 250). In his final section, Adams notes that according to

'Qualia' isn't a term of ordinary language. Neither is 'phenomenal character' nor 'raw feel' nor 'subjective quality'. 'What it's like' or 'how it seems' are ordinary enough – but when used as terms for qualia, they are used in a special technical sense. You can say what it's like to taste New Zealand beer by saying what experience you have when you do, namely a sweet taste. But you can't say what it's like to have a sweet taste in the parallel way, namely by saying that when you do, you have a sweet taste!

Yet despite the lack of a folksy word or phrase, I still say that the concept of qualia is somehow built into folk psychology. My reason is that when philosophers tell us very concisely indeed what they mean by 'qualia', we catch on. I think they never say enough to introduce the concept from scratch to someone who doesn't already have it (whether or not he has the qualia themselves). But maybe they do say enough to serve as a reminder to someone who has the concept already, even if he has it in some inexplicit way.

Now I will say what I think the folk-psychological concept – and hence the definitive role – of qualia is.

Preliminaries: I will say *experiences* when I mean particular events of experiencing. These events are havings of *experiential states*, which are had repeatedly at different times and by different people. These repeatable states also are called 'experiences' – but not in this paper. An experience is of the same *type* as another if it is the having of exactly the same experiential state. An experience is *novel* if the subject hasn't had an experience of the same type before.

It is well known that by having novel experiences we gain mental abilities, often abilities we can gain in no other way. These include the ability to recognize experiences of the same type when they come again, and also the ability to imagine experiences of that type when not having them. Experiences of different types confer different such abilities.[2] Presumably it is because of properties they have that expe-

materialism there is no such correlation to be explained; but this, he says, is because the materialist is committed to a 'radical' and 'desperate' eliminativism about qualia. I disagree.

2 See Laurence Nemirow, 'Physicalism and the Cognitive Role of Acquaintance', and David Lewis, 'What Experience Teaches', both in William G. Lycan (ed.), *Mind and*

riences confer these abilities; and experiences of different types must differ in their ability-conferring properties. A concept of qualia – a materialistically acceptable concept, but perhaps not the whole of the folk concept – is the concept of properties of experiences apt for causing abilities to recognize and to imagine experiences of the same type.

Maybe there is more to the concept than that, even before we get to the part I think is trouble. Maybe, for instance, it is part of the concept that the qualia of experiences are responsible for responses of pleasure, disgust, etc. And maybe it is part of the concept that the qualia of experiences are responsible for judgements of similarity-distance, e.g., the judgement that these two colour-samples nearly match whereas those two contrast strikingly; and in this way, the qualia of experiences constitute something akin to a metric space.

It may well be redundant to speak of both experiential states and of qualia. If E, F,.... are various experiential states, then being a having of E, being a having of F, ... are corresponding properties of particular experiences. Might it just be these properties that occupy the functional role of qualia (insofar as the role described so far is rightly so-called)? If so, no harm. Then these properties corresponding to experiential states are candidates – the best candidates around, in my view – to deserve the name of qualia. So if the state pain is C-firing, to take a toy example, then the distinctive quale of pains would be the property: being an event of C-firing.

Unfortunately there is more to the folk-psychological concept of qualia than I have yet said. It concerns the *modus operandi* of qualia. Folk psychology says, I think, that we *identify* the qualia of our experiences. We know exactly what they are – and that in an uncommonly demanding and literal sense of 'knowing what'. If I have an experience with quale Q, I know that I am having an experience with quale Q, and I will afterwards remember (unless I happen to forget) that on that occasion I had an experience with quale Q. It is by producing this identifying knowledge that a novel experience confers abilities to recognize and imagine. Recognition: when Fred first tasted Vegemite, he found out that it caused an experience with quale Q.

Cognition: A Reader (Oxford: Blackwell, 1990) pp. 490–519 (the latter is reprinted in this volume as Chapter 17).

Afterwards, when he has an experience that has quale Q, he knows he is having an experience that has quale Q, so he infers that he is having an experience of the same type as before; and so he may at least guess that he is again tasting Vegemite. Imagination: Fred knew all along, supposedly, how to imagine an experience having quale Q. But only when he had tasted Vegemite did he know that by imagining an experience with quale Q, he would be imagining an experience of tasting Vegemite.

Call this the *Identification Thesis*. Why do I think it must be part of the folk theory of qualia? Because so many philosophers find it so very obvious.[3] I think it seems obvious because it is built into folk psychology. Others will think it gets built into folk psychology because it is so obvious; but either way, the obviousness and the folk-psychological status go together.

I spoke of 'an uncommonly demanding and literal sense of "knowing what"'. Let me elaborate. I say that according to the Identification Thesis, the knowledge I gain by having an experience with quale Q enables me to know what Q is – identifies Q – in this sense: any possibility not ruled out by the content of my knowledge is one in which it is Q, and not any other property instead, that is the quale of my experience. Equivalently, when I have an experience with quale Q, the knowledge I thereby gain reveals the essence of Q: a property of Q such that, necessarily, Q has it and nothing else does. If, for instance, Q is essentially the physical property of being an event of C-firing, and if I identify the qualia of my experience in the appropriate 'demanding and literal' sense, I come to know that what is going on in me is an event of C-firing. Contrapositively: if I identify the quale of my experience in the appropriate sense, and yet know nothing of the firing of my neurons, then the quale of my experience cannot have been essentially the property of being an event of C-firing.

---

3 Adams, for instance, speaks of our 'first-person' way of identifying qualia (*op. cit.*, p. 259). And Saul Kripke seems to be relying on the Identification Thesis in *Naming and Necessity* (Oxford: Blackwell, 1980) p. 152, when he writes that 'pain . . . is picked out by its immediate phenomenological quality . . .' and concludes that 'pain' can be a rigid designator although it is not introduced by rigidifying any accidental description of pain.

A materialist cannot accept the Identification Thesis. If qualia are physical properties of experiences, and experiences in turn are physical events, then it is certain that we seldom, if ever, identify the qualia of our experiences. Making discoveries in neurophysiology is not so easy![4] So if the Identification Thesis is indeed built into folk psychology, then those physical properties are imperfect occupants of the definitive folk-psychological role of qualia, and imperfect deservers of the name. They may yet deserve the name well enough.

Should a materialist believe in qualia? Yes: he should believe in imperfect but good-enough deservers of the name, occupants of the part of the folk-psychological role we get by leaving out the Identification Thesis. And no: he should not believe in perfect deservers of the name, occupants of the entire role. It is not altogether wrong to call him an 'eliminativist'. But see how little he eliminates, how much he retains.

To conclude, I distinguish the Identification Thesis itself from two harmless look-alikes. A materialist can and should accept these look-alike theses. That makes his position seem less radical; it softens the blow of rejecting the Identification Thesis in its full-strength, materialistically unacceptable form.

First, there is no reason to deny that the broad, *de re* content of my knowledge does, in the strongest sense, identify the qualia. Hitherto, I have been denying that the narrow *de se* and *de dicto* content of my knowledge identifies the qualia. But broad content is constituted partly

---

4 If we know exactly what the qualia of our experiences are, they can have no essential hidden structure — no 'grain' — of which we remain ignorant. (If we didn't know whether their hidden 'grain' ran this way or that, we wouldn't know *exactly* what they were. Whatever we might know about them, we would not fully know their essence.) But if nothing essential about the qualia is hidden, then if they seem simple, they *are* simple. We may assume that if a property is structural, then it is so essentially. Then it is a consequence of the Identification Thesis that if we fail to notice structure, there is no structure there to notice. But we do fail to notice structure. So the simplicity of the qualia is a consequence of the Identification Thesis (*inter alia*), and so a derivative part of the folk-psychological concept of qualia. Here is another part of that concept that a materialist should disown.

The simplicity of the qualia is a premise of Adams' argument that we cannot hope to explain the correlation of qualia and physical states within a future science of dualistic psychophysics (*op. cit.,* p. 253).

by my narrow *de se* self-ascriptions involving acquaintance, partly by the identity of the objects of acquaintance. Thus I may know *de re* of Fred that he is a burglar, but without in any sense identifying Fred.[5] Likewise I may know *de re* of a certain physical property that it is among the qualia of my present experience, but without identifying the property in question.

Second, there is no reason to deny that we know what the qualia of our experiences are in a not-so-demanding, not-so-literal, everyday sense of 'knowing what'. Suppose that the essence of a chemical element is its atomic number. I have forgotten the atomic number of potassium. So in the demanding sense, I no longer know exactly which element potassium is. Yet I still know what it is in the sense that I have a rich cluster of descriptions of potassium. These include ego-centric descriptions in terms of the relations of acquaintance, linguistic and otherwise, that I bear to potassium. By some everyday standards, that counts as knowing what potassium is. Likewise, 'individuating by acquaintance',[6] I know who various people are even though I do not know their essences – anyway, not under any plausible version of essentialism I can think of.[7] And likewise, though I don't know the

5 I self-ascribe the property: staring at a burglar; I am in fact staring at Fred, though neither in the demanding sense nor in any everyday sense do I know who I am staring at. That is how I believe (and maybe also know) *de re* of Fred that he is a burglar. See David Lewis, 'Attitudes *De Dicto* and *De Se*', *The Philosophical Review* 88 (1979) pp. 513–543, esp. pp. 538–543.

6 See Jaakko Hintikka, 'Knowledge by Acquaintance – Individuation by Acquaintance' in D. F. Pears (ed.), *Bertrand Russell: A Collection of Critical Essays* (Garden City, NY: Doubleday, 1972); and David Lewis, 'Individuation by Acquaintance and by Stipulation', *The Philosophical Review* 92 (1983) pp. 3–32 (reprinted in this volume as Chapter 22).

7 The case of identifying a person (or a thing) is unlike the case of identifying potassium, or identifying a quale. But how to describe the difference is a controversial question in the metaphysics of modality. Potassium is spread over many possible worlds; there is a clear candidate – atomic number – for being its essence; and this essence can be known. Likewise for qualia, at least if they are indeed physical properties such as the property of being an event of C-firing. On my own view people are strictly speaking confined to single worlds, though they have other-worldly counterparts; their essences consist of properties they share with their counterparts; the counterpart relation suffers from semantic indecision, and so likewise does the line

essences of the various qualia of my experiences, I do know what relations of acquaintance I bear to these qualia. So in some not-so-demanding everyday sense I know what these qualia are, even if the full-strength Identification Thesis is false.

between essential and accidental descriptions; essences are knowable insofar as they are determinate, but the line between knowing someone's essence and simply being well-informed about him (which is the line between identifying him in the 'demanding' and in the 'not-so-demanding' sense) disappears. On another view, someone's essence is a non-qualitative haecceity; that essence never can be known. So the only *useful* sense of identification is the 'not-so-demanding' sense. On yet another view, the essence of a person is the property of originating from a certain sperm and egg; you might hope to know who someone essentially is at least if you are the technician who presides over the *in vitro* conception of a test-tube baby; but no, you only swap the problem of knowing the person's essence for the problem of knowing the essence of the sperm and egg seen under your microscope. You gain nothing. Again, the only useful sense of identification is the 'not-so-demanding' sense.

20

Naming the colours

I. MANIFESTO

An adequate theory of colour must be both materialistic[2] and com-
mensensical. The former demand is non-negotiable. The latter can be
compromised to some degree. We need not be 'ever so inclusive' in
advancing all our offhand folk-theoretical opinions as conditions of
adequacy on a theory.[3] Imperfect occupants of the folk-theoretical role
of colour will be imperfect deservers of the name, but may nevertheless
deserve it quite well enough.

But compromise has its limits. It won't do to say that colours do
not exist; or that we are unable to detect them; or that they never are
properties of material things; or that they go away when things are

First published in *The Australasian Journal of Philosophy* 75 (1997), pp. 325–342. Reprinted with kind permission from *The Australasian Journal of Philosophy*.

1 Thanks are due to Ian Gold, Frank Jackson, J. J. C. Smart, Michael Smith, and others;
and to the Boyce Gibson Memorial Library.

2 I say 'materialistic' where some would rather say 'physicalistic': an adequate theory
must be consistent with the truth and completeness of some theory in much the style
of present-day physics. ('Completeness' is to be explained in terms of supervenience.)
Some fear that 'materialism' conveys a commitment that this ultimate physics must
be a physics of matter alone: no fields, no radiation, no causally active spacetime.
Not so! Let us proclaim our solidarity with forebears who, like us, wanted their
philosophy to agree with ultimate physics. Let us not chide and disown them for
their less advanced ideas about what ultimate physics might say.
3 See Mark Johnston, 'How to Speak of the Colors', *Philosophical Studies* 68 (1992)
pp. 221–263, esp. pp. 221–222.

unilluminated or unobserved; or that they change with every change in the illumination, or with every change in an observer's visual capacities; or that the same surface of the same thing has different colours for different observers. Compromise on these points, and it becomes doubtful whether the so-called 'colours' posited in your theory are rightly so-called. Yet it is a Moorean fact that there are colours rightly so-called. Deny it, and the most credible explanation of your denial is that you are in the grip of some philosophical (or scientific) error.

II. FOLK PSYCHOPHYSICS

In other words, it is a Moorean fact that the folk psychophysics of colour is close to true.

Like other folk theories, the folk psychophysics of colour is a generally shared body of tacit belief. It concerns not only colours themselves, but also the inner states of colour experience that the colours tend to cause in us, and further inner states and behaviour that these colour experiences cause in turn. It is not to be supposed that we go around with careful formulations of folk psychophysics in mind, though perhaps with enough patience it might be possible to elicit such formulations Meno-fashion.

Folk psychophysics should, for instance, afford an explanation of why we can sort dyed bits of wool, and then shuffle them together, and then sort them again into just the same heaps as before.[4] This folk-psychophysical explanation will involve many causal chains, each running from the colour of a bit of wool to a colour experience in the sorter, and thence to a desire to put that bit of wool on a certain heap, and thence to the desired behaviour.

The folk psychophysics of colour is doubtless a fragment of some larger folk theory. Elsewhere in that larger theory we might find the explanation of why our wool-sorter wanted to succeed at his task. We need not worry about demarcation, so long as we agree to include all that will be needed for what follows.

The folk psychophysics of colour is common knowledge among us. In the same tacit way in which we believe the theory itself, we

4 See J. J. C. Smart, 'Colours', *Philosophy* 36 (1961) pp. 128–142.

likewise believe that others around us all believe it too; and that they in turn ascribe belief in it to those around them in the same way we do; and so on *ad infinitum*, or at least as far as is humanly possible.[5]

A theory implicitly defines its theoretical terms. If, without benefit of any prior definition of 'entropy', thermodynamics says that entropy does this, that, and the other, we may factor that into two parts. There is an existential claim – a 'Ramsey sentence' – to the effect that there exists some quantity which does this, that, and the other (or near enough). And there is a semantic stipulation: let that which does this, that, and the other (or near enough), if such there be, bear the name 'entropy'.[6] Here is another way to say it: the theory associates with the term 'entropy' a certain theoretical role. It claims that this role is occupied. And it implicitly defines 'entropy' as a name for the occupant of the role.

What thermodynamics can do, the folk psychophysics of colour can likewise do. The situation is messier, of course, because the theory is tacit. Lacking an authoritative codification, we have no sharp way to tell what is non-negotiably part of the theory, what is provisionally part of it, and what is no part of it at all. Nor are these matters of secret fact. When folk psychophysics defines its theoretical terms, we run a risk of semantic indecision. Yet within limits, that indecision is harmless. We can hope – indeed we can be confident, as a matter of Moorean fact! – that the safe limits are not exceeded.

Central to the folk psychophysics of colour are a multitude of principles connecting colours and corresponding colour experiences. They go roughly as follows.

When a red thing is before someone's eyes, it typically causes in him an experience of redness

or better

5 See my *Convention: A Philosophical Study* (Cambridge, MA: Harvard University Press, 1969) pp. 52–60; Stephen Schiffer, *Meaning* (Oxford: Oxford University Press, 1972) pp. 30–42; Margaret Gilbert, *On Social Facts* (London: Routledge, 1989) pp. 186–197 and elsewhere.

6 See my 'How to Define Theoretical Terms', *The Journal of Philosophy* 67 (1970) pp. 427–446.

When a red thing illuminated by normal light is a suitable distance before the eyes of someone with normal visual capacities in normal surroundings, it typically causes in him an experience of redness.

'Normal light' can be explained in terms of the range of illumination that most people – actually, nowadays, and hereabouts – mostly encounter. Likewise, *mutatis mutandis*, for normal capacities and normal surroundings. Some examples of the abnormal are: sodium vapour light; eyes adapted to sodium vapour light; a room with purple walls, floor, and ceiling, filled with purple furniture, with purple curtains over the windows. I do not suppose it is incumbent on folk psychophysics to do much by way of listing abnormal cases – if it tried, it would soon outrun common knowledge. A statistical conception, rigidified to actuality and nowadays and hereabouts, should suffice. It is otherwise with distance: I dare say that folk psychophysics has a lot to tell us about which distances are 'suitable', but for me that part of the theory remains tacit.

Further, it should really have been

When a red thing is at such-and-such direction before someone's eyes, it typically causes in him an experience of redness-in-such-and-such-direction

or

When a red thing fills such-and-such solid angle . . .

None of these refinements will prove relevant to the principal topic of this paper, so for the most part I shall ignore them.

Drawing on these connecting principles, and also on the part of folk psychophysics that classifies colours as properties (for the most part) of the surfaces of opaque things, and colour experiences as inner states of people (and perhaps other animals), we have folk-psychophysical roles for the colours and for the colour experiences. When we take the theoretical terms to name the occupants of the theoretical roles, we arrive at 'definitions' such as these.

335

D1 *Red* is the surface property of things which typically causes experience of red in people who have such things before their eyes.

D2 *Experience of red* is the inner state of people which is the typical effect of having red things before the eyes.

If, as a matter of contingent fact, the surface property that causes experience of red is a certain reflectance property – that is, a property that supervenes on the thing's reflectance spectrum – then *D1* may serve as a premise for a chromophysical identification: red is, as a matter of contingent fact, that reflectance property. And if, as a matter of contingent fact, the inner state which is the typical effect of red things before the eyes is a certain pattern of neuron firings in the visual cortex, then *D2* may serve as a premise for a psychophysical identification: experience of red is, as a matter of contingent fact, that pattern of neural firings.

D1 and *D2* are all very well as truths; as widely shared tacit beliefs, and even as items of our common knowledge; and as premises for chromophysical and psychophysical identifications. But as a pair of definitions they are almost totally useless, by reason of circularity. Anyone who needed definitions both of 'red' and of 'experience of red' would be little wiser if we gave him both *D1* and *D2*. That circularity, its remedy, and the new problem that arises out of that remedy, shall be our principal business in the rest of this paper.

III. OBJECTIONS AND REPLIES

But first I stop to address some other likely worries, apart from circularity, about what I have already said.

Objection. Our colour experiences do not depend solely on the colours of things before the eyes. They depend also on the illumination, the visual capacities of the observer, and the surroundings. And it is not good enough just to make an exception for 'abnormal' cases, understood simply as infrequent cases (infrequent actually, nowadays, and hereabouts). There is no range of 'normal' cases such that we only seldom find ourselves outside that range, and also such that within that range the effects of differing illumination, etc., are entirely absent.[7]

Reply. No; but there is a range such that we seldom find ourselves outside it, and such that within it the effects of differing illumination, etc., are so small that they are hard to notice. Go from noonday sun to a cloudy afternoon to sunset; go from any of these to incandescent lighting to fluorescent lighting (but not to sodium or mercury vapour lighting); go from the room painted yellow to the room painted purple (but not to a room where almost everything in sight is purple); go from one to another so suddenly that your eyes are maladapted at first. Take with you a book with a green cover. It will continue throughout to cause experience of green, and will not start to cause experience of blue instead. Indeed, if it is the right book, it will continue throughout to cause experience of some fairly specific shade of green: Brunswick green, not malachite green or apple green.

(To be sure, it does not continue throughout to cause *precisely* the same sort of colour experience. And if our topic were not the naming of the colours that we name in daily life, but instead the naming – or rather, numbering – of the myriad precise shades that must be distinguished by matchers of paint, we would have to be much more fussy.)

In short, the barely noticeable differences in colour experience due to frequently encountered differences in illumination are not a problem. The much more striking differences in experience that are caused by much less frequently encountered differences in illumination are not a problem either: we need only say, for instance, that sodium vapour light causes colour illusions. It is only if we conflate these two non-problems, and we try to discuss the entire range of dependence of experience on illumination in a uniform way, that we get a problem. It would be daft to deny that sodium vapour light causes illusions. It would be still more daft to say that *all* light causes colour illusions,

7 See Keith Campbell, 'Colours' in *Contemporary Philosophy in Australia* (eds.) R. Brown and C. D. Rollins (London: Allen and Unwin, 1969); but for a somewhat different view, see also Campbell, 'The Implications of Land's Theory of Colour Vision' in *Logic, Methodology, and Philosophy of Science* (ed.) L. J. Cohen (Amsterdam: North-Holland, 1982).

with the sole exception of cloudy Scottish daylight (or some other precisely and arbitrarily chosen standard).

Another way to create an illusory problem is to ignore our daily experience, follow where theory leads, and then back an oversimple theory. Imagine that the eye is simply a spectrometer that measures the intensities at various wavelengths of the light coming from the thing seen, and produces colour experiences that depend just on those intensities. Then the experience produced by something with an unchanging reflectance spectrum would depend a lot on illumination – even for illumination within the frequently encountered range. The colours of things could not seem as constant as they manifestly do.

So should we assume severe and ubiquitous inconstancy when we philosophize about colour? Of course not! Rather, we should stop assuming that the eye is simply a spectrometer. We should think of it, perhaps, as a *calibrated* spectrometer.[8] If the spectrometer's measurements are corrected to compensate for differences in illumination, they will indeed measure reflectance properties, and experience that depends on the corrected measurements will indeed exhibit constancy of colour. And if the spectrometer shares information with similar spectrometers aimed in different directions (or if it spends some of its own time scanning around the scene), and if it has definite preconceptions about the sort of distribution of reflectance values to be expected, then it will be in a position to calculate the proper correction factors. Of course the method has its limitations. No amount of calibration will permit measurement of reflectance values in a band of wavelengths that is missing from the illumination; when the preconceptions used to calculate correction factors are mistaken, the reflectance measurements will likewise be mistaken; and recalibration after a change of illumination will not be instantaneous. Nevertheless, this fallible method may be good enough to yield approximate constancy throughout a wide range of frequently encountered cases. And that suffices.

8 Here I follow the lead of David Hilbert, *Color and Color Perception* (Chicago: Center for the Study of Language and Information. 1987). One theory that treats the eye as a calibrated spectrometer capable of measuring reflectance properties is Land's well-known 'retinex' theory. But it is by no means the only such theory on offer.

Objection. A brown expanse on the television is composed of diversely coloured pixels – none of them brown. The brown expanse and a certain blue pixel are before the eye in the same direction, at the same distance, at the same time. Should they not cause a colour experience of blue and brown in the very same direction? Yet they do not.

Reply. The pixel and the expanse are not both at a 'suitable distance', even though they are at the same distance, because the suitability of a viewing distance depends on the size of the thing viewed.

Follow-up objection. Then consider a pixel-sized part of the brown expanse. Now the brown thing and the blue thing are the same in size as well as distance, so if one is at a suitable viewing distance then so is the other.

Reply. A pixel-sized part of a brown expanse is not necessarily brown. In this case it is blue. In fact, it is the blue pixel already considered. If the pixel is at a suitable distance, no *brown* part of the brown expanse is at a suitable distance and also in the same direction as the pixel. Colours are imperfectly 'dissective' properties: they are not always shared between a thing and its proper parts.[9]

Objection. Some ostensible facts about the colours – for instance, that there cannot be a reddish green, or that there cannot be a shade of yellow that is closer to various shades of blue than it is to any other shade of yellow – are best explained in terms of the way our colour vision works, rather than in terms of relations between physical properties of surfaces. Then if colours are physical properties of surfaces, how can these facts of exclusion and proximity be facts about colours?

Reply. Our account provides a correspondence between colours and colour experiences. (Various rival accounts also provide such correspondences.) For now, that correspondence takes the form of a set of definitional circles, but soon we shall give it a more satisfactory form. Whatever form it takes, the correspondence yields relations among colours in the image of relations among colour experiences (or vice versa). So no matter where the relations of exclusion and

9 See Hilbert, *Color and Color Perception*, pp. 29–42.

proximity may originate, in the end we have them twice over: as relations among colour experiences and also as relations among the corresponding colours.

(We might have had an offhand opinion that these relations originated as relations among surface properties. If so, we were wrong. But I am not sure we had any such opinion at all; and if we did, we have no business elevating it into a Moorean fact of folk psychophysics.)

If it is absolutely impossible to have an experience of reddish green (or if it is nomically impossible, or if it is unimaginable, or if it is just very difficult to arrange); and if reddish green is by definition the surface property that typically causes experience of reddish green; then the desired exclusion among colours follows. Then it is absolutely impossible (or nomically impossible, or unimaginable, or difficult) for there to be a reddish green surface.[10] *Quod erat demonstrandum.* Likewise for the yellow in the midst of blue.

Objection. Not only surfaces of opaque things are coloured, but also transparent volumes, light sources, the sky,. . . . Colours are not always surface properties. *A fortiori* they are not always reflectance properties.

Reply. I have no opinion about whether the blue of the sky and the blue of an opaque picture of the sky are one shared non-disjunctive property, or whether they are two different, but saliently related, properties.

But even in the first case there is a colour property – *surface blue,* or rather a certain shade thereof – that the picture has and that the sky itself lacks. (It is the conjunction of the shared property with the property of being a surface of an opaque thing.) And in the second case also, we have a surface blue that the picture has and the sky lacks. It is these surface colours that are my present concern, and that well might be identical to reflectance properties. My restriction of topic

10 It is not absolutely or nomically impossible to arrange for an experience of reddish green. But it is difficult, at least by the method presently known: that of H. Crane and T. P. Plantida, 'On Seeing Reddish Green and Yellowish Blue', *Science* 221 (1983) pp. 1078–1080. That method does not involve any special surface property before the eyes. I do not know whether those who have the experience acquire an ability to imagine it afterward when they are no longer having it.

leaves unfinished business. But I doubt that it leads to error within my restricted topic.

Objection. If colours are reflectance properties, they supervene on reflectance spectra. A reflectance spectrum is a disposition, or a bundle of dispositions, to reflect various proportions of light at various wavelengths. A disposition requires a 'causal basis'. For instance, something is disposed to break when struck if it has some property – some intrinsic property, at least in the clearest cases – which, together with striking, would cause breaking. In the case of reflectance properties, the causal basis is a matter of surface microstructure. It turns out that a given reflectance property can have any of many microstructural bases, different ones in different actual cases. Now we face a nasty four-way choice.[11]

Shall we say (1) that the colour is not the reflectance property after all, but rather it is the microstructural causal basis thereof? Or shall we say (2) that the colour is the reflectance property, but that a reflectance property – and any other disposition likewise – is identical to its causal basis? Either way, we end up concluding that what we thought was one single colour, indeed one single shade of one colour, is really many different microstructural properties, different ones in different cases. That is seriously uncommonsensical. Or shall we rather say that a colour is a reflectance property, a reflectance property is a disposition, a disposition is not identical to any of its causal bases, but rather a disposition is the property of having some suitable causal basis or other? Then what shall we say about how the selective reflection of light – or more generally, the manifestation of any disposition – is caused? We cannot deny that the causal basis does the causing. That is how we defined 'causal basis', after all. Shall we say (3) that only the causal basis does the causing, and the disposition itself is impotent? In the present case, that would mean denying that surface colours cause selective reflection of light; and denying also that they cause more distant effects, such as colour experiences or colour-discriminating behaviour, via causal chains that begin with selective reflection of light. And it is

11 See Elizabeth W. Prior, Robert Pargetter, and Frank C. Jackson, 'Three Theses About Dispositions', *American Philosophical Quarterly* 19 (1982) pp. 251–257.

safe to say that colours do not cause colour experiences some other way! But to deny that colours cause colour experiences is seriously uncommonsensical.

Or shall we say that a disposition and its basis, for instance a colour and a microstructure, *both* cause the manifestation? What kind of multiple causation is this? It seems wrong to say that the basis causes the manifestation by first causing the disposition, or vice versa, or that the basis and the disposition jointly cause the manifestation. The remaining alternative is to say (4) that we must have a case of over-determination: the disposition and its basis redundantly cause the manifestation. For instance, the colour and the microstructure re-dundantly cause the selective reflection of light, and thereby they re-dundantly cause the colour experience. This alternative, too, is seriously uncommonsensical.

Reply. Alternatives (1), (2), and (3) should be discarded. Alternative (4) is close to right, but needs correction. The key to sorting out this mess is that we should not have been talking about properties as causes in the first place. That is loose talk. (Most of the time it is harmlessly loose talk, and I do not propose to give it up just because it got us into trouble this once.) Really, the causing is done by particular *havings* of properties – particular 'events', as we call them. (But that name is not meant to imply that all events are short-lived or involve change. If something in a frozen world is changeless throughout some short or long interval, or indeed throughout all time, its changelessness during the interval is still called an 'event'.) The very same event that is es-sentially a having of some causal basis of a certain disposition is also accidentally a having of the disposition itself.[12] So an effect of this event is caused by a having of the basis, and caused also by a having of the disposition. But since these havings are one and the same event, there is no redundant causation. So a colour experience may be caused by a colour, and also by the microstructural causal basis of the reflectance values that comprise that colour, without having a case of causal over-determination.

12 See my 'Events' in *Philosophical Papers, Vol. II* (Oxford: Oxford University Press, 1986) pp. 247–254.

Objection. If we do not want to say that what we thought was one single colour is really many different properties, different ones in different cases, then we also have a problem about *metamers*: different reflectance spectra that cause the same colour experience.[13] What to say about them?

Reply. At worst, we have a problem about *some* metamers. I note, first, that even if we think that the colours will turn out to be reflectance properties, we have no reason to think that all reflectance properties – all properties that supervene on reflectance spectra – will turn out to be colours. Metamers that differ in their reflectance spectra, but do not differ in those reflectance properties that participate in causing colour experience, are no problem. We have the same colour, exactly as in the case where there are different microstructural causal bases of the same reflectance spectrum.

Suppose, for example, that there is a certain division of the visible spectrum into long-wave, middle-wave, and short-wave intervals such that, if we take the triple of integrals of reflectance over the three intervals, the colours will turn out to supervene not only on reflectance spectra but on the triples of integrals.[14] When the spectra differ but the triples do not differ, we have the same colour. Only if different triples caused the same colour experience would we have a problem; only then would we face a choice between denying the identity of colours with triples of reflectance integrals and admitting, uncommonsensically, that some colours cannot be distinguished by sight. (Not without varying the illumination, anyway. Metamers under one illumination may look different under another, especially if we resort to illuminations not frequently encountered.)

I note, second, that it would not be so very bad to acknowledge

---

13 See David Hilbert, *Color and Color Perception*, pp. 81–100; C. L. Hardin, *Color for Philosophers: Unweaving the Rainbow* (Indianapolis: Hackett, 1988) pp. 28, 46, and elsewhere.

14 Perhaps the three intervals should be 'fuzzy' intervals. These are taken as functions – bell curves, or similar – measuring the degree to which a given point is deemed to fall within the interval. To integrate a quantity over a fuzzy interval, we multiply the quantity by the function just mentioned, and we integrate that product *simpliciter*.

some cases of indistinguishable colours, so long as such cases were uncommon. David Hilbert reports an encouraging consequence of one well-developed model of colour constancy (that is, of how the spectrometer gets calibrated in accordance with preconceptions):

Although there are possible differences of colour that are undetectable in normal circumstances, the actual occurrence of such differences appears to be relatively rare.[15]

Objection. When the purple people eater comes out of hiding to stalk its prey, it uses its powers of telehypnosis to disrupt the colour vision of victim and bystanders. In this way it manages to be mistaken for a benign brown beast. The deception always works. The purple people eater, though it is purple from tail to teeth, never causes experience of purple. Is this a counter-example?

Reply. No. The question what the eater itself typically causes is the wrong question. We were supposed instead to ask what the surface properties of the eater typically cause. Does it have a surface property such that this property – or rather, particular havings thereof – will typically cause experience of purple? It does. The same property that occurs on the people eater occurs, or at least could occur, elsewhere: before the eyes of a normal perceiver with undisrupted colour vision. In that case it typically causes, or would cause, experience of purple. Accordingly, that property is the colour purple, and the purple people eater is rightly so called.

Objection. The yellow killer is a more problematic predator. It too disrupts the colour vision of anyone who sets eyes on it; and it disrupts all other brain processes as well, thereby causing instant death. But in this case, it is the killer's colour that does the damage. Its special shade of yellow, 'killer yellow', is fatal regardless of what the coloured thing may be. This colour does not typically cause colour experience. It never does, and never could so long as we retain our vulnerability to it.[16]

15 Hilbert, *Color and Color Perception*, pp. 130–131.
16 The example of killer yellow is due to Saul Kripke, in lectures many years ago. I

Reply. The case is consistent if, but only if, we can subsume killer yellow as a special case under some broader property that does typically cause experience of yellow; and that is not an artificial gerrymander, but rather is unified by appropriate resemblances between its various subcases. If so, we can repeat the strategy that worked in the case of the purple people eater: we distinguish a broader property which deserves the colour name from a narrower property which, if considered just on its own, does not.

To put the point another way: killer yellow deserves to be so called, if indeed it does, in virtue of its resemblance to other shades of yellow that do cause experience of yellow. For instance, it might resemble other shades of yellow in respect of the values of its triple of long-wave, middle-wave, and short-wave integrals of reflectance, if those turn out to be the reflectance properties on which colour experiences normally depend.

In that case, the relation that unites the killer property with non-lethal shades of yellow, and thereby justifies us in classifying the killer property itself as a shade of yellow, is colour resemblance in a doubly derivative sense. First, we have resemblance among colour experiences. That resemblance does not apply directly, since there are no experiences of killer yellow. Second, we have the image among colours of this first relation among experiences, under the causal correspondence between surface properties and the experiences they typically cause: the derivative relation that holds between colours just when the colour experiences they typically cause stand in the first relation. This second resemblance also does not apply directly, since killer yellow does not cause any colour experience at all. Finally, it may be that this second relation typically correlates with a third relation: resemblance in respect of the triple of reflectance integrals. If that turns out to be so (and whether it is so is an empirical question, even supposing that the colours do turn out to be triples of reflectance integrals) then in a still more derivative sense we may regard this third relation also as a relation of colour resemblance. So, finally, we have a relation that can unite killer yellow with other yellows.

am obliged to note that what I say here may not correspond to the whole of what Kripke said in those lectures.

IV. FROM CIRCULARITY TO MULTIPLICITY

I return at last to our principal difficulty: the definitional circle between the name of a colour and the name of the corresponding colour experience. Red is the surface property apt for causing experience of red, which is the inner state that red things before the eyes are apt for causing. Likewise for green, for magenta, . . .

A manoeuvre due mainly to Carnap often works to cure such circularities, but in the present case it proves disappointing.[17] Here is how it works, when it works. Suppose thermodynamics has *two* theoretical terms, 'entropy' and 'temperature'; and without benefit of prior definition of either, it says that entropy does this, that, and the other; temperature does so and so; temperature and entropy are related thus. Then any ordered pair of X and Y is called a *realization* of thermodynamics iff X does this, that, and the other; Y does so and so; X and Y are related thus. (Equivalently: X and Y make thermodynamics true, if taken as referents of the respective terms 'entropy' and 'temperature'.) Now we define our terms without circularity: *entropy* is the first component of the unique realization of thermodynamics, if such there be; *temperature* is the second component of the unique realization.

What to do if there is no realization, not even a near-enough imperfect realization? Here different versions of the method disagree. Carnap's version falls silent about what referents, if any, the theoretical terms have; my version and Bedard's version say that the terms fail to refer. What to do if there are two (or more) different realizations, say the pair of X_1 and Y_1 and also the pair of X_2 and Y_2? Again there is disagreement. Carnap's version says that either the terms refer respectively to X_1 and Y_1 or else they refer respectively to X_2 and Y_2, but falls silent about which. My version says again that the terms fail to refer. Bedard's version says that the terms become indeterminate in reference, so that there is no fact of the matter about whether they refer respectively to X_1 and Y_1 or instead to X_2 and Y_2; and as usual

17 Rudolf Carnap, 'Replies and Systematic Expositions' in *The Philosophy of Rudolf Carnap*, (ed.) P. A. Schilpp (La Salle: Open Court, 1963), pp. 963–966; my 'How to Define Theoretical Terms', op. cit.; and Katherine Bedard, 'Partial Denotations of Theoretical Terms', *Noûs* 27 (1993) pp. 499–511.

we resort to van Fraassen's method of supervaluations and say that what is true (or false) on both resolutions of the indeterminacy alike is true (or false) *simpliciter*.[18] Nowadays I am inclined to split the difference between my version and Bedard's: when the two realizations are sufficiently different we get reference failure; when they are sufficiently alike we get indeterminacy of reference; in between it is indeterminate which one we get.

Now suppose our term-introducing theory is a fragment of the folk psychophysics of colour. It has just one pair of a colour name and a colour-experience name: 'red' and 'experience of red'. It says nothing to distinguish this pair of a colour and a corresponding colour experience from all other corresponding pairs. So we have a very severe problem of multiple realization: *every* corresponding pair of a colour and a colour experience is a realization of our theory. But it will not do to fall silent about the reference of 'red' and 'experience of red'; or to say that these terms fail to refer; or to say that these terms are radically indeterminate in reference. Our method for curing circularities, in all its versions, has been defeated by the multiplicity of realizations.

But at least we are now in a position to do some useful redefining. A *corresponding pair* is any realization of the theory just considered. A *colour* is any first component of a corresponding pair. A *colour experience* is any second component.

If we take a bigger fragment of folk psychophysics that mentions n different colours and their corresponding experiences, we make matters worse. Now we have as many realizations as there are ordered n-tuples of corresponding pairs!

Instead of our definitional circle, we have no definitions at all. We are worse off than before.

V. PAROCHIAL SOLUTIONS

The remedy is that the folk psychophysics of colour, as we have envisaged it so far, is too abstract and general. It has a lot to say about

---

18 See Bas van Fraassen, 'Singular Terms, Truth-Value Gaps, and Free Logic', *Journal of Philosophical Logic* 63 (1966) pp. 481–495.

the causal relations between colours and their corresponding colour experiences. But it needs another chapter to tell us what distinguishes each colour from all the others (or each colour experience from all the others). Then the problem of multiplicity will be solved. Once we add the missing chapter, the folk psychophysics of colour will have a unique realization. (Or near enough. Maybe there will still be multiple realizations, but they will differ so little from one another that if we follow Bedard and say that the theoretical terms are indeterminate in reference, their indeterminacy will be far from radical. Some mild indeterminacy about the exact boundaries of the colours is credible enough. In fact, it is perfect determinacy that would be hard to believe.)

When we add the chapter that distinguishes the colours by name, how shall we do it? Most simply, we could give examples. 'Red is the colour of pillar boxes' has been a philosophers' favourite, in England at least. Others might prefer to mention the people's flag. I myself would rather say that red is the colour of the diagonal stripe on an Essendon Football Club jumper.

Likewise for more specific shades. Brunswick green, for instance, was the colour of locomotives of the Great Western Railway. (Of faded ones and freshly painted ones; of those painted before and after certain changes in the recipe for the paint; wherefore it cannot be a perfectly specific shade.)

Sometimes the examples are particular and soon forgotten. I ask you 'What's magenta?' You make a mark with a crayon and say 'This is.' I trust you to have been cooperative and truthful in answering my question. So now I can say that magenta is the colour of the mark you made when I asked you what magenta was.

A week later I can no longer say that: I have forgotten the lesson. No harm done, if I retain the mental abilities which the lesson imparted to me. Any time I like, I can put myself into a state in which I can truly say 'Magenta is the colour that typically causes the colour experience I am right now imagining'. Or I can use myself (and others can use me) as a living instrument: magenta is the colour such that I am disposed to say 'magenta' if you point to it and ask 'What colour is that?'; and if I am disposed to be cooperative and truthful, and if the magenta thing is at a suitable distance, and if the light and my visual capacities are normal.

(In calling myself a 'living instrument', I do not at all mean to suggest that my responses are mere mindless reflexes, rather than the reasoned judgements they might seem to be. No – bizarre cases aside, surely they are the latter. But for present purposes it does not matter which they are, so long as they are reliable indicators that magenta is present.)

The general chapter of the folk psychophysics of colour told us about the relations of resemblance among colour experiences, and about the derivative relations of resemblance among the colours themselves. So once we have distinguished some colours by the methods already mentioned, we can distinguish further colours by interpolation or triangulation: orange is reddish yellow; lemon yellow is ever-so-slightly greenish, and not at all reddish, yellow; and so on.

In these ways, I can add a chapter to the folk psychophysics of colour that will distinguish all the colours to which I have been properly introduced. And so can you, and so can almost anyone. (Even a blind man, except that he cannot use the methods that depend on his own abilities to imagine colour and to serve as a living instrument.) Once the chapter on distinguishing the colours has been added, we no longer have a severe problem of multiple realization. Now it is safe to say that our colour names and our colour-experience names refer to the approximately unique occupants of theoretical roles. Such moderate multiplicity as remains will result at worst in semantic indeterminacy regarding the exact boundary between one colour (or one colour experience) and another. All is well.

Or is it? The trouble is that I (or you, or almost anyone) drew upon ever so much parochial knowledge: information that is not common knowledge throughout the linguistic community. In Ballybunnion where the pillar boxes are green, or in New Haven where they are blue and not in the shape of pillars, people may or may not know about the red pillar boxes in far-off lands. And even if they do, does everyone else in the English-speaking world know that they do? Does everyone know that everyone else knows that everyone else knows that they do? Does . . . Surely not!

Likewise it is common knowledge among certain people – call them *footy people* – that Essendon wears a red diagonal stripe. But this is probably not known at all to certain other people, call them *rugby people*. So it is not common knowledge throughout the linguistic community. It takes all kinds to make the English-speaking world.

Surely very few other people know of the lesson whereby I was introduced to magenta, especially if I myself forgot it in a week. Nor do people who have never heard of me know anything about my ability to imagine magenta or to serve as an instrument for indicating its presence. Here too, the chapter on distinguishing the colours was built not upon common knowledge but upon parochial knowledge.

Maybe it is common knowledge that orange is reddish yellow. But interpolations and triangulations are useless by themselves. They only serve to distinguish more colours after we have distinguished some already. How to get started?

Our parochial solution is not good enough because language is a conventional, rational system of semantic coordination.[19] I say something I take to be true under semantic interpretation I_1; you trust me to be truthful under I_1 and also to be well-informed; and in this way you come to share my information – something that both of us wanted to happen. Coordination of truthfulness under I_2 with trust under I_2 would have worked just as well, even if I_1 and I_2 assigned opposite truth conditions to the same sentences. But miscoordination – of truthfulness under I_1 with trust under I_2 or vice versa – would have deprived us of the benefits of communication.

Any conventional system of coordination, semantic or otherwise, is rationalised by a potentially endless system of mutual expectations. Why do you drive on the left? Because you expect me to. Why do you expect me to? Because you expect me to expect you to. Why . . . In short: we both drive on the left because it is common knowledge between us that we both will. (Likewise *mutatis mutandis* if there are more drivers sharing the roads than two.) Our coordination is rationally sustained. It is not hard-wired and it is not mere luck. Even if we drive on the left by habit, as surely we do, the habit is sustained by

19 See my *Convention*.

reason. If our common knowledge were eroded by doubt, or undermined by counter-evidence, we would swiftly change our ways.

So here is the current state of the problem: if we distinguish and name the colours by recourse to parochial information, how can we have the semantic common knowledge that is required if our talk about colour is to be part of a conventional, rational system of coordination?

VI. A SOLUTION THAT RELIES TOO MUCH ON LUCK

A few examples of a few colours are common knowledge throughout the linguistic community. Blood is red, well-watered leaves are green, the sky is blue, and flames are yellow. (Or rather, since we agreed to confine ourselves to surface colours, pictures of the sky are blue and pictures of flames are yellow. But let us waive the point.) These few examples will do to begin the job of distinguishing the colours, and maybe we can do the rest by interpolation and triangulation. Then the chapter of folk psychophysics that distinguishes the colours will not rely on parochial knowledge. It will be common knowledge throughout the linguistic community. So when we name the colours and colour experiences as occupants of theoretical roles, that naming will be a matter of semantic common knowledge. Our problem will be solved.

This solution is all very well for today, but consider the future. Leaves, well-watered or otherwise, will be long gone and forgotten. We will resort to brute force methods, powered by fusion, to regain oxygen from carbon dioxide. Flames will be forbidden. The polluted sky will occasionally be blue, when the smog clears, but just as often it will be red with nitric oxide, yellow with sulphur dust, or green with noxious scum never yet seen in our own time. People will have to spend their lives encased in protective armour, and so their blood never will be seen except by police and medical robots that have neither language nor colour vision. All records of better times will long since have been destroyed by the Hedonic Legion because of their tendency to sadden those who read them. Yet there will still be colour – lots of it. Graffiti will cover everything.

Could there still be semantic common knowledge of colour language? I think so. That means that our presently proposed solution, though it may well succeed under fortunate conditions, cannot be the only possible solution.

VII. A SOLUTION THAT IS UNAVAILABLE TO MATERIALISTS

Some philosophers think that each sort of colour experience has a simple, ineffable, unique essence that is instantly revealed to anyone who has that experience. When I was shown the crayon mark and told that it was magenta (and I believed what I was told, and it was true) straightway I knew all there is to know about experience of magenta. I knew that it was the experience with the simple, ineffable, unique essence E. And that is all there is to it.[20] (Or perhaps it is the colour magenta itself that has the simple, ineffable, unique essence that is instantly revealed to each beholder, or anyway to each beholder with normal visual capacities in normal light.)

If this doctrine of revelation were true, presumably it would be obviously true. Even those philosophers who denied it would know it in their hearts, once they had seen a few colours and experienced the workings of revelation for themselves. Thanks to its obviousness, the general doctrine of revelation could readily become common knowledge throughout the linguistic community. Then if it were also common knowledge that everyone in the community becomes acquainted with magenta early in life (and if the community were properly dismissive of sceptical doubts about inverted spectra, etc.) it would be common knowledge throughout the community that magenta is the colour that typically causes experience with essence E. (Or perhaps, according to the other version of the story, that magenta is the colour that itself has the simple, ineffable, unique essence E.) The same would go, of course, for all the other colours that we become acquainted with

20 See Galen Strawson, '"Red" and Red', *Synthese* 78 (1989) pp. 193–232; Mark Johnston, 'How to Speak of the Colors', op. cit., pp. 223–224 and elsewhere; David Lewis, 'Should a Materialist Believe in Qualia?', *Australasian Journal of Philosophy* 73 (1995) pp. 140–144 (reprinted in this volume as Chapter 19).

and have names for. So here we would have the requisite common knowledge of the semantics of the language of colour. It would be ineffable common knowledge, but what is the harm in that? The doctrine of revelation would solve our problem.

The only remaining difficulty is that the doctrine is false. At any rate, it is false for colour experiences (and colours themselves).[21] At any rate, it is false by materialist lights – and we have pledged ourselves non-negotiably to materialism. The essence of a colour experience is not at all simple, not at all ineffable, not at all easily known. Probably it is a matter of neural firing patterns; but if not that, something equally esoteric. Likewise for the essences of the colours themselves.

The doctrine of revelation is tailor-made to solve our problem. But we materialists must dismiss this 'solution' as a useless piece of wishful thinking.[22]

---

21 Maybe revelation is true in some other cases – as it might be for the part–whole relation.

22 You should have noticed that my continuing difficulties result from a continuing effort to associate descriptive senses with the names of the colours and the colour experiences. Is that effort misguided? Did not Kripke and his allies refute the description theory of reference, at least for names of people and places? Then why should we expect descriptivism to work any better for names of colours and colour experiences? For the supposed refutation of descriptivism, see *inter alia* Saul Kripke, 'Naming and Necessity' and Keith Donnellan, 'Proper Names and Identifying Descriptions', both in *Semantics of Natural Language* (eds.) Donald Davidson and Gilbert Harman (Dordrecht: Reidel, 1972); and Michael Devitt, *Designation* (New York: Columbia University Press, 1981) pp. 3–25.

I disagree. What was well and truly refuted was a version of descriptivism in which the descriptive senses were supposed to be a matter of famous deeds and other distinctive peculiarities. A better version survives the attack: *causal descriptivism*. The descriptive sense associated with a name might for instance be 'the place I have heard of under the name "Taromeo"' or maybe 'the causal source of this token: Taromeo', and for an account of the relation being invoked here, just consult the writings of the causal theorists of reference. A brief mention of causal descriptivism, with credit to Robert Nozick, is to be found in 'Naming and Necessity' itself (p. 349, fn. 38); see also my 'Putnam's Paradox', *Australasian Journal of Philosophy* 62 (1984) pp. 226–227 (reprinted in this volume as Chapter 2); and Fred Kroon, 'Causal Descriptivism', *Australasian Journal of Philosophy* 65 (1987) pp. 1–17.

Causal descriptivism explains, as the causal theory itself does not, (1) how the way reference is fixed by means of causal chains is part of our semantic common

So much the worse for materialism? Not if we have an alternative solution. And we do.

VIII. HOW MUCH COMMON KNOWLEDGE DO WE REALLY NEED?

Consider again the case of the footy people and the rugby people: two subcommunities of the English-speaking linguistic community. For simplicity, I suppose that every English-speaker is either a footy person or a rugby person. Or both? I do not need to say whether or not the two subcommunities overlap. But they do not overlap much. Plenty of footy people know nothing of rugby, and vice versa.

The two subcommunities mingle. Often, you cannot tell whether you are talking to a footy person or a rugby person, so long as you are not talking about sport.

It is common knowledge among the footy people that the diagonal stripe on the Essendon jumper is red, that the widest horizontal stripe on the Footscray jumper is red, that Swans are mostly red, . . . None of these things are known to rugby people, except for those of them, if any, who are footy people as well.

Likewise, some examples of red things are common knowledge among the rugby people. But a footy person like me – a footy person who is not also a rugby person – has no idea what these examples are.

The footy people have their version of the added chapter of folk psychophysics that distinguishes the colours. And when they define theoretical terms as names for the occupants of theoretical roles, they arrive at their version of a definition of 'red'. This definition is part of the semantic common knowledge of the footy people, but it is not common knowledge among the English-speaking community as a whole.

Likewise the rugby people have their version of the chapter and the definition. But the two definitions are parochial. In fact, no definition

knowledge, and (2) how it depends on our contingent semantic conventions. As it does: distinctive-peculiarity descriptivism *could* have been true instead, inconvenient though that would have been, but our actual conventions of language are such as to render it false.

of 'red' is part of the semantic common knowledge of the entire community.

(Not even 'the colour of blood'? After all, the present example is *not* set in the nightmare future previously imagined. Still, these rugby people are peculiar! Look at their funny ideas about the proper shape for goalposts. Might they not also have funny ideas about blood? And even if you know they do not, do you know that everyone knows? Do you know that everyone knows that everyone knows? Do you know . . .)

When footy people and rugby people mingle, they talk. Sometimes they talk about the colours of things. It never seems to happen that there is a misunderstanding. Why not? You might expect that sometimes a footy person, wrongly thinking that his conversational partner was a footy person too, would call something red because it is red in the footy sense. Then the rugby person he was talking to, wrongly thinking that the speaker was another rugby person, would believe that the thing was red in the rugby sense – and he would get a surprise when it turned out not to be.

If such conversational mishaps occurred, we would notice them. (Or at least we would hear from others who noticed them.) And if conversationalists took precautions to prevent mishaps, we would notice that. And we would hope that those who belong to both subcommunities – if there are any of those – would warn the rest of us about the risk of misunderstandings. And yet we never notice mishaps or precautions or warnings. Why? The best explanation is that there is in fact no risk of misunderstanding, because exactly the same things that are red in the footy sense are red also in the rugby sense.

Exactly the same things; or near enough. Disagreement on a few things that both subcommunities alike would treat as borderline cases would be harmless and hard to notice.

In this way, even though neither definition was common knowledge throughout the entire linguistic community, there might still be *existential* common knowledge: common knowledge (1) that some definition of 'red' was common knowledge among the footy people, and (2) that some definition of 'red' was common knowledge among the rugby people, and (3) that these two definitions agreed (or near enough) about which things were red.

If there were only that much common knowledge throughout the entire community, that would suffice. Existential common knowledge, even without fully specific semantic common knowledge, would sustain rational semantic coordination, even between footy people and rugby people conversing about what is red.

If the footy and rugby definitions of 'red' agree in extension, that will avoid the simplest sort of mishap in communication. But if the two definitions differ in intension, is there not still some risk of a more subtle sort of mishap? Suppose two people are talking; and unbeknownst to them, one is a footy person and one is a rugby person. So long as they talk about which things *are* red, they have no problem. But what happens if they talk instead about which things *would* be red under various counterfactual circumstances? Suppose the footy definition of red is simply: 'the colour of the Essendon diagonal stripe'. Now if the Essendon Football Club were taken over by the Environmentalist Party, who are no respecters of tradition and never pass up a chance for self-advertisement, what would then be red: blood or leaves? If leaves would then be red in the footy sense yet blood would remain red in the rugby sense, our conversationalists would be in trouble if they were to try to discuss this hypothetical case. Their mismatched definitions would cause a failure of communication after all.

Yet this sort of mishap also is never observed. Why not? Because the footy definition of 'red' is not simply 'the colour of the Essendon stripe'. Rather it is: 'the colour of the Essendon stripe actually, nowadays, and hereabouts'. The latter definition is 'rigidified'. Unlike the simple one, it can be relied upon not to shift its reference when we talk about unactualized hypothetical cases, or about actualities at remote times and places.[23] The rugby definition, whatever it may be, is likewise rigidified. And it is common knowledge throughout the entire linguistic community that both definitions are rigidified. In this

23 See Hans Kamp, 'Formal Properties of "Now"', *Theoria* 40 (1971) pp. 76–109; my 'Anselm and Actuality', *Noûs* 4 (1970) pp. 175–188; Saul Kripke, 'Naming and Necessity', pp. 273–278 and elsewhere; David Kaplan, 'Dthat' and Robert Stalnaker 'Assertion', both in *Syntax and Semantics 9: Pragmatics* (ed.) P. Cole (New York: Academic Press, 1978).

way mishaps of communication are averted even when conversation ranges beyond the actual or beyond the here and now.

(I do not say that the simple phrase 'the colour of the Essendon stripe' is definitely *un*rigidified. Rather, I suppose it to be ambiguous with respect to rigidification. Hence the custom of rigidification has two separate advantages. One is that, as we have already seen, it can prevent failures of communication between conversational partners who use different definitions. The other is that it prevents ambiguity in the speech of a single person. The cost of a custom of rigidification is that it makes unrigidified things harder to say. To gain the advantage, and pay the cost, it is not of course required that we always signal rigidification with some special form of words.)

Do the footy people's rigidified 'red' and the rugby people's rigidified 'red' have the same intension or do they not? A straight answer would be unwise. The two have something beyond their extension in common, and something not in common. But whether 'intension' is the word for what they have in common or the word for what they have not in common is an unsettled matter.

It is a simplification to imagine that the footy people define 'red' as 'the colour of the Essendon stripe' (duly rigidified). Many examples of red are common knowledge among them. Any selected one of these, or any selection of several of these, would do for a definition. It would serve no good purpose for them to make an official choice. If they have not done so, that is only to be expected.

Or perhaps there is a default choice: the biggest class of examples that does not overstep the bound of their common knowledge. If all the examples that are common knowledge among them are mentioned in their version of the chapter of folk psychophysics that distinguishes the colours, and if red is defined to be the occupant of the resulting folk-theoretical role, that is just what will happen.

But there might be a few rotten apples in the barrel: items of common knowledge that are not knowledge at all but rather error. I said that one example of red was the widest horizontal stripe on the Footscray jumper. But that begged a question about what is a stripe and what is a stripe-shaped part of the background. Arguably, the widest stripe of all is not the red stripe, but rather the very wide blue stripe right at the bottom.

As already noted, we should be prepared to say that red is a *near-enough* occupant of a role. But which one? Once we retreat from demanding perfection, there might in principle be competing near-enough occupants. So even given a default choice, there is still some risk of semantic indecision in naming the colours. Doubtless the risk is slight, doubtless the indecision risked is also slight. Yet we can still ask what to do about it. Answer: nothing. Not unless there turns out to be a real problem. The advantage of being prepared is not worth the bother of solving countless problems in advance when most of them will never arise.

The footy people and the rugby people were two linguistic subcommunities, both large. Of course the subcommunities could be smaller and more numerous, so long as the necessary existential common knowledge was available. In the extreme case, I do not see why we could not have very many subcommunities of one person each, each one with his own private collection of coloured box-beetles. At that limit, the specific common knowledge within the subcommunity would vanish. Existential common knowledge would have to do the whole job of sustaining a rational system of linguistic coordination. I see no reason why this extreme case would be impossible in principle. But certainly it would be a far cry from the real world.

21

Percepts and color mosaics in visual experience

Professors Firth's "Sense-Data and the Percept Theory"[1] examines a disagreement over the nature of visual experience. Those in the traditions of British empiricism[2] and introspectionist psychology[3] hold that the content of visual experience is a sensuously given mosaic of color spots, together with a mass of interpretive judgments injected by the subject. Firth calls this the Sense-Datum Theory, but I shall call it the *Color-Mosaic Theory* (since the opposing theory also accepts something we might call a sense datum). Those in the newer traditions of linguistic phenomenology,[4] Husserlian phenomenology,[5] and Gestalt psychology[6] agree that visual experience consists rather of sensuously given *percepts* – presentations of ostensible constituents of the external world. Firth calls this the *Percept Theory*, as shall I. He himself is one of a growing number of epistemologists who accept it.

As we shall see in the next section, Firth shows how the difference

First published in *The Philosophical Review* 75 (1966), 357–368. Copyright 1966 Cornell University. Reprinted with kind permission from the publisher of *The Philosophical Review*.

1 *Mind*, 58 (1949), 434–465; 59 (1950), 35–56.

2 See Berkeley, *An Essay towards a New Theory of Vision*.

3 See Titchener, *A Textbook of Psychology* (New York, 1928), pp. 1–92.

4 See Austin, *Sense and Sensibilia* (Oxford, 1962).

5 See Husserl, *Ideas: General Introduction to Pure Phenomenology*, trans. by W. R. Boyce Gibson (London, 1931), pp. 101–111.

6 See Koehler, *Gestalt Psychology* (New York, 1947), pp. 67–99.

between the two theories may be stated as a disagreement over a certain thesis: the *Exposure Hypothesis*. Color-mosaic theorists implicitly accept the Exposure Hypothesis; percept theorists such as Firth reject it.

I claim that the Exposure Hypothesis, properly understood, does not conflict with Firth's Percept Theory. I shall propose an interpretation of the Exposure Hypothesis and the central thesis of the Color-Mosaic Theory within the terms of the Percept Theory itself. If I am right, disagreement over the Exposure Hypothesis is not disagreement over the nature of visual experience, but only over the value of a certain way of speaking.

THE EXPOSURE HYPOTHESIS

The Percept Theory introduces percepts as presentations of objects ostensibly in the external world before the subject. These objects need not be concrete. They may be qualities or processes: in a brief glance I may have a percept of roundness, or out of the corner of my eye I may have a percept of a sudden movement, but in neither case do I necessarily have a percept of any definite round or moving thing. Perhaps we do best to understand percepts as presentations of ostensible *facts*:[7] I have a percept of a tree when I am ostensibly seeing that there is a tree before me, of roundness when I am ostensibly seeing that there is something round before me, of a movement when I am ostensibly seeing that there is something moving before me.

Whether concreta, abstracta, or facts, the objects of percepts are intentional *Gegenstaende*, presented qua falling under specific descriptions. They are no more or less determinate than the descriptions under which they are presented. If I see the speckled hen and do not count the speckles, my percept is of an ostensible hen which is many-speckled, but is not n-speckled for any number n. If I see an "E" and do not see it as containing an "F" (even if I know it does) the ostensible "E" which is the object of my percept cannot be said to contain an

7 See D. M. Armstrong, "A Theory of Perception," *Scientific Psychology: Principles and Approaches*, ed. by B. B. Wolman (New York, 1965), pp. 489–505.

"F." If I see a reversing cube as slanting up, I have a percept of an ostensible up-slanting cube. If later I count the speckles, or see the "F," or reverse the aspect of the cube, I have changed a percept of one ostensible object into a new percept of a new (more or otherwise determinate) ostensible object. When I notice something new – say, a snake in the grass – I get a new percept. When I so much as shift my visual attention – say, from the foreground to the background of the scene around me – I lose old percepts and gain new ones. The Percept Theory aims to cover the whole content of visual experience, leaving no residue to be covered under catchall headings of noticing, attending to, and seeing as.

It aims likewise to cover every variety of ordinary or extraordinary visual experience. Among the extraordinary varieties it includes that very color-mosaic experience which color-mosaic theorists regard as all-pervasive.

Percept and color-mosaic theorists would agree that visual experience may be made to contain nothing but a mosaic of color spots – a visual experience which could be reported exhaustively by a set of "I am ostensibly seeing that something of color c is located in direction d" clauses for all discriminable directions. To produce this pure color-mosaic experience we must concentrate, to the exclusion of all else, on the visual qualities of the smallest discriminable regions considered in isolation from their surroundings. Firth calls this the operation of *perceptual reduction*. It is a difficult task practiced by artists and by introspectionist psychologists.

A color-mosaic theorist must admit that he needs to perform perceptual reduction before he can (easily and with confidence) observe the sensuously given color mosaic which he claims is present in all visual experience. The color mosaic observed is notoriously often not what one might have expected beforehand. He may explain that perceptual reduction is needed because we do not ordinarily notice the color mosaic, since it is of no practical importance, but attend instead to our own interpretive judgments based on it. Perceptual reduction is a redirection of attention in which we dispel the judgments that occupy our attention and expose to observation what remains: their hitherto unnoticed *sensory core*.

The Exposure Hypothesis is the essential thesis in this account of perceptual reduction: the thesis that the color-mosaic experience someone has after he performs perceptual reduction is somehow *the same as* something that was already present in his visual experience before reduction.

In Firth's own words:

According to the Exposure Hypothesis, the operation of perceptual reduction does not produce a state of consciousness which is simply *other than* the original state of perception on which it is performed. It produces, on the contrary, a state of direct awareness which was contained in the original perception.[8]

Since the Exposure Hypothesis invokes the notion of unnoticed aspects of experience it is prima facie contrary to the Percept Theory. Why should a percept theorist regard perceptual reduction as "anything more than one method among many of substituting one state of consciousness for another"[9] with any special claim to yield "the real but previously unobservable content of the original state?"[10] Why not say that when someone adopts the special standpoint of perceptual reduction he just creates a percept of a color mosaic in place of whatever percepts he had before?

The Color-Mosaic Theory requires the Exposure Hypothesis, since all parties agree that the color mosaic can be observed only after perceptual reduction. Conversely, if we assume that perceptual reduction is always in principle possible, the Exposure Hypothesis seems to imply the Color-Mosaic Theory. This is to say that the issue between the theories is acceptance or rejection of the Exposure Hypothesis; and if Firth is right, the Hypothesis is no more than a misdescription of perceptual reduction.

I find this diagnosis unconvincing. Why was the Color-Mosaic Theory once generally accepted, and why is it still plausible, unless there is more behind it than Firth recognizes?

---

8 *Op. cit.*, Pt. I, p. 462.
9 Firth, *op. cit.*, Pt. I, p. 463.
10 *Ibid.*

Now I must digress to introduce some concepts within the terms of the Percept Theory, to be used in interpreting the Exposure Hypothesis and the Color-Mosaic Theory.

We first distinguish between changes of percept and percepts of change. There is a change of percept whenever one gains or loses a percept – that is, whenever there is any change in the content of one's visual experience as reported in "I am ostensibly seeing that . . ." clauses. Change of percept is not itself part of the content of visual experience. Indeed, it may go unnoticed and not be part of the content of experience at all. Changes of percept take place all the time; usually there are some due to changes in the external world, and always there are some due to one's own noticings, attention shifts, or (less often) aspect shifts.

A percept of change, on the other hand, *is* part of the content of visual experience. It is the visual presentation of some sort of ostensible change – a movement or a change in light or color – in the external world. It is what occurs when one is ostensibly seeing that something before him is somehow changing. The manner and the subject of change may be more or less determinate: one may ostensibly see that the trees are swaying, or one may ostensibly see just that something or other is happening to something or other.

A percept of change is normally accompanied by a corresponding change of percept, since any large change in the pattern of light impinging on the eye produces both. There is a percept of change because the process of change itself is perceived. There is a change of percept because the change leaves things changed. When it does *not* leave things changed, as when a lamp flickers too fast to follow, there is a percept of change without a change of percept. Or if the ostensible change is illusory, as when one is dizzy and the world turns, or as in the waterfall illusion,[11] there is a percept of change without a change of percept. Such cases show that percepts of change cannot always be analyzed as noticings of changes of percept.

11 Described by William James in *The Principles of Psychology*, II (New York, 1890), pp. 245–246.

Although a percept of change is normally accompanied by a corresponding change of percept, many changes of percept are not accompanied by corresponding percepts of change: namely, at least all those changes of percept which are due to one's own noticings, attention shifts, or aspect shifts. These unaccompanied changes of percept may go unnoticed; and even if one of them is noticed, the noticing of it is not a percept of change since it is not a *visual* presentation of ostensible *external* change.

Indeed, no change of percept is accompanied by a corresponding percept of change if it is slow enough. If I watch the minute hand of a clock, I have several changes of percept every minute, but no percepts of change. But any change of percept could presumably occur suddenly; and among sudden changes of percept a clear distinction appears between those which are accompanied by corresponding percepts of change and those which are not.

MODIFICATION EQUIVALENCE

Let us call a change of percept a *modification* of visual experience just in case it is sudden but is not accompanied by a corresponding percept of change. Let us say that one (actual or possible) particular[12] visual experience (E_1) is *directly modifiable* into another one (E_2) just in case they are experiences belonging to the same person and he can in principle (he can or he could but for his inadequate powers of concentration) go from E_1 to E_2 by one modification. Let us likewise say that E_1 is *modifiable* into E_2 just in case they are experiences belonging to the same person and he can in principle go from E_1 to E_2 by finitely many modifications. (Thus direct modifiability is a – presumably proper – subrelation of modifiability.) Let us further say that any two (actual or possible) particular visual experiences $(E_1$ and $E_2)$ are *modification-equivalent* just in case there is some finite sequence (S) of (actual or possible) particular visual experiences, such that E_1 and E_2 are the first and last terms of S, and such that if E_j and E_k are adjacent

12 I.e., one which happens – or could happen or could have happened – to a definite person at a definite time. We will consider only the experiences of any one person, not the relations between experiences of different people.

terms of S then either E_j is directly modifiable into E_k or E_k is directly modifiable into E_j. Expressing the definition of modification equivalence by a recursion: (1) E_1 is modification-equivalent to E_1; (2) if E_1 is modification-equivalent to E_m, and if either E_m is directly modifiable into E_n or E_n is directly modifiable into E_m, then E_1 is modification-equivalent to E_n; and (3) visual experiences are modification-equivalent only if they are so by virtue of (1) and (2).

Whatever the logical properties of the underlying relation of direct modifiability may be, modification equivalence is an equivalence relation – reflexive, symmetric, and transitive. It divides a person's visual experiences (unless they are all modification-equivalent) into several disjoint *modification-equivalence classes*, such that a visual experience is modification-equivalent to all and only members of its own class.

Modifiability is a subrelation of modification equivalence. It is a proper subrelation; for modifiability implies precedence in time and so must be asymmetric, whereas modification equivalence is symmetric. If E_1 is modifiable into E_2, E_1 precedes E_2, so E_2 is not modifiable into E_1; but E_2 is modification-equivalent to E_1. What is more, if some modifications – for example, some noticings – are in principle irreversible, there may be pairs of visual experiences which are modification-equivalent although neither is modifiable into the other. Let E_0 be my visual experience just before I notice a snake in the grass; let E_1 be my visual experience just after I notice the snake; let E_2 be the visual experience I would have had slightly later, had I not noticed the snake. E_1 and E_2 are modification-equivalent because E_0 is modifiable into both. E_2 is not modifiable into E_1 because E_1 precedes E_2. And E_1 is not modifiable into E_2 because my noticing of the snake is – so far as I know – irreversible; I cannot *disnotice* the snake.

A performance of perceptual reduction is, in general, a finite sequence of modifications[13] going from some original visual experience to a pure color-mosaic experience. The original experience is therefore

13 If perceptual reduction could be performed gradually, it would not be a sequence of modifications, since modifications are by definition sudden. But so far as we know, the results of gradual perceptual reduction could always be duplicated by jerky perceptual reduction. So we can confine ourselves, with no loss of generality, to the case of jerky perceptual reduction.

modifiable into, and a fortiori modification-equivalent to, the color-mosaic experience which is its reduction product.

In trying to say how the operation of perceptual reduction may be said to leave visual experience the same, I do not claim that it is radically unlike other "methods of substituting one state of consciousness for another." I claim rather that it belongs to a large family of operations, *all* of which may be said to leave visual experience the same: namely, operations which change visual experience only by producing modifications.

THE DISTRIBUTION PREMISE

The observation that perceptual reduction changes visual experience only by modifications will permit me to interpret the Exposure Hypothesis. But to interpret the Color-Mosaic Theory I shall also need the following *Distribution Premise*: pure color-mosaic experiences are distributed among modification-equivalence classes in such a way that each class includes instances of one and only one pure *color-mosaic percept* (that being defined as a percept of a color mosaic and of nothing else). This is to say that every visual experience is modification-equivalent to some pure color-mosaic experience, and that all those pure color-mosaic experiences which are modification-equivalent to any one visual experience are pure experiences of the same color mosaic – that is, instances of the same pure color-mosaic percept. Since modification equivalence is reflexive, it follows that pure color-mosaic experiences are modification-equivalent only if they are instances of the same pure color-mosaic percept.

The Distribution Premise implies that there is precisely one color mosaic which can be observed after perceptual reduction of any given visual experience, even if the reduction can be performed via several alternative routes. Perceptual reduction is the operational counterpart to the well-defined function which assigns to each visual experience E that unique color mosaic C, such that E is modification-equivalent to pure experiences of C. It is for this reason that color-mosaic experience and the operation of perceptual reduction have a special importance – not because perceptual reduction produces change in some *sui generis* way.

366

The Distribution Premise is, clearly, an empirical thesis. We find it somewhat plausible because it fits our rough understanding of the way visual experience is caused. We suppose that a sudden change of percept is accompanied by a corresponding percept of change – is not a modification – just in case it is produced directly by a change in the pattern of impinging light. If so, the distinction between those sudden changes of percept which are modifications and those which are not is a correlate in phenomenal terms of the distinction between those which are internally produced and those which are externally produced. It follows that a modification-equivalence class should comprise just those visual experiences which can occur under some one pattern of light. We also suppose that pure color-mosaic percepts correspond precisely to the patterns of light under which they can occur. The two suppositions jointly imply that every modification-equivalence class should contain instances of precisely one pure color-mosaic percept: that one corresponding to the pattern of light under which members of the class can occur.

But our real reasons for accepting the Distribution Premise do not matter. The Premise was stated in purely phenomenal terms. In principle we could forget our causal preconceptions and test the Premise just by examining enough experience (though in reality we would never take the time to do so). So if the Distribution Premise is true, it is available even if (as phenomenologists or epistemologists) we insist on confining ourselves to pure description of visual experience without mention of its causal conditions.

CLASSIFICATION OF VISUAL EXPERIENCE

Let us call two (actual or possible) particular visual experiences *percept-equivalent* just in case they are instances of precisely the same percepts—that is, just in case they could be reported exhaustively by precisely the same "I am ostensibly seeing that . . ." clauses. Percept equivalence is an equivalence relation and therefore divides a person's visual experiences into several disjoint *percept-equivalence classes*, such that a visual experience is percept-equivalent to all and only members of its own class.

The Percept Theory may suggest that we ought to interpret the relation of *identity in kind* between visual experiences as percept equivalence, thereby classifying visual experiences according to the percepts they contain. But we are free to adopt whatever principle of classification we find convenient for our purposes at hand. The choice of a principle of classification is nothing more than a choice between alternative ways of speaking. Any salient equivalence relation which can be defined within the terms of the Percept Theory is a possible principle of classification and might, if convenient, be adopted. Percept equivalence and modification equivalence are two such equivalence relations. I suggest that for some purposes we have reasons to adopt the latter – to interpret identity in kind as modification equivalence and thus to classify visual experiences according to their modification-equivalence classes. There is nothing incorrect in classifying by percept equivalence; but classifying by modification equivalence is *as* correct, and sometimes more convenient.

Classification by percept equivalence does capture all discriminable differences in content. This sensitivity is both a virtue and a fault. We sometimes want judicious omission of detail in order to emphasize what we think important – diagrams instead of photographs. Just as we may not want to distinguish all the discriminable colors, so we may not want to distinguish all visual experiences which are not percept-equivalent. If identity in kind is to be a useful concept it must often be applicable. We cannot afford to set too high a standard.

In particular, we may often wish to ignore the perpetual flux of modifications: the noticings, attention shifts, and aspect shifts. We may regard the important features of visual experience as those which vary between modification-equivalence classes but not within them. Consider especially the context of epistemology: we might want to ignore differences within a modification-equivalence class because – unofficially speaking[14] – we suppose they are not due to differences in the impinging light and hence carry no information about the external world.

14 Officially, we cannot give this reason for ignoring such differences, since we are trying to describe visual experience prior to explaining it by causal conditions. But we can just ignore them for *no* legitimate reason and hope to be justified afterward by success in reaching a simple and adequate epistemology.

There seems to be no way of classifying by partial percept equivalence which would ignore all and only differences within modification-equivalence classes. So far as we know, any percept or any number of percepts in a visual experience may be changed by modifications. What is invariant under all modifications must be something very complicated, unless we are prepared to say it is just modification-equivalence class affiliation itself.

But modification equivalence does not just ignore some differences which percept equivalence captures. It also captures other differences which percept equivalence ignores. Neither is a subrelation of the other. Two percept-equivalent visual experiences may have quite different potentialities for modification. When I glance at the grass on two occasions I may have the very same percept of tall, brown, ragged grass; but on one occasion I can notice a snake in the grass if I look harder, whereas on the other occasion I cannot, since there is no snake to be seen. The two visual experiences are percept-equivalent but they are not modification-equivalent. Percept equivalence is the strongest possible equivalence relation between visual experiences on the basis of actual content alone. But modification equivalence sacrifices some sensitivity to actual content in return for some sensitivity to potential content. There is no reason to exclude potentialities from our account of the nature of visual experience, so long as they are potentialities within the realm of experience itself, described without mention of the external causes and effects of experience.

A RATIONALE FOR THE COLOR-MOSAIC THEORY

If we do choose to take identity in kind as modification equivalence, we have adopted a way of speaking on which we must say that perceptual reduction leaves visual experience the same. For perceptual reduction is just a sequence of modifications, of changes of the sort we have chosen to ignore. We shall therefore say that the original visual experience and the pure color-mosaic experience which is its reduction product, being modification-equivalent, are identical in kind. In fact, "the operation of perceptual reduction does not produce a state of consciousness which is simply *other than* the original state of perception on which it was performed. It produces, on the contrary, a state of direct awareness which was contained in" – we might better say, "which is the same as a state contained in" – "the original perception." This is the Exposure Hypothesis.

Not only is a visual experience identical in kind to its product under a particular performance of perceptual reduction; granted the Distribution Premise, any visual experience is identical in kind to instances of precisely one pure color-mosaic percept. In this sense every visual experience can be described as experience of some definite color mosaic, so color-mosaic experience is all-pervasive. This is the Color-Mosaic Theory.

It would indeed be just as true to say that *non*-color-mosaic experience is all-pervasive. For a visual experience is in general modification-equivalent both to color-mosaic experiences and to non–color-mosaic experiences. (Thus we must take some properties of visual experience as compatible when we classify by modification equivalence which are not compatible when we classify by percept equivalence: namely, properties which vary between modification-equivalent visual experiences. Being color-mosaic experience and being non-color-mosaic experience are two such properties.) The point of describing all visual experience as color-mosaic experience is not that it can be described as *nothing but* color-mosaic experience; rather, that it can be described *inter alia* as definite color-mosaic experience, and so described it is especially amenable to systematic comparison and causal explanation.

If we have chosen to classify by modification equivalence only, and it turns out that now and then we must speak of the differences in percept between modification-equivalent visual experiences, we can get by in a clumsy way without resorting to classification by percept equivalence (which would be better if we had *much* need to speak of those differences). We can think of the differences in percept between any visual experience and some modification-equivalent reference experience (or between any visual experience and the members of some class of mutually percept-equivalent experiences, all of which are modification-equivalent to it) as being itself an element superimposed on the sensuously given in visual experience. These difference elements are the interpretive judgments which, according to the Color-

Mosaic Theory, surround the sensory core. Since these difference elements are differences from the reference experience(s), a reference experience itself can contain none. Under the Distribution Premise, the pure color-mosaic experiences which are modification-equivalent to a given visual experience make an especially convenient reference class; for there are always some such, and they are always mutually percept-equivalent. Thus it is understandable that color-mosaic experience should seem to be visual experience purified of its nongiven elements. I think, however, that the Exposure Hypothesis and the Color-Mosaic Theory are wrong on this point: the difference elements have an equal claim to be regarded as part of the given, and color-mosaic experience has no other special status than that which it has by virtue of the Distribution Premise and by virtue of the supposed precise correspondence between color mosaics and patterns of impinging light. I have tried to make sense of two doctrines: that perceptual reduction leaves visual experience the same, and that color-mosaic experience is all-pervasive. I take it that these two doctrines, not the mistaken notion of nonsensuous interpretive judgments, are the essential content of the Exposure Hypothesis and the Color-Mosaic Theory.

I have been defending the Exposure Hypothesis and the Color-Mosaic Theory by attempting to show how they might be restated in the percept theorist's own terms. It might seem that Firth himself does no less:

We can say that the statement, "These two perceptions are different interpretations of the same sensory core," should be understood to mean: "If these two perceptions were perceptually reduced exactly similar states of direct awareness would be produced in the two cases." And to understand this second statement, of course, we do not need any concepts which are incompatible with the Percept Theory. . . . By means of this definition in use, then, philosophers and psychologists who accept the Percept Theory can translate into an empirical language statements about the given which would otherwise be verifiable only if the Exposure Hypothesis were valid. In preferring this definition, moreover, they do not necessarily belittle the importance for psychology of either the operation of perceptual reduction or the concept of the sensory core which is defined in terms of it. To deny the existence of the sensory core as traditionally conceived, therefore, is not necessarily to discredit the empirical science erected by psychologists who have assumed its existence, nor even to disparage their method.[15]

But to interpret the Color-Mosaic Theory (excluding the notion of nonsensuous interpretive judgments) and to show that the color-mosaic theorist is justified in speaking as he does, it is not enough to find substitutions which turn part of what the color-mosaic theorist says into something we, as percept theorists, can accept. We could turn part of phlogiston chemistry into something we can accept by substituting "combines with oxygen" for "releases phlogiston," but that is to *correct* phlogiston chemistry, not to translate or interpret it, and not to justify it as a way of speaking. The "translation" Firth prescribes is so called only by a euphemism, for it is not complete enough to exhibit any rationale for the way the color-mosaic theorist speaks – to show any reason except erroneous understanding for speaking that way. I believe my more elaborate correlation between the color-mosaic theorist's way of speaking and the percept theorist's way has shown legitimate reasons for even a percept theorist to speak in the color-mosaic theorist's way on occasion.

Finally, how can this line of defense help the traditional color-mosaic theorist who had no theory of modification equivalence? Did he reach a defensible conclusion only by accident, for entirely indefensible reasons? I think we can give him more credit than that. A typical color-mosaic theorist, if challenged, might well have agreed that we do in a sense change visual experience in order to observe a color mosaic, and then might have gone on to say that this change is one of many which we can safely ignore because they are changes which are not ostensibly due to changes in the external world, and because they are changes which cannot take us from one color mosaic to another. If he could say this much – even if he misdescribed the nature of those changes – then he would have had the essential point.

15 *Op. cit.*, Pt. II, pp. 39–40.

22

Individuation by acquaintance and by stipulation

I. THE CASE OF THE MISSING DAGGER

What do we see when we see what isn't there?

Macbeth the hallucinator sees a dagger. There is no dagger there to be seen: no ordinary steel dagger before his eyes, no miniature dagger on his retina or inside his brain, no ghostly dagger of spook-stuff. There is no reason to think that our world contains any such thing. But the lack of a dagger makes it mysterious how we can describe Macbeth's state, as we do, by means of predicates applying to the dagger he seems to see – it is bloody, it has a wooden handle – and not to the nerve signals, brain states, and other nondaggers that really exist. Notoriously, if we try to describe Macbeth adverbially – he is appeared to dagger-ishly, bloody-and-wooden-handled-daggerishly, and so on – it becomes plain that we only understand our Macbeth-descriptions by understanding the dagger-descriptions that are built into them. How so, if there is no dagger there to describe?

The case of the missing dagger has been solved by inspector Hintikka.[1] I accept his solution, differing only on points of detail, and I shall begin this paper by restating it in my own way.

First published in *The Philosophical Review* 92 (1983), 3–32. Copyright 1983 Cornell University. Reprinted with kind permission from the publisher of *The Philosophical Review*.

I thank many friends for valuable discussion; and I thank the Australian National University and La Trobe University for their hospitality while this paper was written.
1 Jaakko Hintikka, "On the Logic of Perception," in his *Models for Modalities* (Reidel,

When Macbeth is appeared to daggerishly, his experience has in-formational content, and part of that content is that there is a dagger before him. His experience tends to modify his belief, and if he is fooled by his hallucination, then also part of the content of his belief is that there is a dagger before him. An ordinary dagger, not a spooky one; and before the eyes, not inside the head.

The dagger Macbeth seems to see has the same status as Sherlock Holmes; or as the planet Vulcan, mistakenly posited to explain the perturbations of Mercury. The dagger, or Holmes, or Vulcan, exists according to something with false informational content, but does not actually exist.

Informational content can be explained in terms of possibilities. The information admits some possibilities and excludes others. Its content is given by the division of possibilities into the admitted ones and the excluded ones. The information is that some one of *these* possibilities is realized, not any one of *those*.

Besides the daggerless Macbeth of this world, there are countless other possible Macbeths who inhabit countless other possible worlds. Some of them have daggers before their eyes − just the right sort, bloody and wooden-handled, in just the right orientation with the handle toward the hand, against just the right background,. . . . What Macbeth's experience tells him is that he himself is one of these pos-sible Macbeths. The possibility that is realized, according to the con-tent of his visual experience, is some one of the ones in which there is a suitable dagger before him. Let us call the possibilities admitted by Macbeth's present visual experience his *visual alternatives*. Likewise his *perceptual alternatives* give the content of his complete perceptual expe-rience; his *doxastic alternatives* give the content of his system of beliefs; his *epistemic alternatives* give the content of his knowledge; and so on.

To solve the case of the missing dagger, we need only look for it in the right place. It is not some very peculiar brain-dagger or spook-

1969); "On Attributions of 'Self-Knowledge,'" *Journal of Philosophy* 67 (1970) 73–87; "Knowledge by Acquaintance − Individuation by Acquaintance," in D. F. Pears, ed., *Bertrand Russell: A Collection of Critical Essays* (Doubleday Anchor, 1972); and Chapters 1–4 of *The Intentions of Intentionality and other New Models for Modalities* (Reidel, 1975).

dagger hidden somewhere in this world. It is a perfectly ordinary dagger. But it is part of another world, floating before the eyes of an otherworldly alternative Macbeth whom the real Macbeth wrongly takes himself to be. By describing the ostensible dagger, we specify which alternatives are admitted or excluded by the informational content of Macbeth's state. And thus by trafficking in mere possibilities we describe actuality; for it is in virtue of what is actually going on in Macbeth that he is in a state with a certain content, rather than in a different state with different content.[2]

But now a question arises: one dagger or many? We speak of *the* dagger Macbeth seems to see. We ascribe properties to *it*. We regard it as a definite individual. Yet how can that be? The otherworldly daggers of Macbeth's visual or doxastic alternatives are many, or so it

---

2 The right assignment of content to Macbeth's states will be the one given by the best general rule of assignment. The best rule will be the one that does best at assigning contents that rationalize behavior, according to the principles of common sense psychology. We want the rule that does best generally: for Macbeth now and at other times, for Macbeth as he actually is and as he would have been under different circumstances, for Macbeth himself and for others of his kind. See my "Radical Interpretation," *Synthese* 23 (1974) 331–44; however, that account is too individualistic and should be corrected in that respect.

Note that it is not a question of Macbeth's states gaining causal powers by entering into relations with unactualized *possibilia*. Rather, the states are related as they are to *possibilia* in virtue of their causal powers. Compare the case of numerical magnitudes. When water boils because it reaches a temperature of 100° that is not a case of a number managing to cause physical effects.

I allow that the best rule for assigning content may be one that leaves the assignment somewhat indeterminate. Indeed it must be so if we are to treat moderately irrational – that is, normal – belief systems. If someone thinks that a certain restaurant is so crowded nowadays that nobody goes there any more, we need not assign him impossible doxastic alternatives, where the restaurant is crowded and deserted, as possibilities admitted by his belief system! Instead, his confusion amounts to indeterminacy between a belief system – an alternative set – in which the restaurant is crowded and one in which it is deserted. In a sense, he believes each half (though not the whole) of a contradiction; in a sense, he believes neither half. Someone who looks at a *trompe d'oeil* version of Escher's "Belvedere" might suffer a like indeterminacy between conflicting sets of visual alternatives. See the discussion of fragmented belief in my "Logic for Equivocators," *Noûs* 16 (1982) 431–41, and Nicholas Rescher and Robert Brandom, *The Logic of Inconsistency* (Blackwell, 1980).

would seem. Unless Macbeth enjoys a godlike view of all of space and time, his visual experience leaves many questions unanswered and so admits many alternative possibilities. Unless he is opinionated to an absurd degree, his doxastic alternatives likewise are many. Each alternative has its dagger, but there is no reason to think that one and the same dagger runs through them all. Macbeth has little notion where the dagger before him comes from, or whose it is, or when and where it was forged, or what famous stabbings it has been involved in, or what it is made of. Still less does his present visual experience tell him these things. He has little notion which of all the possible and actual daggers there are is the one before his eyes – unless we count it an answer just to say "Which one? Why, *this* one!" The identity of the dagger is one of the many questions left open by the content of his experience and belief, and differently answered by the different alternatives.

II. CROSS-IDENTIFICATION BY DESCRIPTION AND BY ACQUAINTANCE

At this point we have struck the famous problem of identity across possible worlds, or *cross-identification*. It is the problem of what we mean in saying, for instance, that a dagger present at one world and a dagger present at another are the same. The problem divides into two parts. (1) Is cross-identification literally a matter of identity, in that one and the same thing is wholly present at each of two worlds? Or is it a matter of relations that unite distinct things, each confined to its own world, so that we may treat them together as one although they are not really the same? Hintikka and I take the latter view, and regard cross-identification as the uniting of suitably related, but distinct, individuals from different worlds. (2) Are cross-identifications determined entirely by the qualitative character of the things and worlds in question?[3] Or do they depend at least partly on some other aspect or relation of things or worlds, something else that might differ

3 Here I use "qualitative character" in a broad enough sense to cover the causal relations, laws, and chances that prevail at the world in question, whether or not these things supervene on qualitative character more narrowly construed.

even between perfect qualitative duplicates? Hintikka and I see no need for this mysterious something else. We regard cross-identifications as holding in virtue of qualitative matching or resemblance, either in the intrinsic character of the cross-identified things or in their relations to the worldmates that surround them.

These answers to questions (1) and (2) lead to something like the counterpart theory I have proposed elsewhere.[4] We have a multitude of daggers, or whatever. Each one is "world-bound": it belongs wholly to one single world, and never appears at any other world. However, some of these daggers resemble others in various ways, and sometimes we think of distinct but similar daggers as if they were identical. Although a dagger cannot itself appear at worlds other than its own, it may have counterparts at other worlds, united to it by bonds of resemblance. Questions of cross-identification are to be understood not in terms of literal identity (in which case they would be trivialized) but in terms of counterpart relations. For instance, a certain dagger might have been used to stab Caesar if it has a counterpart that was used to stab a counterpart of Caesar. A dagger has some property essentially if it shares that property with all its counterparts. A "singular proposition" predicating a certain property of a certain actual dagger holds at just those worlds where some counterpart of that dagger has that property. A counterfactual conditional about a certain dagger is to be assessed by considering certain of the worlds where that dagger has a counterpart that satisfies the antecedent supposition. And so on.

A counterpart theorist must say that, strictly and literally speaking, the daggers of Macbeth's alternatives are many. The question is whether these many daggers are counterparts. The closest we can come to saying that the dagger is a definite individual, reappearing throughout the alternatives, is to say that the daggers of any two alternatives are counterparts united by the common role they play. The diversity of the daggers – their differing origins, history, composition, and so on – is what originally put us off calling them the same. Shall it now likewise put us off calling them counterparts?

---

4 In "Counterpart Theory and Quantified Modal Logic," *Journal of Philosophy* 65 (1968) 113–26; "Counterparts of Persons and Their Bodies," *Journal of Philosophy* 68 (1971) 203–11; and section 1.9 of *Counterfactuals* (Blackwell, 1973).

So stated, the difficulty will not puzzle us for long. Things resemble and differ from one another in many different respects. There are countless ways to amalgamate similarities and differences into a resultant relation of overall similarity. Hence we are not stuck with one fixed counterpart relation. Our daggers can be noncounterparts in one way and counterparts in another, and so can be a multitude in one way and a definite individual in another. One big advantage of counterpart theory is that it has no trouble providing for more than one kind of cross-identification; strict identity across worlds could replace at most one of all the different counterpart relations we need.[5]

Hintikka speaks of cross-identification by description and by acquaintance. In the language of counterpart theory, we have two different counterpart relations. Or better, we have two families of counterpart relations; both kinds of cross-identification may be further subdivided. The daggers of Macbeth's alternatives are not, in most cases, counterparts by description: they are not alike in their descriptions. But they are counterparts by acquaintance, being alike in the way Macbeth is acquainted with them. Cross-identifying by strict identity, they are a multitude. Cross-identifying by description, they are still a multitude. Cross-identifying by acquaintance, however, they are a definite individual, united by resemblance in a way that entitles us to regard them as if they were one.

Counterparts by description are united partly by similarity in their intrinsic character; and partly by similarity in their place in the world – their places in their worlds, I might better say – which is a matter of their relations to their surroundings. There is no special part of the surrounding world which has a privileged role; counterparts by description are alike *vis-à-vis* the world at large. (That will make it hard for things to be counterparts if their surrounding worlds differ too much.) One especially weighty sort of resemblance is match of ori-

---

5 A harmless multiplicity of counterpart relations (by description) can solve problems about *de re* modality that would otherwise require an objectionable multiplicity of mysteriously related entities. I discuss one such case in "Counterparts of Persons and Their Bodies." Several others have been discussed by Denis Robinson, "Re-Identifying Matter," *The Philosophical Review* 91 (1982) 317–341.

gins.[6] Suppose two worlds are just alike in their initial temporal segments, and diverge thereafter. Within the region of match, it is easy to find counterparts. They are perfect duplicates. Outside the region of match, we can still find counterparts that are alike in the way they are connected, by lines of spatiotemporal and causal continuity, to things inside the region of match. If I had remained a chemist, I might be very different today. But I and my counterpart the chemist would be continuations of duplicate initial segments, situated in duplicate surroundings, with duplicate histories. I doubt that our counterpart-by-description relations always give decisive weight to match of origins (when it is present) but certainly there is a tendency that way.

Counterparts by acquaintance, on the other hand, are united by resemblance in their relations to a subject of attitudes. In particular, the relations that govern the subject's epistemic access are alike. The subject plays a privileged role: the relations of the counterparts to him matter in a way that their relations to other things don't. Switch the subject, therefore, and you switch the cross–identification. So whereas cross–identification by description employs a two–place relation between counterparts, it seems that cross–identification by acquaintance requires a three–place relation. We must say that X and Y are counterparts by acquaintance for subject Z, meaning by this that X is related to Z at X's world in much the same way that Y is related to Z at Y's world.

The perceptual cases are simplest. The counterparts are similar in the way the subject perceives them. For instance, they are situated alike in what Hintikka calls the subject's "visual geometry." As it might be: straight ahead, about two feet away, the handle toward the hand.

6 I have reported Hintikka as agreeing with me that cross-identification by description is governed by similarity. Yet Hintikka denies this: see pages 127–29 and 209 of *The Intentions of Intentionality*. He insists that besides, or instead of, similarity, we need to use "continuity principles." Counterparts are to be related alike by continuity to individuals in a region of good match where cross–identification is especially easy. Yes indeed, say I; but why is this not one kind of similarity? If Hintikka's point is that purely intrinsic similarity is not enough, and we also must consider certain kinds of relational similarity, then we have never disagreed. I said at the start "your counterparts resemble you closely in content *and context* . . ." (page 114, "Counterpart Theory and Quantified Modal Logic," italics added).

To this, I would add a causal similarity. Perceptual counterparts are to be similar in the contribution they make to the subject's perceptual experience, and in the way that the subject's experience causally depends on them. (Here I depart to some extent from Hintikka's account.)[7]

The case of Macbeth's dagger required cross-identification by acquaintance between his perceptual alternatives. We also may consider cross-identification between the subject's alternatives and reality. Reality may indeed supply one of the alternatives, if the content of the subject's perceptual experience is free of all error. But if not, then although his perceptual alternatives are all of them unactualized possibilities, he may yet be perceiving real things. Not so in the case of Macbeth's hallucinatory dagger; but in other cases, the things present in the alternatives may be counterparts by acquaintance of real things that the subject is perceiving or misperceiving. Each of my visual alternatives has a sheet of paper contributing in a certain distinctive way to my visual experience. This world has an actual sheet of paper contributing to my experience in just that way, or near enough. So even if this world does not quite succeed in supplying one of my perceptual alternatives – thanks to a deceptive afterimage, let us say – there is a good sense in which the actual sheet of paper is the very one I seem to see. Not only are the sheets of paper of the alternatives counterparts by acquaintance, for me, of one another; they also are counterparts by acquaintance, for me, of the real sheet of paper before my eyes.

Perceptual cross-identification may be generalized in virtue of the analogy between relations of perceptual acquaintance and other, more

7 Hintikka uses causal relations for cross-identification between the actual world and its perceptual alternatives, but not for cross-identification between these alternatives. (See *The Intentions of Intentionality*, Chapter 4, especially page 71.) I think my use of causal relations even in cross-identifying between alternatives has its uses in the perceptual case (for instance, in handling the problem about mirrors noted on page 67, *op. cit.*) and is indispensable in the doxastic and epistemic cases. It has its price: suitably ordinary causal relations must prevail in the perceptual alternatives, making causal information part of the content of perceptual experience. But I think that is objectionable only given the forlorn hope that we can speak sensibly of the pure content of perceptual experience, separated from all collateral information.

tenuous, relations of epistemic rapport. There are the relations that someone bears to me when I get a letter from him, or I watch the swerving of a car he is driving, or I read his biography, or I hear him mentioned by name, or I investigate the clues he has left at the scene of his crime. In each case, there are causal chains from him to me of a sort which would permit a flow of information. Perhaps I do get accurate information; perhaps I get misinformation, but still the channel is there. I shall call such relations as these *relations of acquaintance*. Just as perceptual counterparts are alike in the way they are linked to the subject by perceptual relations, so, in general, counterparts by acquaintance are alike in the way they are linked to the subject by relations of acquaintance of all sorts.

For cross-identification by acquaintance, match of origins does not matter at all. Neither does similarity of intrinsic character, except insofar as it would be hard for things of quite different kinds to be alike in the relations of acquaintance into which they enter. And that is not so very hard. Waxworks and people may be perceptual counterparts, or shadows and spooks, or puddles and layers of hot air.

Cross-identification by acquaintance can be put to good use in describing the subject's state. Holmes begins his investigation with an open mind: each of his doxastic alternatives has some murderer or other, since he believes that someone is the murderer, but in no sense is it the same murderer throughout the alternatives. Later there is someone in particular whom he believes to be the murderer: the murderers of the alternatives that remain uneliminated are counterparts by acquaintance for Holmes of one another, and in that sense they comprise a definite individual. (They need not be counterparts by description. It is not part of Holmes' task to discover the murderer's right name, his famous deeds, his origins, or even whether he is man or spook.) Holmes comes to believe: the murderer is the one I am acquainted with in such-and-such ways. Holmes being what he is, doubtless he is right in this belief, in which case the real-world murderer also is a counterpart by acquaintance of the murderers of Holmes' doxastic alternatives. (He might even be one of them, if Holmes is wrong about nothing at all.) It is otherwise with the imaginative and deluded Scholmes. He is dead wrong, completely out of touch with reality. But his belief system is not unlike Holmes', and his doxastic alternatives have narrowed down in much the same way. We may say of Scholmes too that after much "investigation" there is someone in particular whom he believes to be the murderer, though in Scholmes' case this is not anyone real.

For Scholmes, as for Holmes, the murderers of his doxastic alternatives are counterparts by acquaintance of one another. Thus they comprise a definite individual for him, a "vivid character in his inner story."[8] What makes this character fictitious – a mere figment of Scholmes' imagination – is that there is no cross-identification by acquaintance between the *possibilia* that comprise it and anyone real.

Likewise in perceptual cases we may use cross-identification by acquaintance to make familiar distinctions. I see the famous speckled hen. Or I hallucinate it – no matter, the distinctions we want cut across the difference between successful perception and hallucination. At first I do not pay close attention. The content of my visual experience is not very detailed: it tells me that there are speckles, but it does not tell me their number or distribution or size or shape. Each visual alternative has speckles, but no single speckle is present throughout them. The alternatives differ too much. Then I focus my attention on one of the speckles. My visual experience becomes more informative and my new set of alternatives is less diverse. That speckle, with its distinctive location in my visual geometry and its distinctive causal contribution to my experience, runs uniformly through my alternatives. Or better: there are speckles, one for each alternative, that are cross-identified for me by perceptual acquaintance. They are perceptual counterparts. I saw at once that there were speckles; only later was there a particular speckle (real or hallucinatory) that I saw. Similarly, Macbeth sees a (hallucinatory) dagger only if the daggers of his alternatives are perceptually cross-identified. That might not have been so if, for instance, he had hallucinated a scene of furious battle. Suppose his eye is on his attacker's axe, and he barely notices that some of those nearby are wielding daggers. Then he sees – or hallucinates – that there are daggers, but there is no dagger that he sees.

8 *Cf.* David Kaplan, "Quantifying In," *Synthese* 19 (1968) 178–214, especially pages 199–203.

III. CROSS-IDENTIFYING THE SUBJECT

Thus far, Hintikka's story, slightly amended. But now I shall raise a problem which seems to me serious, and which Hintikka does not consider. It is simplest to state it as a problem about cross-identification by acquaintance between the subject's own world and his alternatives, though it could be stated instead as a problem about cross-identification between alternatives. I think my problem can be solved if, and only if, we change our thinking about possibilities in a rather fundamental way. I think this change is desirable also on other grounds.

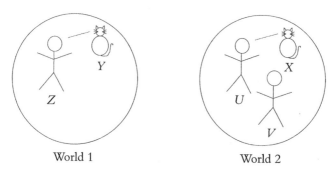

World 1   World 2

Please look through the Verneoscope at these two possible worlds.[9] You see Y and Z, here at world 1. Perhaps that is our world. As you see, Z is a perceiving subject, and Y is something which stands to Z in certain relations of acquaintance. And you see X, here at world 2. Perhaps that is a world that supplies one of Z's perceptual alternatives. Examine these worlds and their inhabitants closely and tell me: is X a counterpart by acquaintance of Y for subject Z?

You see that among X's worldmates at world 2 are U and V. Both of them are perceiving subjects, rather like Z at world 1. And X stands to U in relations of acquaintance just like the relations of Y to Z. But X stands in no relation of acquaintance to V, or at any rate none that resembles any of the relations of Y to Z. Now what do you think?

You say: it depends. If U is the subject Z, then indeed X and Y are

9 The Verneoscope is an impossible device, invented by David Kaplan, for inspecting other worlds. See Kaplan's "Transworld Heir Lines," in Michael J. Loux, ed., *The Possible and the Actual* (Cornell, 1979), especially page 93.

counterparts by acquaintance for Z. But if V is Z, not so. First we must settle which inhabitant of world 2 is Z, then we can answer the question.

I say: strictly speaking, no inhabitant of world 2 *is* Z. We'll have no cross-world identities, if you please. Z is wholly at world 1 and nowhere else, and only his counterparts are at other worlds such as world 2. The best you can do is to settle which inhabitant of world 2 is Z's counterpart.

You say: right. Which kind of counterpart?

Here's the problem in a nutshell. Before we can cross-identify anything by acquaintance for a certain subject, we must first cross-identify the subject. As good counterpart theorists, we cannot do that by strict identity. In fact, I shall argue that we cannot do it at all, given the way I posed the problem. Neither kind of counterpart relation does the job.

Let us first try cross-identification by acquaintance. As you see, Z bears certain relations of acquaintance to himself. Foremost among these is identity, which indeed is a relation that provides plenty of epistemic rapport. (But also there are others: relations which Z bears to himself, although it is possible for someone to bear them to something else. Like the famous hero, Z studies records of his own past exploits; like the unfortunate man with his pants on fire, Z unwittingly watches himself in a mirror.)[10] So Z's counterpart by acquaintance at world 2 must be linked to Z by much the same relations of acquaintance as Z himself is. Linked to Z himself? – No, to Z's counterpart at world 2, whoever that is. The most we will get this way, I think, is that Z's counterpart by acquaintance at world 2 has the same sort of epistemic self-rapport that Z has. This is too easy a condition to satisfy. Both U and V satisfy it. For instance both of them are self-identical, just as Z is.

Perhaps we'd do better to try cross-identification by description.

---

10 The hero appears in Hector-Neri Castañeda, "On the Logic of Attributions of Self-knowledge to Others," *Journal of Philosophy* 65 (1968) 439–56, especially pages 446–47; the man with his pants on fire appears in David Kaplan, "Demonstratives," in Joseph Almog, John Perry, and Howard Wettstein, eds., *Themes from Kaplan* (Oxford, 1989).

But that way, we get a condition that may be too hard to satisfy. Suppose Z is rather badly mistaken in his opinions, and suppose world 2 is the sort of world that Z wrongly supposes himself to inhabit. It is one of his *belief worlds*, a world of just the kind that we must consider in order to characterize the content of Z's system of beliefs by assigning him a set of doxastic alternatives. Then world 2 may contain no counterpart by description of Z. No inhabitant of world 2 matches Z in origins: Z came from a certain sperm and egg, but he is convinced that the myth of sperms and eggs is scientistic tommyrot and that a rival hypothesis is correct. The inhabitants of Z's belief worlds are all brought by storks. There is nobody at world 2 who matches Z in intrinsic character: Z himself is a complicated physical object like you and me, whereas his belief worlds are populated entirely by embodied spirits who conform to his philosophy of mind. Although Z has many famous deeds to his name, he refuses to believe that anyone – least of all, he himself – could have done all those things. He is kind but cynical, so that nobody at Z's belief worlds is as nice as Z himself. And so it goes. If we cross-identify by description, Z is nowhere to be found at his own belief worlds. Shall we conclude that Z does not believe that he himself exists? No, Z's opinions are a mite peculiar, sure enough, but they're not that peculiar.

The case was extreme, but more realistic cases would be bad enough. We might well have counterparts by description of Z at only some of his belief worlds, not all. For this to happen he needn't be wrong about anything, only open-minded. We should not conclude from this that Z is uncertain whether he himself exists.

In the more and the less extreme cases alike, it may be that world 2 contains no counterparts by description of Z. If so, we still have no answer to our question whether X and Y are counterparts by acquaintance for Z. But that is a question we need to answer if world 2 provides one of Z's perceptual or doxastic or what-not alternatives. We can't just ignore the alternatives that make trouble. To leave out some of the alternatives would impute richer content to Z's state than is really there.

It could also happen that Z has two different counterparts by description at a single world: U and V, say. They are twins from the same sperm and egg, and they are leading similar lives. If we cross-identify by description, they have equal claim to be taken as Z. Honor both claims, and we get conflicting answers about whether X and Y are counterparts by acquaintance for Z.

So if we cross-identify the subject by description preparatory to cross-identifying other things by acquaintance, we hit trouble. But even if the proposal could work, still it is unsound in principle. When we cross-identify by acquaintance between the subject's alternatives, we are doing so in order to describe the informational content of his state. If two subjects are psychological duplicates – if they believe alike, or are alike in their visual experience, or whatever – we should assign them the same sets of alternative possibilities, with the same cross-identification by acquaintance between these alternatives. But if we first cross-identified the subject by description, we might get answers that depend not only on the state we intend to describe, but also on such irrelevancies as the subject's origins, intrinsic character, and so on. If two subjects who are psychologically alike are different in ways that give them different counterparts by description, that should not matter at all. But on the present proposal it will matter. It may matter a lot, as we have seen; but it is bad if it matters even a little bit. Irrelevancies intrude into what was meant to be a purely psychological characterization.

What makes it wrong to cross-identify the subject by description is that the subject may be wrong about his own description. Take the doxastic case. The subject has a certain conception of himself. He believes that he has such-and-such intrinsic properties and stands in such-and-such relations to his surroundings. (He also believes that he inhabits such-and-such a kind of world; if we count this as part of his self-conception, as I think we should, his self-conception subsumes his entire belief system.)[11] Since the subject's doxastic alternatives are to be exactly the possibilities admitted by the content of his belief, they must in particular conform to his beliefs about himself. No matter how we cross-identify the subject into his doxastic alternatives, we always must find someone who fits his self-

11 See my "Attitudes *De Dicto* and *De Se*," *The Philosophical Review* 88 (1979) 513–43, especially page 518.

conception. His counterparts by description cannot be relied on to do so; for his self-conception might be wrong in essential ways, as we have seen. Further, the discrepancies between the subject's true description and his self-conception are something that might differ between psychological duplicates. That is why irrelevancies intrude into our attempted psychological characterization if we cross-identify the subject by description.

It may seem that we have solved our problem *en passant*. Perhaps we should cross-identify the subject not by acquaintance and not by description but by self-conception. Let us search world 2 through the Verneoscope for someone who fits Z's self-conception; the one who does is the one we will cross-identify with Z. He is the one we will take as a point of reference in cross-identifying other things by acquaintance. (If world 2 supplies one of Z's doxastic alternatives, there will indeed be at least one of its inhabitants who fits his self-conception. But what if there are two, for instance both of U and V? And what if it supplies not a doxastic alternative but, for instance, a visual alternative? Let us ignore these problems.) I say that this is no solution at all. It is circular. The subject's self-conception is (at least) part of the content of his belief system, which content is supposed to be given by his set of doxastic alternatives. To find out his self-conception, we look to see what is true of him throughout these alternatives. To find out what is true of him, with respect to any given one of the alternatives, we must first find him. And which one is he? – the one who fits the self-conception! Either we need an independent way to find the self-conception, in which case the alternatives are unfit for their work, or else we still need an independent way to find the subject.

IV. STIPULATION AND HAECCEITISM

No matter how we try to cross-identify the subject, we meet both technical difficulties and difficulties of principle. We can't win. But we Yanks have a way with unwinnable wars: we simply declare them won, go home, celebrate the victory, and live happily ever after. (*We* live happily ever after.) Saul Kripke has proposed that we conquer the problem of cross-identification in the same way. He invites us to consider questions of identity across possible worlds unproblematic, and to settle them by declaration.[12] Kripke advises us not to stare at another world through the Verneoscope in search of something that will tell us which, if any, of its inhabitants is Nixon – is he, perhaps, this inept politician over here who has never won an election? Rather, we should simply stipulate: let us consider a world where Nixon invariably loses elections.

Kripke makes it fairly clear that these stipulations are not meant as acts of mental worldmaking, or of mental identification-making. What we make are not worlds, with or without built-in cross-identifications, but rather are (partial) specifications of worlds. When we stipulate we are selecting. Out of all the worlds there are, we stipulate which ones we wish to consider. And in doing this, Kripke insists, it is perfectly right and proper to specify worlds in terms of cross-identification.

Certainly we are free to stipulate that the world under consideration shall be one where Nixon invariably loses. Anyone can agree to that, whatever his views on cross-identification (unless his views provide no way at all to cross-identify Nixon with an otherworldly loser). Even a counterpart theorist like myself can be happy with such a stipulation, rightly understood. It comes to this: let us consider a world such that the qualitative character of that world and its inhabitants, plus the qualitative character of our world and its Nixon, together make some election-loser in that world be a counterpart by description of our Nixon. In brief: let us consider a world that bears certain relations of qualitative likeness and difference to ours. It is not in dispute that stipulations involving cross-identification are proper. The real issue is whether these always can be replaced, in principle, by purely qualitative stipulations (perhaps making reference, as above, to the unspecified qualitative character of our own world). We have already raised this issue. Are cross-identifications determined entirely by the qualitative character of the things and worlds in question, as counterpart theorists believe? Then stipulations in terms of cross-identification are

<hr>

12 In his "Naming and Necessity," in Donald Davidson and Gilbert Harman, eds., *Semantics of Natural Language* (Reidel, 1972), especially pages 264–69.

just a convenience. They add nothing to our resources. Or do cross-identifications depend at least partly on some other aspect or relation of things or worlds, as Haecceitists (in approximately David Kaplan's sense)[13] believe? Then indeed stipulations in terms of cross-identification can do something that no amount of purely qualitative stipulation can do. They can specify the alleged non-qualitative determinants of cross-identification.

Our problem in finding the subject was that nothing we could see through the Verneoscope seemed to help. Now we are advised simply to stipulate: let world 2 be a world where U is Z. Or: where V is Z. Or somebody else, or nobody. Any of these stipulations would solve our problem, and put us in a position to cross-identify by acquaintance. But if such stipulations are to make sense, it cannot have been fully settled beforehand just which world we had in mind. Our Verneo-scopic, purely qualitative view of the so-called "world 2" must have been a view not of one world but of many: many worlds exactly alike qualitatively but differing in some other way. The nonqualitative differences among these duplicate worlds must somehow be relevant to cross-identification, so that some of them are worlds where U is to be cross-identified with Z, some are worlds where V is to be cross-identified with Z, and so on. Stipulation is beside the point. We are invited to give up on counterpart theory, join the Haecceitists, believe in nonqualitative determinants of cross-identification, and rely on these to solve our problem of finding the subject.

13 David Kaplan, "How to Russell a Frege-Church," *Journal of Philosophy* 72 (1975) 716–29, especially pages 722–23. Haecceitism as Kaplan defines it, however, is a package deal consisting of several independent theses. I shall concentrate on the central thesis of the package: namely, that there are nonqualitative determinants of cross-identification. I shall use "Haeccetism" simply as a name for this thesis. Thus a Haecceitist could hold any of various opinions about what the nonqualitative determinants of cross-identification are, and how they do their work. In particular, he might or might not believe in identities between inhabitants of different worlds. He might not even believe in the irreducibly nonqualitative haecceities that give the package its name, for he might be a nominalist and believe in no properties at all. Conversely, someone who rejects Haecceitism might believe in nonqualitative haecceities for reasons having nothing to do with cross-identification (as indeed I do); see Robert M. Adams, "Primitive Thisness and Primitive Identity," *Journal of Philosophy* 76 (1979) 5–26.

I decline the invitation. My reason is that Haecceitism in any form will lead us into intolerable mysteries. But different versions will lead us into different mysteries, so we must take them separately.

I first consider the version that is suggested by Kripke's discussion of cross-identification. (I do not say that Kripke himself is committed to all of it.) This kind of Haecceitism disagrees with counterpart theory on two points, but it does not sever cross-identification from resemblance altogether. Its theses are as follows. (1) Cross-identification is literally a matter of identity. When something in one world is cross-identified with something in another, one and the same thing is wholly present at each of two worlds. (2) There are nonqualitative determinants of cross-identification, differing between worlds that are qualitatively alike: namely, these identities between the inhabitants of the worlds. Duplicate worlds may differ by having different individuals in common with, for instance, our world. However, (3) there are qualitative constraints on cross-identification, limits on how different a thing could have been from the way it actually is. Things have nontrivial qualitative essences. Cross-identification enforces certain resemblances in qualitative character, particularly match of origins; contrapositively, certain dissimilarities preclude cross-identification. Saul Kripke being what he is, there is no world where he himself is present and is a puddle, or a poached egg, or someone originally brought by a stork.

This version of Haecceitism cannot solve our problem of finding the subject. Because of its essentialism, it fails in the same way as our previous proposal to cross-identify the subject by description. Anyone too different from the subject as he actually is, anyone who lacks his qualitative essence, cannot be him. So again it may turn out that the subject is nowhere to be found at his own belief worlds, thanks to his mistakes. Or he may be found at only some of them, thanks to his open-mindedness. Stipulation might select among too many eligible candidates for cross-identification, but stipulation cannot help if there are too few. (If there is no world where Saul Kripke himself was brought by a stork, it's no use stipulating that we are to consider such a world.) Further, I object again that irrelevancies are intruding into what was meant as a purely psychological description. Our cross-identification by acquaintance will depend as before on the subject's actual qualitative character. That will now enter by way of essentialistic constraints on identity across worlds, rather than by way of a descriptive counterpart relation, but it ought not to enter in any way.

It would therefore be a step in the right direction to drop the essentialism, and switch to a more extreme version of Haecceitism in which cross-identification depends not at all on qualitative character: any individual can have any character.[14] We might of course worry that such a Haecceitism cannot account for certain facts, such as the fact that I could not possibly have been a poached egg. But that is no real difficulty. We counterpart theorists can offer the loan of our own account, suitably adapted. The limits to difference that no longer constrain identity across worlds may reappear, optionally, in the form of an accessibility relation. It is common enough to say modal things that disregard some of all the possibilities there are; and so long as we disregard those worlds where things differ too much from the way they actually are, there are no worlds where I am a poached egg.

Consider an extreme version of Haecceitism, without essentialism, which retains both the theses (1) that cross-identification is literally a matter of identity, and (2) that identities across worlds serve as non-qualitative determinants of cross-identification. On this view we have things wholly present at more than one world, and there is no limit to the qualitative difference between something at one world and that same thing at another. For example – and it is not a very extreme example – we may have something wholly present at one world, where it is square, and at another, where it is round.

How can this be? I know what it is to be square, or to be round; but this thing is supposed to be both. "But at different worlds!" – How does that help? I know what it is to have a square part and a round part – as may happen when something changes its shape over time – but this thing is supposed to be *wholly* square and *wholly* round. Presumably, the thing is supposed to bear the square-at relation to one world, and the round-at relation to another. There is no contradiction

<hr>

14 Such a theory has been defended by Pavel Tichý in lectures and in conversation. I am grateful to him for persuading me that it is worthy of consideration.

because these relations are born to different *relata*. But what are these alleged relations? – Not shapes! Shapes are properties, not relations. We cannot just be told to think of them now as relations but understand them exactly as before. An explanation is required. What is it to be square at a world? What has that to do with simply being square?

If *I* say that something is square at a world, most likely I just mean that it is square, and it is at that world. Or I might be speaking of something composed of parts from several worlds, in which case I would mean that the part at the world in question is square. Also, I could say that seven numbers the circles at one world but not at another, meaning by this that seven bears the numbering relation to the class comprising the circles that are at one world, but not to the class comprising the circles that are at the other. So my problem is not that I cannot understand the adverbial phrase "at such-and-such world." I can; but not in a way that allows something to be wholly present at two worlds without having exactly the same intrinsic properties at both.[15]

It is as if someone said that Ted and Ned are Siamese twins; they share a hand; as Ted's right hand it has five fingers but as Ned's left hand it has six fingers. We would not put up with such double-talk, but would ask once and for all how many fingers are on the hand. "Five if you're Ted, six if you're Ned" would not be an acceptable answer.

(Doubtless I shall be told that my mistake is to suppose that something present at a world is literally part of that world, like the twins' hand. I shall be advised that worlds are like stories. Rather special stories: maximally detailed, infinitely long, hence untold. [Or perhaps they're like pictures, or models, or mental images, or belief systems, or representations of some other sort – again, infinitely rich ones, and

---

15 Nothing I have said here is an objection to identity across worlds in the special case in which the cross-identified thing is exactly alike in intrinsic properties at all the worlds where it appears. Likewise, the usual objection to identity across worlds determined by qualitative resemblance – identity is transitive, resemblance isn't – does not apply to that special case. Cross-identification of this special sort is of course not enough to solve our problem of finding the subject; it suffers from essentialistic constraints to an extreme degree.

hence unrealized.] If conflicting stories are told about someone, all of them are about *him*: about one and the same individual. And they are about the whole of him, not different parts. There is no problem about how he can be different in different stories, for he isn't literally *in* any of them. Nobody is literally part of a story. Likewise – so goes the advice – something can be square according to one world-story and round according to another one, although no part of either story is either square or round. The proposal that we should construe worlds as story-like, or [as I would put it] that we should use world-stories as substitutes for the worlds themselves, is a popular one. Fortunately, we need not consider its merits here. For it rejects a presupposition of the problem we are trying to solve. Hence it cannot solve that problem, though perhaps it might circumvent it. Remember how we began: we can describe Macbeth by describing his dagger because his state puts him into a relation with otherworldly daggers that fit our descriptions. No world-story theory can accept this solution to the case of the missing dagger. According to any such theory, there are no otherworldly daggers to be described – only false stories according to which there are daggers. However well they might succeed on their own terms, world-story theories are irrelevant to our present problem, and I shall consider them no further.)

If identity across worlds requires a mysterious wholesale transformation of properties into relations, perhaps the Haecceitist will decide that it is more trouble than it is worth. He might then give up on the identities, but continue to maintain that cross-identification varies independently of qualitative character. According to this version of Haecceitism, when something in one world is cross-identified with something in another, the two never are identical. Each is confined to its own world. Yet these two things are somehow linked, as many other pairs are not, in virtue of something nonqualitative.

I ask what the nonqualitative determinants of cross-identification are, and how they do their work. So long as the Haecceitist believes in identity across worlds, he has a good answer to me. But if he gives up on the identities, he throws that answer away and he owes me another.

He might say that when two things are cross-identified, that is because they stand in a certain relation. Or they share a certain property.

Or they are both included as parts of a certain mereological aggregate, one that is not entirely in any one world. But this tells me nothing at all. *Any* two things stand in infinitely many relations, share infinitely many properties, and are both included as parts of infinitely many aggregates. For any class of ordered pairs, however miscellaneous, there is the relation of being paired by a member of that class; for any class of things, however miscellaneous, there is the property of belonging to that class and there is the mereological sum of that class. Perhaps the Haecceitist thinks that some of all these relations or properties or aggregates are somehow special, and he meant to speak only of the special ones. (Perhaps he also thinks that only the special ones exist.) Then he must tell me which of all the relations and properties and aggregates I believe in are the special ones. He cannot draw on my (sadly partial) understanding of what it is for some of them to be special by cutting along the qualitative joints; and he must avoid circularity. I do not think he can answer me. If he cannot, he leaves it entirely mysterious how cross-identification is supposed to be determined.

Since I do not see how honest toil can solve my problem of finding the subject, I should like to accept the Haecceitist's invitation to solve it by other means. Further, there is a certain amount of direct intuitive evidence for Haecceitism, which we will consider shortly. But do we really want the mysterious Haecceitistic differences among duplicate worlds? Or the transformation of familiar properties into unfamiliar relations? I say not. We should not buy the Haecceitist's costly wares, even if they would solve our problem,[16] until we have made sure that no cheaper substitute can be had.

---

16 And would the Haecceitist's wares solve our problem? Suppose that somehow we have a satisfactory, anti-essentialistic version of Haecceitism, and we use it to cross-identify the subject. I complain once again that irrelevancies intrude into our psychological descriptions of the subject. This time it is not the subject's qualitative character that wrongly intrudes, but his very identity. Suppose we have two subjects, *S* and *T*; we have a certain set of alternative possibilities; and at each alternative *S* and *T* are present (let the Haecceitist tell us what this means) and *S* is wise and *T* is foolish. Now: if someone had this as his set of doxastic alternatives, would he think himself wise? Or foolish? This question about his self-conception seems like a purely psychological one, so the alternative set ought to answer it. But on the present proposal, the answer depends on whether the subject is *S* or *T*, and it

One uncustomary distinction, and our problem solves itself. We shall have a cheap quasi-Haecceitism, and we shall be free to find the subject by stipulation.

From the outset I have spoken of the subject's perceptual or doxastic or what-not alternatives as *possibilities* – not as *possible worlds* (except in discussing proposals due to be rejected). Let me distinguish: *possibilities are not always possible worlds*. There are possible worlds, sure enough, and there are possibilities, and possible worlds are some of the possibilities. But I say that *any* possible individual is a possibility, and not all possible individuals are possible worlds. Only the biggest ones are.[17,18]

The world is the totality of things. It is the actual individual that includes every actual individual as a part. Likewise a possible world is a possible individual big enough to include every possible individual that is compossible with it. It is a way that an entire world might possibly be. But lesser possible individuals, inhabitants of worlds, proper parts of worlds, are possibilities too. They are ways that something less than an entire world might possibly be. A possible person, for instance, is a way that a person might possibly be. A possible dagger is a way that a dagger might possibly be.

A central thesis of the metaphysics of modality is that the unit of possibility is the possible world. I divide the thesis, retain part, and

shouldn't. See also my discussion of a similar point on pages 522–24 of "Attitudes *De Dicto* and *De Se*."

17 My point is not that possible worlds are maximal specific possibilities, and there are also less specific ones. That is so, but here I am speaking always of maximally specific possibilities. A possible individual, whether or not it is a possible world, is a maximally specific possibility.

18 Quine's "centered worlds," or some slight generalization of them, might indeed correspond to all the possibilities. But centered worlds are not just worlds, much as stuffed cabbage is not just cabbage; centered worlds amount to presentations of possible individuals, so a proposal to use centered worlds differs little from my proposal to use the individuals themselves. See W. V. Quine, "Propositional Objects," in his *Ontological Relativity and Other Essays* (Columbia, 1969): and see Section X of my "Attitudes *De Dicto* and *De Se*."

reject part. It is true, and important, that possibilities are invariably provided by whole possible worlds. There are no free-floating *possibilia*. Every possibility is part of a world – exactly one world – and thus comes surrounded by worldmates, and fully equipped with relational properties in virtue of its relations to them. What is not true is that we should count distinct possibilities by counting the worlds that provide them. A single world may provide many possibilities, since many possible individuals inhabit it.

To illustrate, consider these two possibilities for me. I might have been one of a pair of twins. I might have been the firstborn one, or the secondborn one. These two possibilities involve no qualitative difference in the way the world is. Imagine them specified more fully: there is the possibility of being the firstborn twin in a world of such-and-such maximally specific qualitative character. And there is the possibility of being the secondborn twin in exactly such a world. The Haecceitist says: two possibilities, two worlds. They *seem* just alike, but they must differ somehow. They differ in their cross-identification of David Lewis, hence they must differ with respect to the determinants of cross-identification; and these must be nonqualitative, since there are no qualitative differences to be had. I say: two possibilities, sure enough. But they are two possibilities within a single world. The world in question contains twin counterparts of me. (Counterparts by description, under a counterpart relation that stresses match of origins and personal continuity.) Each twin is a possible way for a person to be, and in fact is a possible way for me to be. I might have been one, or I might have been the other. These are two distinct possibilities for me. But they involve only one possibility for the world: it might have been the world inhabited by two such twins. The Haecceitist was quite right when he thought that purely qualitative worlds gave us too narrow a range of distinct possibilities. He concluded that worlds must not be purely qualitative. He'd have done better to conclude that *worlds* gave us too narrow a range of possibilities. The parts of worlds also must be put to use.

For a second illustration, consider the thought that I might have been someone else. Here am I, there goes poor Fred: there but for the grace of God go I; how lucky I am to be me, not him. Where there is luck there must be contingency. I am contemplating the possibility of my being poor Fred, and rejoicing that it is unrealized. I am not contemplating a possibility that involves any qualitative difference in the world – not, for instance, a world where someone with origins just like mine suffers misfortunes just like Fred's. Rather, I am contemplating the possibility of being poor Fred in a world just like this one. The Haecceitist will suggest that I have in mind a qualitative duplicate of this world where the nonqualitative determinants of cross-identification somehow link me with the qualitative counterpart of Fred. But this distorts my thought: I thought not just that I might have lived Fred's life, but that I might have been Fred living Fred's life. Maybe I misunderstood my own thought – it's hard to be sure – but let's see if the Haecceitist's amendment is really needed. I think not. I suggest that the possibility I have in mind is not a world that is like ours qualitatively but differs from ours Haecceitistically. Instead it is a possible individual, in fact an actual individual, namely poor Fred himself. Like any other possible person, he is a possible way for a person to be. And in a sense he is even a possible way for me to be. He is my counterpart by description under an extraordinarily generous counterpart relation, one which demands nothing more of counterparts than that they be things of the same kind.[19] Any property that one of my counterparts does have is a property that I might have; being Fred – being literally identical with him – is such a property; and so there is a sense in which I might have been him. That is not to say that the world might have been such that I was Fred – it makes no sense to thank God for His gracious favoritism in making the world be as it is, rather than some different way such that I would have been poor Fred! The possibility in question is a possibility for me, not for the world.[20]

---

19 This counterpart relation is one that permits things to have counterparts in their own worlds, other than themselves, *contra* a requirement I took as axiomatic in "Counterpart Theory and Quantified Modal Logic."

20 Thomas Nagel, in "The Objective Self," in Carl Ginet and Sydney Shoemaker, eds., *Mind and Knowledge: Essays in Honor of Norman Malcolm* (Oxford, 1983), discusses the thought that I might have been someone else. He writes "my being *TN* (or whoever I in fact am) *seems* accidental . . . it seems as if I just *happen* to be the publicly identifiable person *TN*." He insists that this thought should be respected at face value, and not converted into the more tractable thought that I might have lived a different life. I in turn insist that it should not be converted, as Nagel himself

Besides possible individuals, world-sized and smaller, there are still other possibilities: joint possibilities for two or more individuals. These are ordered pairs, triples, etc. . . . or even infinite sequences of possible individuals, all from the same world. An ordered pair of compossible individuals, for instance, is a way that a pair of individuals might possibly be. Imagine that we live in a spatially symmetric world. The entire history of one side is replicated on the other side. But it didn't have to be so. An alternative possibility for the world starts out symmetric, just as this world supposedly is; but tomorrow one side is destroyed by a catastrophe and the other side survives. I have my twin, J, on the other side. One joint possibility for me and my twin is that I am killed in the catastrophe and he survives. Another, which I prefer, is that he is killed and I survive. The Haecceitist has his way of distinguishing these two possibilities. I have my cheaper way. The world of the catastrophe has its pair of twins, K who gets killed and L who lives. Therefore it provides two ordered pairs of compossible individuals: $<K,L>$ and $<L,K>$. These are two different ways for an ordered pair of individuals to be. In particular, they are two different ways for the ordered pair $<I,J>$ to be, two different joint possibilities for me and my twin. Both K and L are counterparts by description of both I and J; further, the relations between K and L are like the relations between I and J so there is a natural sense in which both the pairs $<K,L>$ and $<L,K>$ are counterparts by description of the pair $<I,J>$. Of these two joint possibilities for $<I,J>$, $<L,K>$ is the one I prefer. Other cases require sequences with repetitions or gaps (which we can fill, artificially, with a "null individual" denoted by *). There might have been a world with no duplication, but only one shared counterpart H of the twins I and J. One joint possibility for I and J is that they might have both existed and been identical; this is the pair $<H,H>$. Another is that I alone might have existed; this is the pair $<H,*>$. A third is that J alone might have existed; this is the pair $<*,H>$. Once

proposes, into the thought that I might have born some relation other than identity to someone other than the one to whom I actually bear this relation. The treatment I suggest here is due, in essentials, to Allen Hazen; see his "Counterpart-theoretic Semantics for Modal Logic," *Journal of Philosophy* 76 (1979) 319–38, especially page 331, footnote 17.

again, we have our desired difference of possibilities without any difference of worlds.[21]

This is my first argument that not all possibilities are possible worlds. By accepting the thesis, we satisfy the Haecceitist's intuitions on the cheap, giving him the distinctions among possibilities that he rightly demands without buying into any mysterious non-qualitative aspects of worlds.

VII. INDIVIDUALS AS ALTERNATIVES

The possibilities that are a subject's perceptual or doxastic or epistemic alternatives will almost never be possible worlds. ("Almost" because of solipsistic possibilities, in which the subject is the whole of his world.) The subject's alternatives will typically be possible people, or subjects rather like people; or better, they will be temporal stages thereof. The informational content of the subject's state will be: I am one of such-and-such alternative possible individuals. It will not just be: I inhabit one of such-and-such alternative possible worlds. As I have argued elsewhere,[22] the objects of attitudes in general are *properties*, defined as sets of possible individuals; only in special cases can we take them as *propositions*, defined as sets of possible worlds. Alternative worlds will do to characterize content having to do with the way the subject's world is. They will not do to characterize further content having to do with the subject's place in the world. To see what this further content is, imagine being without it. You have been told that there are two duplicate dungeons. The door of the one on the left leads to freedom. The door of the one on the right leads to the gallows. Open the door and there's no going back. In the duplicate dungeons are two duplicate prisoners. One of them is you. You know, well enough, what sort of world you live in. Narrowing down the alternative worlds won't help you to decide whether to open your

---

21 The problem of the symmetric world and its asymmetric alternative is presented by Robert M. Adams in "Primitive Thisness and Primitive Identity," pages 22–23. The treatment I suggest for it is again due, in essentials, to Allen Hazen, "Counterpart-theoretic Semantics for Modal Logic."

22 In "Attitudes *De Dicto* and *De Se*."

door. Nevertheless you need to narrow down your alternative possibilities. You urgently need to know which of two alternative possible individuals – both actual, as it happens – is the real you.

This is my second argument that not all possibilities are possible worlds: alternative worlds cannot be used to characterize the whole of the informational content of perceptual experience, belief, knowledge, and other such states.

My third argument, of course, is that replacing alternative worlds by alternative possible subjects does away with the problem of cross-identifying the subject from one alternative to another, or from actuality to the alternatives. Thereby it does away with the main trouble that confronts cross-identification by acquaintance.

We did not know how to identify the subject and his acquaintances across worlds. But we don't have to do that. We have to identify them across the subject's alternatives, and those alternatives aren't worlds. They are alternative possible individuals. In the doxastic case, they're exactly those possible individuals who, according to the content of the subject's beliefs, he himself might be. They're the ones who fit his self-conception, since his self-conception consists of the properties he has throughout his doxastic alternatives. They may or may not be counterparts by description of the subject; they may or may not share his essence, which need not be part of his self-conception; so in that sense, they may or may not really be possibilities for him. We keep all the essentialism we want, but we don't let it restrict the range of doxastic alternatives.

Likewise the subject's visual alternatives are those possible individuals who, according to the content of his visual experience, he himself might be; they share just those properties that he sees himself to have. These will mostly be relational properties: properties of facing such-and-such an arrangement of nearby things. Likewise the subject's epistemic alternatives are those possible individuals who, according to the content of his knowledge, he himself might be; they share just those properties that he knows himself to have. He is one of them. Likewise, *mutatis mutandis*, for other attitudes having content that can be described by means of sets of alternatives.

We might usefully borrow some terminology usually applied to possible worlds. In the broadest sense, all possible individuals without exception, even the poached eggs, are possibilities for me. (Here we echo the extreme Haecceitist.) But some possibilities are accessible to me in various ways, others are not. My counterparts by description are *metaphysically accessible* to me; or better, each counterpart-by-description relation is a relation of metaphysical accessibility. My alternatives are *visually, perceptually, doxastically, epistemically, . . . accessible* to me. Metaphysical and (for instance) epistemic possibilities for me are not things of two different sorts. They are *possibilia* out of the same logical space. The difference is in the accessibility.

If the subject has two alternatives in a single world, we need not wonder which is the right one. That is a question to settle by stipulation: if we want to consider one of them we may, if we want to consider the other we may. We stipulate which, just as Kripke invited us to. But we are selecting among possible individuals, not among duplicate worlds that differ somehow. We are finding the subject by stipulation, sure enough. But we are not cross-identifying the subject by stipulation. Our problem of finding the subject is not, after all, a problem of cross-identification. That is why we could not find any approach to cross-identification that would solve it.

In trying to settle whether X and Y are counterparts by acquaintance for subject Z, we had come this far: taking U as the subject they are but taking V as the subject they are not. *And that is far enough.* We sought in vain for a three-place relation, asking whether X and Y were counterparts by acquaintance for subject Z. But all the while we had a four-place relation, and that is all we need for cross-identification by acquaintance. We can say it this way: *X for U is a counterpart by acquaintance of Y for Z.* (And X for V isn't.) This means that X and U are worldmates, as are Y and Z, and that the relations of acquaintance of X to U sufficiently resemble those of Y to Z. (Perhaps we also want a competitive condition: there is no rival worldmate of U whose relations of acquaintance to U resemble those of Y to Z even better.)

It is not written into the four-place counterpart relation that U is related to Z in any particular way; but in the applications we have in mind, they will be related in one or both of two ways. (1) It may be that Z himself is the subject whose state we are describing, and U is one of his alternatives. Then the four-place relation serves to cross-identify things in the subject's own world with things in the worlds of his alternatives. (2) It may be that Z and U are two of the alternatives for a certain subject. Then the four-place relation serves to cross-identify things between the worlds of different alternatives.

The worlds of different alternatives need not be different worlds, nor need they be different from the subject's own world. It may happen, then, that a thing is or isn't cross-identified by acquaintance with itself. Consider, for instance, the situation in world 2 of our example: X for U is not a counterpart by acquaintance of X for V.

A subject of attitudes can scarcely fail to be intimately acquainted with himself, and the subject's alternatives will be likewise self-acquainted. So we will have cases that are reflexive in the first two places and in the last two. Normally, perhaps invariably, when U is one of Z's alternatives, then U for U is a counterpart by acquaintance of Z for Z. It is an interesting question whether we can have reflexivity in the last two places only: T for U is a counterpart by acquaintance of Z for Z, where T and U are not identical. Such would be a case where some of Z's major channels of self-acquaintance are relations which he could have born to something other than himself: he watches himself in the mirror he mistakes for a window, he follows his own trail, or what have you. Shall we permit such cases? Or shall we rule them out, giving identity predominant weight among channels of self-acquaintance?[23] I know of no evidence that we have settled this question. Nor need we settle it; we can allow that different versions of the four-place counterpart-by-acquaintance relation go different ways.

23 This question is relevant to Hintikka's proposal, in his "On Attributions of 'Self-Knowledge,'" to represent self-knowledge using formulas that are to be interpreted using cross-identification by acquaintance. The proposal succeeds only if we do give identity predominant weight. At this point I am indebted to discussions with Mark Johnston.

23

Why conditionalize?

INTRODUCTION (1997)

This paper presents what is nowadays called the 'diachronic Dutch book argument'. I wrote it in 1972 as a handout for a course, with no thought of publication. I thought then that the argument was well-known.[1] Yet I could not find it presented in print, so I had to reconstruct it for myself. I showed my handout to Paul Teller; he presented the argument, with my permission and with full acknowledgement, in his article 'Conditionalization and Observation'.[2] Teller's article has become the standard source for the argument. But it seems to leave a question in some readers' minds: why does the argument call for conditionalizing on the subject's total increment of experiential evidence, no more and no less? Since my handout had addressed just that question, I decided there was some reason to publish it after all. Apart from a little editing to simplify notation, it appears here in its original form.

The diachronic Dutch book argument can be broken into two halves. Consider a conditional bet: that is, a bet that will be null and void unless its condition is met. We note, first, that the conditional

---

1 Hilary Putnam alludes to, but does not state, a diachronic Dutch book argument in his 'Probability and Confirmation' in *Philosophy of Science Today*, ed. by Sidney Morgenbesser (Basic Books, 1967), p. 113. He says that if one follows a certain learning rule, it can be shown 'that even if one's bets at any one time are coherent, one's total betting strategy through time will not be coherent'.

2 *Synthese* 26 (1973), pp. 218–258.

bet is equivalent in its outcome, come what may, to a certain pair of unconditional bets. We note, second, that the conditional bet is also equivalent in its outcome, come what may, to a certain contingency plan whereby one's future betting transactions are made to depend on the arrival of new evidence. The first equivalence yields a well-known synchronic argument relating the prices of conditional and unconditional bets. The second equivalence yields a diachronic argument relating the present prices of conditional bets to the future prices, after various increments of evidence, of unconditional bets. We can stitch both halves together and leave the conditional bet unmentioned; and that is the argument presented here.

Richard Jeffrey has suggested that we should respond to experiential evidence not by conditionalizing, but rather by a less extreme redistribution of degrees of belief.[3] Despite appearances, I do not disagree. He and I are considering different cases. My advice is addressed to a severely idealized, superhuman subject who runs no risk of mistaking his evidence, and who therefore can only lose if he hedges against that risk. Jeffrey's advice is addressed to a less idealized, fallible subject who has no business heeding counsels of perfection that he is unable to follow.

Similarly, it seems that we should sometimes respond to conceptual discoveries by revising our beliefs. If first you divide your belief between hypotheses H_1, H_2, H_3, and 'none of the above', and then you discover that 'none of the above' includes a hitherto unnoticed H_4 that is far nicer than the other three, you would be wise to shift some of your belief to H_4, even though you would not be conditionalizing on experiential evidence. Our ideal subject, who never changes his belief except by conditionalizing, will never do that. Is he pig-headed? No – being ideal, he has left no conceptual discoveries unmade. He made them all in his cradle. So he has no occasion to respond to new conceptual discoveries. But we, who are not so smart, would be unwise to emulate him. Some of our departures from ideal rationality are just what we need to compensate for other departures.

Note also that the point of any Dutch book argument is not that it

3 Richard C. Jeffrey, *The Logic of Decision* (McGraw-Hill, 1965; University of Chicago Press, 1983), Chapter 11.

would be imprudent to run the risk that some sneaky Dutchman will come and drain your pockets. After all, there aren't so many sneaky Dutchmen around; and anyway, if ever you see one coming, you can refuse to do business with him. Rather, the point is that if you are vulnerable to a Dutch book, whether synchronic or diachronic, that means that you have two contradictory opinions about the expected value of the very same transaction. To hold contradictory opinions may or may not be risky, but it is in any case irrational.

$$* \qquad * \qquad *$$

Suppose that at time 0, you have a coherent belief function M. Let $E_1, \ldots, E_n$ be mutually exclusive and jointly exhaustive propositions that specify, in full detail, all the alternative courses of experience you might undergo between time 0 and time 1. For each i from 1 to n, let M_i be the belief function you would have at time 1 if you had the experience specified by E_i – that is, if E_i were the true one of $E_1, \ldots, E_n$. You would *conditionalize* if, for any proposition P (in the domain of M),

$$M_i(P) \; = \; C(P/E_i) \; =^{\mathrm{df}} M(PE_i)/M(E_i)$$

Why would it be irrational to respond to experience in any other way?

Assume that your belief functions both at times 0 and 1 can be measured by your betting behavior, as follows: your degree of belief that P is the price at which you would be willing either to buy or to sell the bet [\$1 if P, 0 otherwise]. Assume also that if any betting transactions are acceptable to you, so are any sums or multiples thereof.

Suppose $M_i(P)$ is less than $C(P/E_i)$. Then I can follow this three-step plan to exploit the fact.

(1) Sell you the two bets

      [\$1 if PE_i, \$0 otherwise]
      [\$x if not-E_i, \$0 otherwise]

where $x = C(P/E_i)$, for the maximum price you will pay: *viz.* \$M(PE_i) + \$xM(not-E_i) = \$C(P/E_i).

(2) Wait and see whether E_i is true. (Thus I need to have as much

405

knowledge as you, but no more; for you also will know by time 1 whether E_i is true.)

(3) If E_i is true, buy from you at time 1 the bet

[\$1 if P, \$0 otherwise]

for the minimum price you will accept: *viz.* \$$M_i(P)$.

If E_i is false, your net loss will be \$0. If E_i is true (regardless of P) your net loss will be \$$C(P/E_i)$ − \$$M_i(P)$, which by hypothesis is positive. As a result of your failure to conditionalize, I can inflict on you a risk of loss uncompensated by any chance of gain; and I can do this without at any point using knowledge that you do not have.

Likewise if $M_i(P)$ is greater than $C(P/E_i)$ I can exploit that by the opposite plan: buy at step (1), sell at step (3).

If you can be thus exploited you are irrational; so you are rational only if you conditionalize.

Why doesn't a parallel argument work for *any* set $D_1, \ldots, D_n$ of mutually exclusive and jointly exhaustive propositions, showing that your belief function ought to evolve by conditionalization on the true one of *this* set? If $M_j(P)$ is less than $C(P/D_j)$, why can't I take advantage of this?

(1) Suppose D_j is wholly contained in (implies) some E_i, but $D_j \neq E_i$. Then to carry out my plan of exploitation, I must learn that D_j while you learn only that E_i. It proves nothing derogatory about your rationality that I can exploit you by taking advantage of my greater knowledge.

(2) If $D_j = E_i$, I can take advantage of you, but this adds nothing to the argument that you should conditionalize on the true one of $E_1, \ldots, E_n$.

(3) Otherwise D_j overlaps two or more distinct E's; thus you can distinguish two or more ways for D_j to come true, and it is not legitimate to assume that there is a *unique* new belief function M_j that you will end up with if D_j is true. We should consider separately the various belief functions determined by the different

406

distinguishable ways for D_j to be true; we thus revert to cases (1) and (2).

It has been pointed out[4] that if you fail to conditionalize, I still have no safe strategy for exploiting you unless I *know* in advance what you do instead of conditionalizing. That is: I must know whether $M_i(P)$ is less than or greater than $C(P/E_i)$. But suppose you don't know this yourself. Then I can reliably exploit you only with the aid of superior knowledge, which establishes nothing derogatory about your rationality. – Granted. But I reply that if you can't tell in advance how your beliefs would be modified by a certain course of experience, that also is a kind – a different kind – of irrationality on your part.

4 By D. Kaplan, a student at Princeton in 1972; and by Gilbert Harman.

24

What puzzling Pierre does not believe

Kripke's puzzle about belief refutes a certain simple analysis of belief sentences. This analysis fails for another reason as well, since it requires believers to have a knowledge of essences which they do not in fact possess.

THE LESSON OF PIERRE

The case of Pierre is presented by Saul Kripke. It runs as follows.[1]

Suppose Pierre is a normal French speaker who lives in France and speaks not a word of English or of any other language except French. Of course he has heard of that famous distant city, London (which he of course calls '*Londres*') though he himself has never left France. On the basis of what he has heard of London, he is inclined to think that it is pretty. So he says, in French, '*Londres est jolie.*' On the basis of his sincere French utterance, we will conclude:

(1). Pierre believes that London is pretty.

First published in *The Australasian Journal of Philosophy* 59 (1981), pp. 283–289. Reprinted with kind permission from *The Australasian Journal of Philosophy*.

I am grateful to the Australian National University for research support, and to several philosophers there and elsewhere for valuable discussion. Special thanks are due to Nathan Salmon.

1 Saul A. Kripke, 'A Puzzle about Belief', in Avishai Margalit, ed., *Meaning and Use* (Reidel, 1979). The quoted material comes from pp. 254–257, with deletions and renumbering of sentences.

Later, Pierre, through fortunate or unfortunate vicissitudes, moves to England, in fact to London itself, though to an unattractive part of the city with fairly uneducated inhabitants. He, like most of his neighbours, rarely ever leaves this part of the city. None of his neighbours knows any French, so he must learn English by 'direct method'; by talking and mixing with the people he eventually begins to pick up English. In particular, everyone speaks of the city, 'London', where they all live. Pierre learns from them everything they know about London, but there is little overlap with what he heard before. He learns, of course, to call the city he lives in 'London'. Pierre's surroundings are unattractive, and he is unimpressed with most of the rest of what he happens to see. So he is inclined to assent to the English sentence: 'London is not pretty'. Of course he does not for a moment withdraw his assent from '*Londres est jolie*'; he merely takes it for granted that the ugly city in which he is now stuck is distinct from the enchanting city he heard about in France. After Pierre lived in London for some time, he did not differ from his neighbours either in his knowledge of English or in his command of the relevant facts of local geography. Now Pierre's neighbours would surely be said to use 'London' as a name for London and to speak English. Since, as an English speaker, he does not differ at all from them, we should say the same of him. But then, on the basis of his sincere assent to 'London is not pretty', we should conclude:

(2) Pierre believes that London is not pretty.

So now it seems that we must respect both Pierre's French utterances and their English counterparts. So we must say that Pierre has contradictory beliefs. But there seem to be insuperable difficulties. We may suppose that Pierre is a leading philosopher and logician. He would *never* let contradictory beliefs pass. And surely anyone is in principle in a position to notice and correct contradictory beliefs if he has them. But it is clear that Pierre, as long as he is unaware that the cities he calls 'London' and '*Londres*' are one and the same, is in no position to see, by logic alone, that at least one of his beliefs must be false. He lacks information, not logical acumen.

(3) He cannot be convicted of inconsistency; to do so would be incorrect.

Kripke presents the case as an unsolved puzzle. His principal moral is that whatever is responsible for this puzzle may also be the source of difficulties commonly blamed on failures of substitutivity.

To solve the puzzle would be to show how (1), (2), and (3) are compatible. That would require an adequate analysis of (1) and (2) that would not represent them as ascribing inconsistent beliefs. I have no such solution to offer, in part because some of the makings of the sort of solution I might favour are not mine to present.[2]

Instead, I shall make a negative point. There is a natural and straightforward analysis of (1) and (2) that does represent them as ascribing inconsistent beliefs. The case of Pierre refutes this analysis, thus clearing the way – let us hope – for some less simple but more accurate successor. The refuted analysis consists of three parts.

(4) 'Pierre believes that F(A)', where A is an ordinary proper name and F is an easily understood predicate, ascribes to Pierre a belief whose object is the proposition (actually) expressed by 'F(A)'.

(5) This proposition holds at exactly those possible worlds where the thing which is (actually) denoted by A has the property which is (actually) expressed by F.

(6) Beliefs are jointly inconsistent if there is no possible world where their propositional objects hold true together.

Given that we accept (1), (2), and (3), as I think we clearly must, this analysis stands refuted. For 'London' is an ordinary proper name, which (actually, and in this context) denotes the city London; 'is pretty' and 'is not pretty' are easily understood predicates which (actually, and in this context) express strictly contradictory properties; so there is no possible world where anything, be it London or anything else, has the properties expressed by those two predicates.

I think the refuted analysis has been held, but let me not stop to point the finger. It surely deserves to be held, but for its failures: it is simple and plausible, and it fits perfectly into a systematic program for compositional semantics. If it did not exist, it would be necessary to invent it – and to refute it.

Several remarks before we go on. First, the refuted analysis as I stated it is limited in scope, and thereby dodges some extra problems that would plague its generalizations. Since A is an ordinary proper name, it is not a fictitious name with no actual denotation. Likewise it is not first-person or present-tensed, so we avoid problems about self-

2 I have in mind some ideas about the analysis of belief sentences suggested by Robert Stalnaker (personal communication, 1979).

descriptive belief. Since F is easily understood, it is not one of those semi-technical terms like 'elm', 'water', or 'arthritis', that are used at least somewhat competently by laymen who lack full mastery of their meanings; neither does it have any confusingly complex internal structure.

Second, the refuted analysis has variants which equally stand refuted. There is the counterpart-theoretic variant: we amend (5) to consider not worlds where the thing denoted by A is itself present to have the property expressed by F, but rather worlds where that thing has that property vicariously, through a unique counterpart which is united to it by some sort of resemblance and which stands in for it at that world.[3] (A variant permitting multiple, rather than unique, counterparts would so far escape refutation on a technicality; but would fall victim to the considerations discussed in the next section.) Thus the London of our world is vicariously pretty at a world where it does not exist, strictly speaking, if it has at that world a unique counterpart and that counterpart is pretty. Such a world might well be counted as one where the proposition (actually) expressed by 'London is pretty' holds.

Also there is the ersatz variant: we systematically replace possible worlds and individuals, and properties thereof, by stand-ins constructed entirely out of the resources of this world.[4] An ersatz variant will be counterpart-theoretic as well, unless the ersatz worlds are so constructed that London itself, for instance, always is used as the ersatz for any unactualised alternative London.

Third, notice that to refute the analysis given by (4)–(6) is not yet to refute the theory that beliefs have propositional objects, where a proposition is something fully characterised by the set of worlds where it holds. It is one question what the objects of belief are, another question how the 'that'-clause of a belief sentence specifies the object of the ascribed belief. In fact, I think the refuted analysis is wrong on

---

3 See my 'Counterpart Theory and Quantified Modal Logic', *Journal of Philosophy* **65** (1968), pp. 113–126; and *Counterfactuals* (Blackwell, 1973), pp. 39–43.
4 See, for instance, the construction of ersatz worlds in W. V. Quine, 'Propositional Objects', in his *Ontological Relativity and Other Essays* (Columbia University Press, 1969).

both points,[5] but in this paper I shall be content to show that there's something wrong with it somewhere. And there is, as witness Kripke's puzzle.

IGNORANCE OF ESSENCE

However, we do not really need the whole of the puzzle of Pierre to see that the refuted analysis goes wrong. False accusations of inconsistency between beliefs are but a symptom. The cause of the trouble can be seen even if we consider beliefs one at a time. Let us stick to the case of Pierre, and consider whether the refuted analysis accounts even for the truth of (1). I say it does not. (It likewise fails to account for the truth of (2).) Pierre does not have as an object of his belief the proposition (actually) expressed by 'London is pretty'. For there is a possible world which fits Pierre's beliefs perfectly – it is one of his 'belief worlds' – at which that proposition is false.

I have in mind a world where the beautiful city Pierre heard about was not London but Bristol. Imagine a world just like ours until fairly recently (except to the extent that it must differ to fit Pierre's misconceptions about earlier history, if any). Then the beautification of Bristol was undertaken, and at the same time it was renamed in honour of Sir Ogdred Londer. The French called this famous city *'Londres'*; they spoke often of its beauty, and all they said was true. In due course Pierre heard of the beauty of Bristol, lately called 'Londer' in England and *'Londres'* in France, and he came to assent sincerely to *'Londres est jolie'*. What happened at his end was just like what happened at the real world.

While Bristol was beautified, London fell into decay. The better parts were demolished – copies sometimes were built in Bristol, alias 'Londer' – and only the slums remained. London became ugly through and through. Also, nothing of consequence happened there. The French had little occasion to speak of the place under any name, and indeed it never was mentioned in Pierre's presence. It was to this place that the unfortunate Pierre was made to go. Again, what happened at

5 On objects of belief, but not the analysis of belief sentences, see my 'Attitudes *De Dicto* and *De Se'*, *The Philosophical Review* **88** (1979), pp. 513–543.

Pierre's end of his encounters with London was just like what happened at the real world.

This world fits Pierre's beliefs perfectly. For all that he believes, it might very well be the world he lives in. Tell him and show him all about it, claiming that it is the real world; he will never be at all surprised, unless it surprises him to find that he has turned out to be right in all his beliefs without exception. Nothing he believes – no propositional object of his belief – is false at this world.

However, the proposition (actually) expressed by 'London is pretty' according to (5), or a counterpart-theoretical or ersatz-theoretic variant thereof, is false at this world. 'London' denotes London and 'is pretty' expresses the property of being pretty, and this is a world where London, or a good counterpart or ersatz, is present and is not at all pretty.

(In a parallel way, we could find a world which fits Pierre's beliefs, but in which the proposition expressed according to (5) by 'London is not pretty' is false. We could even find a belief world for Pierre where the propositions expressed by 'London is pretty' and 'London is not pretty' both are false. Let the city he heard of in France be a beautified Bristol, renamed 'Londer' or *'Londres'*; let the city he fetches up in be a worsened Manchester, renamed 'London'; and let London itself be absent altogether.)

Therefore (4) and (5) are not both true. ((6) is not involved in this refutation.) I see no grounds for blaming the trouble on (5); I take (5) to be correct, either as it stands or when restated in terms of counterparts. The culprit is (4). The role of the 'that'-clause in a belief sentence is not, in such cases as this, to express the proposition which is the object of the ascribed belief.

The error of (4) amounts to ascribing a knowledge of essences that we may not in fact possess. Let us define the *essence* of London as that property that belongs to London at every world where it exists, and to nothing else at any world. (Or it belongs to all and only counterparts of London, or to all and only ersatz Londons.) What Pierre's belief that London is pretty is about is that which plays the role of London for him; or rather, that which plays one of the London-roles for him. It may or may not be London. If being the X is London's essence, it may or may not be the X. Having London's essence is not a prerequisite for playing the London-role. Thus Pierre does not believe that London is the X, or even that London is the X if anything is; and this despite the fact that he believes the proposition that holds at every world, and every world is a world where London is the X if anything is. Because of this ignorance, he is unable to get from his belief that London is pretty to a belief having as object the proposition that the X is pretty – or in other words, to the proposition expressed by 'London is pretty'.

OBJECTIONS AND REPLIES

Objection. Why are you entitled to assume that the so-called Bristol (or 'Londer', or *'Londres'*) of the counterexample world is not really London? *I reply*: on my view of these matters, it isn't London because there is no identity across worlds; and it isn't a counterpart of London because it isn't very much like London, and because there is a rival candidate that resembles the real London very much better. This is so if we consider location; or match of origins; or resemblance of histories; or resemblance of present geography; or even, not completely but to a sufficient degree, resemblance of landmarks. (All the ugly landmarks of London and all the pretty landmarks of Bristol remain. Although Bristol does have its copies of the Houses of Parliament and Tower Bridge and one or two more, these being the ones Pierre was shown pictures of when he was in France, they're quite poor copies – he was shown quite poor pictures.) On an opposite view, according to which there is identity across worlds and it varies quite independently of qualitative character, there are worlds of the sort I imagined where the so-called Bristol is really London, and others where it isn't. I hereby stipulate that the counterexample world is one of the latter ones. On an intermediate view, essentialist but Haecceitist, there are no qualitative conditions sufficient for identity across worlds, but match of origins is a necessary condition; and the so-called Bristol fails to satisfy this qualitative prerequisite for identity with the real London. It may or may not be the real Bristol, but London it definitely isn't. These three views seem to cover the spectrum of reasonable positions fairly well.

Objection. The so-called Bristol is a counterpart of London at least *for Pierre.* His epistemic rapport with it at the counterexample world is just like one part of his epistemic rapport with London at the real world. In this respect, the otherworldly Bristol resembles the real London. It is London if, in Jaakko Hintikka's terminology, we cross-identify by acquaintance.[6] *I reply:* yes. This is true, and relevant, and perhaps something that would figure in a satisfactory analysis of (1) and (2). But it cannot save the refuted analysis. A counterpart by acquaintance for Pierre is not a counterpart *simpliciter;* the relativity to Pierre is not provided for in (4) and (5). They are stated in terms of a sentence expressing a proposition, and our notion of expressing includes no such relativity. Other relativities, yes: to language, and to context. But not the relativity involved in cross-identification by acquaintance for Pierre.

Objection. You forget Kripke's emphatic stipulation (*op. cit.,* pp. 242 and 246) that he is speaking always of belief *de dicto*, never of belief *de re.* Given this stipulation, (1) and (2) *must* be interpreted according to (4) and (5). *I reply* that Kripke may stipulate that (1) and (2) are to be interpreted according to a certain analysis, or he may invite us to rely on our intuitions about their truth. But he cannot do both without begging the question in favour of the preferred analysis. However, it is not at all clear to me what Kripke is stipulating. The notion that ordinary language belief sentences divide into *de dicto* and *de re*, without residue or overlap, may be part of an oversimplified semantic analysis. The stipulation that (1) and (2) are not *de re* seems clearer and safer than the stipulation that they are *de dicto*; for we can support it by a parallel puzzle in which no *res* is available. (Pierre has been told in France that *'Pere Noel'* brings presents to all the children, and has been told in England that Father Christmas brings presents only to the good children. He reckons that good children get double shares.) But the stipulation that (1) and (2) are something other than *de re*, even if

---

6 See his 'The Logic of Perception', in his *Models for Modalities* (Reidel, 1969), and in Norman S. Care and Robert M. Grimm, eds., *Perception and Personal Identity* (Case Western Reserve University Press, 1969).

legitimate, is not enough by itself to settle that we must interpret them by (4) and (5).

Objection. 'Believes that' and 'believes the proposition that' are synonymous. *I reply*: maybe so. But in that case, 'believes the proposition that' must not be analysed as 'has a belief with the propositional object expressed by' (with quotation marks supplied), at least not if the latter bears the meaning I have given it in this paper.

Objection. The counterexample world is not a world that fits Pierre's beliefs. For Pierre believes that London is pretty, whereas the counterexample world is one where London is not pretty. *I reply* by posing a dilemma. When we characterise the content of belief by assigning propositional (or other) objects, are we characterising an inner, narrowly psychological state of the believer? Are beliefs in the head? Or are we characterising partly the believer's inner state, partly the relations of that state to the outer world?[7] If it is the latter, the objection may succeed; however, Kripke's puzzle vanishes. For if the assignment of propositional objects characterises more than the believer's inner state, then there is no reason to suppose that a leading philosopher and logician would never let contradictory beliefs pass, or that anyone is in principle in a position to notice and correct contradictory beliefs if he has them. Anyone is in principle in a position to notice and correct a state of the head which can be characterised by assigning contradictory propositional objects, but why should philosophical and logical acumen help him if the trouble lies partly outside? As soon as we accept the consistency of Pierre's beliefs as a datum – as I did, on Kripke's invitation – we are committed to the narrowly psychological conception of belief and its objects. (I would like to think that this was what Kripke intended in instructing us to consider belief *de dicto*.) But on the narrowly psychological conception, the counterexample world does fit Pierre's beliefs, as witness the fact that it would not at all surprise him to be persuaded that the world was just that way. To be sure, it is not a world where London is pretty. That only means that

---

7 Compare characterising perceptual experience without regard to whether it is veridical versus characterising the perceiver's accomplishments in gaining information about the world around him. I owe this comparison to John Perry.

(1) is not a narrowly psychological characterisation. Indeed not; we can see that directly. Someone might be exactly like Pierre psychologically and yet not believe that London is pretty. The Pierre-counterpart at the counterexample world is one such person. Another is an actual Pierre-counterpart on Twin Earth, long ago in a galaxy far, far away. His neighbours might say of him 'He believes that London is pretty'; but *we* have no business saying it, given what 'London' means in our mouths and given his isolation both from our London and from our 'London'. Since (1) is not a narrowly psychological characterisation of Pierre's beliefs, it is irrelevant to the question whether the counterexample world fits Pierre's beliefs on the narrowly psychological conception.

25

Elusive knowledge

We know a lot. I know what food penguins eat. I know that phones used to ring, but nowadays squeal, when someone calls up. I know that Essendon won the 1993 Grand Final. I know that here is a hand, and here is another.

We have all sorts of everyday knowledge, and we have it in abundance. To doubt that would be absurd. At any rate, to doubt it in any serious and lasting way would be absurd; and even philosophical and temporary doubt, under the influence of argument, is more than a little peculiar. It is a Moorean fact that we know a lot. It is one of those things that we know better than we know the premises of any philosophical argument to the contrary.

Besides knowing a lot that is everyday and trite, I myself think that we know a lot that is interesting and esoteric and controversial. We know a lot about things unseen: tiny particles and pervasive fields, not to mention one another's underwear. Sometimes we even know what an author meant by his writings. But on these questions, let us agree to disagree peacefully with the champions of 'post-knowledgeism'.

First published in *The Australasian Journal of Philosophy* 74 (1996), pp. 549–567. Reprinted with kind permission from *The Australasian Journal of Philosophy*.

Thanks to many for valuable discussions of this material. Thanks above all to Peter Unger; and to Stewart Cohen, Michael Devitt, Alan Hájek, Stephen Hetherington, Denis Robinson, Ernest Sosa, Robert Stalnaker, Jonathan Vogel, and a referee for *The Australasian Journal of Philosophy*. Thanks also to the Boyce Gibson Memorial Library and to Ormond College.

The most trite and ordinary parts of our knowledge will be problem enough.

For no sooner do we engage in epistemology – the systematic philosophical examination of knowledge – than we meet a compelling argument that we know next to nothing. The sceptical argument is nothing new or fancy. It is just this: it seems as if knowledge must be by definition infallible. If you claim that S knows that P, and yet you grant that S cannot eliminate a certain possibility in which not-P, it certainly seems as if you have granted that S does not after all know that P. To speak of fallible knowledge, of knowledge despite uneliminated possibilities of error, just *sounds* contradictory.

Blind Freddy can see where this will lead. Let your paranoid fantasies rip – CIA plots, hallucinogens in the tap water, conspiracies to deceive, old Nick himself – and soon you find that uneliminated possibilities of error are everywhere. Those possibilities of error are farfetched, of course, but possibilities all the same. They bite into even our most everyday knowledge. We never have infallible knowledge.

Never – well, hardly ever. Some say we have infallible knowledge of a few simple, axiomatic necessary truths; and of our own present experience. They say that I simply cannot be wrong that a part of a part of something is itself a part of that thing; or that it seems to me now (as I sit here at the keyboard) exactly as if I am hearing clicking noises on top of a steady whirring. Some say so. Others deny it. No matter; let it be granted, at least for the sake of the argument. It is not nearly enough. If we have only that much infallible knowledge, yet knowledge is by definition infallible, then we have very little knowledge indeed – not the abundant everyday knowledge we thought we had. That is still absurd.

So we know a lot; knowledge must be infallible; yet we have fallible knowledge or none (or next to none). We are caught between the rock of fallibilism and the whirlpool of scepticism. Both are mad!

Yet fallibilism is the less intrusive madness. It demands less frequent corrections of what we want to say. So, if forced to choose, I choose fallibilism. (And so say all of us.) We can get used to it, and some of us have done. No joy there – we know that people can get used to the most crazy philosophical sayings imaginable. If you are a contented fallibilist, I implore you to be honest, be naive, hear it afresh. 'He knows, yet he has not eliminated all possibilities of error.' Even if you've numbed your ears, doesn't this overt, explicit fallibilism *still* sound wrong?

Better fallibilism than scepticism; but it would be better still to dodge the choice. I think we can. We will be alarmingly close to the rock, and also alarmingly close to the whirlpool, but if we steer with care, we can – just barely – escape them both.

Maybe epistemology is the culprit. Maybe this extraordinary pastime robs us of our knowledge. Maybe we do know a lot in daily life; but maybe when we look hard at our knowledge, it goes away. But only when we look at it harder than the sane ever do in daily life; only when we let our paranoid fantasies rip. That is when we are forced to admit that there always are uneliminated possibilities of error, so that we have fallible knowledge or none.

Much that we say is context-dependent, in simple ways or subtle ways. Simple: 'it's evening' is truly said when, and only when, it is said in the evening. Subtle: it could well be true, and not just by luck, that Essendon played rottenly, the Easybeats played brilliantly, yet Essendon won. Different contexts evoke different standards of evaluation. Talking about the Easybeats we apply lax standards, else we could scarcely distinguish their better days from their worse ones. In talking about Essendon, no such laxity is required. Essendon won because play that is rotten by demanding standards suffices to beat play that is brilliant by lax standards.

Maybe ascriptions of knowledge are subtly context-dependent, and maybe epistemology is a context that makes them go false. Then epistemology would be an investigation that destroys its own subject matter. If so, the sceptical argument might be flawless, when we engage in epistemology – and only then![1]

---

1 The suggestion that ascriptions of knowledge go false in the context of epistemology is to be found in Barry Stroud, 'Understanding Human Knowledge in General' in Marjorie Clay and Keith Lehrer (eds.), *Knowledge and Skepticism* (Boulder: Westview Press, 1989); and in Stephen Hetherington, 'Lacking Knowledge and Justification by Theorising About Them' (lecture at the University of New South Wales, August

If you start from the ancient idea that justification is the mark that distinguishes knowledge from mere opinion (even true opinion), then you well might conclude that ascriptions of knowledge are context-dependent because standards for adequate justification are context-dependent. As follows: opinion, even if true, deserves the name of knowledge only if it is adequately supported by reasons; to deserve that name in the especially demanding context of epistemology, the arguments from supporting reasons must be especially watertight; but the special standards of justification that this special context demands never can be met (well, hardly ever). In the strict context of epistemology we know nothing, yet in laxer contexts we know a lot.

But I myself cannot subscribe to this account of the context-dependence of knowledge, because I question its starting point. I don't agree that the mark of knowledge is justification.[2] First, because justification is not sufficient: your true opinion that you will lose the lottery isn't knowledge, whatever the odds. Suppose you know that it is a fair lottery with one winning ticket and many losing tickets, and you know how many losing tickets there are. The greater the number of losing tickets, the better is your justification for believing you will lose. Yet there is no number great enough to transform your fallible opinion into knowledge – after all, you just might win. No justification is good enough – or none short of a watertight deductive argument, and all but the sceptics will agree that this is too much to demand.[3]

Second, because justification is not always necessary. What (non-circular) argument supports our reliance on perception, on memory,

1992). Neither of them tells the story just as I do, however it may be that their versions do not conflict with mine.

2 Unless, like some, we simply define 'justification' as 'whatever it takes to turn true opinion into knowledge' regardless of whether what it takes turns out to involve argument from supporting reasons.

3 The problem of the lottery was introduced in Henry Kyburg, *Probability and the Logic of Rational Belief* (Middletown, CT: Wesleyan University Press, 1961), and in Carl Hempel, 'Deductive-Nomological vs. Statistical Explanation' in Herbert Feigl and Grover Maxwell (eds.), *Minnesota Studies in the Philosophy of Science*, Vol. II (Minneapolis: University of Minnesota Press, 1962). It has been much discussed since, as a problem both about knowledge and about our everyday, non-quantitative concept of belief.

and on testimony?[4] And yet we do gain knowledge by these means. And sometimes, far from having supporting arguments, we don't even know how we know. We once had evidence, drew conclusions, and thereby gained knowledge; now we have forgotten our reasons, yet still we retain our knowledge. Or we know the name that goes with the face, or the sex of the chicken, by relying on subtle visual cues, without knowing what those cues may be.

The link between knowledge and justification must be broken. But if we break that link, then it is not – or not entirely, or not exactly – by raising the standards of justification that epistemology destroys knowledge. I need some different story.

To that end, I propose to take the infallibility of knowledge as my starting point.[5] Must infallibilist epistemology end in scepticism? Not quite. Wait and see. Anyway, here is the definition. Subject S *knows* proposition P iff P holds in every possibility left uneliminated by S's evidence; equivalently, iff S's evidence eliminates every possibility in which not-P.

The definition is short, the commentary upon it is longer. In the first place, there is the proposition, P. What I choose to call 'propositions' are individuated coarsely, by necessary equivalence. For instance, there is only one necessary proposition. It holds in every possibility; hence in every possibility left uneliminated by S's evidence, no matter who S may be and no matter what his evidence may be. So the necessary proposition is known always and everywhere. Yet this known proposition may go unrecognised when presented in impenetrable linguistic disguise, say as the proposition that every even number is the sum of two primes. Likewise, the known proposition that I have two hands may go unrecognised when presented as the proposition that the number of my hands is the least number n such that every even number is the sum of n primes. (Or if you doubt the necessary existence of numbers, switch to an example involving equiv-

---

4 The case of testimony is less discussed than the others; but see C. A. J. Coady, *Testimony: A Philosophical Study* (Oxford: Clarendon Press, 1992) pp. 79–129.

5 I follow Peter Unger, *Ignorance: A Case for Skepticism* (New York: Oxford University Press, 1975). But I shall not let him lead me into scepticism.

alence by logic alone.) These problems of disguise shall not concern us here. Our topic is modal, not hyperintensional, epistemology.[6]

Next, there are the possibilities. We needn't enter here into the question whether these are concreta, abstract constructions, or abstract simples. Further, we needn't decide whether they must always be maximally specific possibilities, or whether they need only be specific enough for the purpose at hand. A possibility will be specific enough if it cannot be split into subcases in such a way that anything we have said about possibilities, or anything we are going to say before we are done, applies to some subcases and not to others. For instance, it should never happen that proposition P holds in some but not all sub-cases; or that some but not all sub-cases are eliminated by S's evidence.

But we do need to stipulate that they are not just possibilities as to how the whole world is; they also include possibilities as to which part of the world is oneself, and as to when it now is. We need these possibilities *de se et nunc* because the propositions that may be known include propositions *de se et nunc*.[7] Not only do I know that there are hands in this world somewhere and somewhen. I know that *I* have hands, or anyway I have them *now*. Such propositions aren't just made true or made false by the whole world once and for all. They are true for some of us and not for others, or true at some times and not others, or both.

Further, we cannot limit ourselves to 'real' possibilities that conform to the actual laws of nature, and maybe also to actual past history. For propositions about laws and history are contingent, and may or may not be known.

Neither can we limit ourselves to 'epistemic' possibilities for S – possibilities that S does not know not to obtain. That would drain our definition of content. Assume only that knowledge is closed under strict implication. (We shall consider the merits of this assumption later.) Remember that we are not distinguishing between equivalent

---

6 See Robert Stalnaker, *Inquiry* (Cambridge, MA: MIT Press, 1984) pp. 59–99.

7 See my 'Attitudes *De Dicto* and *De Se*', *The Philosophical Review* 88 (1979) pp. 513–543; and R. M. Chisholm, 'The Indirect Reflexive' in C. Diamond and J. Teichman (eds.), *Intention and Intentionality: Essays in Honour of G. E. M. Anscombe* (Brighton: Harvester, 1979).

propositions. Then knowledge of a conjunction is equivalent to knowledge of every conjunct. *P* is the conjunction of all propositions not-*W*, where *W* is a possibility in which not-*P*. That suffices to yield an equivalence: *S* knows that *P* iff, for every possibility *W* in which not-*P*, *S* knows that not-*W*. Contraposing and cancelling a double negation: iff every possibility which *S* does not know not to obtain is one in which *P*. For short: iff *P* holds throughout *S*'s epistemic possibilities. Yet to get this far, we need no substantive definition of knowledge at all! To turn this into a substantive definition, in fact the very definition we gave before, we need to say one more thing: *S*'s epistemic possibilities are just those possibilities that are uneliminated by *S*'s evidence.

So, next, we need to say what it means for a possibility to be eliminated or not. Here I say that the uneliminated possibilities are those in which the subject's entire perceptual experience and memory are just as they actually are. There is one possibility that actually obtains (for the subject and at the time in question); call it *actuality*. Then a possibility *W* is *uneliminated* iff the subject's perceptual experience and memory in *W* exactly match his perceptual experience and memory in actuality. (If you want to include other alleged forms of basic evidence, such as the evidence of our extrasensory faculties, or an innate disposition to believe in God, be my guest. If they exist, they should be included. If not, no harm done if we have included them conditionally.)

Note well that we do not need the 'pure sense-datum language' and the 'incorrigible protocol statements' that for so long bedevilled foundationalist epistemology. It matters not at all whether there are words to capture the subject's perceptual and memory evidence, nothing more and nothing less. If there are such words, it matters not at all whether the subject can hit upon them. The given does not consist of basic axioms to serve as premises in subsequent arguments. Rather, it consists of a match between possibilities.

When perceptual experience *E* (or memory) eliminates a possibility *W*, that is not because the propositional content of the experience conflicts with *W*. (Not even if it is the narrow content.) The propositional content of our experience could, after all, be false. Rather, it is the existence of the experience that conflicts with *W*: *W* is a possibility in which the subject is not having experience *E*. Else we would need to tell some fishy story of how the experience has some sort of infallible, ineffable, purely phenomenal propositional content. . . . Who needs that? Let E have propositional content P. Suppose even – something I take to be an open question – that E is, in some sense, fully characterized by P. Then I say that E eliminates W iff W is a possibility in which the subject's experience or memory has content different from P. I do *not* say that E eliminates W iff W is a possibility in which P is false.

Maybe not every kind of sense perception yields experience; maybe, for instance, the kinaesthetic sense yields not its own distinctive sort of sense-experience but only spontaneous judgements about the position of one's limbs. If this is true, then the thing to say is that kinaesthetic evidence eliminates all possibilities except those that exactly resemble actuality with respect to the subject's spontaneous kinaesthetic judgements. In saying this, we would treat kinaesthetic evidence more on the model of memory than on the model of more typical senses.

Finally, we must attend to the word 'every'. What does it mean to say that every possibility in which not-P is eliminated? An idiom of quantification, like 'every', is normally restricted to some limited domain. If I say that every glass is empty, so it's time for another round, doubtless I and my audience are ignoring most of all the glasses there are in the whole wide world throughout all of time. They are outside the domain. They are irrelevant to the truth of what was said.

Likewise, if I say that every uneliminated possibility is one in which P, or words to that effect, I am doubtless ignoring some of all the uneliminated alternative possibilities that there are. They are outside the domain, they are irrelevant to the truth of what was said.

But, of course, I am not entitled to ignore just any possibility I please. Else true ascriptions of knowledge, whether to myself or to others, would be cheap indeed. I may properly ignore some uneliminated possibilities; I may not properly ignore others. Our definition of knowledge requires a *sotto voce* proviso. *S knows* that P iff S's evidence eliminates every possibility in which not-P – Psst! – except for those possibilities that we are properly ignoring.

Unger suggests an instructive parallel.[8] Just as P is known iff there are no uneliminated possibilities of error, so likewise a surface is flat

8 Peter Unger, *Ignorance*, chapter II. I discuss the case, and briefly foreshadow the

iff there are no bumps on it. We must add the proviso: Psst! – except for those bumps that we are properly ignoring. Else we will conclude, absurdly, that nothing is flat. (Simplify by ignoring departures from flatness that consist of gentle curvature.)

We can restate the definition. Say that we *presuppose* proposition Q iff we ignore all possibilities in which not-Q. To close the circle: we *ignore* just those possibilities that falsify our presuppositions. *Proper* presupposition corresponds, of course, to proper ignoring. Then S knows that P iff S's evidence eliminates every possibility in which not-P – Psst! – except for those possibilities that conflict with our proper presuppositions.[9]

The rest of (modal) epistemology examines the *sotto voce* proviso. It asks: what may we properly presuppose in our ascriptions of knowledge? Which of all the unelimated alternative possibilities may not properly be ignored? Which ones are the 'relevant alternatives'? – relevant, that is, to what the subject does and doesn't know?[10] In reply, we can list several rules.[11] We begin with three prohibitions: rules to tell us what possibilities we may not properly ignore.

First, there is the *Rule of Actuality*. The possibility that actually obtains is never properly ignored; actuality is always a relevant alternative;

present paper, in my 'Scorekeeping in a Language Game', *Journal of Philosophical Logic* 8 (1979) pp. 339–359, esp. pp. 353–355.

9 See Robert Stalnaker, 'Presuppositions', *Journal of Philosophical Logic* 2 (1973) pp. 447–457; and 'Pragmatic Presuppositions' in Milton Munitz and Peter Unger (eds.), *Semantics and Philosophy* (New York: New York University Press, 1974). See also my 'Scorekeeping in a Language Game'.

The definition restated in terms of presupposition resembles the treatment of knowledge in Kenneth S. Ferguson, *Philosophical Scepticism* (Cornell University doctoral dissertation, 1980).

10 See Fred Dretske, 'Epistemic Operators', *The Journal of Philosophy* 67 (1970) pp. 1007–1022, and 'The Pragmatic Dimension of Knowledge', *Philosophical Studies* 40 (1981) pp. 363–378; Alvin Goldman, 'Discrimination and Perceptual Knowledge', *The Journal of Philosophy* 73 (1976) pp. 771–791; G. C. Stine, 'Skepticism, Relevant Alternatives, and Deductive Closure', *Philosophical Studies* 29 (1976) pp. 249–261; and Stewart Cohen, 'How to be A Fallibilist', *Philosophical Perspectives* 2 (1988) pp. 91–123.

11 Some of them, but only some, taken from the authors just cited.

nothing false may properly be presupposed. It follows that only what is true is known, wherefore we did not have to include truth in our definition of knowledge. The rule is 'externalist' – the subject himself may not be able to tell what is properly ignored. In judging which of his ignorings are proper, hence what he knows, we judge his success in knowing – not how well he tried.

When the Rule of Actuality tells us that actuality may never be properly ignored, we can ask: *whose* actuality? Ours, when we ascribe knowledge or ignorance to others? Or the subject's? In simple cases, the question is silly. (In fact, it sounds like the sort of pernicious nonsense we would expect from someone who mixes up what is true with what is believed.) There is just one actual world, we the ascribers live in that world, the subject lives there too, so the subject's actuality is the same as ours.

But there are other cases, less simple, in which the question makes perfect sense and needs an answer. Someone may or may not know who he is; someone may or may not know what time it is. Therefore I insisted that the propositions that may be known must include propositions *de se et nunc;* and likewise that the possibilities that may be eliminated or ignored must include possibilities *de se et nunc.* Now we have a good sense in which the subject's actuality may be different from ours. I ask today what Fred knew yesterday. In particular, did he then know who he was? Did he know what day it was? Fred's actuality is the possibility *de se et nunc* of being Fred on September 19th at such-and-such possible world; whereas my actuality is the possibility *de se et nunc* of being David on September 20th at such-and-such world. So far as the world goes, there is no difference: Fred and I are worldmates, his actual world is the same as mine. But when we build subject and time into the possibilities *de se et nunc*, then his actuality yesterday does indeed differ from mine today.

What is more, we sometimes have occasion to ascribe knowledge to those who are off at other possible worlds. I didn't read the newspaper yesterday. What would I have known if I had read it? More than I do in fact know. (More and less: I do in fact know that I left the newspaper unread, but if I had read it, I would not have known that I had left it unread.) I-who-did-not-read-the-newspaper am here at this world, ascribing knowledge and ignorance. The subject to whom I am ascribing that knowledge and ignorance, namely I-as-I-would-have-been-if-I-had-read-the-newspaper, is at a different world. The worlds differ in respect at least of a reading of the newspaper. Thus the ascriber's actual world is not the same as the subject's. (I myself think that the ascriber and the subject are two different people: the subject is the ascriber's otherworldly counterpart. But even if you think the subject and the ascriber are the same identical person, you must still grant that this person's actuality *qua* subject differs from his actuality *qua* ascriber.)

Or suppose we ask modal questions about the subject: what must he have known, what might he have known? Again we are considering the subject as he is not here, but off at other possible worlds. Likewise if we ask questions about knowledge of knowledge: what does he (or what do we) know that he knows?

So the question 'whose actuality?' is not a silly question after all. And when the question matters, as it does in the cases just considered, the right answer is that it is the subject's actuality, not the ascriber's, that never can be properly ignored.

Next, there is the *Rule of Belief*. A possibility that the subject believes to obtain is not properly ignored, whether or not he is right to so believe. Neither is one that he ought to believe to obtain – one that evidence and arguments justify him in believing – whether or not he does so believe.

That is rough. Since belief admits of degree, and since some possibilities are more specific than others, we ought to reformulate the rule in terms of degree of belief, compared to a standard set by the unspecificity of the possibility in question. A possibility may not be properly ignored if the subject gives it, or ought to give it, a degree of belief that is sufficiently high, and high not just because the possibility in question is unspecific.

How high is 'sufficiently high'? That may depend on how much is at stake. When error would be especially disastrous, few possibilities may be properly ignored. Then even quite a low degree of belief may be 'sufficiently high' to bring the Rule of Belief into play. The jurors know that the accused is guilty only if his guilt has been proved beyond reasonable doubt.[12]

Yet even when the stakes are high, some possibilities still may be properly ignored. Disastrous though it would be to convict an innocent man, still the jurors may properly ignore the possibility that it was the dog, marvellously well-trained, that fired the fatal shot. And, unless they are ignoring other alternatives more relevant than that, they may rightly be said to know that the accused is guilty as charged. Yet if there had been reason to give the dog hypothesis a slightly less negligible degree of belief – if the world's greatest dog-trainer had been the victim's mortal enemy – then the alternative would be relevant after all.

This is the only place where belief and justification enter my story. As already noted, I allow justified true belief without knowledge, as in the case of your belief that you will lose the lottery. I allow knowledge without justification, in the cases of face recognition and chicken sexing. I even allow knowledge without belief, as in the case of the timid student who knows the answer but has no confidence that he has it right, and so does not believe what he knows.[13] Therefore any proposed converse to the Rule of Belief should be rejected. A possibility that the subject does not believe to a sufficient degree, and ought not to believe to a sufficient degree, may nevertheless be a relevant alternative and not properly ignored.

Next, there is the *Rule of Resemblance*. Suppose one possibility saliently resembles another. Then if one of them may not be properly ignored, neither may the other. (Or rather, we should say that if one of them may not properly be ignored *in virtue of rules other than this rule*, then neither may the other. Else nothing could be properly ignored; because enough little steps of resemblance can take us from anywhere to any-

---

12 Instead of complicating the Rule of Belief as I have just done, I might equivalently have introduced a separate Rule of High Stakes saying that when error would be especially disastrous, few possibilities are properly ignored.

13 A. D. Woozley, 'Knowing and Not Knowing', *Proceedings of the Aristotelian Society* 53 (1953) pp. 151–172; Colin Radford, 'Knowledge – by Examples', *Analysis* 27 (1966) pp. 1–11.

where.) Or suppose one possibility saliently resembles two or more others, one in one respect and another in another, and suppose that each of these may not properly be ignored (in virtue of rules other than this rule). Then these resemblances may have an additive effect, doing more together than any one of them would separately.

We must apply the Rule of Resemblance with care. Actuality is a possibility uneliminated by the subject's evidence. Any other possibility W that is likewise uneliminated by the subject's evidence thereby resembles actuality in one salient respect: namely, in respect of the subject's evidence. That will be so even if W is in other respects very dissimilar to actuality – even if, for instance, it is a possibility in which the subject is radically deceived by a demon. Plainly, we dare not apply the Rules of Actuality and Resemblance to conclude that any such W is a relevant alternative – that would be capitulation to scepticism. The Rule of Resemblance was never meant to apply to *this* resemblance! We seem to have an *ad hoc* exception to the Rule, though one that makes good sense in view of the function of attributions of knowledge. What would be better, though, would be to find a way to reformulate the Rule so as to get the needed exception without *ad hoc*ery. I do not know how to do this.

It is the Rule of Resemblance that explains why you do not know that you will lose the lottery, no matter what the odds are against you and no matter how sure you should therefore be that you will lose. For every ticket, there is the possibility that it will win. These possibilities are saliently similar to one another: so either every one of them may be properly ignored, or else none may. But one of them may not properly be ignored: the one that actually obtains.

The Rule of Resemblance also is the rule that solves the Gettier problems: other cases of justified true belief that are not knowledge.[14]

14 See Edmund Gettier, 'Is Justified True Belief Knowledge?', *Analysis* 23 (1963) pp. 121–123. Diagnoses have varied widely. The four examples below come from: (1) Keith Lehrer and Thomas Paxson Jr., 'Knowledge: Undefeated True Belief', *The Journal of Philosophy* 66 (1969) pp. 225–237; (2) Bertrand Russell, *Human Knowledge: Its Scope and Limits* (London: Allen and Unwin, 1948) p. 154; (3) Alvin Goldman, 'Discrimination and Perceptual Knowledge', op. cit.; (4) Gilbert Harman, *Thought* (Princeton, NJ: Princeton University Press, 1973) p. 143.

Though the lottery problem is another case of justified true belief without

(1) I think that Nogot owns a Ford, because I have seen him driving one; but unbeknownst to me he does not own the Ford he drives, or any other Ford. Unbeknownst to me, Havit does own a Ford, though I have no reason to think so because he never drives it, and in fact I have often seen him taking the tram. My justified true belief is that one of the two owns a Ford. But I do not know it; I am right by accident. Diagnosis: I do not know, because I have not eliminated the possibility that Nogot drives a Ford he does not own whereas Havit neither drives nor owns a car. This possibility may not properly be ignored. Because, first, actuality may not properly be ignored; and, second, this possibility saliently resembles actuality. It resembles actuality perfectly so far as Nogot is concerned; and it resembles actuality well so far as Havit is concerned, since it matches actuality both with respect to Havit's carless habits and with respect to the general correlation between carless habits and carlessness. In addition, this possibility saliently resembles a third possibility: one in which Nogot drives a Ford he owns while Havit neither drives nor owns a car. This third possibility may not properly be ignored, because of the degree to which it is believed. This time, the resemblance is perfect so far as Havit is concerned, rather good so far as Nogot is concerned.

(2) The stopped clock is right twice a day. It says 4:39, as it has done for weeks. I look at it at 4:39; by luck I pick up a true belief. I have ignored the uneliminated possibility that I looked at it at 4:22 while it was stopped saying 4:39. That possibility was not properly ignored. It resembles actuality perfectly so far as the stopped clock goes.

(3) Unbeknownst to me, I am travelling in the land of the bogus barns; but my eye falls on one of the few real ones. I don't know that I am seeing a barn, because I may not properly ignore the possibility that I am seeing yet another of the abundant bogus barns. This possibility saliently resembles actuality in respect of the abundance of bogus barns, and the scarcity of real ones, hereabouts.

(4) Donald is in San Francisco, just as I have every reason to think he is. But, bent on deception, he is writing me letters and having them posted to me by his accomplice in Italy. If I had seen the phoney

knowledge, it is not normally counted among the Gettier problems. It is interesting to find that it yields to the same remedy.

letters, with their Italian stamps and postmarks, I would have concluded that Donald was in Italy. Luckily, I have not yet seen any of them. I ignore the uneliminated possibility that Donald has gone to Italy and is sending me letters from there. But this possibility is not properly ignored, because it resembles actuality both with respect to the fact that the letters are coming to me from Italy and with respect to the fact that those letters come, ultimately, from Donald. So I don't know that Donald is in San Francisco.

Next, there is the *Rule of Reliability*. This time, we have a presumptive rule about what *may* be properly ignored; and it is by means of this rule that we capture what is right about causal or reliabilist theories of knowing. Consider processes whereby information is transmitted to us: perception, memory, and testimony. These processes are fairly reliable.[15] Within limits, we are entitled to take them for granted. We may properly presuppose that they work without a glitch in the case under consideration. Defeasibly – *very* defeasibly! – a possibility in which they fail may properly be ignored.

My visual experience, for instance, depends causally on the scene before my eyes, and what I believe about the scene before my eyes depends in turn on my visual experience. Each dependence covers a wide and varied range of alternatives.[16] Of course, it is possible to hallucinate – even to hallucinate in such a way that all my perceptual experience and memory would be just as they actually are. That possibility never can be eliminated. But it can be ignored. And if it is properly ignored – as it mostly is – then vision gives me knowledge. Sometimes, though, the possibility of hallucination is not properly ignored; for sometimes we really do hallucinate. The Rule of Reliability may be defeated by the Rule of Actuality. Or it may be defeated by the Rules of Actuality and of Resemblance working together, in a

---

15 See Alvin Goldman, 'A Causal Theory of Knowing', *The Journal of Philosophy* 64 (1967) pp. 357–372; D. M. Armstrong, *Belief, Truth and Knowledge* (Cambridge: Cambridge University Press, 1973).

16 See my 'Veridical Hallucination and Prosthetic Vision', *Australasian Journal of Philosophy* 58 (1980) pp. 239–249. John Bigelow has proposed to model knowledge-delivering processes generally on those found in vision.

Gettier problem: if I am not hallucinating, but unbeknownst to me I live in a world where people mostly do hallucinate and I myself have only narrowly escaped, then the uneliminated possibility of hallucination is too close to actuality to be properly ignored.

We do not, of course, presuppose that nowhere ever is there a failure of, say, vision. The general presupposition that vision is reliable consists, rather, of a standing disposition to presuppose, concerning whatever particular case may be under consideration, that we have no failure in that case.

In similar fashion, we have two permissive *Rules of Method*. We are entitled to presuppose – again, very defeasibly – that a sample is representative; and that the best explanation of our evidence is the true explanation. That is, we are entitled properly to ignore possible failures in these two standard methods of non-deductive inference. Again, the general rule consists of a standing disposition to presuppose reliability in whatever particular case may come before us.

Yet another permissive rule is the *Rule of Conservatism*. Suppose that those around us normally do ignore certain possibilities, and it is common knowledge that they do. (They do, they expect each other to, they expect each other to expect each other to, . . .) Then – again, very defeasibly! – these generally ignored possibilities may properly be ignored. We are permitted, defeasibly, to adopt the usual and mutually expected presuppositions of those around us.

(It is unclear whether we need all four of these permissive rules. Some might be subsumed under others. Perhaps our habits of treating samples as representative, and of inferring to the best explanation, might count as normally reliable processes of transmission of information. Or perhaps we might subsume the Rule of Reliability under the Rule of Conservatism, on the ground that the reliable processes whereby we gain knowledge are familiar, are generally relied upon, and so are generally presupposed to be normally reliable. Then the only extra work done by the Rule of Reliability would be to cover less familiar – and merely hypothetical? – reliable processes, such as processes that relied on extrasensory faculties. Likewise, *mutatis mutandis*, we might subsume the Rules of Method under the Rule of Conservatism. Or we might instead think to subsume the Rule of Conservatism under the Rule of Reliability, on the ground that what is generally presupposed tends for the most part to be true, and the reliable processes whereby this is so are covered already by the Rule of Reliability. Better redundancy than incompleteness, though. So, leaving the question of redundancy open, I list all four rules.)

Our final rule is the *Rule of Attention*. But it is more a triviality than a rule. When we say that a possibility is properly ignored, we mean exactly that; we do not mean that it *could have been* properly ignored. Accordingly, a possibility not ignored at all is *ipso facto* not properly ignored. What is and what is not being ignored is a feature of the particular conversational context. No matter how far-fetched a certain possibility may be, no matter how properly we might have ignored it in some other context, if in *this* context we are not in fact ignoring it but attending to it, then for us now it is a relevant alternative. It is in the contextually determined domain. If it is an uneliminated possibility in which not-*P*, then it will do as a counter-example to the claim that *P* holds in every possibility left uneliminated by *S*'s evidence. That is, it will do as a counter-example to the claim that *S* knows that *P*.

Do some epistemology. Let your fantasies rip. Find uneliminated possibilities of error everywhere. Now that you are attending to them, just as I told you to, you are no longer ignoring them, properly or otherwise. So you have landed in a context with an enormously rich domain of potential counter-examples to ascriptions of knowledge. In such an extraordinary context, with such a rich domain, it never can happen (well, hardly ever) that an ascription of knowledge is true. Not an ascription of knowledge to yourself (either to your present self or to your earlier self, untainted by epistemology); and not an ascription of knowledge to others. That is how epistemology destroys knowledge. But it does so only temporarily. The pastime of epistemology does not plunge us forevermore into its special context. We can still do a lot of proper ignoring, a lot of knowing, and a lot of true ascribing of knowledge to ourselves and others, the rest of the time.

What is epistemology all about? The epistemology we've just been doing, at any rate, soon became an investigation of the ignoring of possibilities. But to investigate the ignoring of them was *ipso facto* not to ignore them. Unless this investigation of ours was an altogether atypical sample of epistemology, it will be inevitable that epistemology must destroy knowledge. That is how knowledge is elusive. Examine it, and straightway it vanishes.

Is resistance useless? If you bring some hitherto ignored possibility to our attention, then straightway we are not ignoring it at all, so *a fortiori* we are not properly ignoring it. How can this alteration of our conversational state be undone? If you are persistent, perhaps it cannot be undone – at least not so long as you are around. Even if we go off and play backgammon, and afterward start our conversation afresh, you might turn up and call our attention to it all over again.

But maybe you called attention to the hitherto ignored possibility by mistake. You only suggested that we ought to suspect the butler because you mistakenly thought him to have a criminal record. Now that you know he does not – that was the *previous* butler – you wish you had not mentioned him at all. You know as well as we do that continued attention to the possibility you brought up impedes our shared conversational purposes. Indeed, it may be common knowledge between you and us that we would all prefer it if this possibility could be dismissed from our attention. In that case we might quickly strike a tacit agreement to speak just as if we were ignoring it; and after just a little of that, doubtless it really would be ignored.

Sometimes our conversational purposes are not altogether shared, and it is a matter of conflict whether attention to some far-fetched possibility would advance them or impede them. What if some far-fetched possibility is called to our attention not by a sceptical philosopher, but by counsel for the defence? We of the jury may wish to ignore it, and wish it had not been mentioned. If we ignored it now, we would bend the rules of cooperative conversation; but we may have good reason to do exactly that. (After all, what matters most to us as jurors is not whether we can truly be said to know; what really matters is what we should believe to what degree, and whether or not we should vote to convict.) We would ignore the far-fetched possibility if we could – but can we? Perhaps at first our attempted ignoring would be make-believe ignoring, or self-deceptive ignoring; later, perhaps, it might ripen into genuine ignoring. But in the meantime, do we know? There may be no definite answer. We are bending the rules, and our practices of context-dependent attributions of knowledge were made for contexts with the rules unbent.

If you are still a contented fallibilist, despite my plea to hear the sceptical argument afresh, you will probably be discontented with the Rule of Attention. You will begrudge the sceptic even his very temporary victory. You will claim the right to resist his argument not only in everyday contexts, but even in those peculiar contexts in which he (or some other epistemologist) busily calls your attention to far-fetched possibilities of error. Further, you will claim the right to resist without having to bend any rules of cooperative conversation. I said that the Rule of Attention was a triviality: that which is not ignored at all is not properly ignored. But the Rule was trivial only because of how I had already chosen to state the *sotto voce* proviso. So you, the contented fallibilist, will think it ought to have been stated differently. Thus, perhaps: 'Psst! – except for those possibilities we *could* properly have ignored'. And then you will insist that those far-fetched possibilities of error that we attend to at the behest of the sceptic are nevertheless possibilities we could properly have ignored. You will say that no amount of attention can, by itself, turn them into relevant alternatives.

If you say this, we have reached a standoff. I started with a puzzle: how can it be, when his conclusion is so silly, that the sceptic's argument is so irresistible? My Rule of Attention, and the version of the proviso that made that Rule trivial, were built to explain how the sceptic manages to sway us – why his argument seems irresistible, however temporarily. If you continue to find it eminently resistible in all contexts, you have no need of any such explanation. We just disagree about the explanandum phenomenon.

I say S knows that P iff P holds in every possibility left uneliminated by S's evidence – Psst! – except for those possibilities that *we* are properly ignoring. 'We' means: the speaker and hearers of a given context; that is, those of us who are discussing S's knowledge together. It is our ignorings, not S's own ignorings, that matter to what we can truly say about S's knowledge. When we are talking about our own knowledge or ignorance, as epistemologists so often do, this is a distinction without a difference. But what if we are talking about someone else?

Suppose we are detectives; the crucial question for our solution of the crime is whether S already *knew*, when he bought the gun, that he was vulnerable to blackmail. We conclude that he did. *We* ignore various far-fetched possibilities, as hard-headed detectives should. But S does not ignore them. S is by profession a sceptical epistemologist. He never ignores much of anything. If it is our own ignorings that matter to the truth of our conclusion, we may well be right that S already knew. But if it is S's ignorings that matter, then we are wrong, because S never knew much of anything. I say we may well be right; so it is our own ignorings that matter, not S's.

But suppose instead that we are epistemologists considering what S knows. If we are well-informed about S (or if we are considering a well-enough specified hypothetical case), then if S attends to a certain possibility, we attend to S's attending to it. But to attend to S's attending to it is *ipso facto* to attend to it ourselves. In that case, unlike the case of the detectives, the possibilities we are properly ignoring must be among the possibilities that S himself ignores. We may ignore fewer possibilities than S does, but not more.

Even if S himself is neither sceptical nor an epistemologist, he may yet be clever at thinking up far-fetched possibilities that are uneliminated by his evidence. Then again, we well-informed epistemologists who ask what S knows will have to attend to the possibilities that S thinks up. Even if S's idle cleverness does not lead S himself to draw sceptical conclusions, it nevertheless limits the knowledge that we can truly ascribe to him when attentive to his state of mind. More simply: his cleverness limits his knowledge. He would have known more, had he been less imaginative.[17]

Do I claim you can know *P* just by presupposing it?! Do I claim you can know that a possibility *W* does not obtain just by ignoring it? Is that not what my analysis implies, provided that the presupposing and

---

17 See Catherine Elgin, 'The Epistemic Efficacy of Stupidity', *Synthese* 74 (1988) pp. 297–311. The 'efficacy' takes many forms; some to do with knowledge (under various rival analyses), some to do with justified belief. See also Michael Williams, *Unnatural Doubts: Epistemological Realism and the Basis of Scepticism* (Oxford: Blackwell, 1991) pp. 352–355, on the instability of knowledge under reflection.

the ignoring are proper? Well, yes. And yet I do not claim it. Or rather, I do not claim it for any specified P or W. I have to grant, in general, that knowledge just by presupposing and ignoring *is* knowledge; but it is an *especially* elusive sort of knowledge, and consequently it is an unclaimable sort of knowledge. You do not even have to practise epistemology to make it vanish. Simply *mentioning* any particular case of this knowledge, aloud or even in silent thought, is a way to attend to the hitherto ignored possibility, and thereby render it no longer ignored, and thereby create a context in which it is no longer true to ascribe the knowledge in question to yourself or others. So, just as we should think, presuppositions alone are not a basis on which to *claim* knowledge.

In general, when S knows that P some of the possibilities in which not-P are eliminated by S's evidence and others of them are properly ignored. There are some that can be eliminated, but cannot properly be ignored. For instance, when I look around the study without seeing Possum the cat, I thereby eliminate various possibilities in which Possum is in the study; but had those possibilities not been eliminated, they could not properly have been ignored. And there are other possibilities that never can be eliminated, but can properly be ignored. For instance, the possibility that Possum is on the desk but has been made invisible by a deceiving demon falls normally into this class (though not when I attend to it in the special context of epistemology).

There is a third class: not-P possibilities that might either be eliminated or ignored. Take the far-fetched possibility that Possum has somehow managed to get into a closed drawer of the desk – maybe he jumped in when it was open, then I closed it without noticing him. That possibility could be eliminated by opening the drawer and making a thorough examination. But if uneliminated, it may nevertheless be ignored, and in many contexts that ignoring would be proper. If I look all around the study, but without checking the closed drawers of the desk, I may truly be said to know that Possum is not in the study – or at any rate, there are many contexts in which that may truly be said. But if I did check all the closed drawers, then I would know *better* that Possum is not in the study. My knowledge would be better in the second case because it would rest more on the elimination of not-P possibilities, less on the ignoring of them.[18,19]

Better knowledge is more stable knowledge: it stands more chance of surviving a shift of attention in which we begin to attend to some of the possibilities formerly ignored. If, in our new shifted context, we ask what knowledge we may truly ascribe to our earlier selves, we may find that only the better knowledge of our earlier selves still deserves the name. And yet, if our former ignorings were proper at the time, even the worse knowledge of our earlier selves could truly have been called knowledge in the former context.

Never – well, hardly ever – does our knowledge rest entirely on elimination and not at all on ignoring. So hardly ever is it quite as good as we might wish. To that extent, the lesson of scepticism is right – and right permanently, not just in the temporary and special context of epistemology.[20]

What is it all for? Why have a notion of knowledge that works in the way I described? (Not a compulsory question. Enough to observe that

---

18 Mixed cases are possible: Fred properly ignores the possibility W_1 which Ted eliminates; however, Ted properly ignores the possibility W_2 which Fred eliminates. Ted has looked in all the desk drawers but not the file drawers, whereas Fred has checked the file drawers but not the desk. Fred's knowledge that Possum is not in the study is better in one way, Ted's is better in another.

19 To say truly that X is known, I must be properly ignoring any uneliminated possibilities in which not-X; whereas to say truly that Y is better known than X, I must be attending to some such possibilities. So I cannot say both in a single context. If I say 'X is known, but Y is better known', the context changes in mid-sentence: some previously ignored possibilities must stop being ignored. That can happen easily. Saying it the other way around – 'Y is better known than X, but even X is known' – is harder, because we must suddenly start to ignore previously unignored possibilities. That cannot be done, really; but we could bend the rules and make believe we had done it, and no doubt we would be understood well enough. Saying 'X is flat, but Y is flatter' (that is, 'X has no bumps at all, but Y has even fewer or smaller bumps') is a parallel case. And again, 'Y is flatter, but even X is flat' sounds clearly worse – but not altogether hopeless.

20 Thanks here to Stephen Hetherington. While his own views about better and worse knowledge are situated within an analysis of knowledge quite unlike mine, they withstand transplantation.

439

we do have it.) But I venture the guess that it is one of the messy short-cuts – like satisficing, like having indeterminate degrees of belief – that we resort to because we are not smart enough to live up to really high, perfectly Bayesian, standards of rationality. You cannot maintain a record of exactly which possibilities you have eliminated so far, much as you might like to. It is easier to keep track of which possibilities you have eliminated if you – Psst! – ignore many of all the possibilities there are. And besides, it is easier to list some of the propositions that are true in *all* the uneliminated, unignored possibilities than it is to find propositions that are true in *all and only* the uneliminated, unignored possibilities.

If you doubt that the word 'know' bears any real load in science or in metaphysics, I partly agree. The serious business of science has to do not with knowledge *per se*; but rather, with the elimination of possibilities through the evidence of perception, memory, etc., and with the changes that one's belief system would (or might or should) undergo under the impact of such eliminations. Ascriptions of knowledge to yourself or others are a very sloppy way of conveying very incomplete information about the elimination of possibilities. It is as if you had said:

> The possibilities eliminated, whatever else they may also include, at least include all the not-*P* possibilities; or anyway, all of those except for some we are presumably prepared to ignore just at the moment.

The only excuse for giving information about what really matters in such a sloppy way is that at least it is easy and quick! But it *is* easy and quick; whereas giving full and precise information about which possibilities have been eliminated seems to be extremely difficult, as witness the futile search for a 'pure observation language'. If I am right about how ascriptions of knowledge work, they are a handy but humble approximation. They may yet be indispensable in practice, in the same way that other handy and humble approximations are.

If we analyse knowledge as a modality, as we have done, we cannot escape the conclusion that knowledge is closed under (strict) implication.[21] Dretske has denied that knowledge is closed under implication; further, he has diagnosed closure as the fallacy that drives arguments for scepticism. As follows: the proposition that I have hands implies that I am not a handless being, and a *fortiori* that I am not a handless being deceived by a demon into thinking that I have hands. So, by the closure principle, the proposition that I know I have hands implies that I know that I am not handless and deceived. But I don't know that I am not handless and deceived – for how can I eliminate that possibility? So, by *modus tollens*, I don't know that I have hands. Dretske's advice is to resist scepticism by denying closure. He says that although having hands *does* imply not being handless and deceived, yet knowing that I have hands *does not* imply knowing that I am not handless and deceived. I do know the former, I do not know the latter.[22]

What Dretske says is close to right, but not quite. Knowledge *is* closed under implication. Knowing that I have hands *does* imply knowing that I am not handless and deceived. Implication preserves truth – that is, it preserves truth in any given, fixed context. But if we switch contexts midway, all bets are off. I say (1) pigs fly; (2) what I just said had fewer than three syllables (true); (3) what I just said had fewer than four syllables (false). So 'less than three' does not imply 'less than four'? No! The context switched midway, the semantic value of the context-dependent phrase 'what I just said' switched with it. Likewise in the sceptical argument the context switched midway, and the semantic value of the context-dependent word 'know' switched with it. The premise 'I know that I have hands' was true in its everyday context, where the possibility of deceiving demons was properly ignored. The mention of that very possibility switched the context midway. The

---

21 A proof-theoretic version of this closure principle is common to all 'normal' modal logics: if the logic validates an inference from zero or more premises to a conclusion, then also it validates the inference obtained by prefixing the necessity operator to each premise and to the conclusion. Further, this rule is all we need to take us from classical sentential logic to the least normal modal logic. See Brian Chellas, *Modal Logic: An Introduction* (Cambridge: Cambridge University Press, 1980) p. 114.

22 Dretske, 'Epistemic Operators'. My reply follows the lead of Stine, 'Skepticism, Relevant Alternatives, and Deductive Closure', op. cit.; and (more closely) Cohen, 'How to be a Fallibilist', op. cit.

conclusion 'I know that I am not handless and deceived' was false in *its* context, because that was a context in which the possibility of deceiving demons was being mentioned, hence was not being ignored, hence was not being properly ignored. Dretske gets the phenomenon right, and I think he gets the diagnosis of scepticism right; it is just that he misclassifies what he sees. He thinks it is a phenomenon of logic, when really it is a phenomenon of pragmatics. Closure, rightly understood, survives the test. If we evaluate the conclusion for truth not with respect to the context in which it was uttered, but instead with respect to the different context in which the premise was uttered, then truth is preserved. And if, *per impossibile*, the conclusion could have been said in the same unchanged context as the premise, truth would have been preserved.

A problem due to Saul Kripke turns upon the closure of knowledge under implication. *P* implies that any evidence against *P* is misleading. So, by closure, whenever you know that *P*, you know that any evidence against *P* is misleading. And if you know that evidence is misleading, you should pay it no heed. Whenever we know – and we know a lot, remember – we should not heed any evidence tending to suggest that we are wrong. But that is absurd. Shall we dodge the conclusion by denying closure? I think not. Again, I diagnose a change of context. At first, it was stipulated that *S* knew, whence it followed that *S* was properly ignoring all possibilities of error. But as the story continues, it turns out that there is evidence on offer that points to some particular possibility of error. Then, by the Rule of Attention, that possibility is no longer properly ignored, either by *S* himself or by we who are telling the story of *S*. The advent of that evidence destroys *S*'s knowledge, and thereby destroys *S*'s licence to ignore the evidence lest he be misled.

There is another reason, different from Dretske's, why we might doubt closure. Suppose two or more premises jointly imply a conclusion. Might not someone who is compartmentalized in his thinking – as we all are – know each of the premises but fail to bring them together in a single compartment? Then might he not fail to know the conclusion? Yes; and I would not like to plead idealization-of-rationality as an excuse for ignoring such cases. But I suggest that we might take not the whole compartmentalized thinker, but rather each of his several overlapping compartments, as our 'subjects'. That would be the obvious remedy if his compartmentalization amounted to a case of multiple personality disorder; but maybe it is right for milder cases as well.[23]

A compartmentalized thinker who indulges in epistemology can destroy his knowledge, yet retain it as well. Imagine two epistemologists on a bushwalk. As they walk, they talk. They mention all manner of far-fetched possibilities of error. By attending to these normally ignored possibilities they destroy the knowledge they normally possess. Yet all the while they know where they are and where they are going! How so? The compartment in charge of philosophical talk attends to far-fetched possibilities of error. The compartment in charge of navigation does not. One compartment loses its knowledge, the other retains its knowledge. And what does the entire compartmentalized thinker know? Not an altogether felicitous question. But if we need an answer, I suppose the best thing to say is that S knows that P iff any one of S's compartments knows that P. Then we can say what we would offhand want to say: yes, our philosophical bushwalkers still know their whereabouts.

Context-dependence is not limited to the ignoring and non-ignoring of far-fetched possibilities. Here is another case. Pity poor Bill! He squanders all his spare cash on the pokies, the races, and the lottery. He will be a wage slave all his days. We know he will never be rich. But if he wins the lottery (if he wins big), then he will be rich. Contrapositively: his never being rich, plus other things we know, imply that he will lose. So, by closure, if we know that he will never be rich, we know that he will lose. But when we discussed the case before, we concluded that we cannot know that he will lose. All the possibilities in which Bill loses and someone else wins saliently resemble the possibility in which Bill wins and the others lose; one of those possibilities is actual; so by the Rules of Actuality and of Resemblance, we may not properly ignore the possibility that Bill wins. But there is a loophole: the resemblance was required to be salient. Salience, as well as ignoring, may vary between contexts. Before, when I was explaining

23 See Stalnaker, *Inquiry*, pp. 79–99.

how the Rule of Resemblance applied to lotteries, I saw to it that the resemblance between the many possibilities associated with the many tickets was sufficiently salient. But this time, when we were busy pitying poor Bill for his habits and not for his luck, the resemblance of the many possibilities was not so salient. At that point, the possibility of Bill's winning was properly ignored; so then it was true to say that we knew he would never be rich. Afterward I switched the context. I mentioned the possibility that Bill might win, wherefore that possibility was no longer properly ignored. (Maybe there were two separate reasons why it was no longer properly ignored, because maybe I also made the resemblance between the many possibilities more salient.) It was true at first that we knew that Bill would never be rich. And at that point it was also true that we knew he would lose – but that was only true so long as it remained unsaid! (And maybe unthought as well.) Later, after the change in context, it was no longer true that we knew he would lose. At that point, it was also no longer true that we knew he would never be rich.

But wait. Don't you smell a rat? Haven't I, by my own lights, been saying what cannot be said? (Or whistled either.) If the story I told was true, how have I managed to tell it? In trendyspeak, is there not a problem of reflexivity? Does not my story deconstruct itself?

I said: S knows that P iff S's evidence eliminates every possibility in which not-P – Psst! – except for those possibilities that we are properly ignoring. That 'psst' marks an attempt to do the impossible – to mention that which remains unmentioned. I am sure you managed to make believe that I had succeeded. But I could not have done.

And I said that when we do epistemology, and we attend to the proper ignoring of possibilities, we make knowledge vanish. First we do know, then we do not. But I had been doing epistemology when I said that. The uneliminated possibilities were *not* being ignored – not just then. So by what right did I say even that we used to know?[24]

---

24 Worse still: by what right can I even say that we used to be in a position to say truly that we knew? Then, we were in a context where we properly ignored certain uneliminated possibilities of error. Now, we are in a context where we no longer ignore them. If *now* I comment retrospectively upon the truth of what was said

In trying to thread a course between the rock of fallibilism and the whirlpool of scepticism, it may well seem as if I have fallen victim to both at once. For do I not say that there are all those uneliminated possibilities of error? Yet do I not claim that we know a lot? Yet do I not claim that knowledge is, by definition, infallible knowledge?

I did claim all three things. But not all at once! Or if I did claim them all at once, that was an expository shortcut, to be taken with a pinch of salt. To get my message across, I bent the rules. If I tried to whistle what cannot be said, what of it? I relied on the cardinal principle of pragmatics, which overrides every one of the rules I mentioned: interpret the message to make it make sense – to make it consistent, and sensible to say.

When you have context-dependence, ineffability can be trite and unmysterious. Hush! [moment of silence] I might have liked to say, just then, 'All of us are silent'. It was true. But I could not have said it truly, or whistled it either. For by saying it aloud, or by whistling, I would have rendered it false.

I could have said my say fair and square, bending no rules. It would have been tiresome, but it could have been done. The secret would have been to resort to 'semantic ascent'. I could have taken great care to distinguish between (1) the language I use when I talk about knowledge, or whatever, and (2) the second language that I use to talk about the semantic and pragmatic workings of the first language. If you want to hear my story told that way, you probably know enough to do the job for yourself. If you can, then my informal presentation has been good enough.

then, which context governs: the context now or the context then? I doubt there is any general answer, apart from the usual principle that we should interpret what is said so as to make the message make sense.

Index

452